Shojo Beat

ANONYMOUS NOISE

Ryoko
Fukuyama

Anonymous Noise
Volume 16
CONTENTS

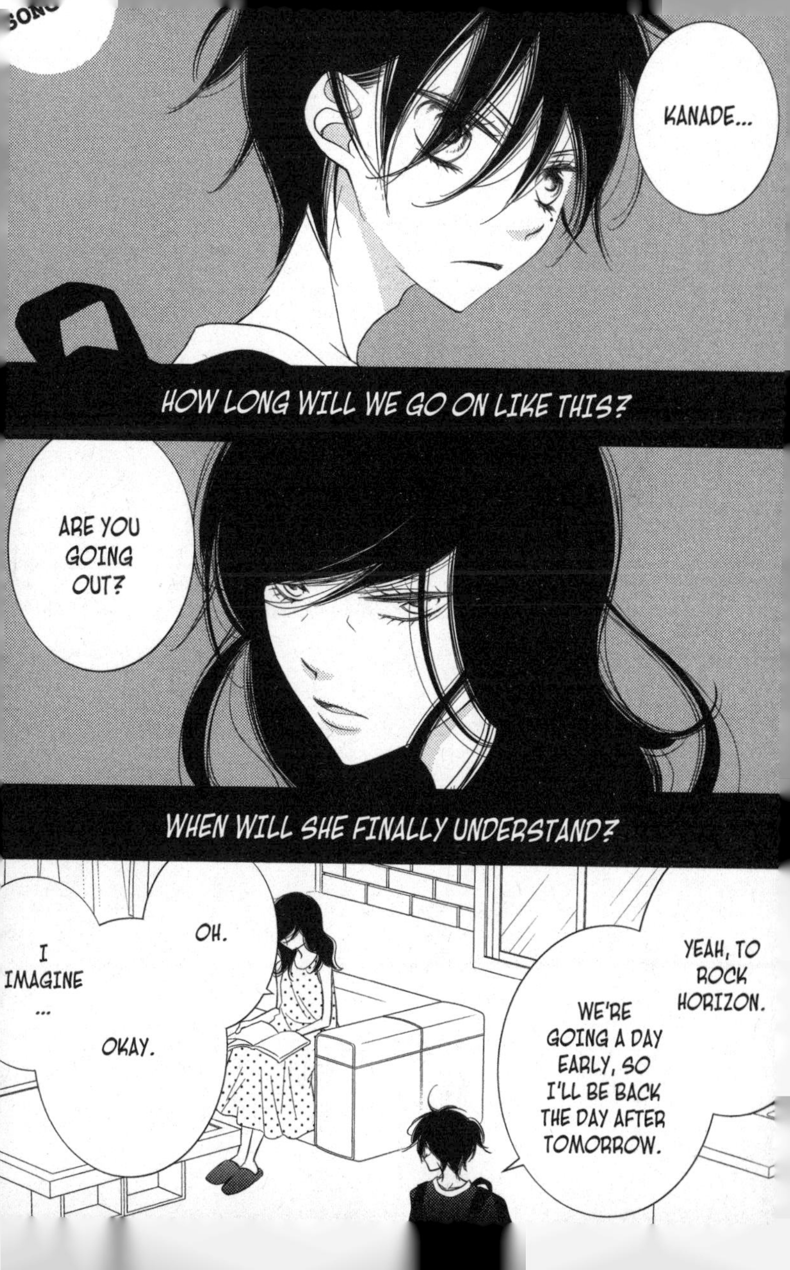
KANADE...
HOW LONG WILL WE GO ON LIKE THIS?
ARE YOU GOING OUT?
WHEN WILL SHE FINALLY UNDERSTAND?
YEAH, TO ROCK HORIZON.
WE'RE GOING A DAY EARLY, SO I'LL BE BACK THE DAY AFTER TOMORROW.
OH.
I IMAGINE ...
OKAY.

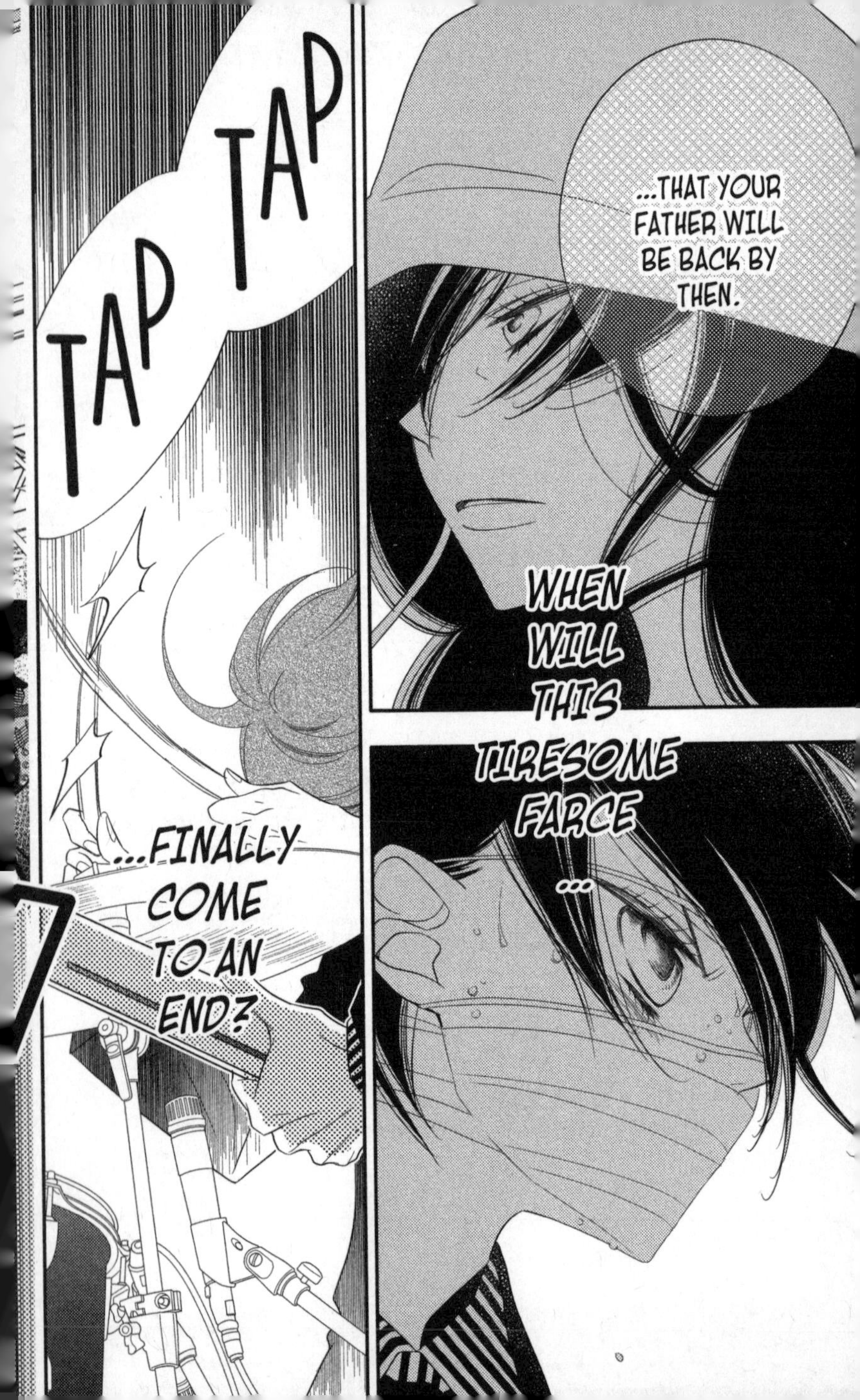
...THAT YOUR FATHER WILL BE BACK BY THEN.
WHEN WILL THIS TIRESOME FARCE ...
TAP TAP
...FINALLY COME TO AN END?

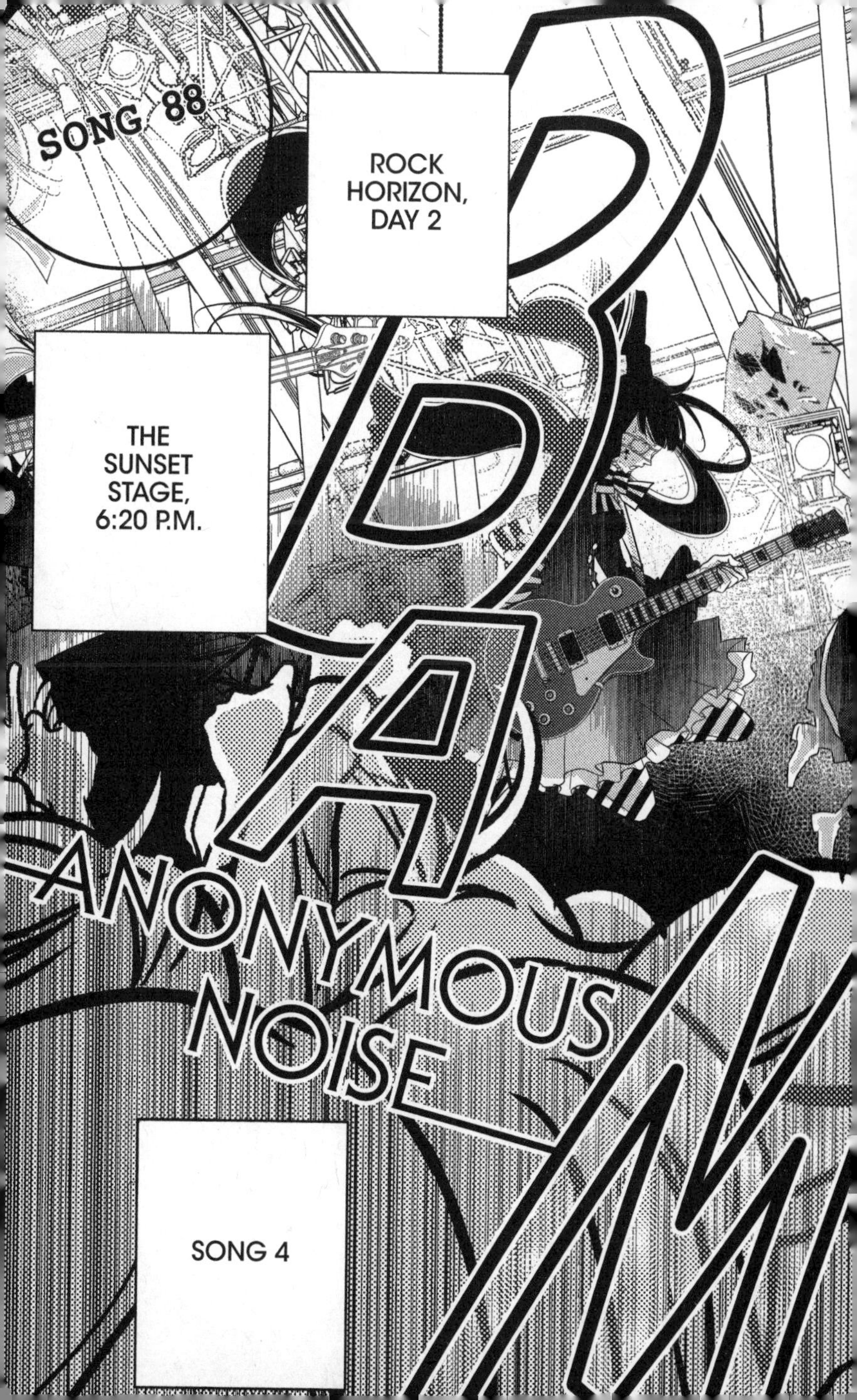
SONG 88
ROCK HORIZON, DAY 2
THE SUNSET STAGE, 6:20 P.M.
ANONYMOUS NOISE
SONG 4

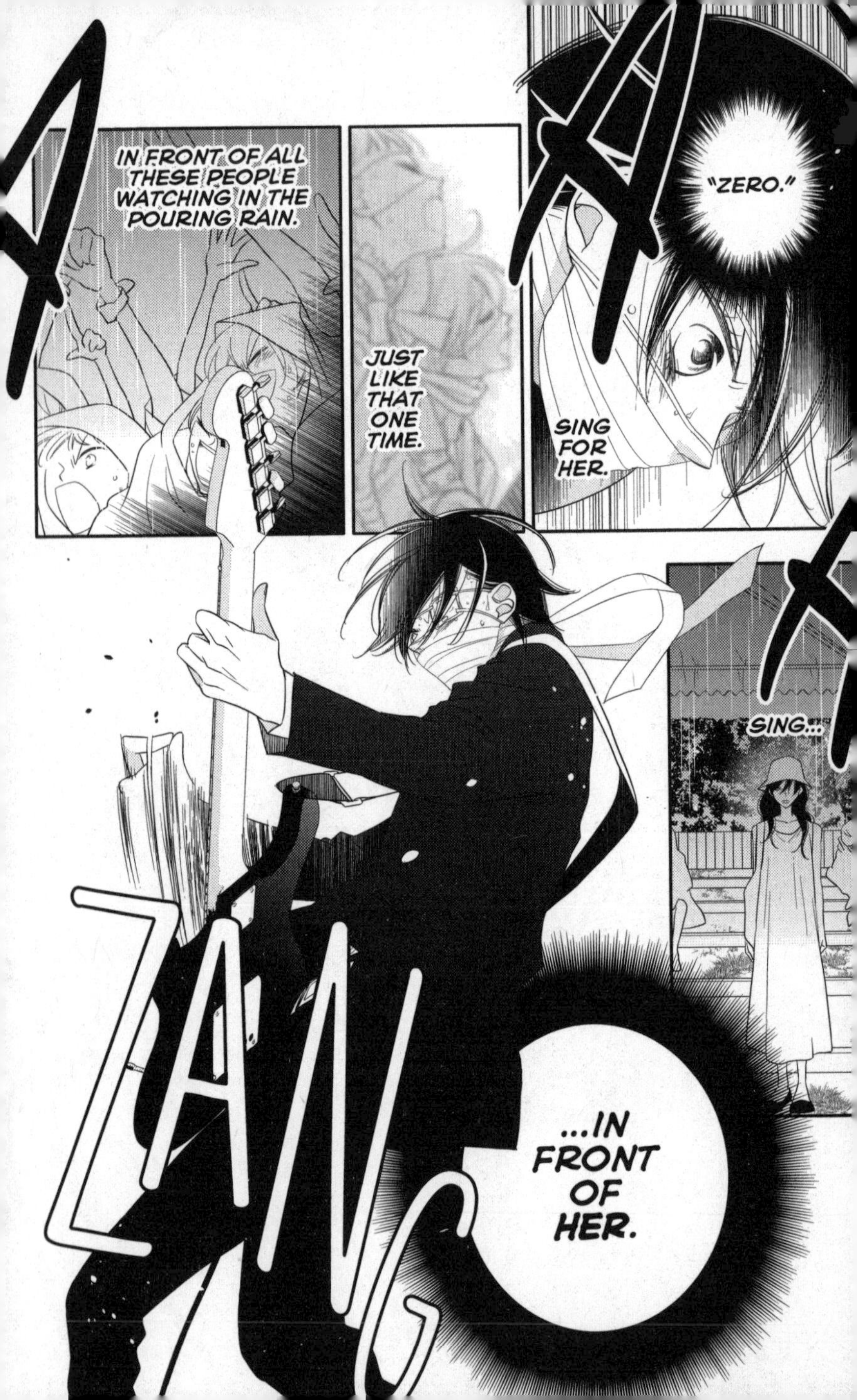
"ZERO."
SING FOR HER.
JUST LIKE THAT ONE TIME.
IN FRONT OF ALL THESE PEOPLE WATCHING IN THE POURING RAIN.
SING...
...IN FRONT OF HER.
ZANG

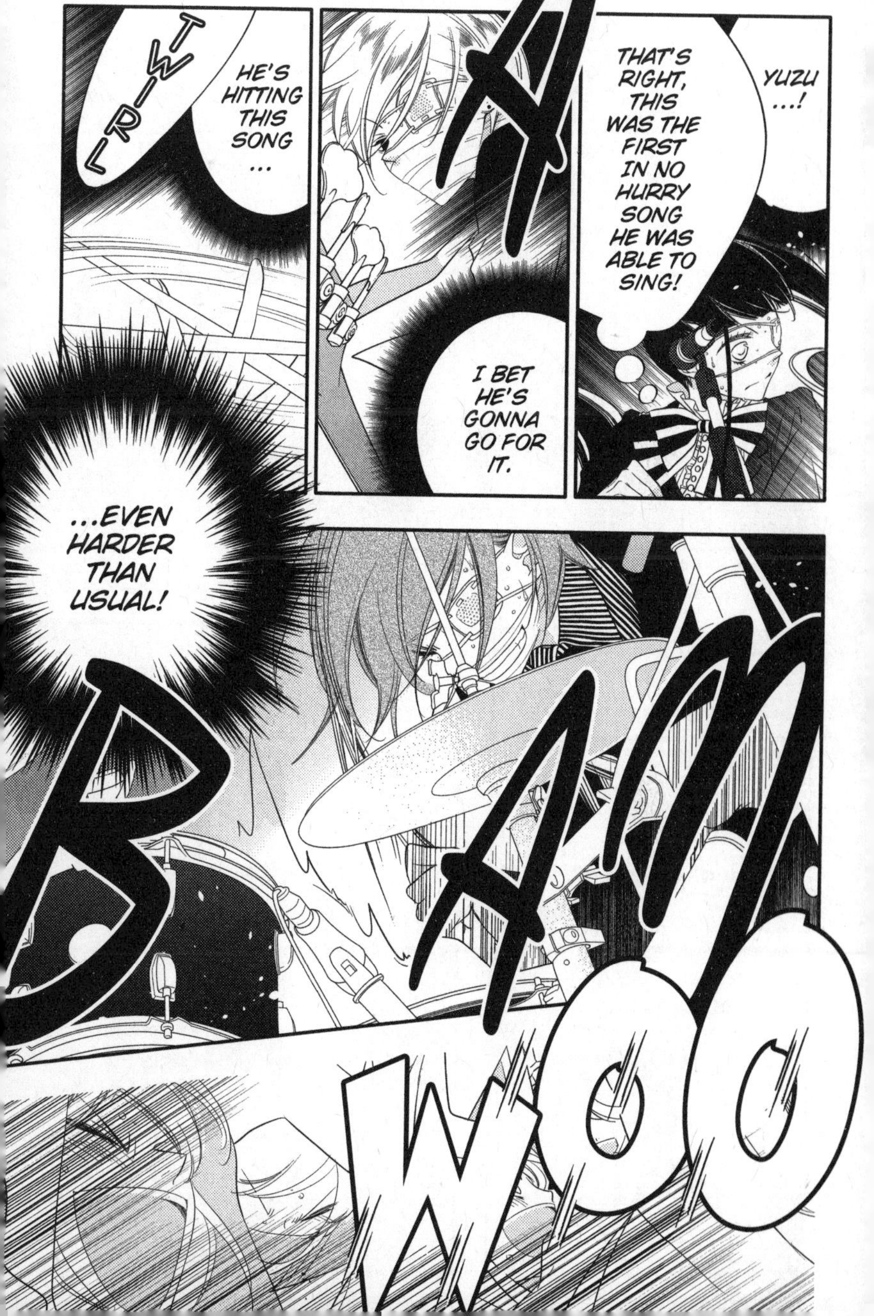
YUZU ...!
THAT'S RIGHT, THIS WAS THE FIRST IN NO HURRY SONG HE WAS ABLE TO SING!
A
I BET HE'S GONNA GO FOR IT.
TWIRL
HE'S HITTING THIS SONG ...
...EVEN HARDER THAN USUAL!
BAM
WOOO

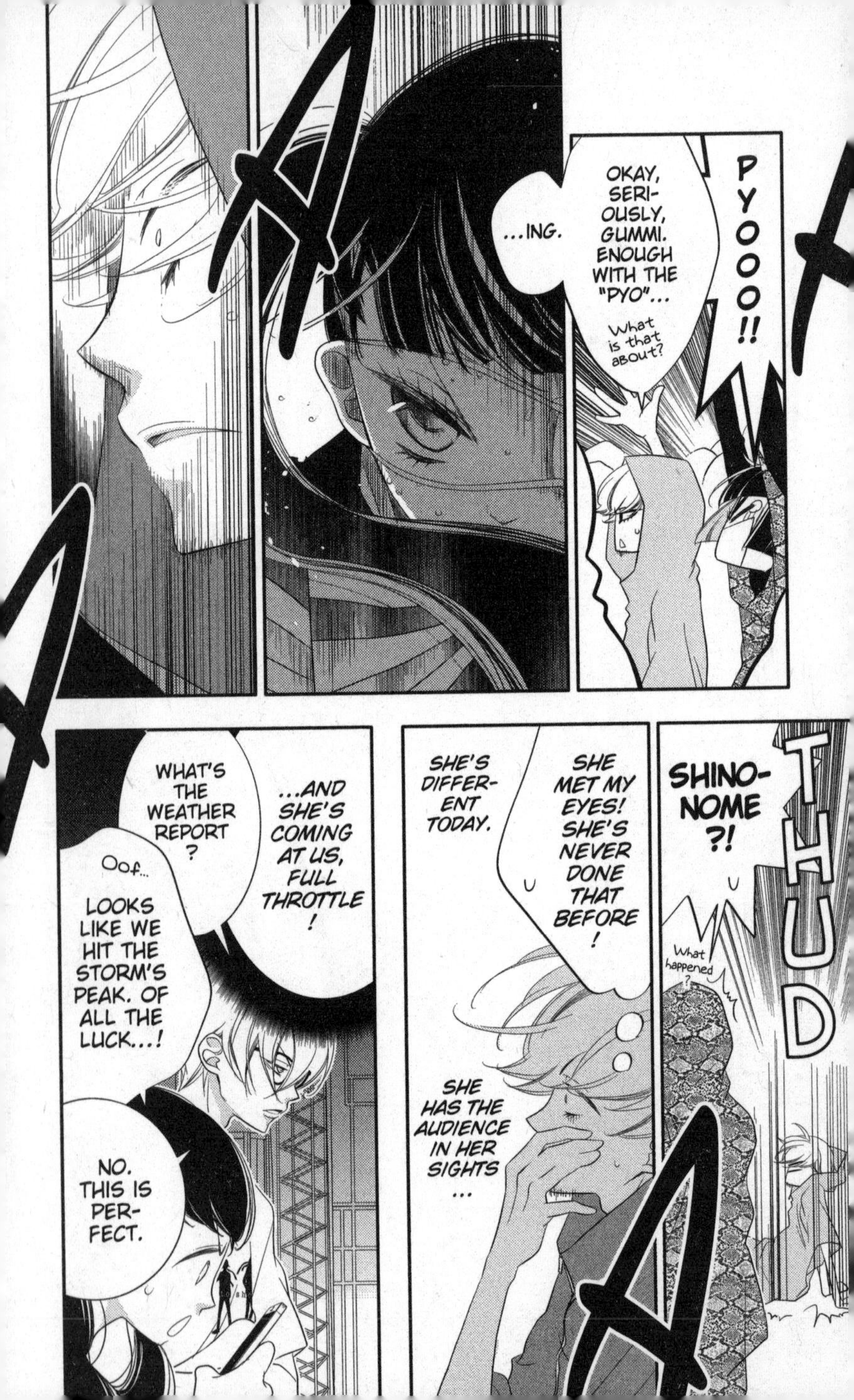
PYOOO!!
OKAY, SERI-OUSLY, GUMMI. ENOUGH WITH THE "PYO"...
What is that about?
...ING.
SHINO-NOME?!
THUD
What happened?
SHE MET MY EYES! SHE'S NEVER DONE THAT BEFORE!
SHE'S DIFFER-ENT TODAY.
SHE HAS THE AUDIENCE IN HER SIGHTS...
...AND SHE'S COMING AT US, FULL THROTTLE!
WHAT'S THE WEATHER REPORT?
Oof...
LOOKS LIKE WE HIT THE STORM'S PEAK. OF ALL THE LUCK...!
NO. THIS IS PER-FECT.

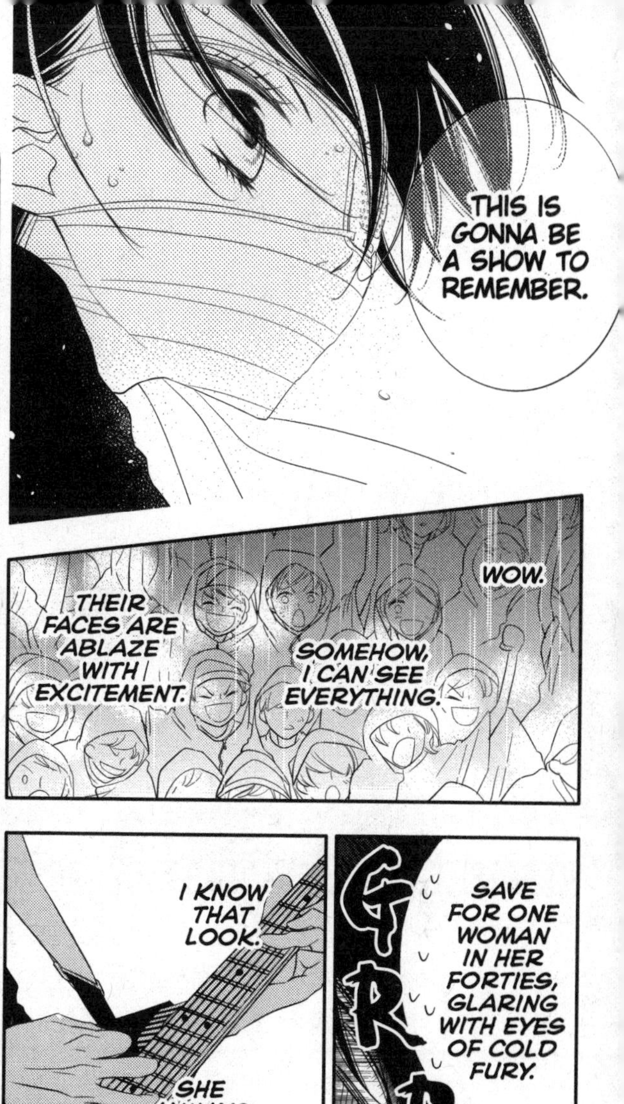
THIS IS GONNA BE A SHOW TO REMEMBER.
WOW.
SOMEHOW, I CAN SEE EVERYTHING.
THEIR FACES ARE ABLAZE WITH EXCITEMENT.
GRRR
SAVE FOR ONE WOMAN IN HER FORTIES, GLARING WITH EYES OF COLD FURY.
I KNOW THAT LOOK.
SHE ALWAYS MAKES THAT FACE WHEN I MAKE MUSIC.

1

Hello, and welcome! I'm Ryoko Fukuyama. Thank you so much for picking up volume 16 of *Anonymous Noise*!

As you can see, I've failed to hand-write the author's columns yet again. And after I'd resolved to do them all by hand this year, no matter what! I'm so sorry.

The columns are due at the publisher in about an hour, and I'm starting to get nervous.

That said, I really hope you enjoy volume 16!

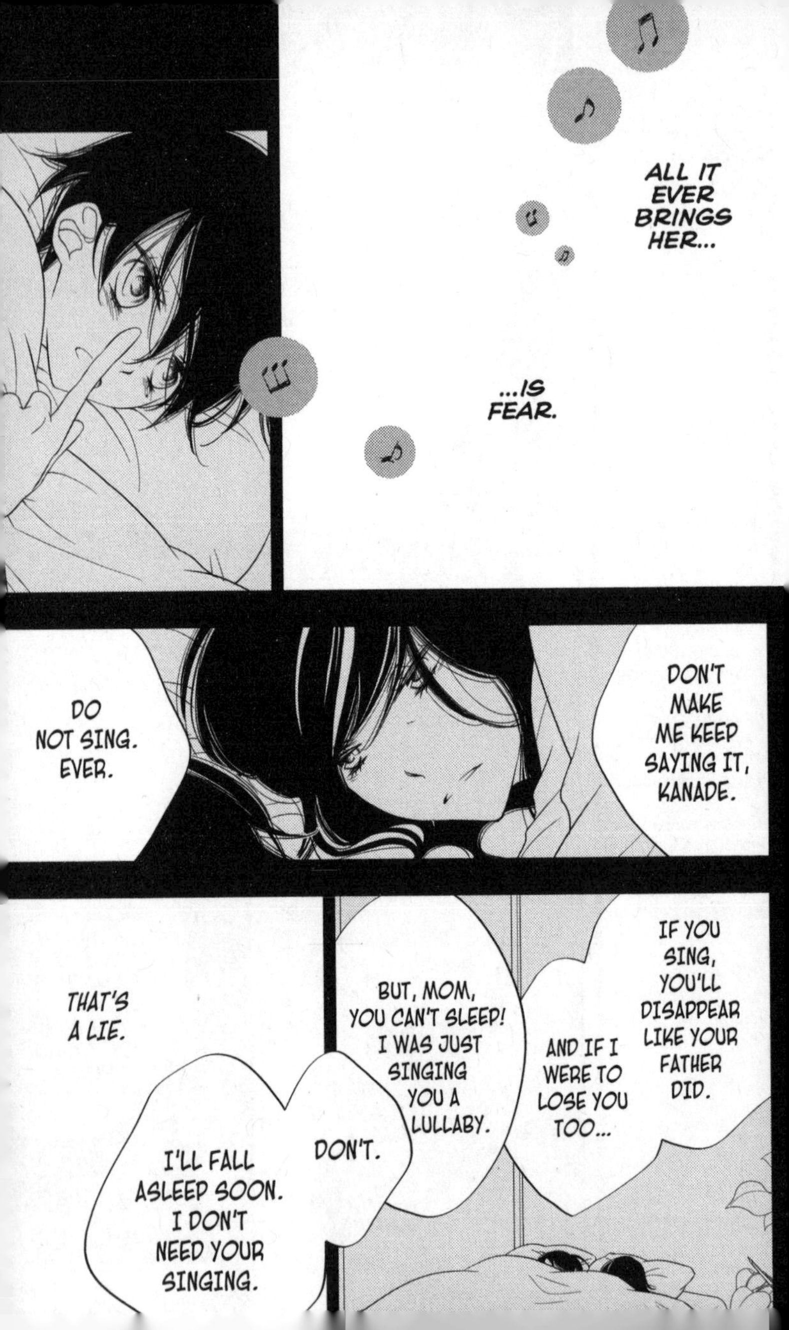
ALL IT EVER BRINGS HER...
...IS FEAR.
DON'T MAKE ME KEEP SAYING IT, KANADE.
DO NOT SING. EVER.
IF YOU SING, YOU'LL DISAPPEAR LIKE YOUR FATHER DID.
AND IF I WERE TO LOSE YOU TOO...
BUT, MOM, YOU CAN'T SLEEP! I WAS JUST SINGING YOU A LULLABY.
DON'T.
I'LL FALL ASLEEP SOON. I DON'T NEED YOUR SINGING.
THAT'S A LIE.

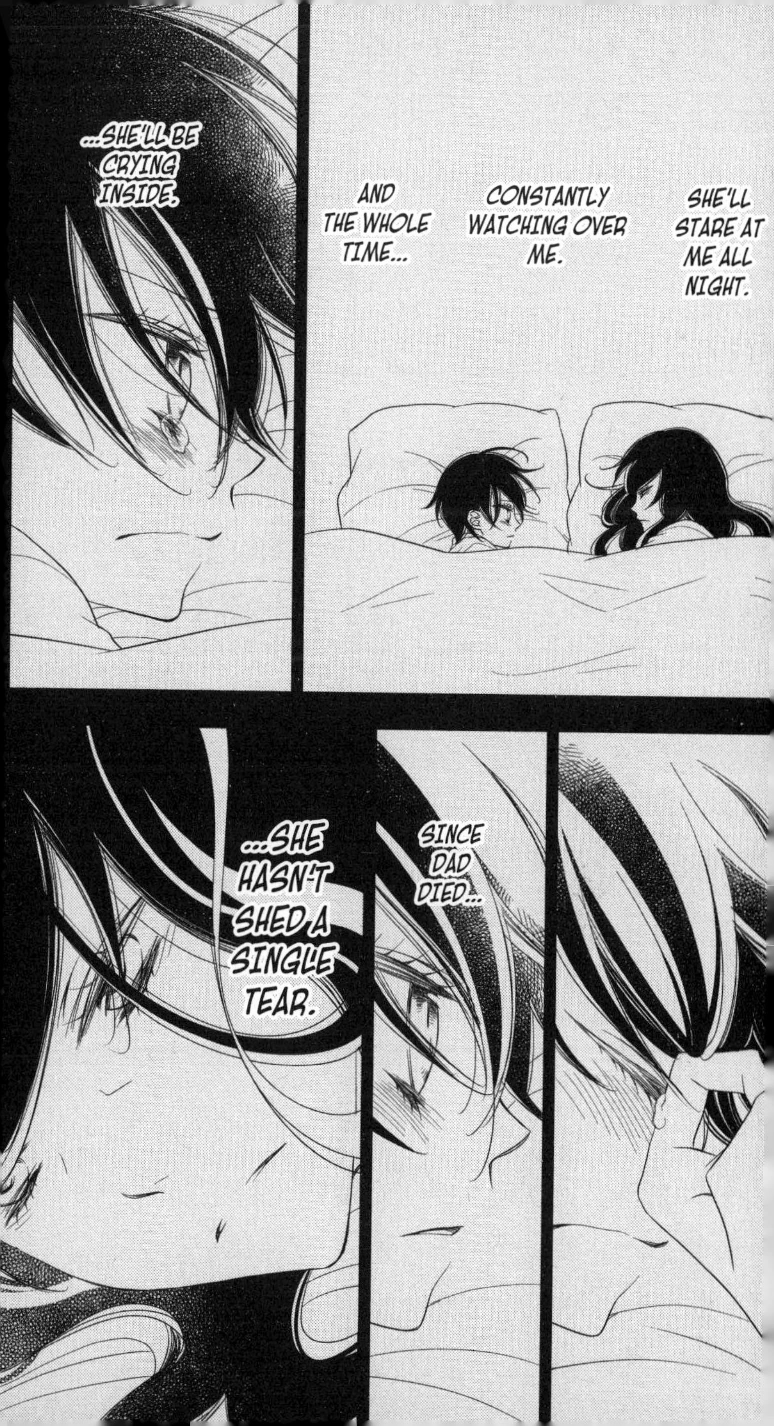
SHE'LL STARE AT ME ALL NIGHT.
CONSTANTLY WATCHING OVER ME.
AND THE WHOLE TIME...
...SHE'LL BE CRYING INSIDE.
SINCE DAD DIED...
...SHE HASN'T SHED A SINGLE TEAR.

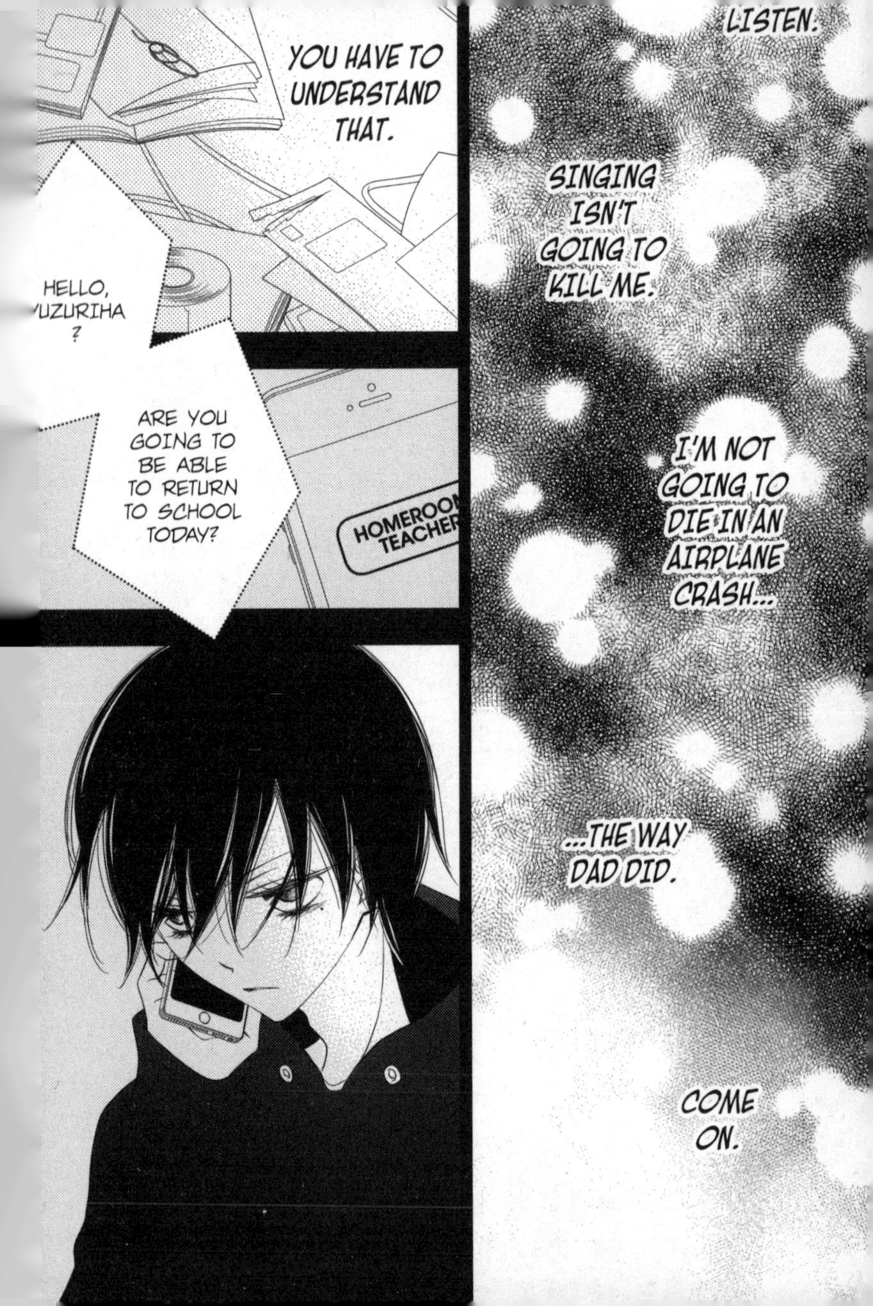
LISTEN.
SINGING ISN'T GOING TO KILL ME.
I'M NOT GOING TO DIE IN AN AIRPLANE CRASH...
...THE WAY DAD DID.
COME ON.
YOU HAVE TO UNDERSTAND THAT.
HELLO, YUZURIHA?
ARE YOU GOING TO BE ABLE TO RETURN TO SCHOOL TODAY?
HOMEROOM TEACHER

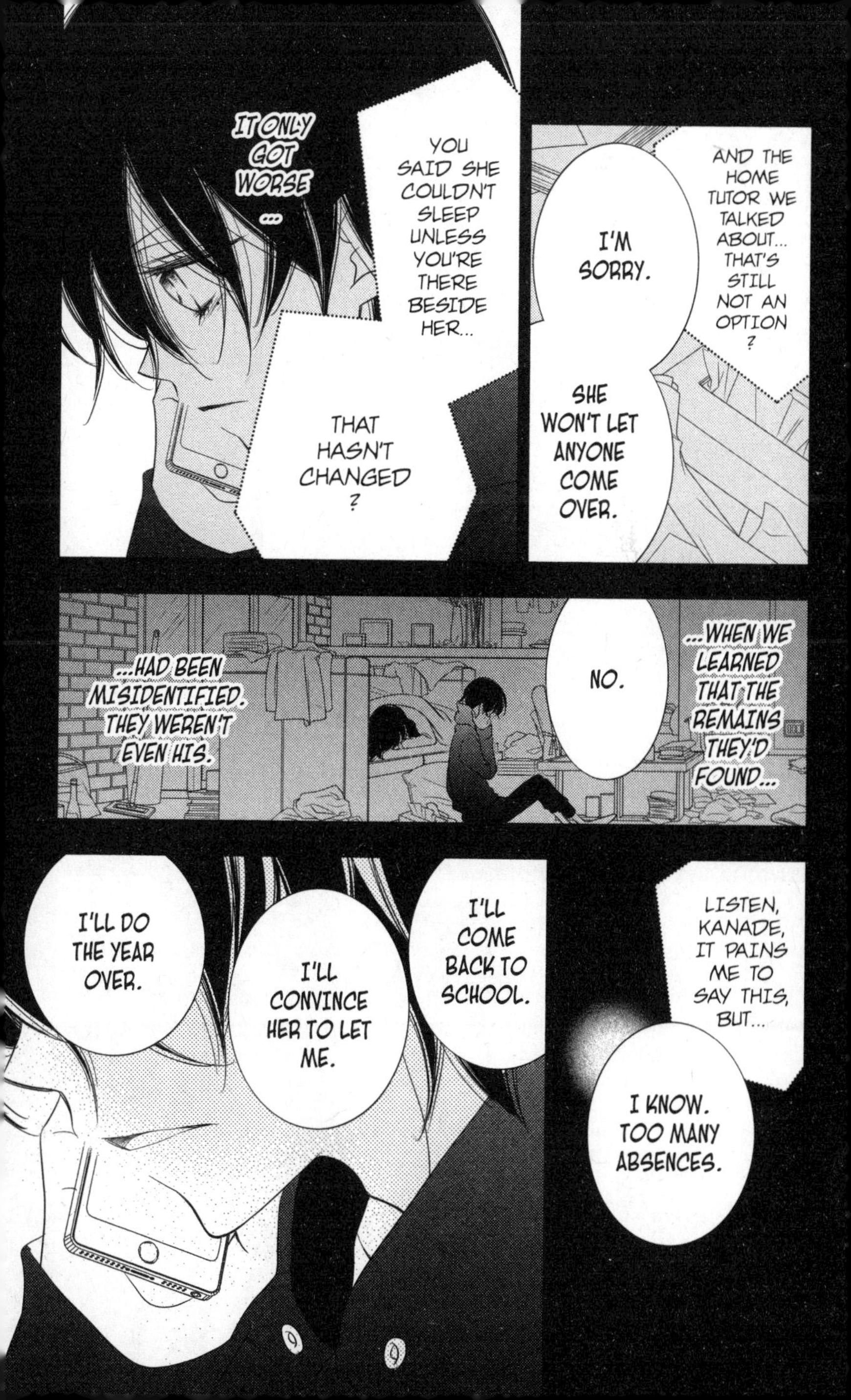
AND THE HOME TUTOR WE TALKED ABOUT... THAT'S STILL NOT AN OPTION?
I'M SORRY.
SHE WON'T LET ANYONE COME OVER.
YOU SAID SHE COULDN'T SLEEP UNLESS YOU'RE THERE BESIDE HER...
THAT HASN'T CHANGED?
IT ONLY GOT WORSE...
...WHEN WE LEARNED THAT THE REMAINS THEY'D FOUND...
NO.
...HAD BEEN MISIDENTIFIED. THEY WEREN'T EVEN HIS.
LISTEN, KANADE, IT PAINS ME TO SAY THIS, BUT...
I KNOW. TOO MANY ABSENCES.
I'LL COME BACK TO SCHOOL.
I'LL CONVINCE HER TO LET ME.
I'LL DO THE YEAR OVER.

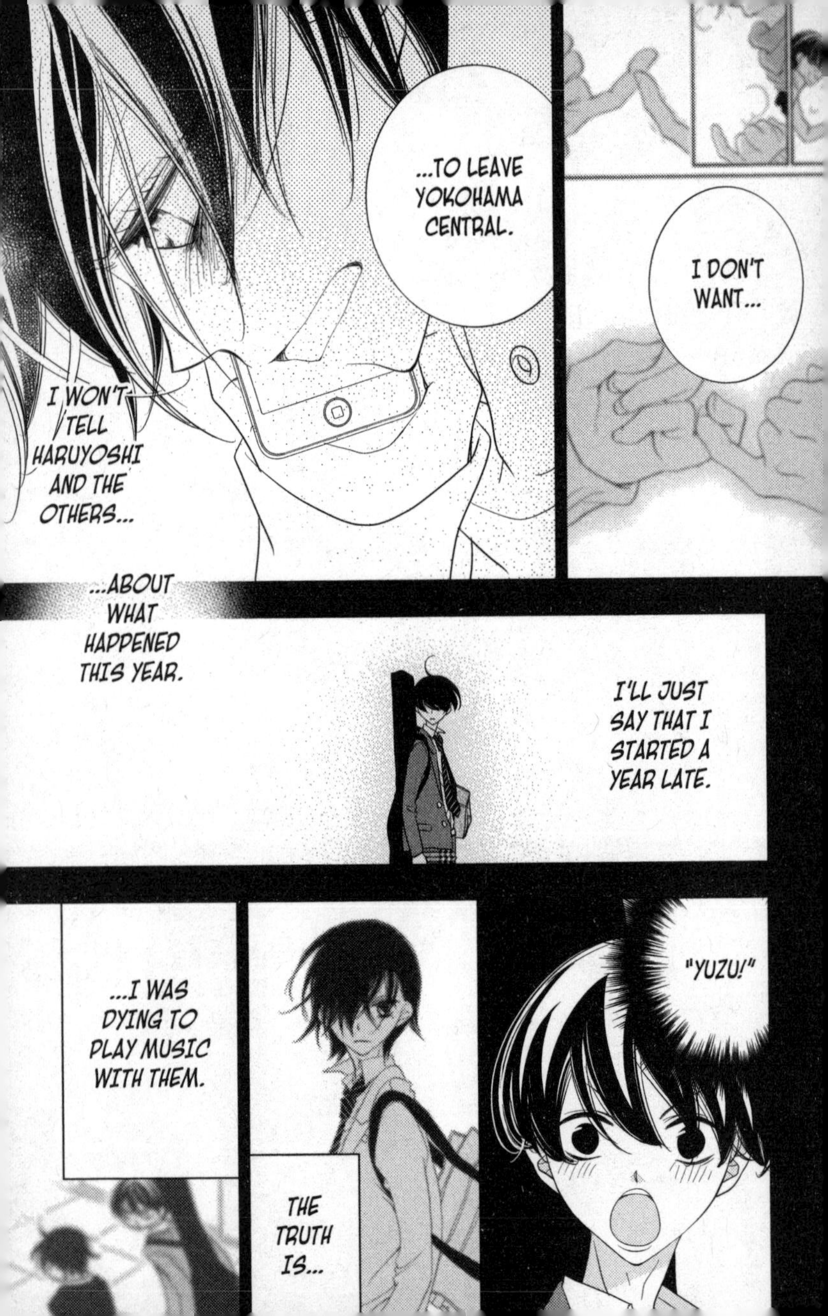
I DON'T WANT...
...TO LEAVE YOKOHAMA CENTRAL.
I WON'T TELL HARUYOSHI AND THE OTHERS...
...ABOUT WHAT HAPPENED THIS YEAR.
I'LL JUST SAY THAT I STARTED A YEAR LATE.
"YUZU!"
THE TRUTH IS...
...I WAS DYING TO PLAY MUSIC WITH THEM.

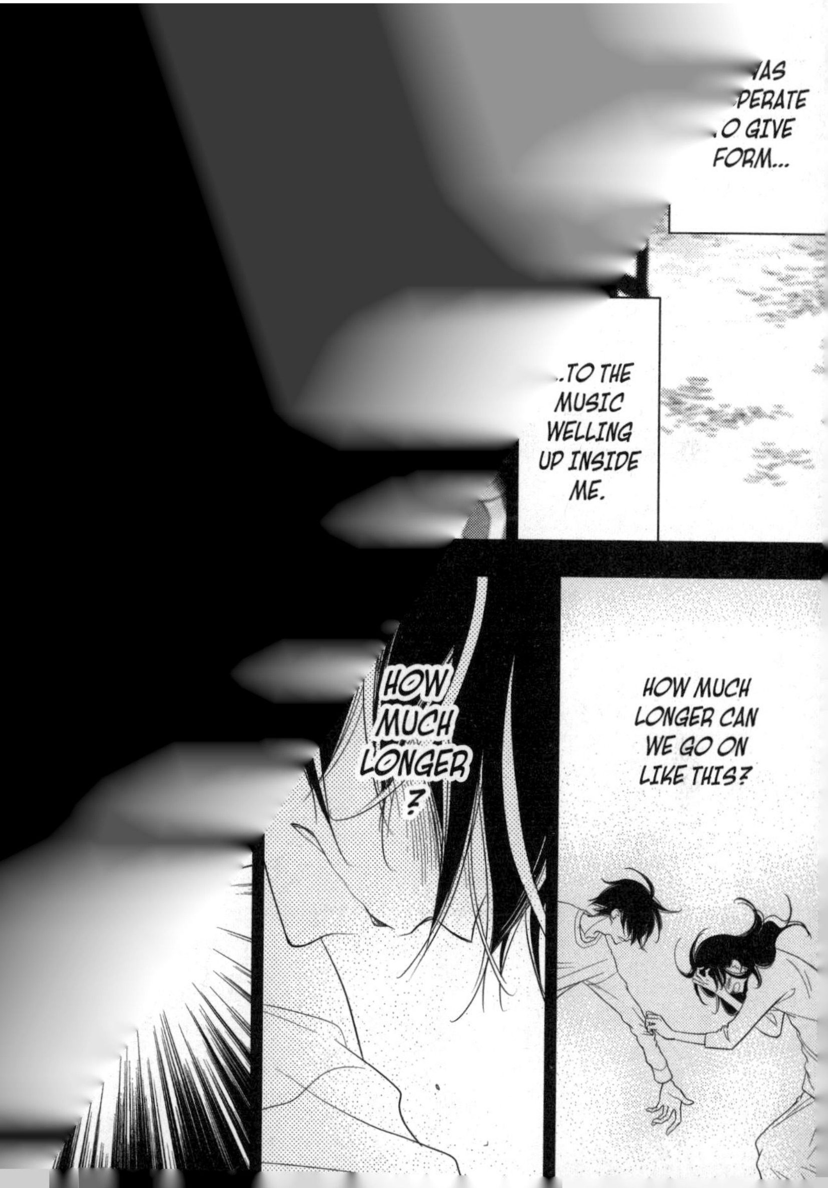

...AS ...PERATE ...O GIVE FORM...
...TO THE MUSIC WELLING UP INSIDE ME.
HOW MUCH LONGER CAN WE GO ON LIKE THIS?
HOW MUCH LONGER?

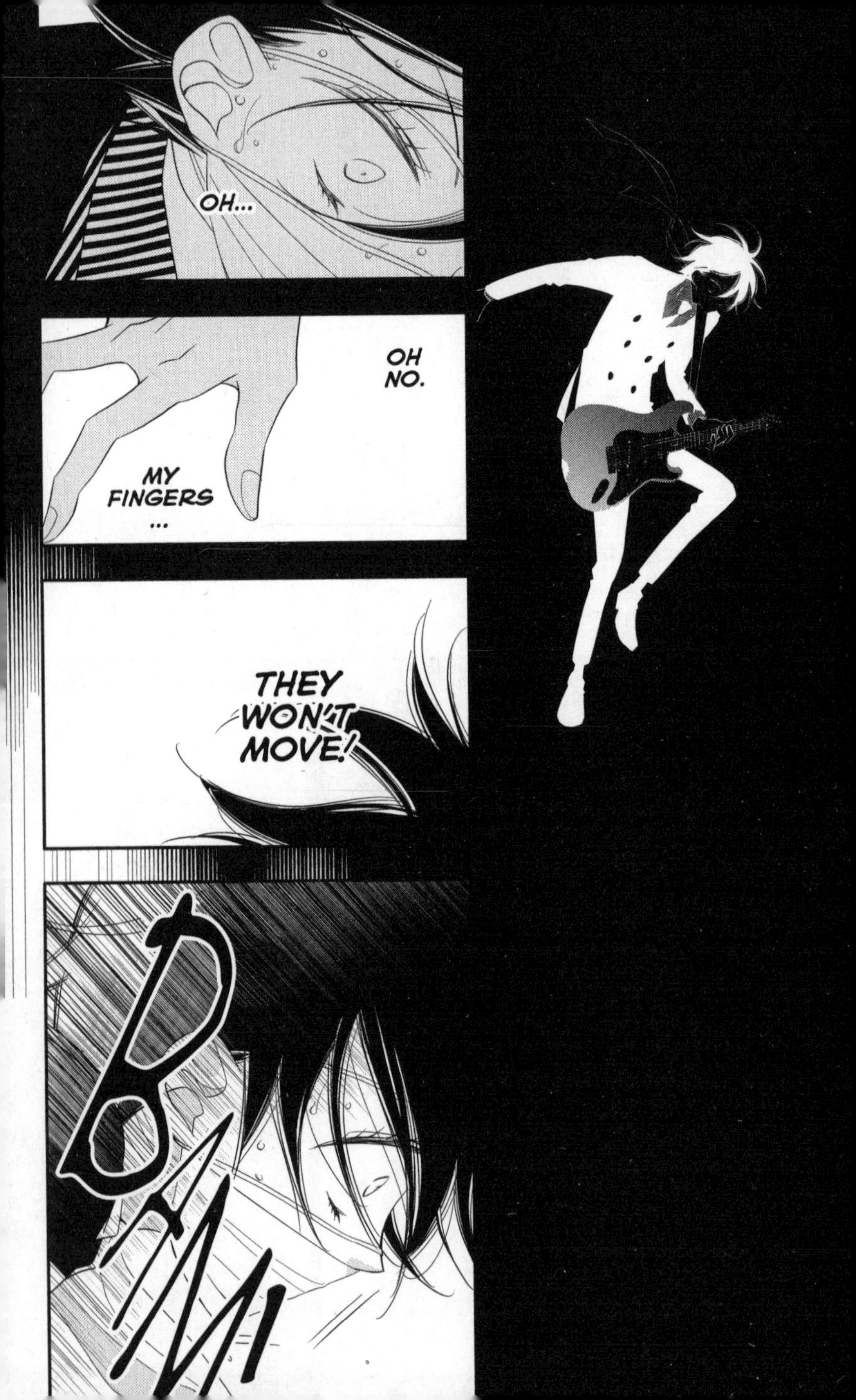
OH...
OH NO.
MY FINGERS ...
THEY WON'T MOVE!
DOM

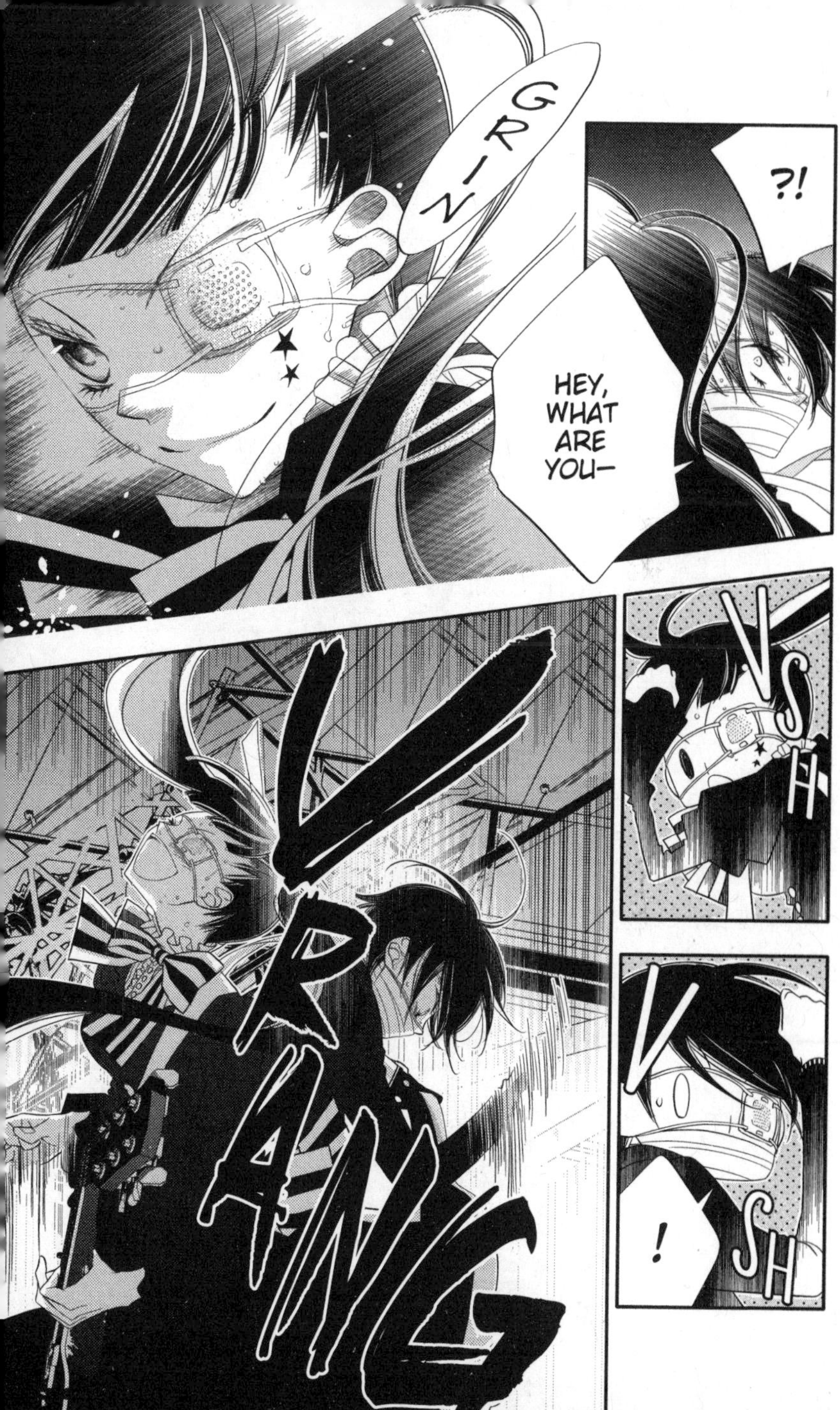
?!
HEY, WHAT ARE YOU–
GRIN
VSH
!
VSH
VRANG

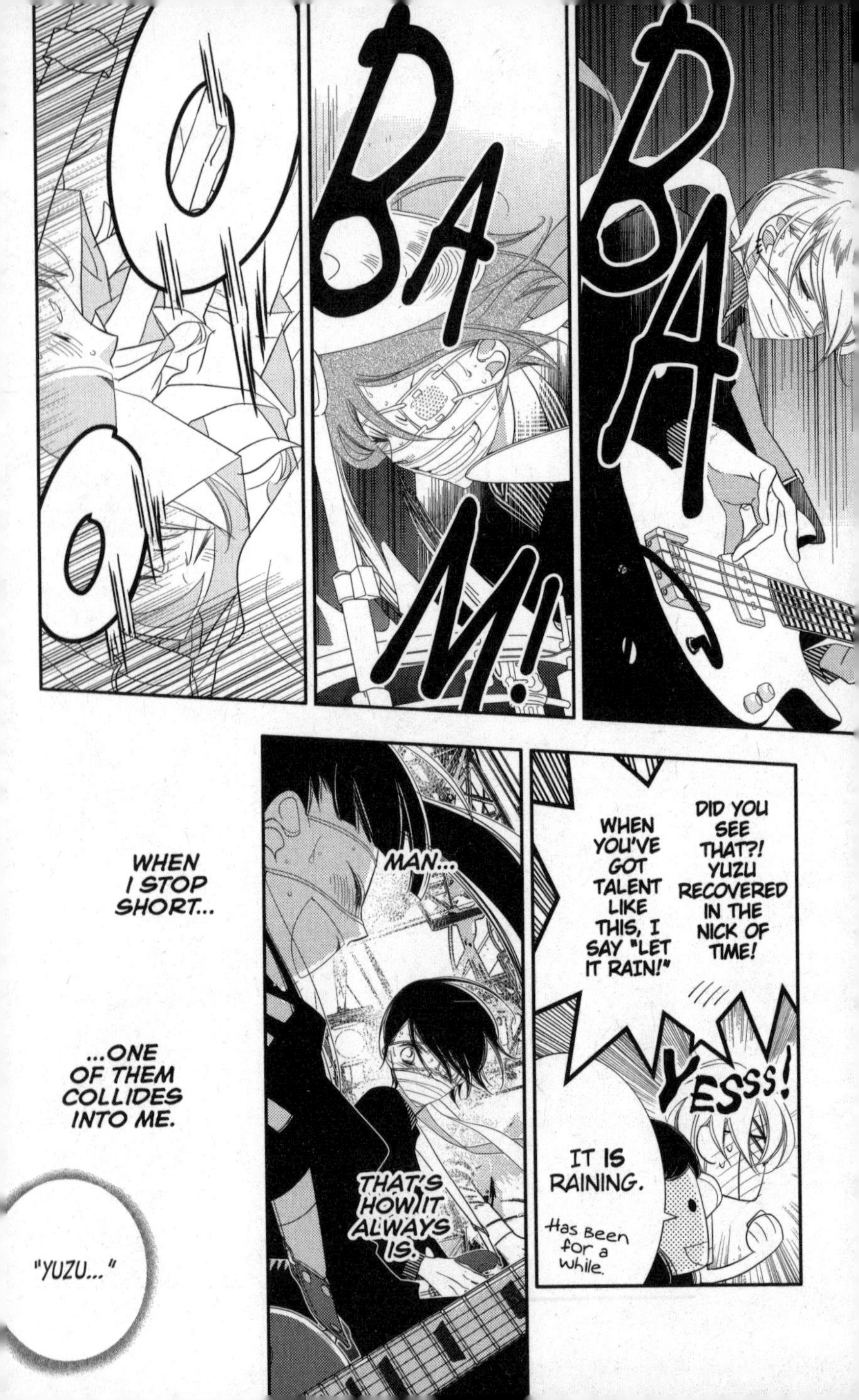
BABAM!
DID YOU SEE THAT?! YUZU RECOVERED IN THE NICK OF TIME!
WHEN YOU'VE GOT TALENT LIKE THIS, I SAY "LET IT RAIN!"
YESSS!
IT IS RAINING.
Has Been for a while.
MAN...
THAT'S HOW IT ALWAYS IS.
WHEN I STOP SHORT...
...ONE OF THEM COLLIDES INTO ME.
"YUZU..."

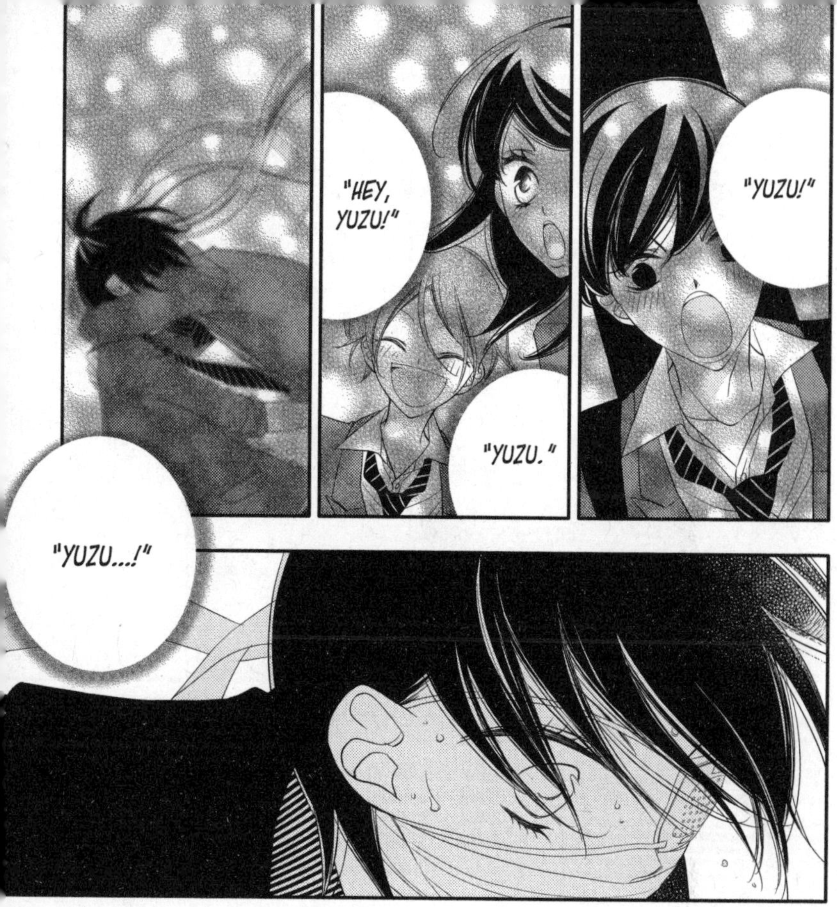
"YUZU!"
"HEY, YUZU!"
"YUZU."
"YUZU...!"

YEAH...

IT'S ALWAYS ME...

...SAYING I CAN'T. MAKING EXCUSES.

PUTTING THINGS OFF. RUNNING AWAY.

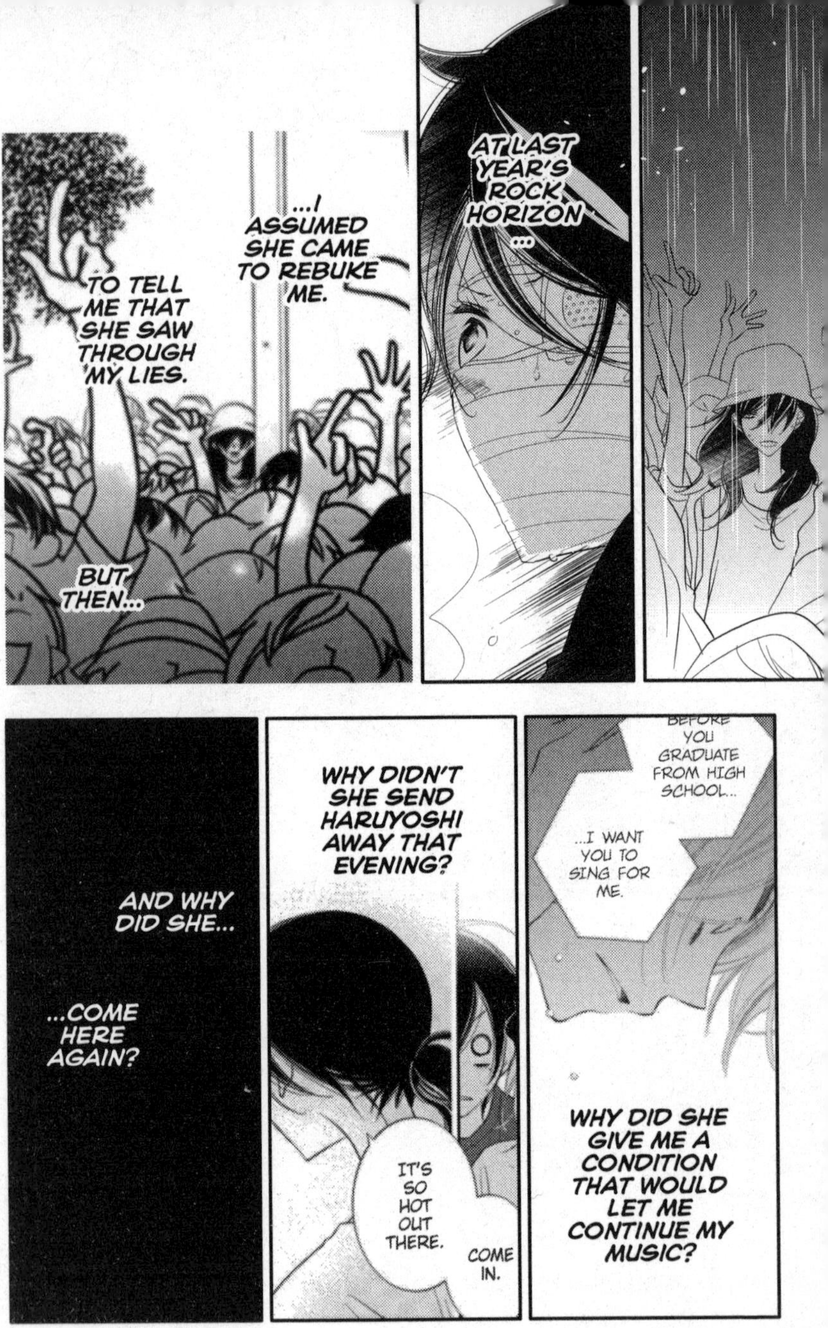
AT LAST YEAR'S ROCK HORIZON...
...I ASSUMED SHE CAME TO REBUKE ME.
TO TELL ME THAT SHE SAW THROUGH MY LIES.
BUT THEN...
BEFORE YOU GRADUATE FROM HIGH SCHOOL...
...I WANT YOU TO SING FOR ME.
WHY DID SHE GIVE ME A CONDITION THAT WOULD LET ME CONTINUE MY MUSIC?
WHY DIDN'T SHE SEND HARUYOSHI AWAY THAT EVENING?
IT'S SO HOT OUT THERE.
COME IN.
AND WHY DID SHE...
...COME HERE AGAIN?

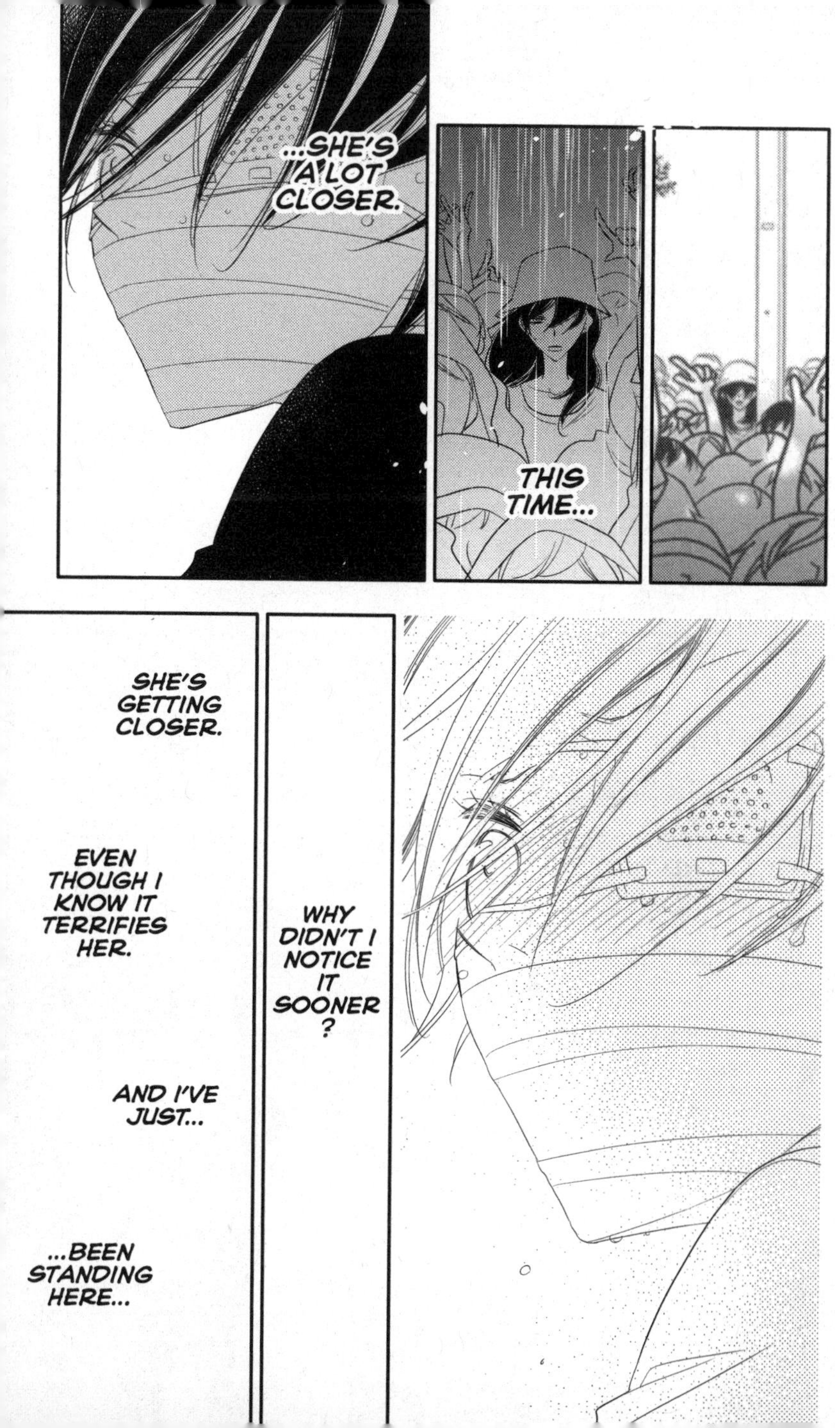
THIS TIME...
...SHE'S A LOT CLOSER.
WHY DIDN'T I NOTICE IT SOONER?
SHE'S GETTING CLOSER.
EVEN THOUGH I KNOW IT TERRIFIES HER.
AND I'VE JUST...
...BEEN STANDING HERE...

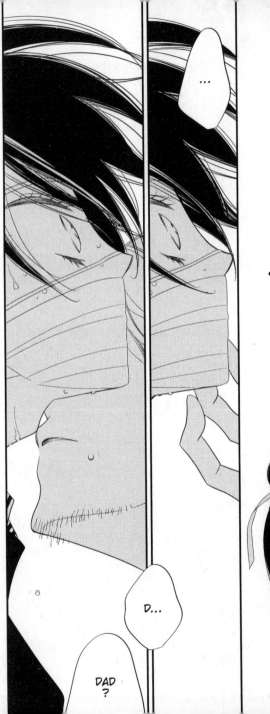

...

...WAITING.

D...

DAD
?

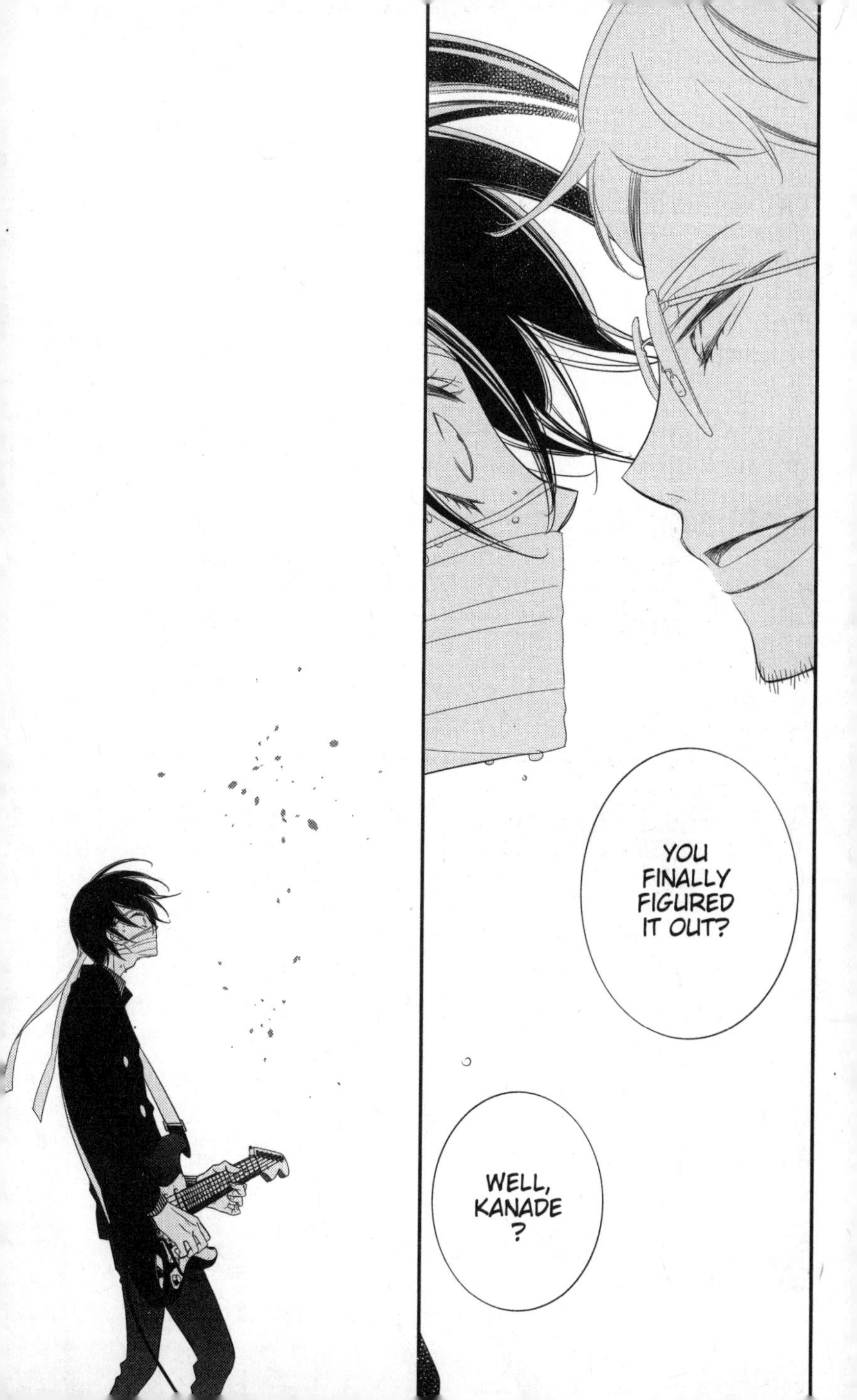
YOU FINALLY FIGURED IT OUT?
WELL, KANADE ?

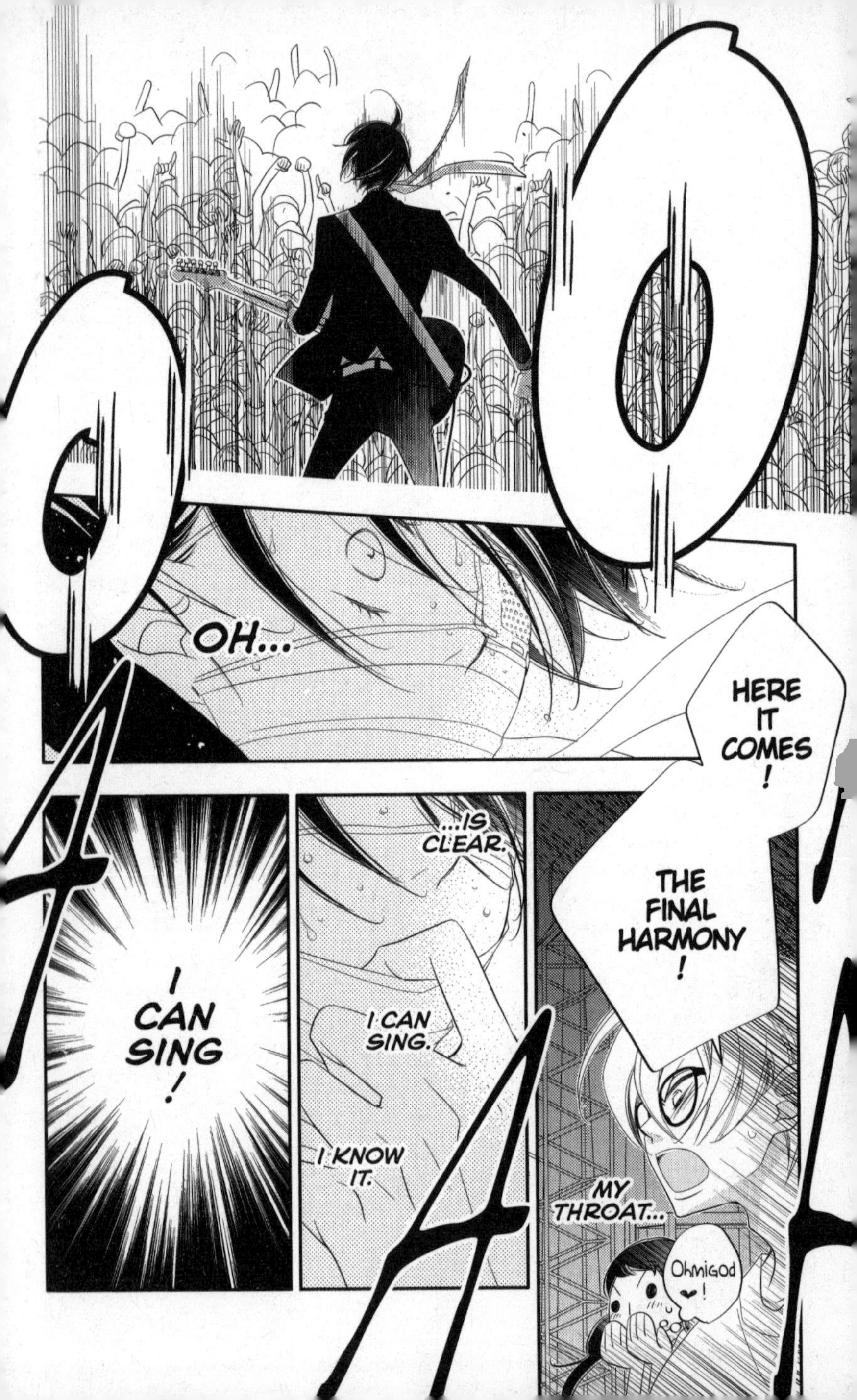
OH...
HERE IT COMES!
THE FINAL HARMONY!
MY THROAT...
Ohmigod!
...IS CLEAR.
I CAN SING.
I KNOW IT.
I CAN SING!

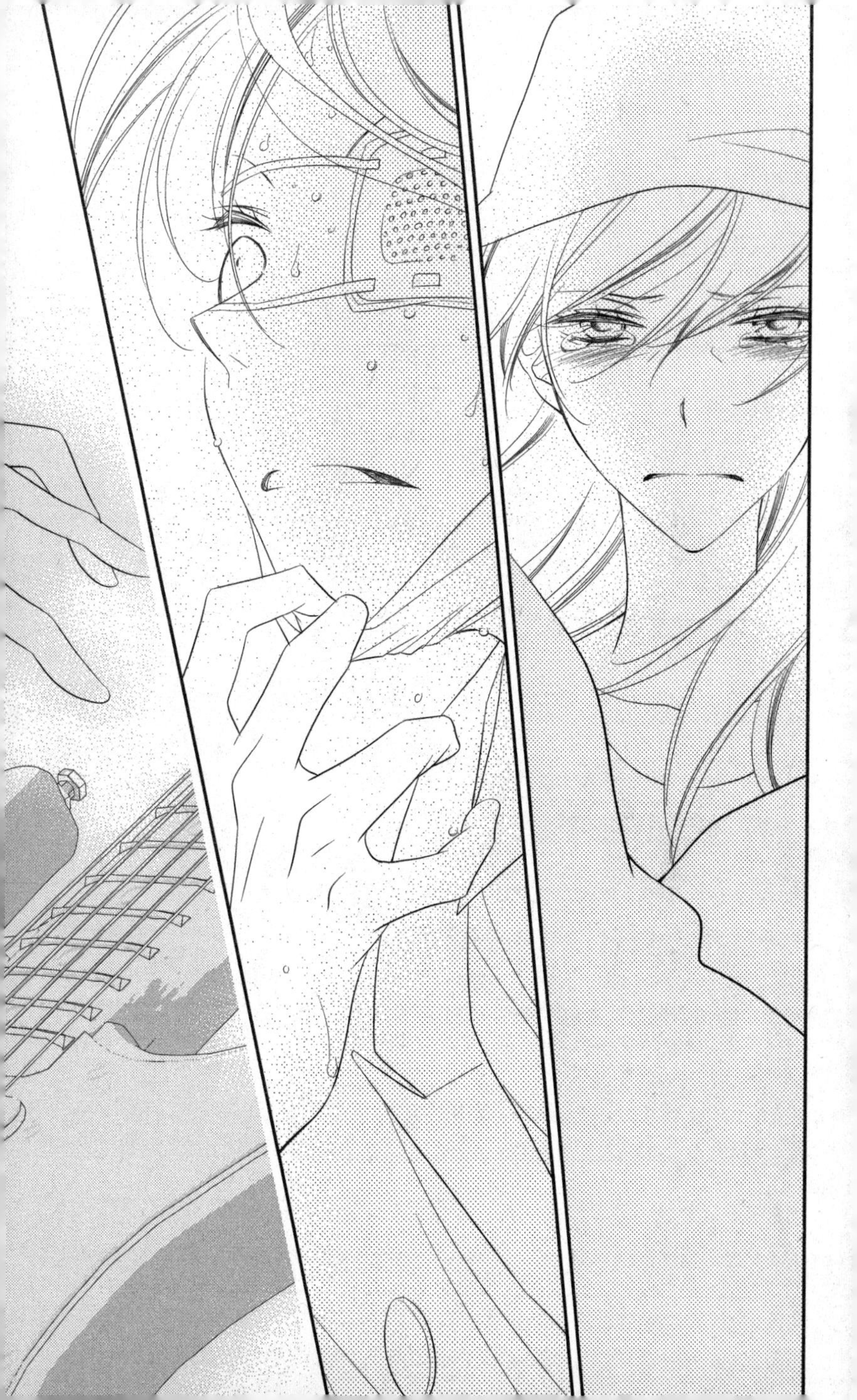

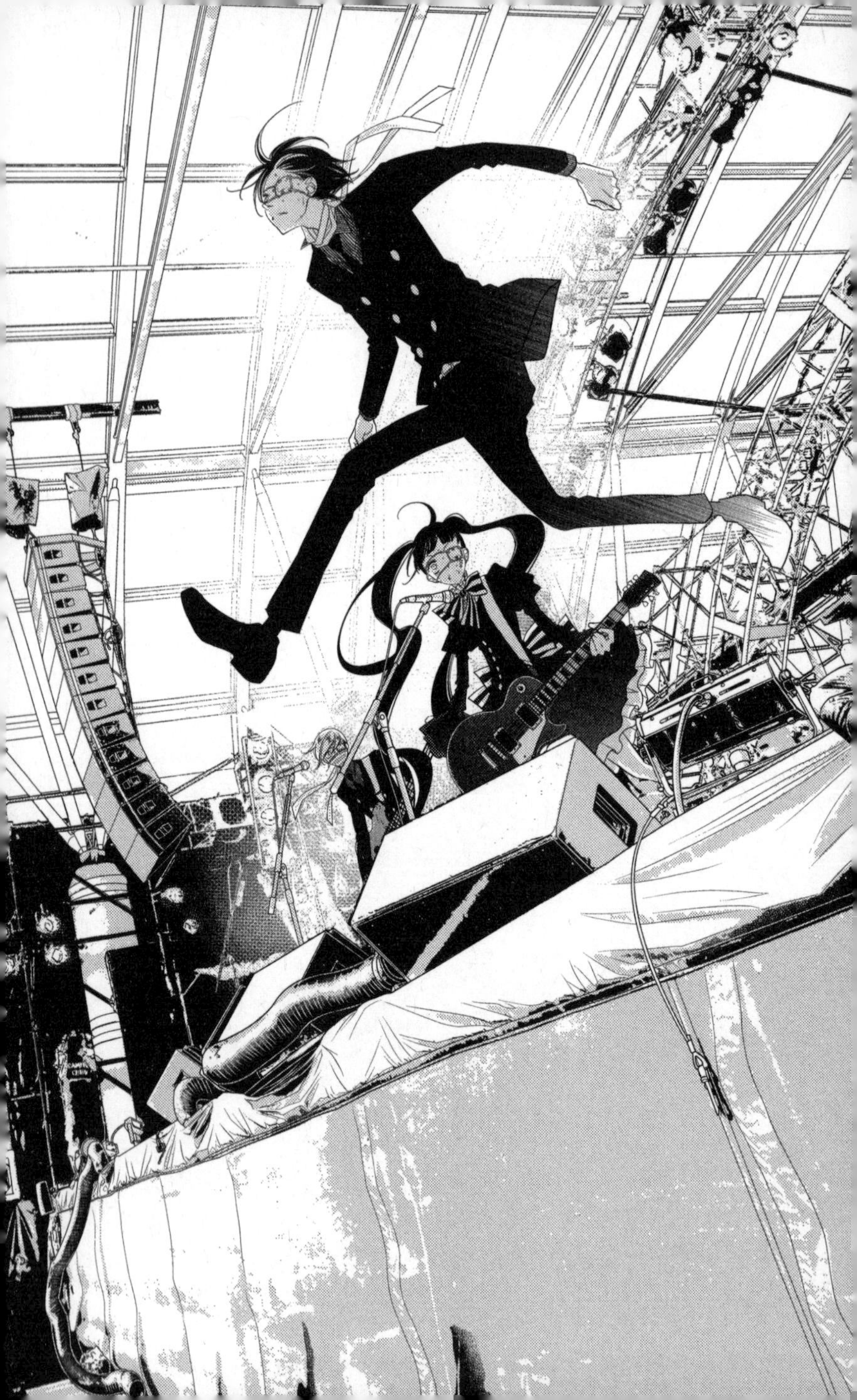

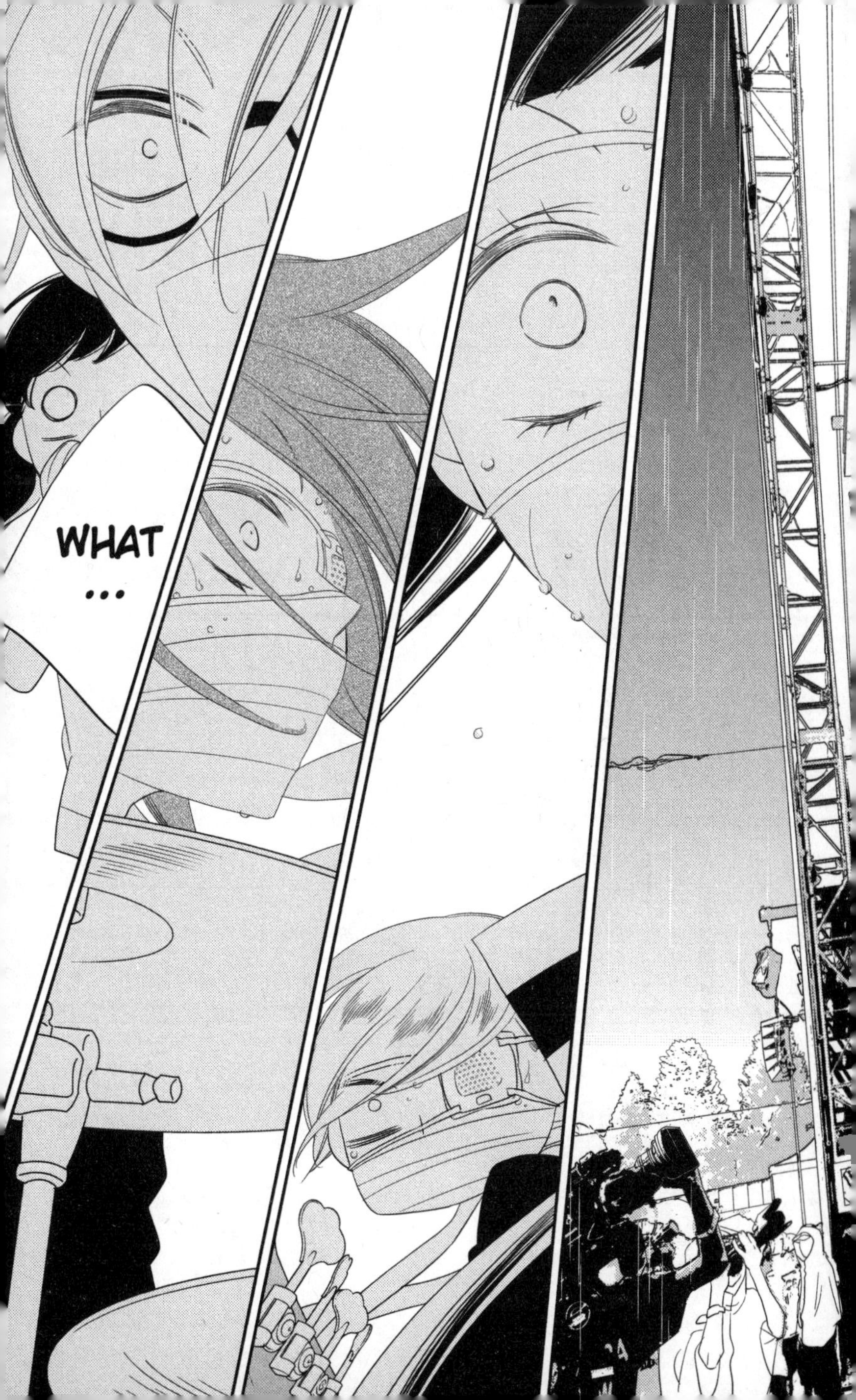
WHAT ...

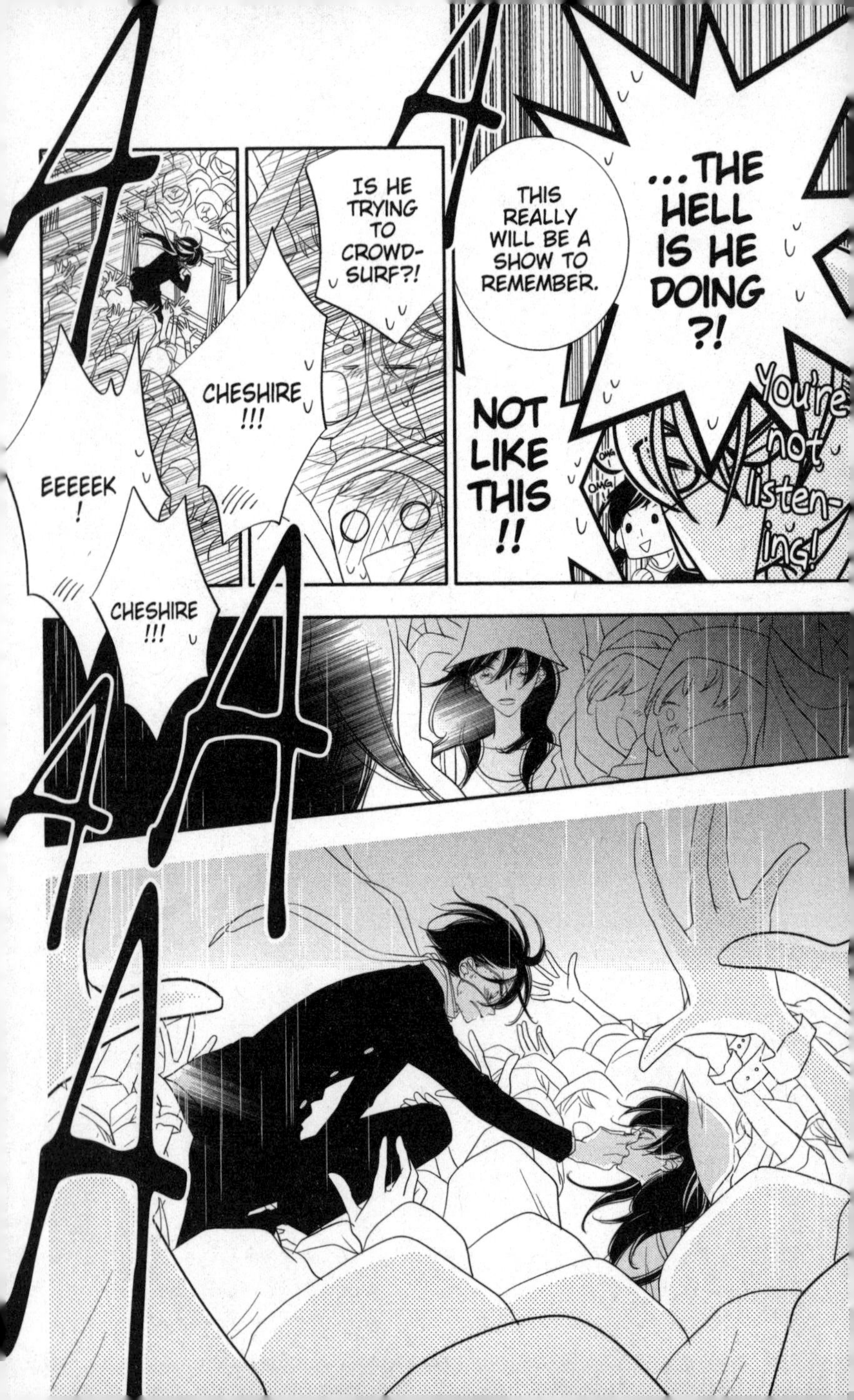
...THE HELL IS HE DOING?!
THIS REALLY WILL BE A SHOW TO REMEMBER.
NOT LIKE THIS!!
You're not listen-ing!
IS HE TRYING TO CROWD-SURF?!
CHESHIRE!!!
EEEEEK!
CHESHIRE!!!

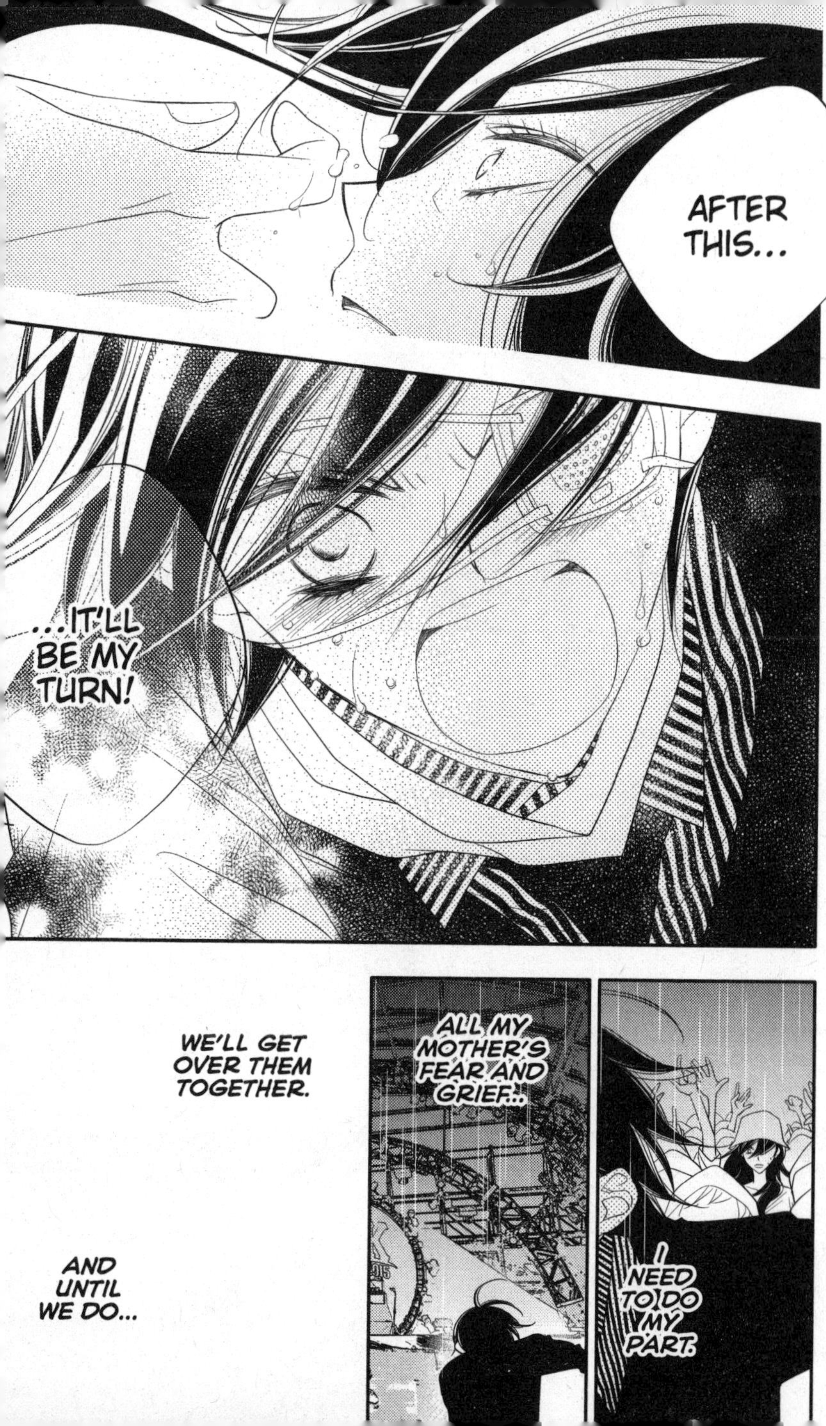
AFTER THIS...
...IT'LL BE MY TURN!
ALL MY MOTHER'S FEAR AND GRIEF...
WE'LL GET OVER THEM TOGETHER.
AND UNTIL WE DO...
I NEED TO DO MY PART.

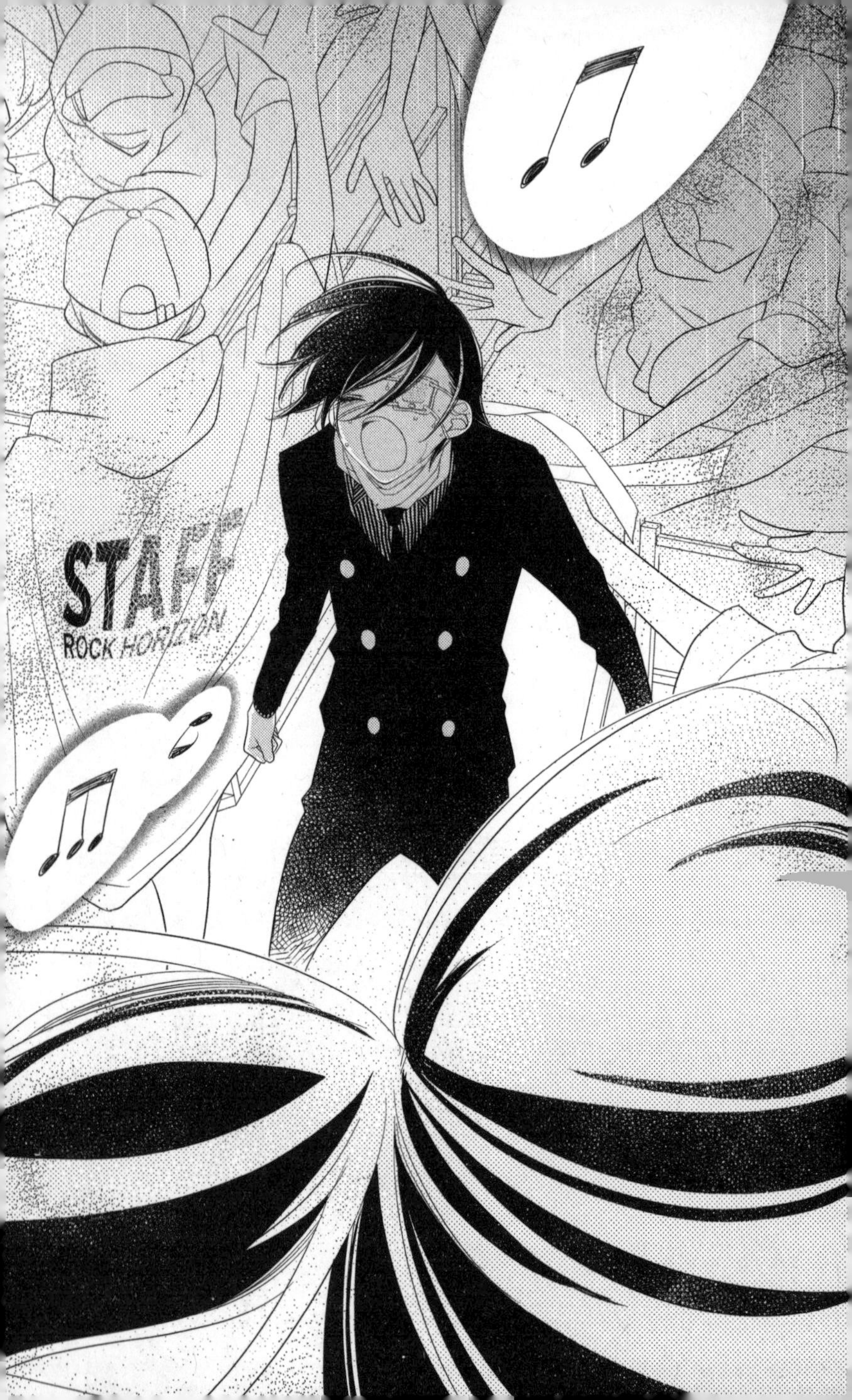
STAFF
ROCK HORIZON

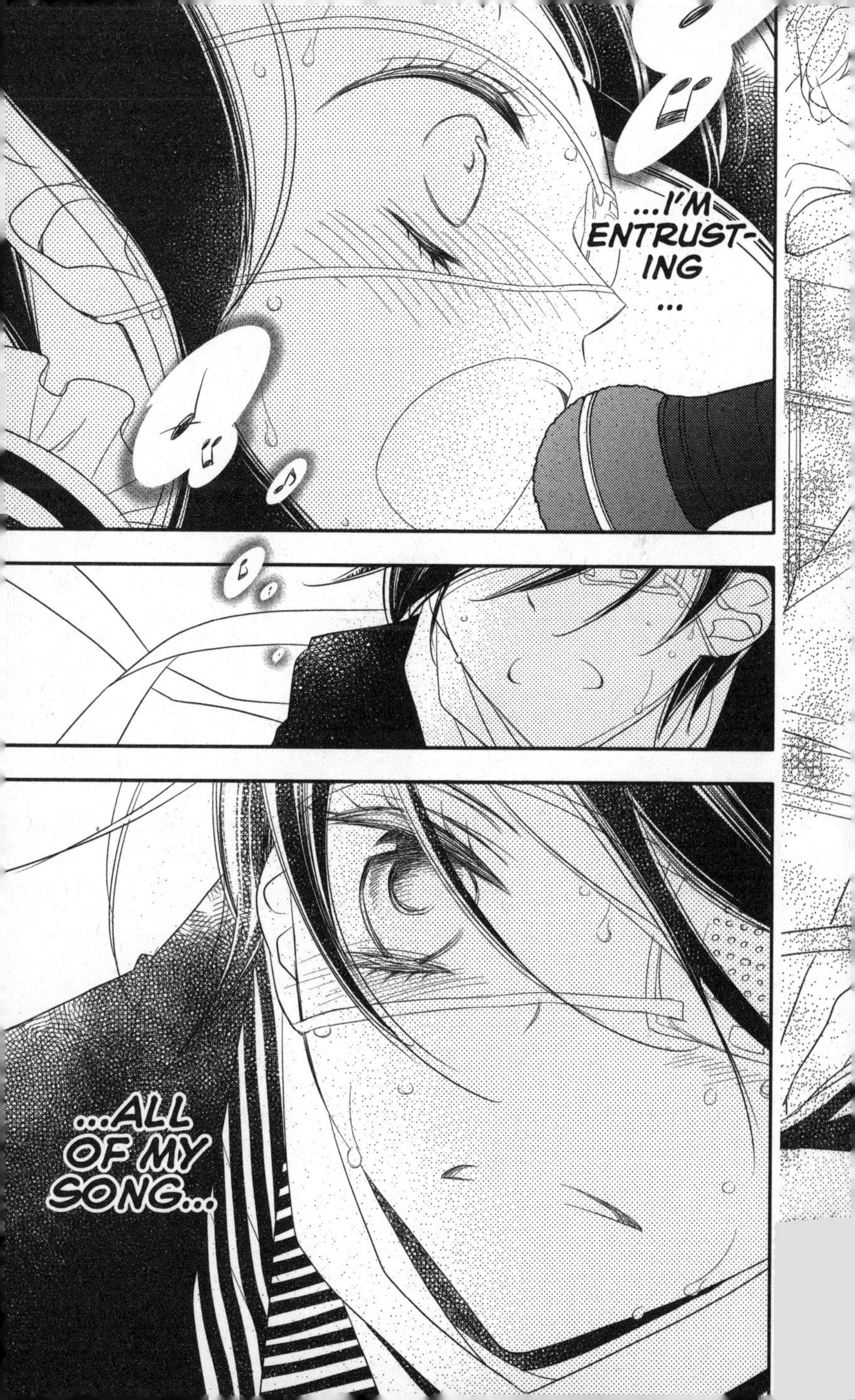
...I'M ENTRUSTING ...
...ALL OF MY SONG...

...TO YOU, ALICE.

in hurry to shout:

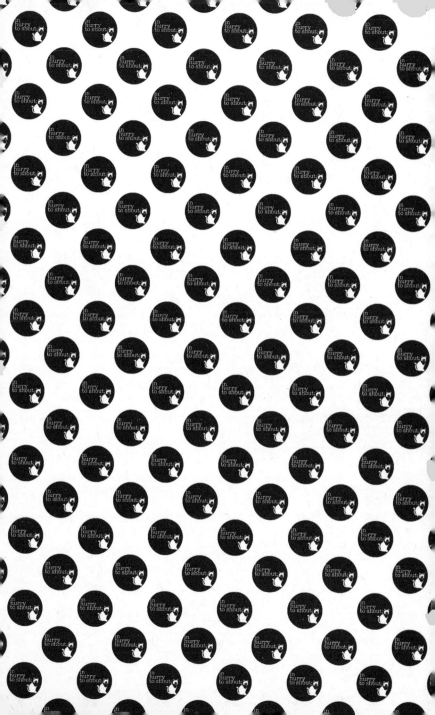

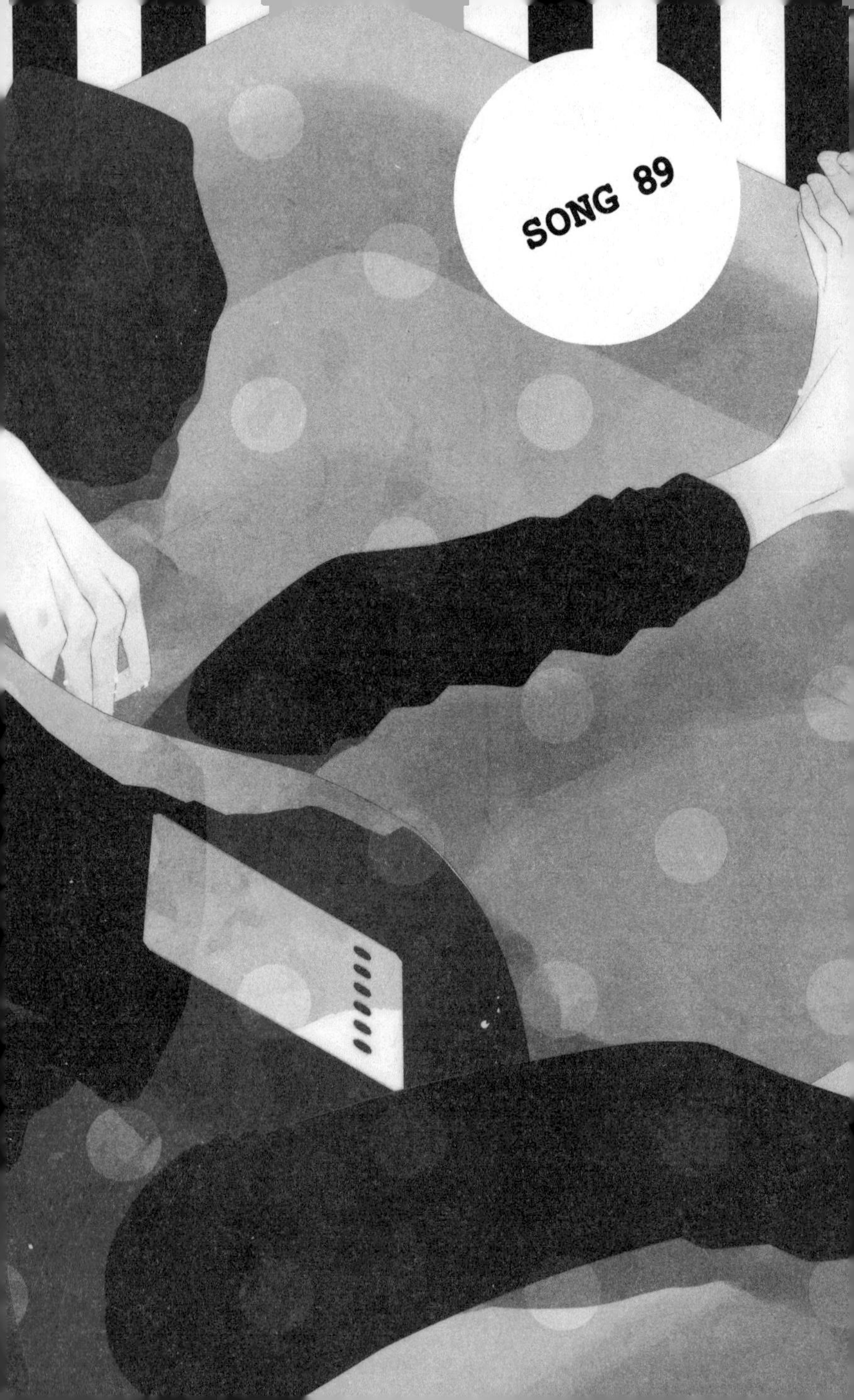
SONG 89

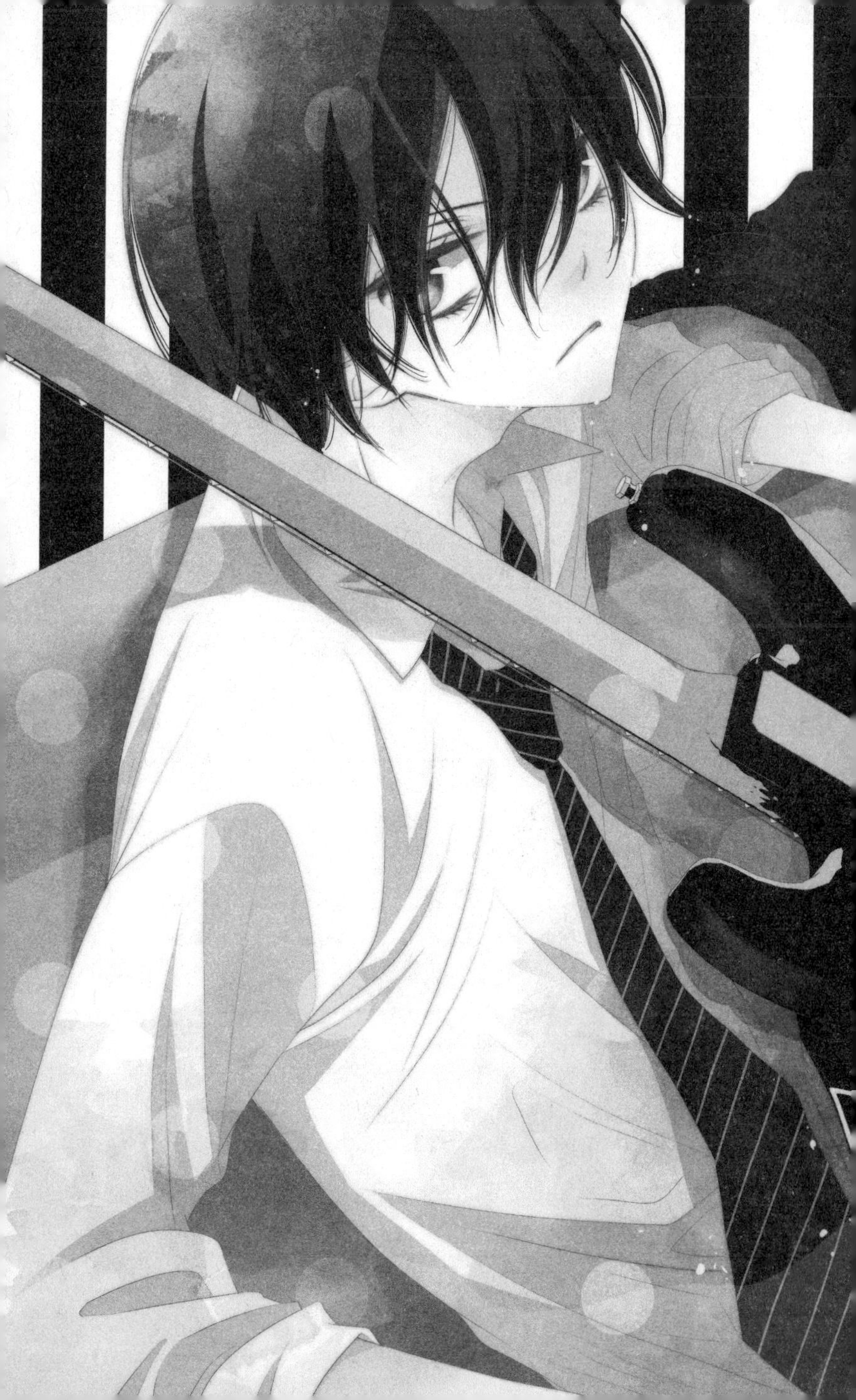

in hurry to shout:

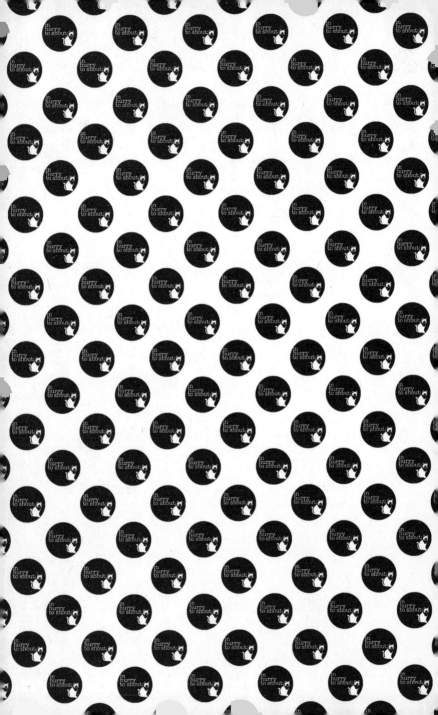

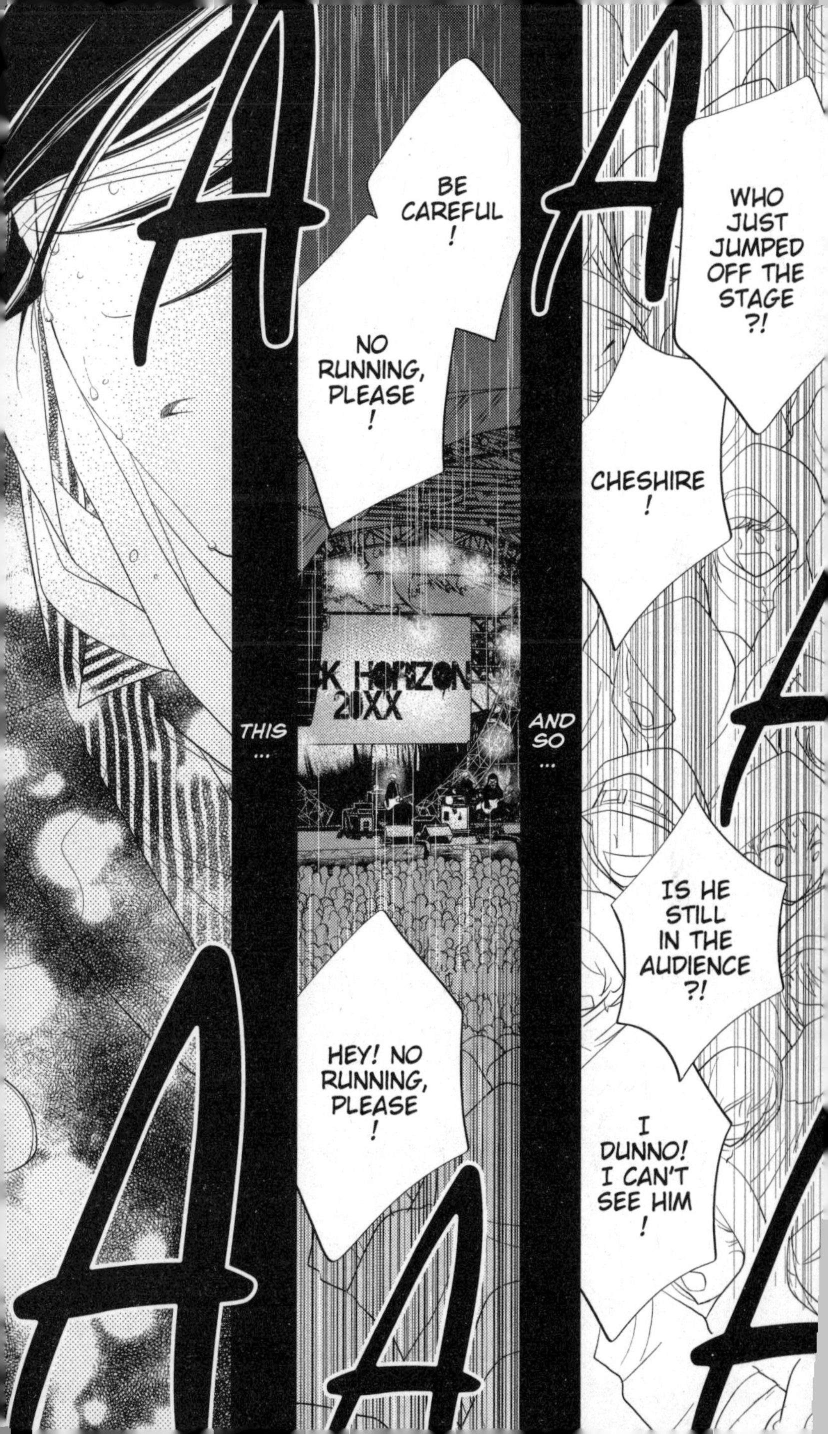
WHO JUST JUMPED OFF THE STAGE ?!
CHESHIRE !
IS HE STILL IN THE AUDIENCE ?!
I DUNNO! I CAN'T SEE HIM !
AND SO ...
BE CAREFUL !
NO RUNNING, PLEASE !
K HORIZON 20XX
HEY! NO RUNNING, PLEASE !
THIS ...

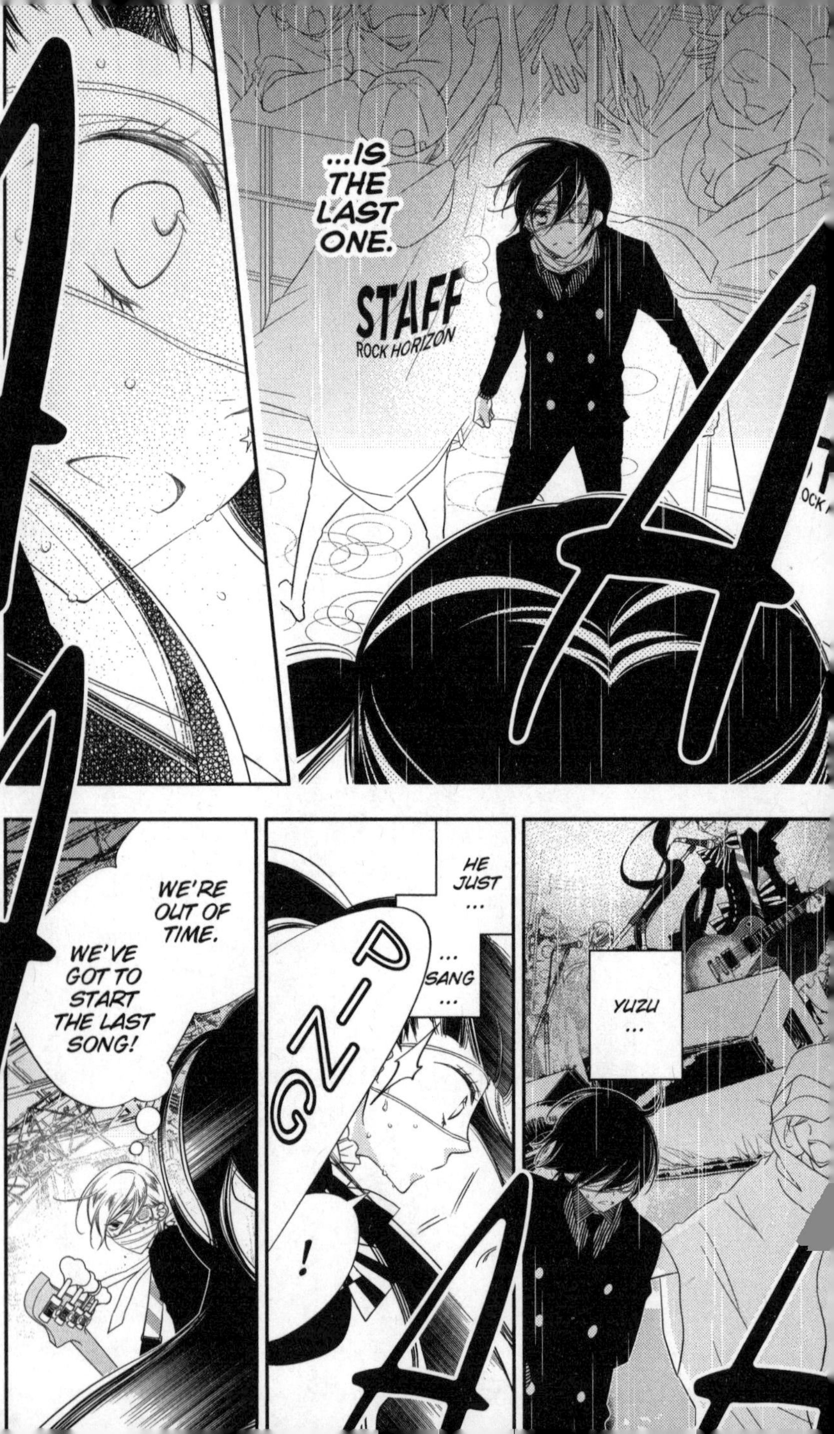
...IS THE LAST ONE.
STAFF
ROCK HORIZON
YUZU ...
HE JUST ...
... SANG ...
PI-N-G
!
WE'RE OUT OF TIME.
WE'VE GOT TO START THE LAST SONG!

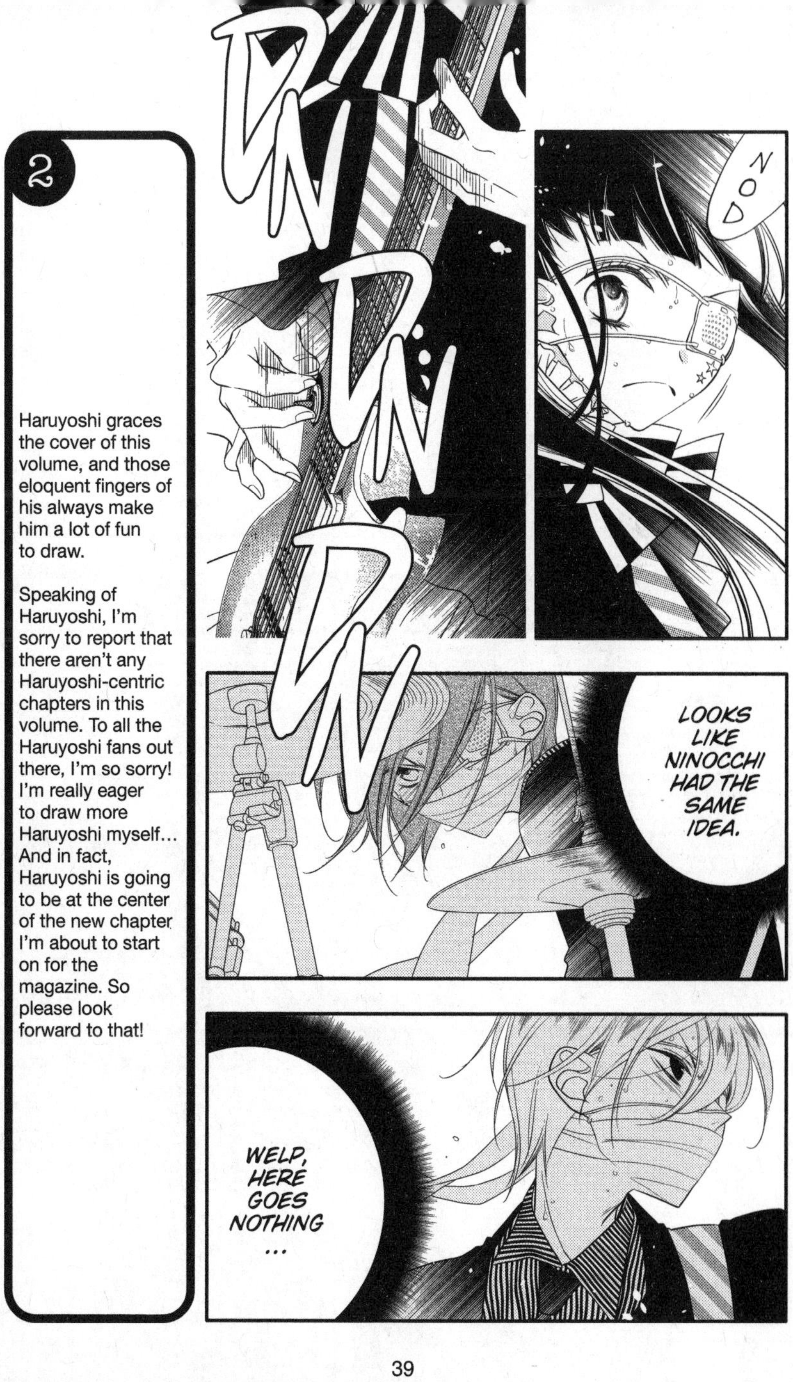
NOD
DUN DUN DUN
LOOKS LIKE NINOCCHI HAD THE SAME IDEA.
WELP, HERE GOES NOTHING...

2

Haruyoshi graces the cover of this volume, and those eloquent fingers of his always make him a lot of fun to draw.

Speaking of Haruyoshi, I'm sorry to report that there aren't any Haruyoshi-centric chapters in this volume. To all the Haruyoshi fans out there, I'm so sorry! I'm really eager to draw more Haruyoshi myself... And in fact, Haruyoshi is going to be at the center of the new chapter I'm about to start on for the magazine. So please look forward to that!

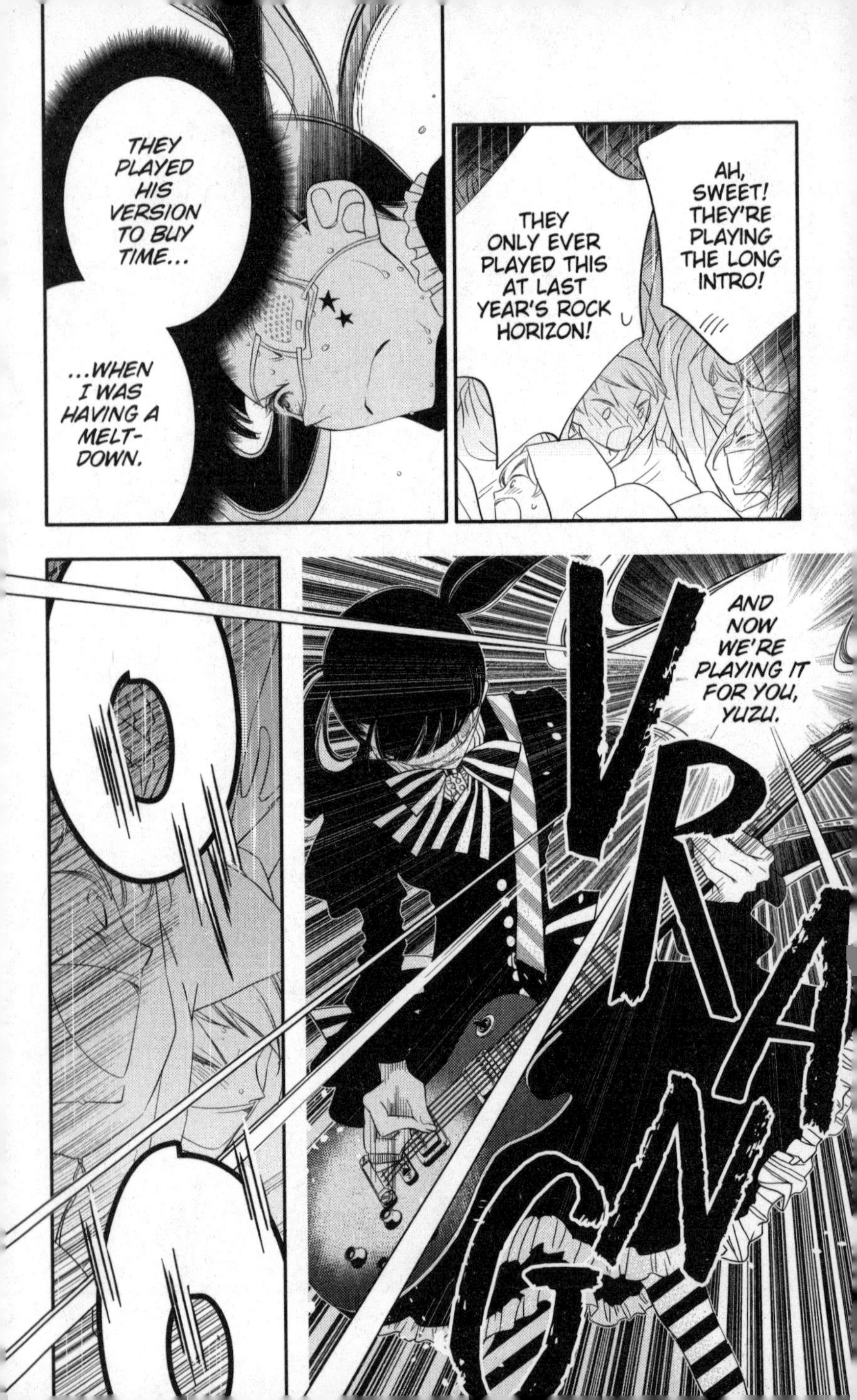
AH, SWEET! THEY'RE PLAYING THE LONG INTRO!
THEY ONLY EVER PLAYED THIS AT LAST YEAR'S ROCK HORIZON!
THEY PLAYED HIS VERSION TO BUY TIME...
...WHEN I WAS HAVING A MELT-DOWN.
AND NOW WE'RE PLAYING IT FOR YOU, YUZU.
VRAANG

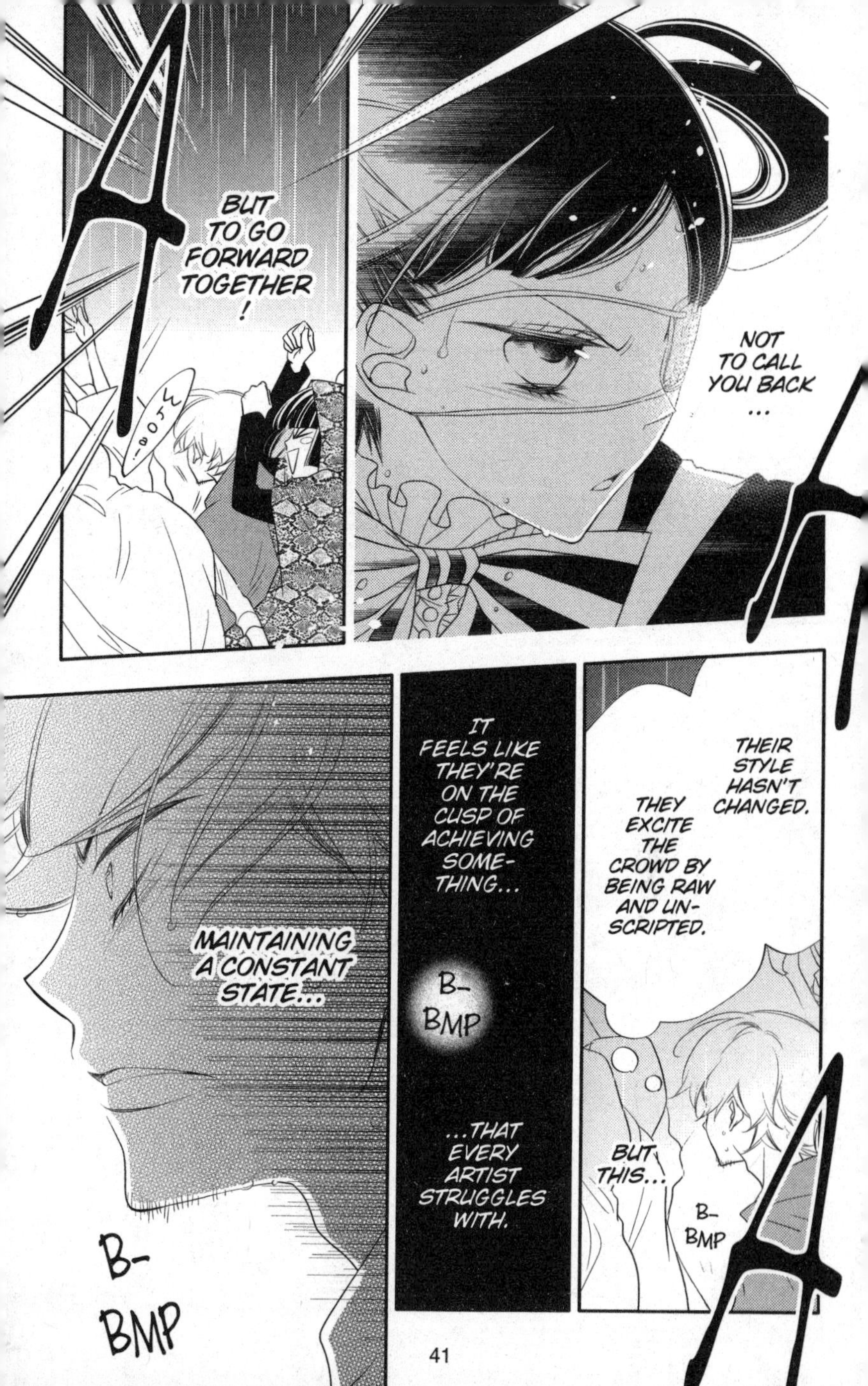
NOT TO CALL YOU BACK...
BUT TO GO FORWARD TOGETHER!
THEIR STYLE HASN'T CHANGED.
THEY EXCITE THE CROWD BY BEING RAW AND UN-SCRIPTED.
BUT THIS...
B-BMP
IT FEELS LIKE THEY'RE ON THE CUSP OF ACHIEVING SOME-THING...
B-BMP
...THAT EVERY ARTIST STRUGGLES WITH.
MAINTAINING A CONSTANT STATE...
B-BMP

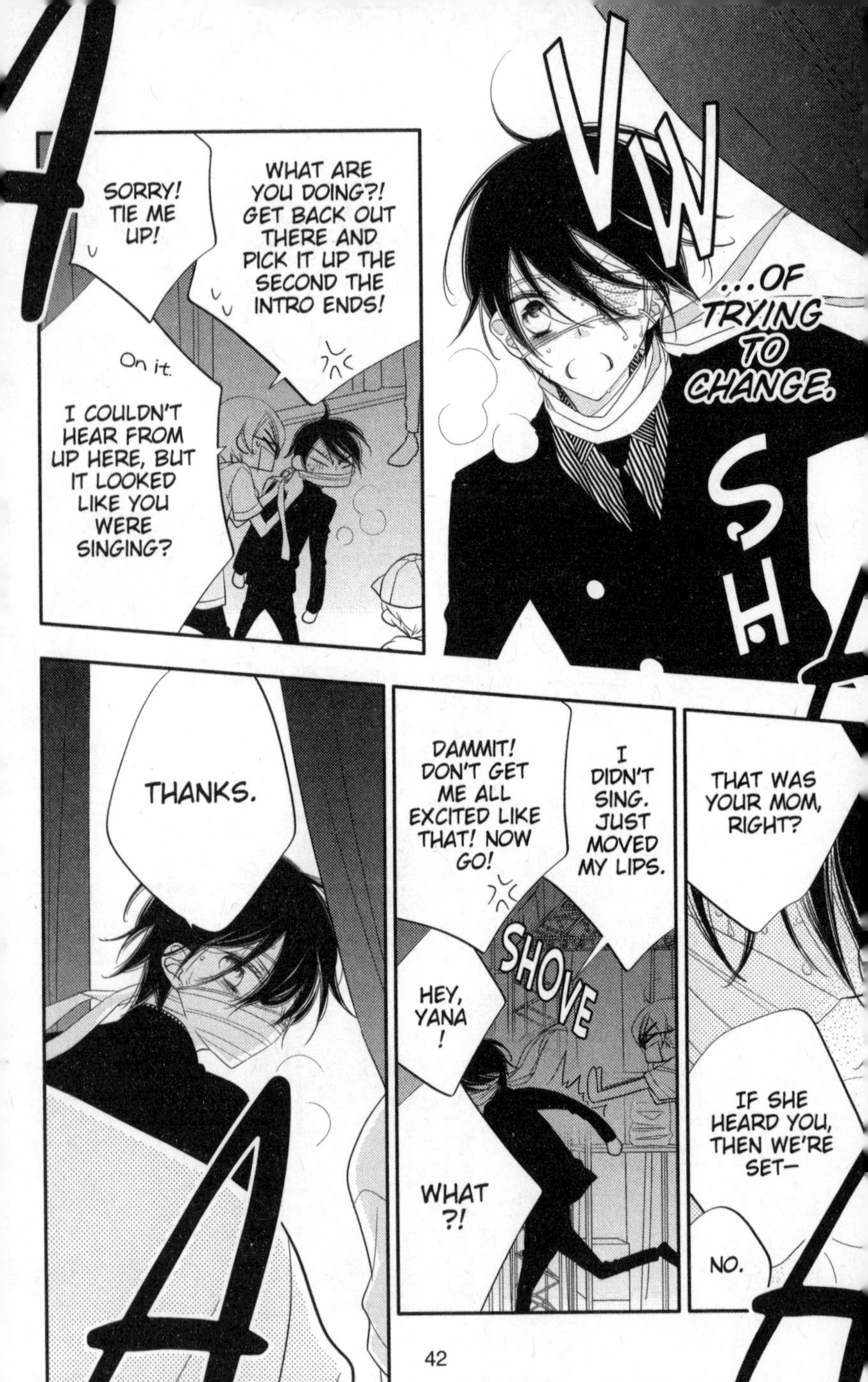
...OF TRYING TO CHANGE.
WHAT ARE YOU DOING?! GET BACK OUT THERE AND PICK IT UP THE SECOND THE INTRO ENDS!
SORRY! TIE ME UP!
On it.
I COULDN'T HEAR FROM UP HERE, BUT IT LOOKED LIKE YOU WERE SINGING?
THAT WAS YOUR MOM, RIGHT?
IF SHE HEARD YOU, THEN WE'RE SET—
NO.
I DIDN'T SING. JUST MOVED MY LIPS.
DAMMIT! DON'T GET ME ALL EXCITED LIKE THAT! NOW GO!
SHOVE
HEY, YANA!
WHAT?!
THANKS.

ROCK
HORIZON
20XX

THE
SUNSET
STAGE

6:25
P.M.

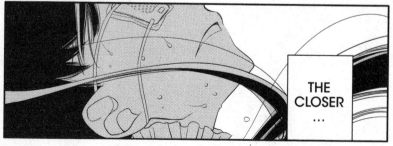

THE
CLOSER
...

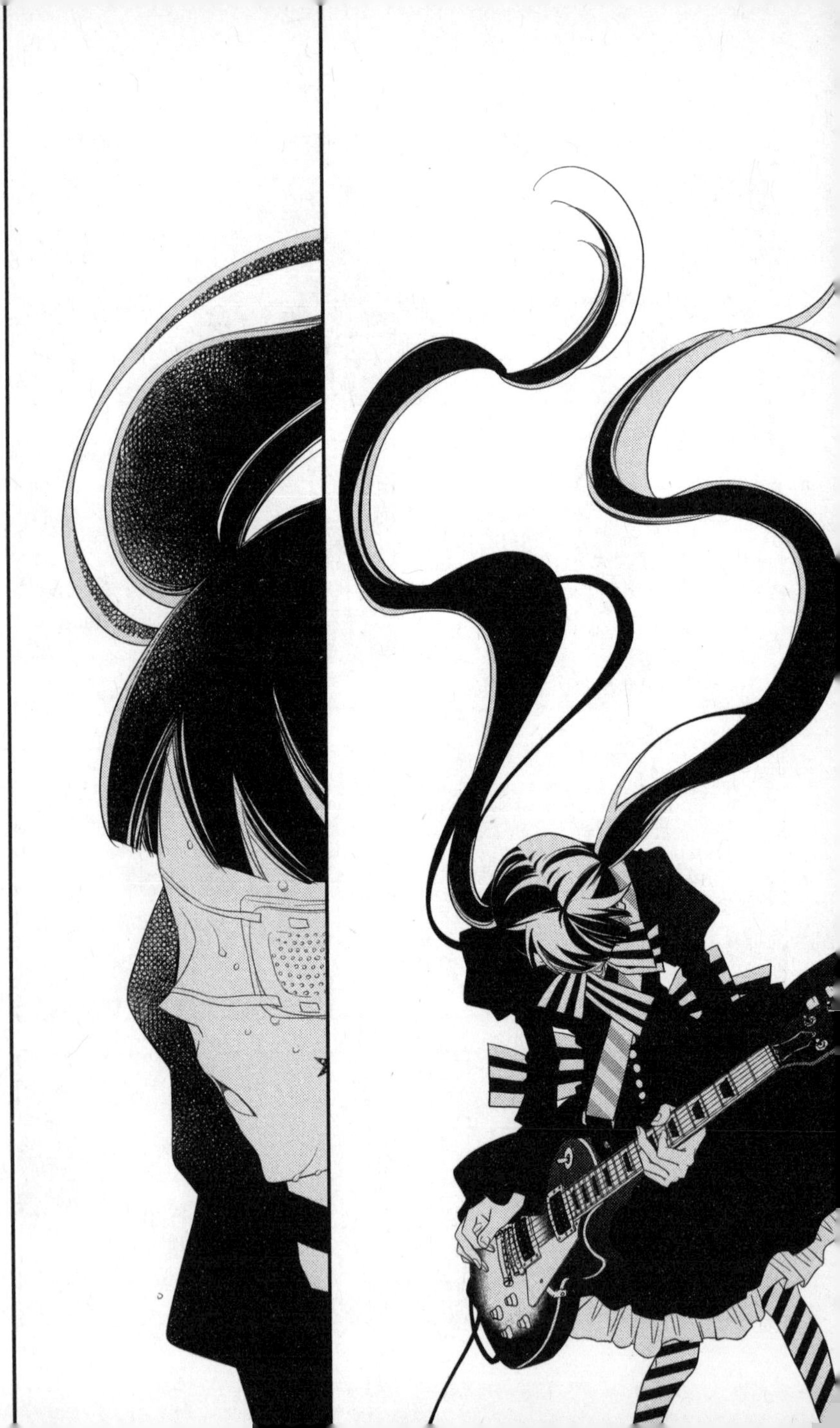

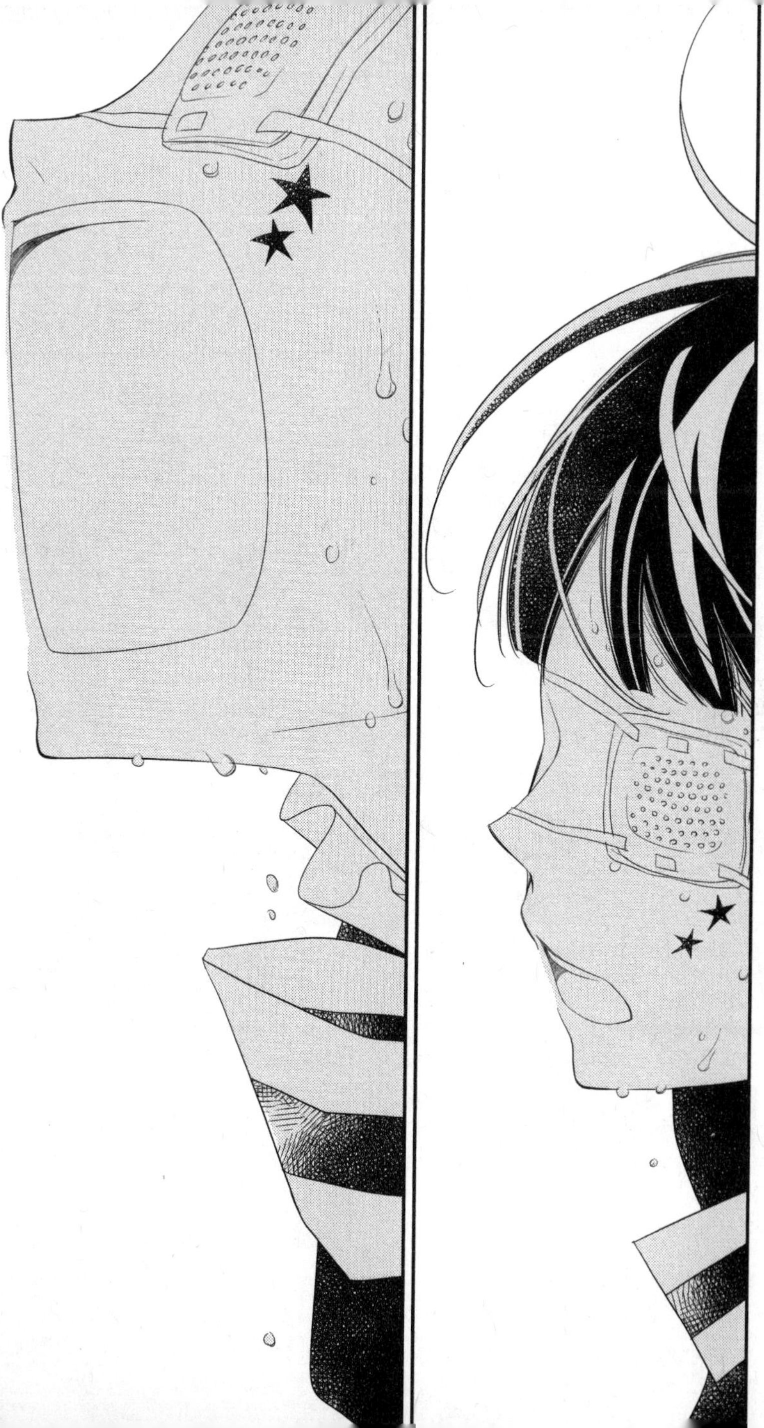

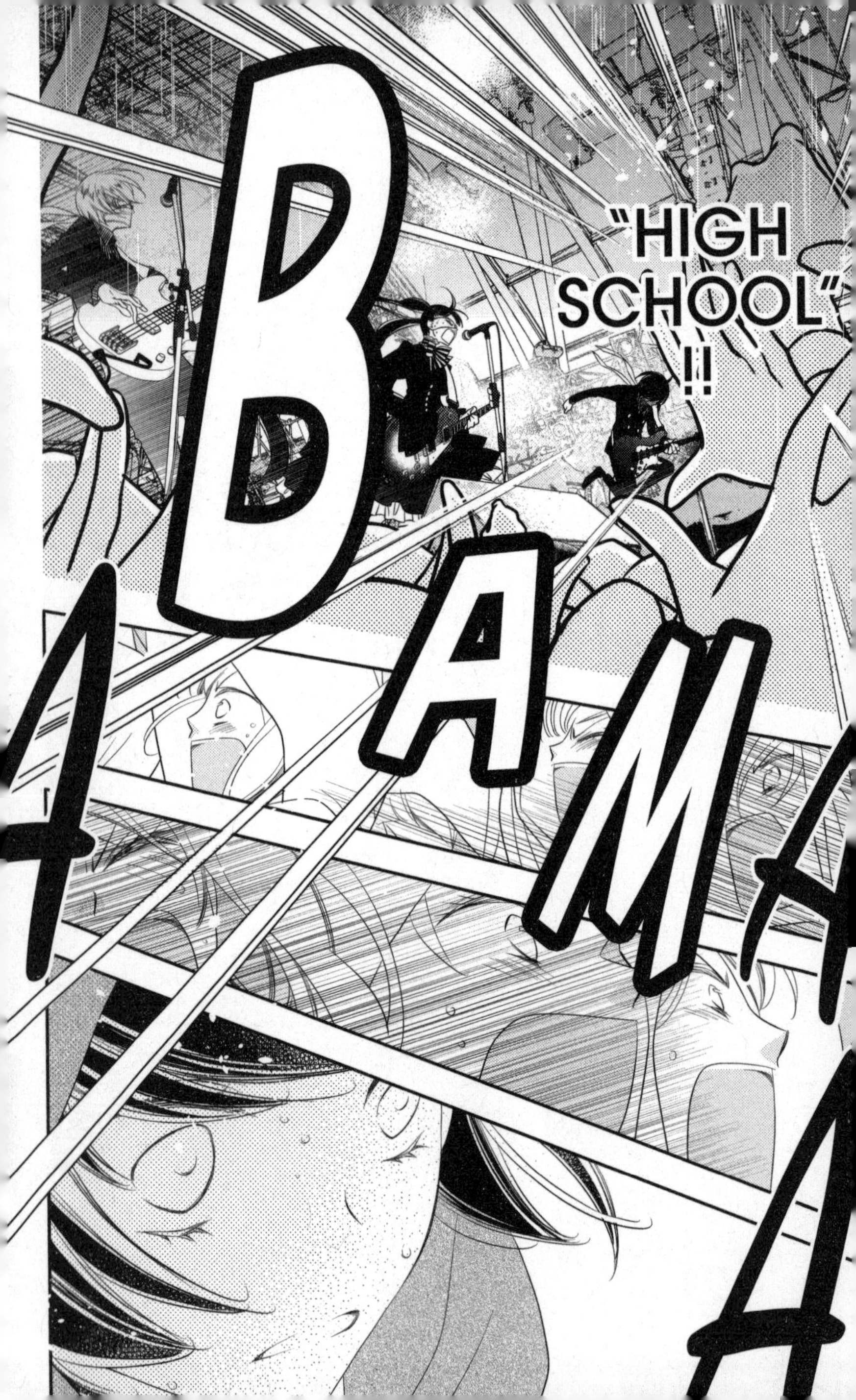
"HIGH SCHOOL"!!
BDAAMMAAA

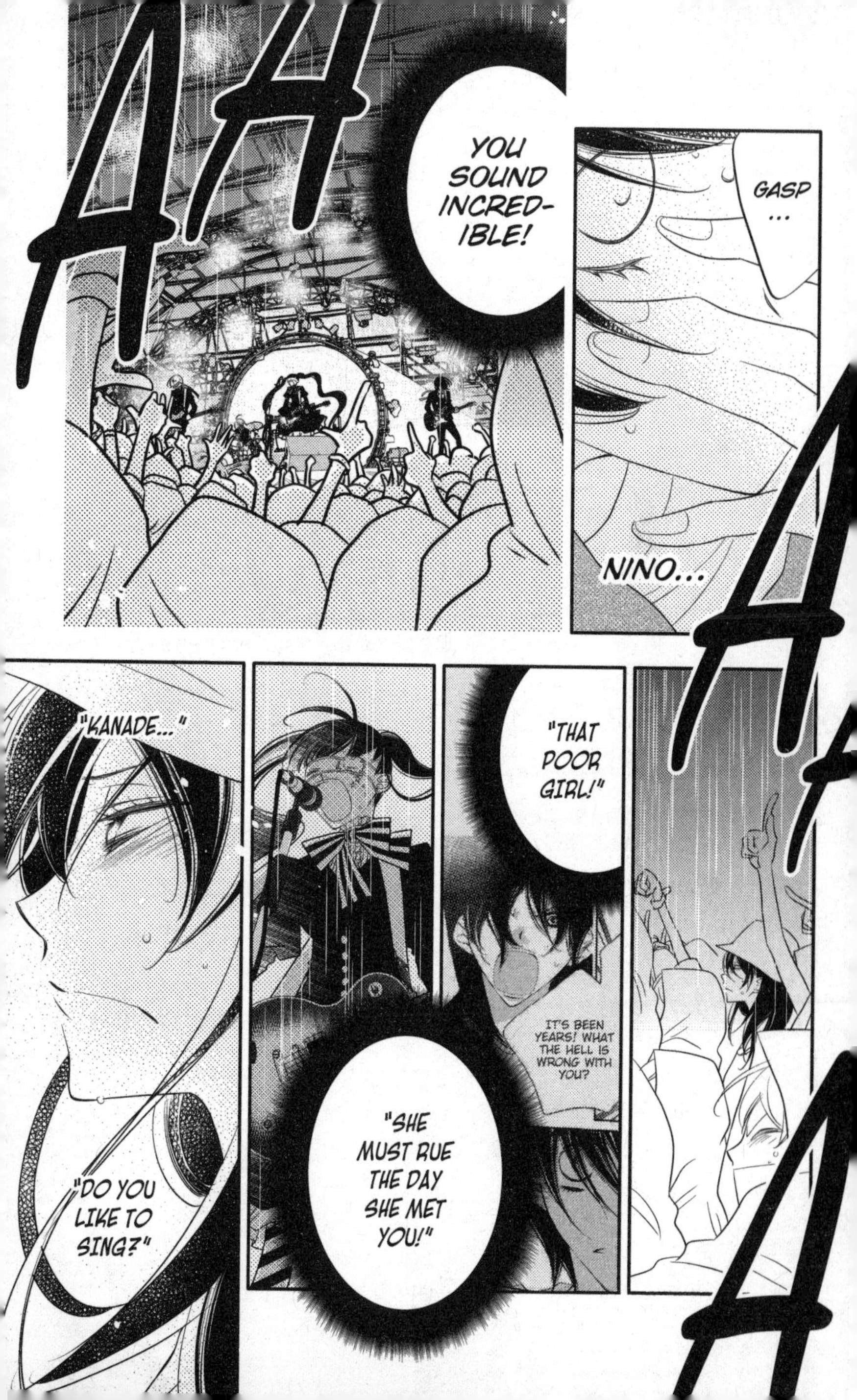
GASP ...
NINO...
YOU SOUND INCREDIBLE!
AH
AAAA
"THAT POOR GIRL!"
IT'S BEEN YEARS! WHAT THE HELL IS WRONG WITH YOU?
"SHE MUST RUE THE DAY SHE MET YOU!"
"KANADE..."
"DO YOU LIKE TO SING?"

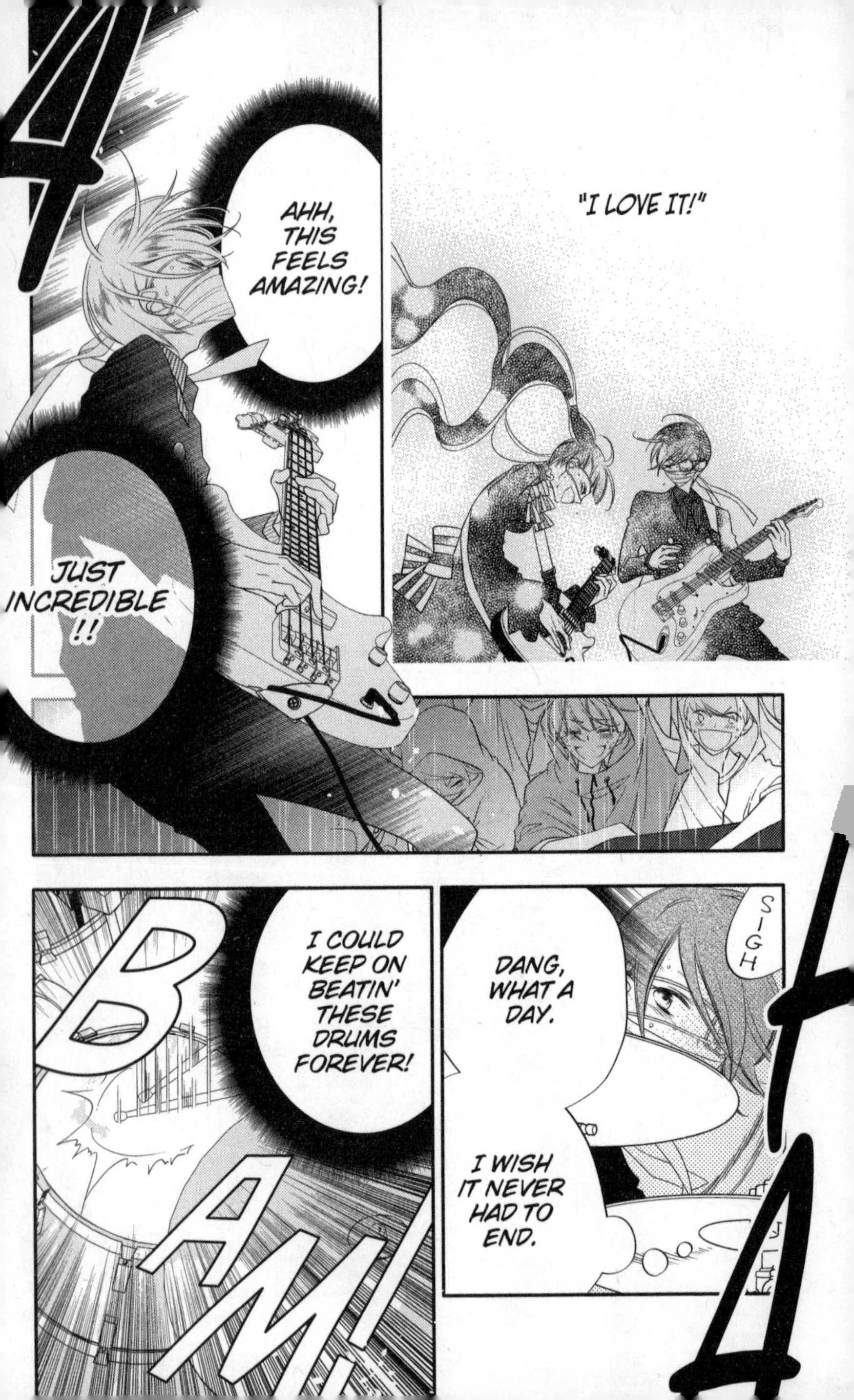
"I LOVE IT!"
AHH, THIS FEELS AMAZING!
JUST INCREDIBLE!!
SIGH
DANG, WHAT A DAY.
I WISH IT NEVER HAD TO END.
I COULD KEEP ON BEATIN' THESE DRUMS FOREVER!
BAM!

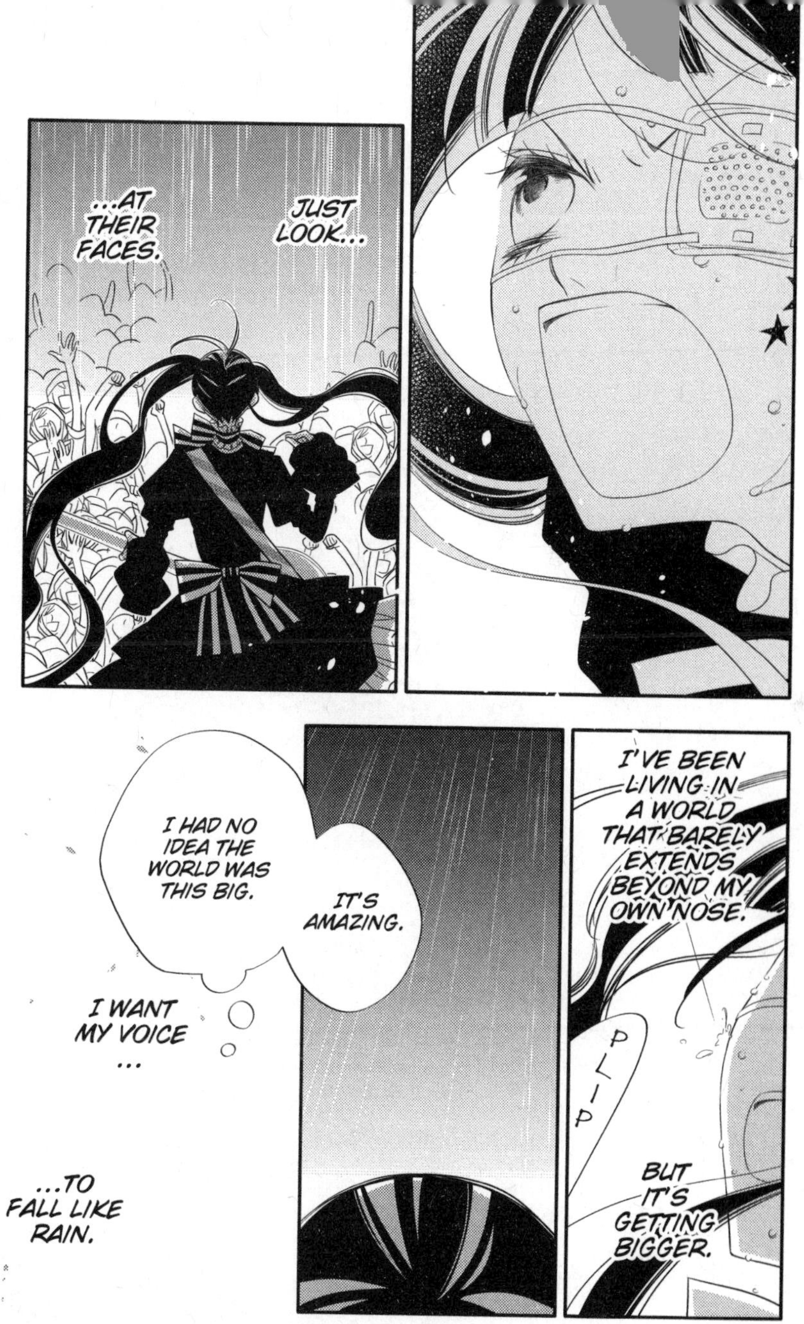
JUST LOOK...
...AT THEIR FACES.
I'VE BEEN LIVING IN A WORLD THAT BARELY EXTENDS BEYOND MY OWN NOSE.
PLIP
BUT IT'S GETTING BIGGER.
IT'S AMAZING.
I HAD NO IDEA THE WORLD WAS THIS BIG.
I WANT MY VOICE ...
...TO FALL LIKE RAIN.

*I
WANT
IT TO
FILL
THE
SKY,
LIKE
SO
MANY
RAINDROPS.*

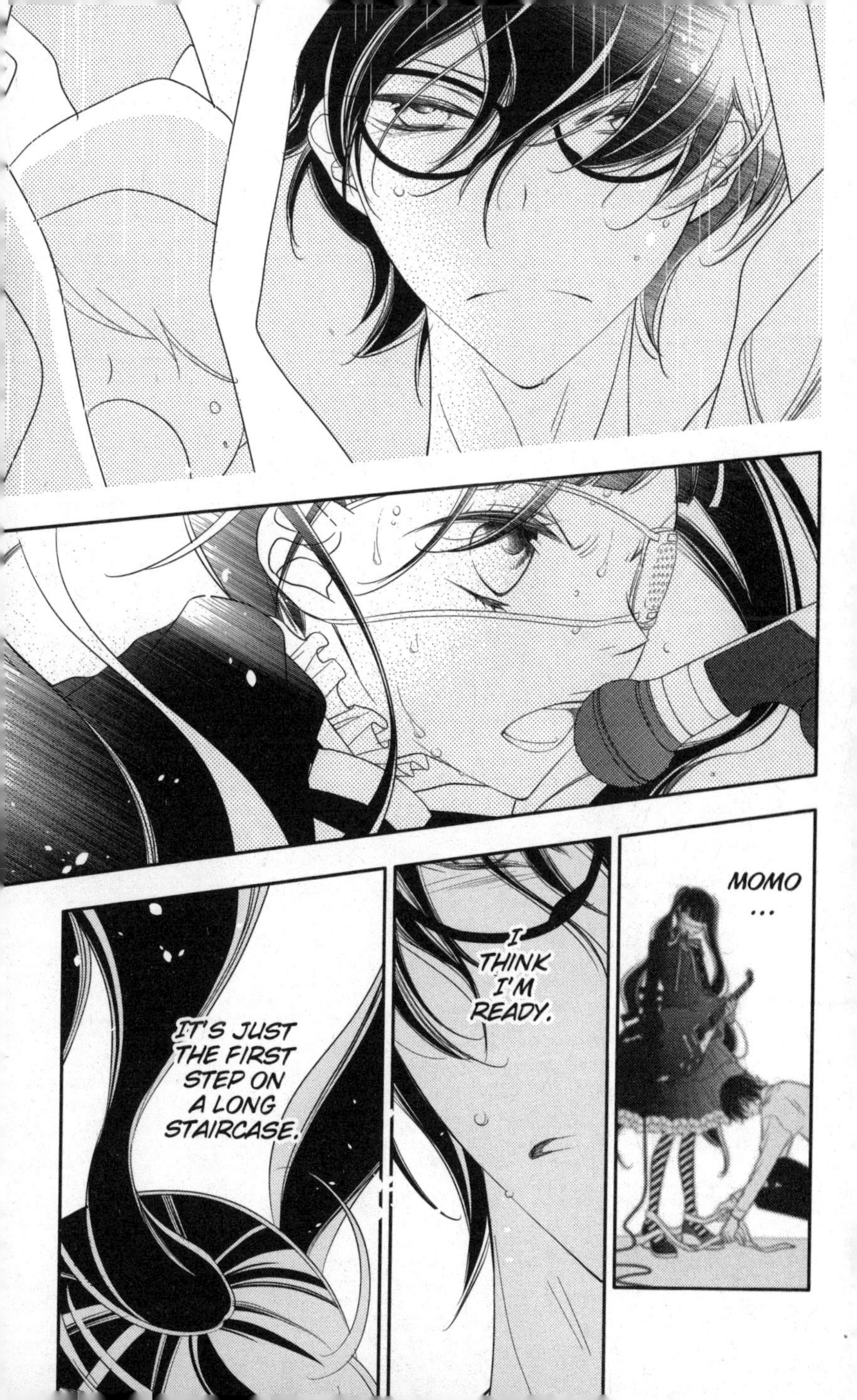
MOMO ...
I THINK I'M READY.
IT'S JUST THE FIRST STEP ON A LONG STAIRCASE.

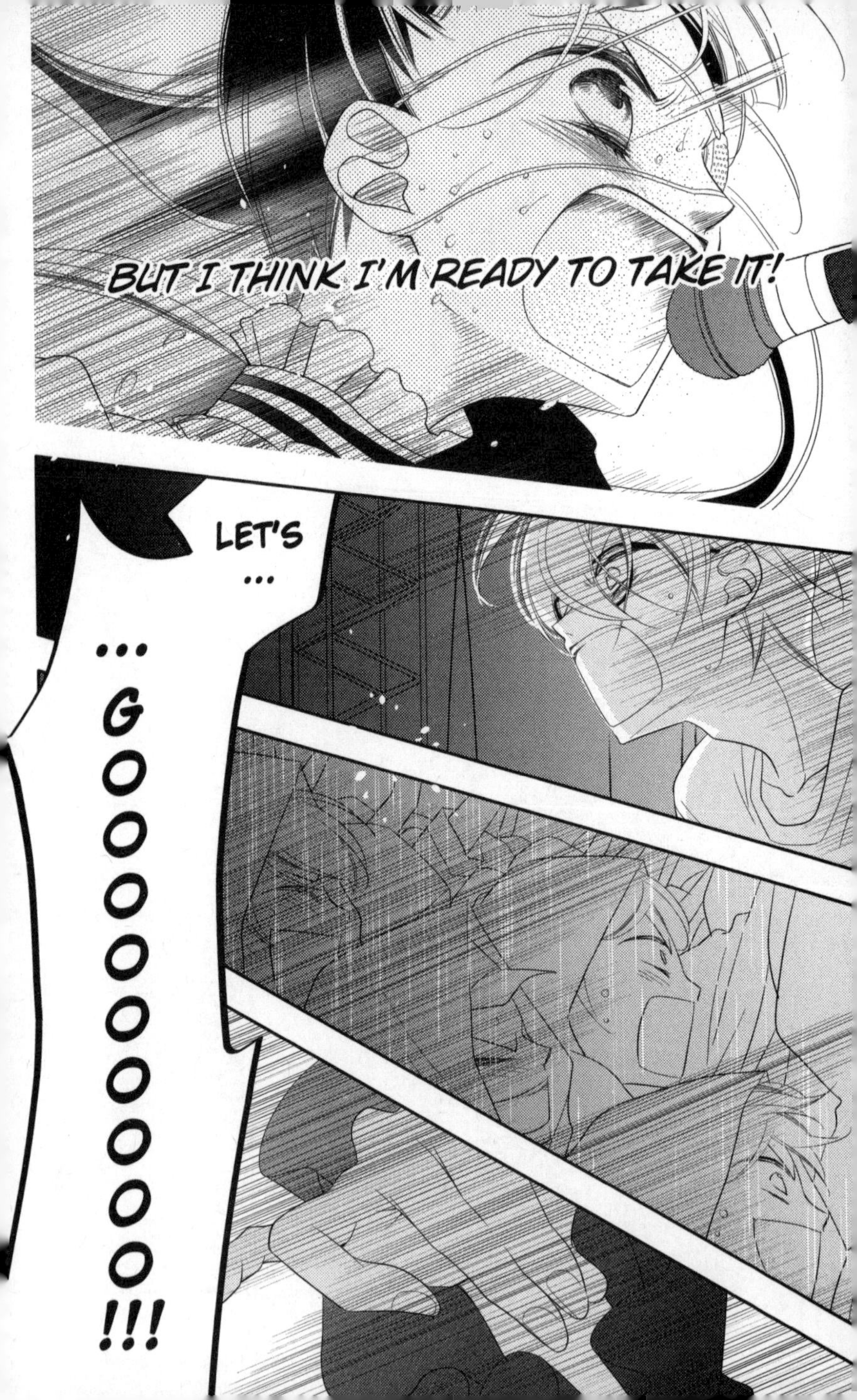
BUT I THINK I'M READY TO TAKE IT!
LET'S ...
... GOOOOOOOOOOOOO!!!

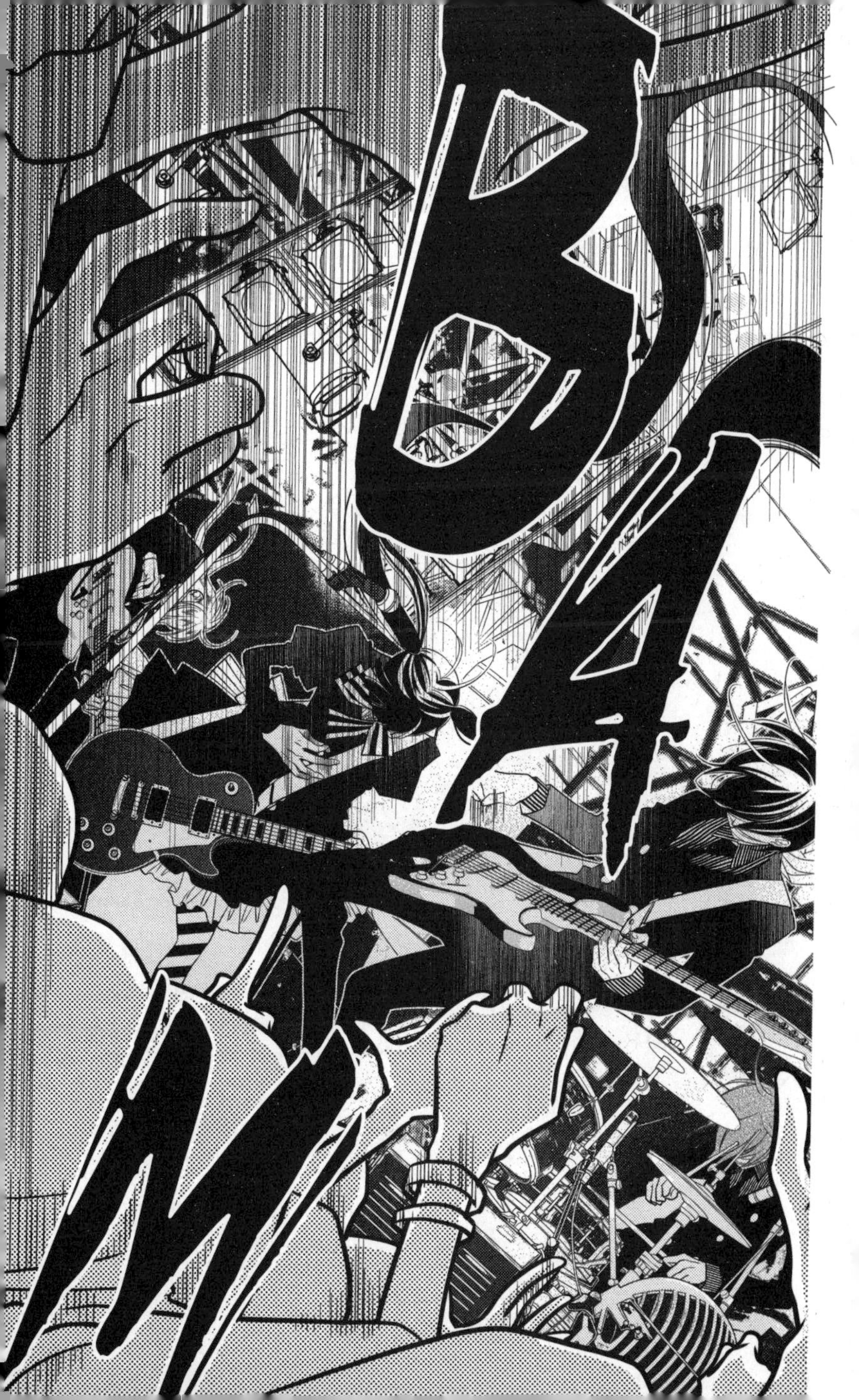

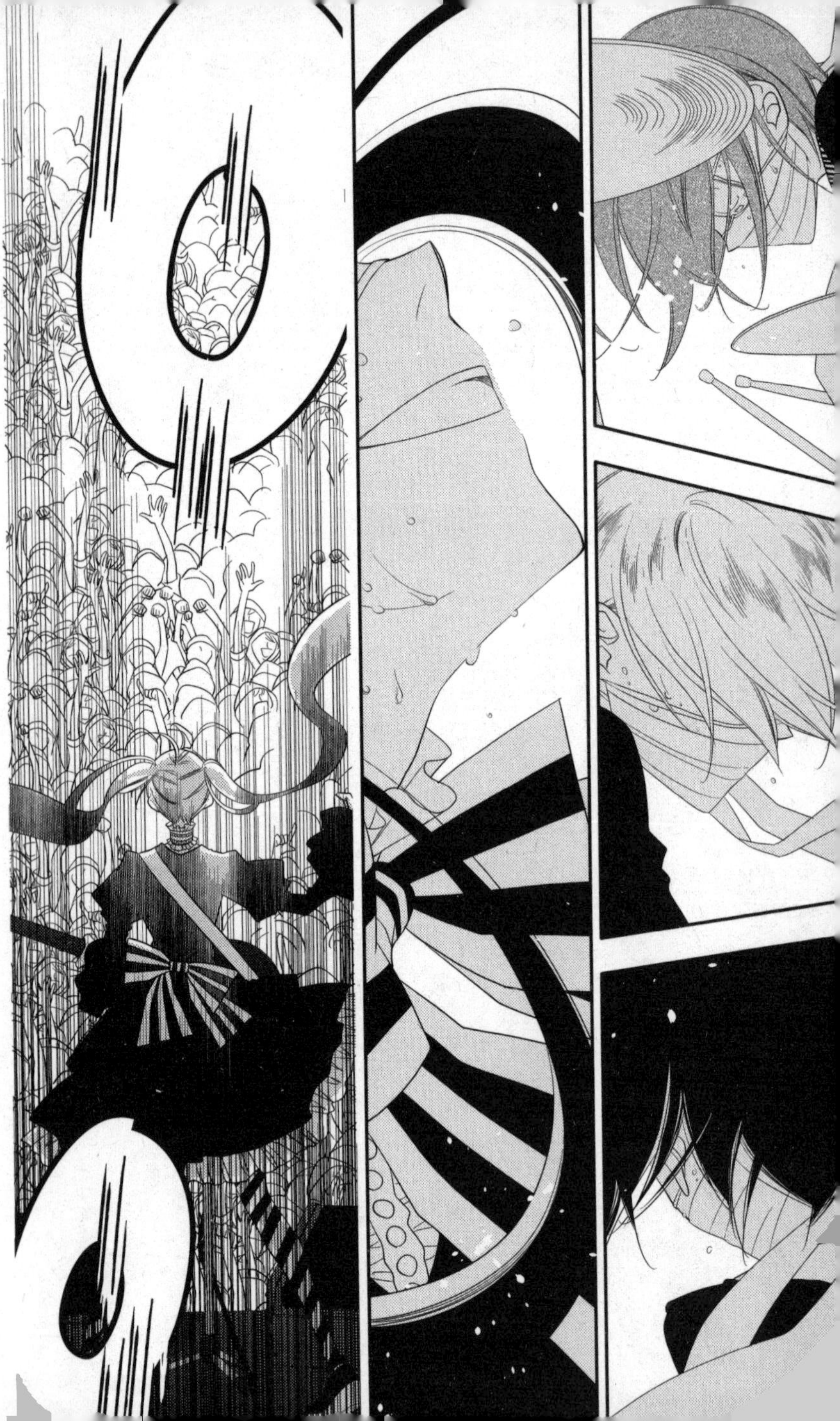

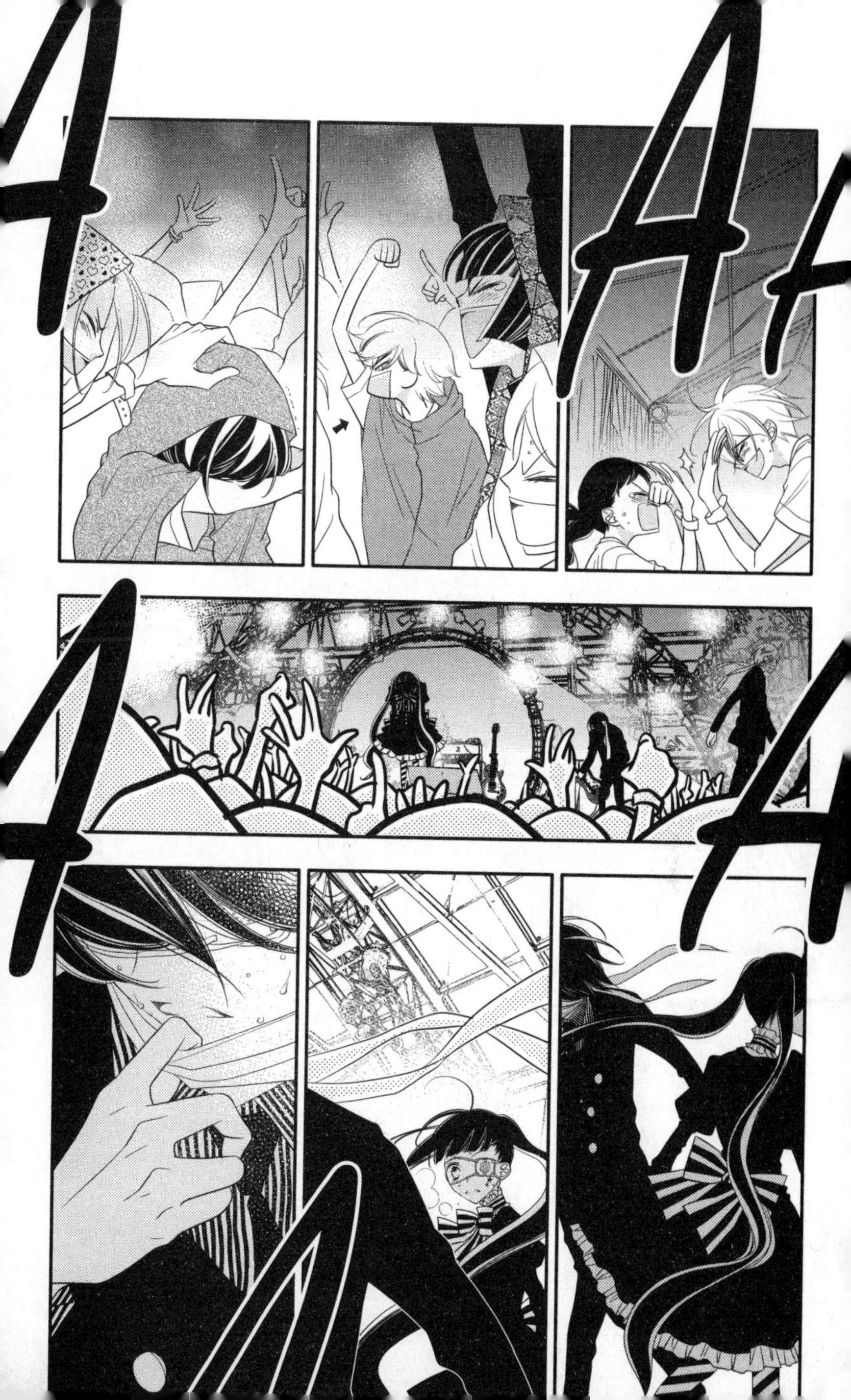
AAAAAAA

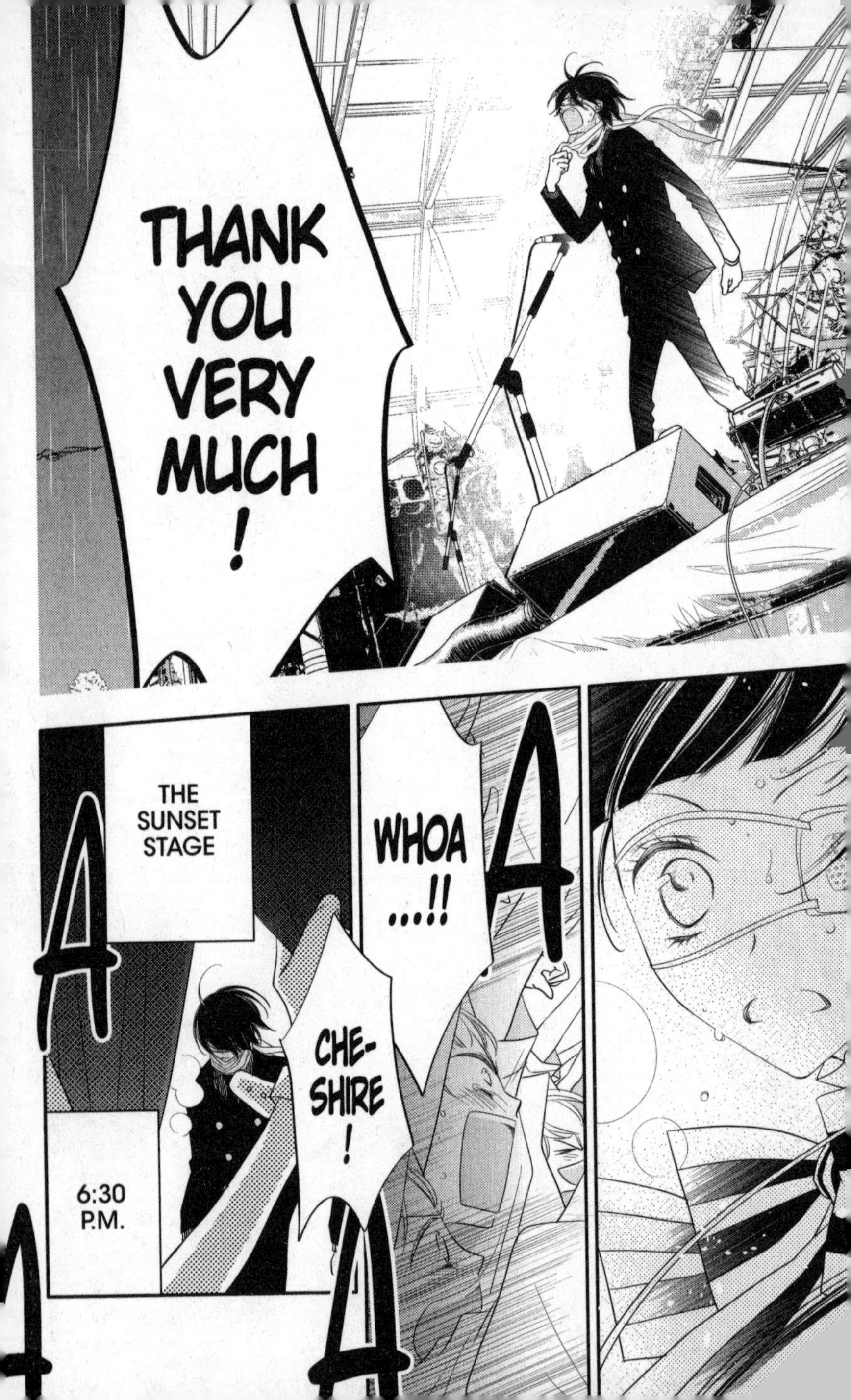
THANK YOU VERY MUCH!
WHOA...!!
THE SUNSET STAGE
CHE-SHIRE!
6:30 P.M.

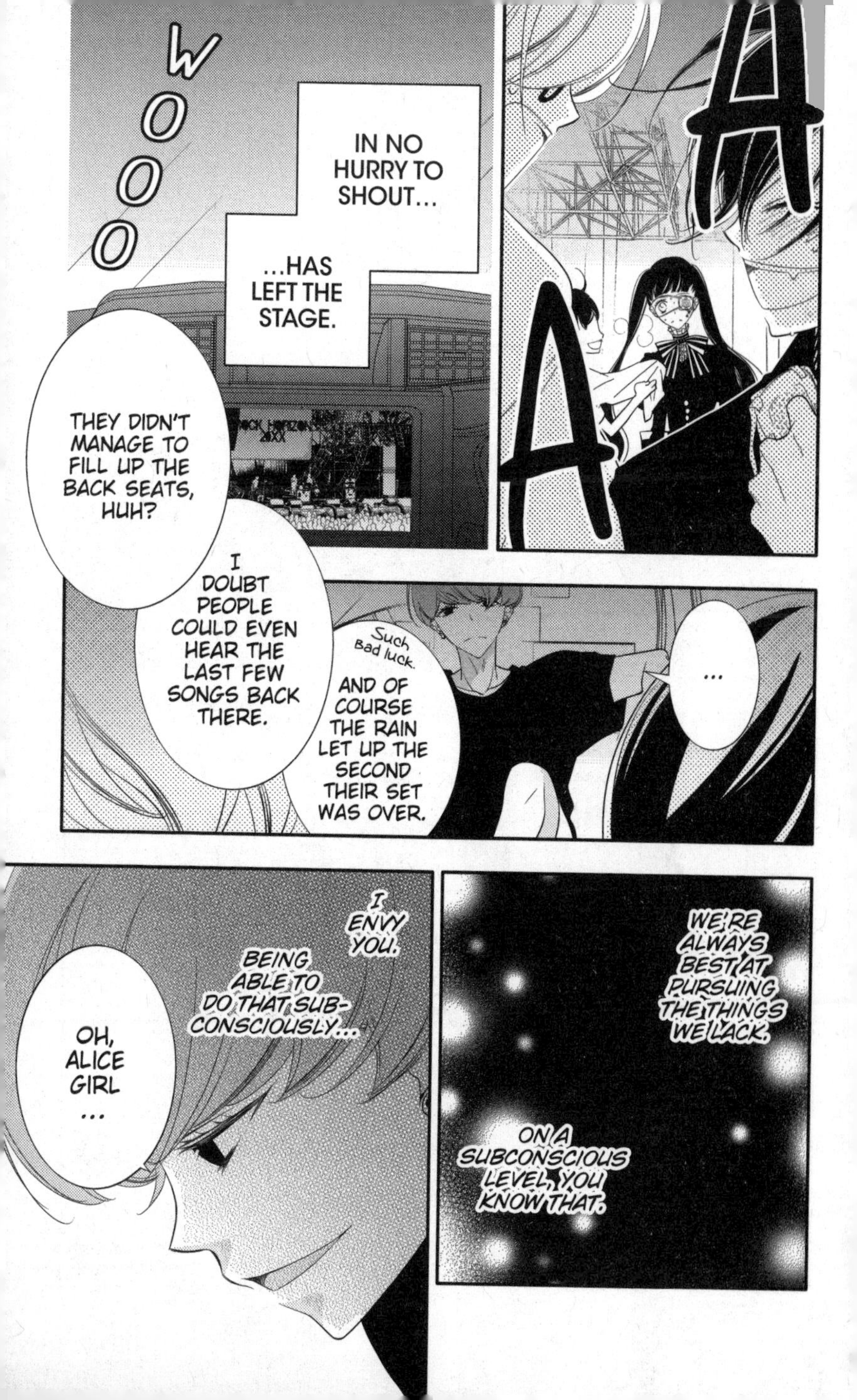
AAA
WOOO
IN NO HURRY TO SHOUT...
...HAS LEFT THE STAGE.
THEY DIDN'T MANAGE TO FILL UP THE BACK SEATS, HUH?
...
Such Bad luck.
AND OF COURSE THE RAIN LET UP THE SECOND THEIR SET WAS OVER.
I DOUBT PEOPLE COULD EVEN HEAR THE LAST FEW SONGS BACK THERE.
WE'RE ALWAYS BEST AT PURSUING THE THINGS WE LACK.
ON A SUBCONSCIOUS LEVEL, YOU KNOW THAT.
I ENVY YOU.
BEING ABLE TO DO THAT SUB-CONSCIOUSLY...
OH, ALICE GIRL ...

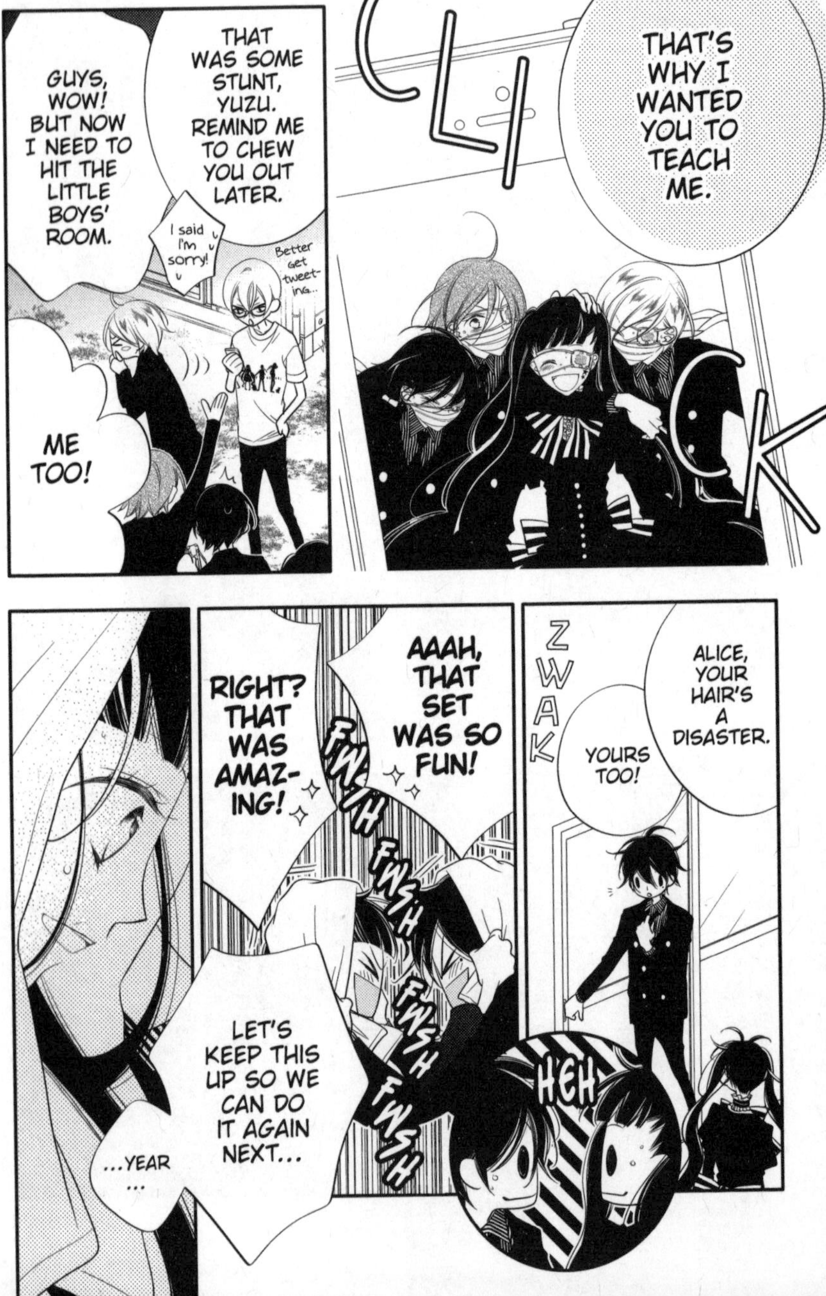

CLI
THAT'S WHY I WANTED YOU TO TEACH ME.
CK
THAT WAS SOME STUNT, YUZU. REMIND ME TO CHEW YOU OUT LATER.
GUYS, WOW! BUT NOW I NEED TO HIT THE LITTLE BOYS' ROOM.
I said I'm sorry!
Better get tweet-ing...
ME TOO!
ZWAK
ALICE, YOUR HAIR'S A DISASTER.
YOURS TOO!
HEH
AAAH, THAT SET WAS SO FUN!
RIGHT? THAT WAS AMAZ-ING!
FWSH
FWSH
FWSH
FWSH
LET'S KEEP THIS UP SO WE CAN DO IT AGAIN NEXT...
...YEAR...

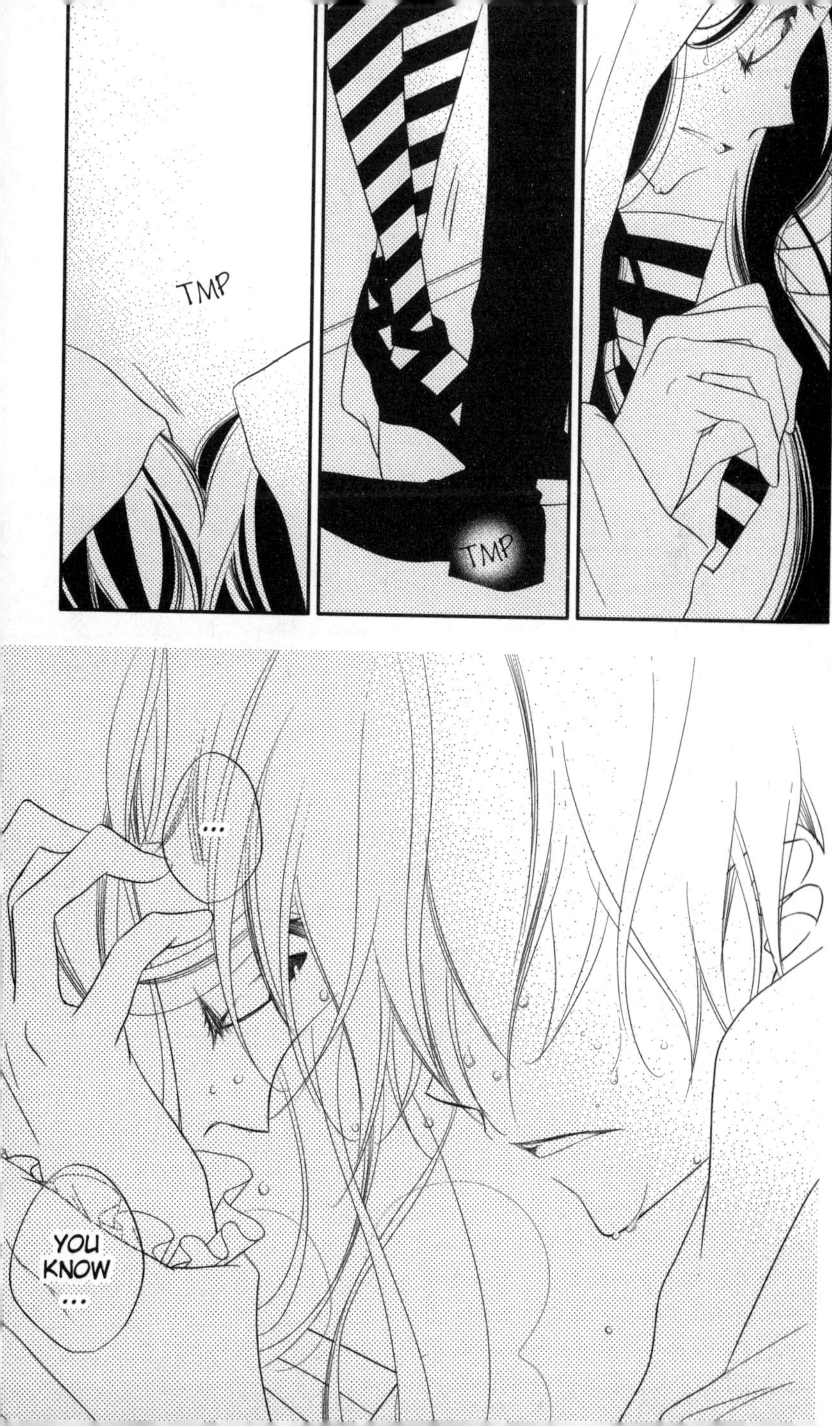
TMP
TMP
...
YOU KNOW ...

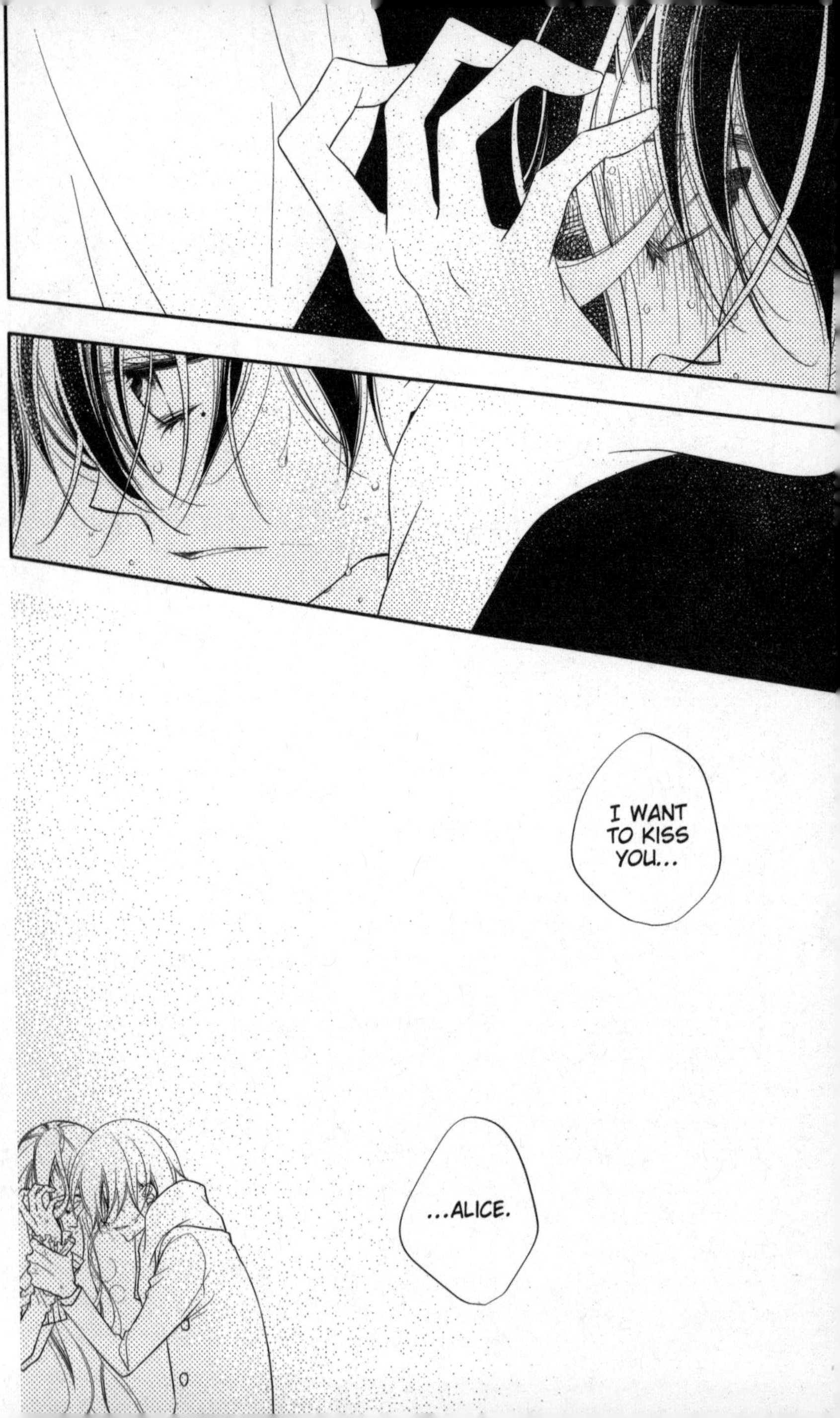
I WANT TO KISS YOU...
...ALICE.

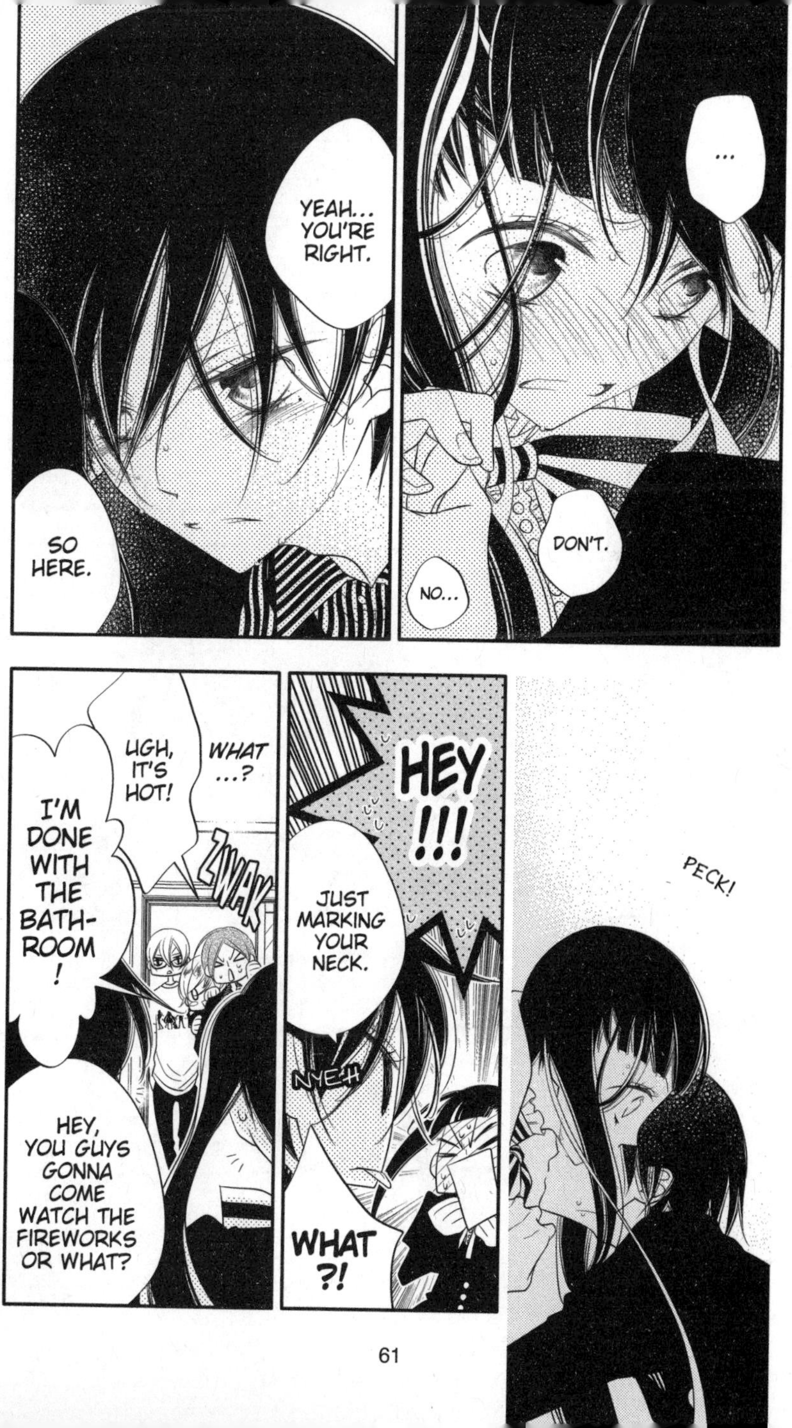
...
DON'T.
NO...
YEAH... YOU'RE RIGHT.
SO HERE.
PECK!
HEY!!!
JUST MARKING YOUR NECK.
NYEH
WHAT?!
WHAT...?
UGH, IT'S HOT!
ZWAK
I'M DONE WITH THE BATH-ROOM!
HEY, YOU GUYS GONNA COME WATCH THE FIREWORKS OR WHAT?

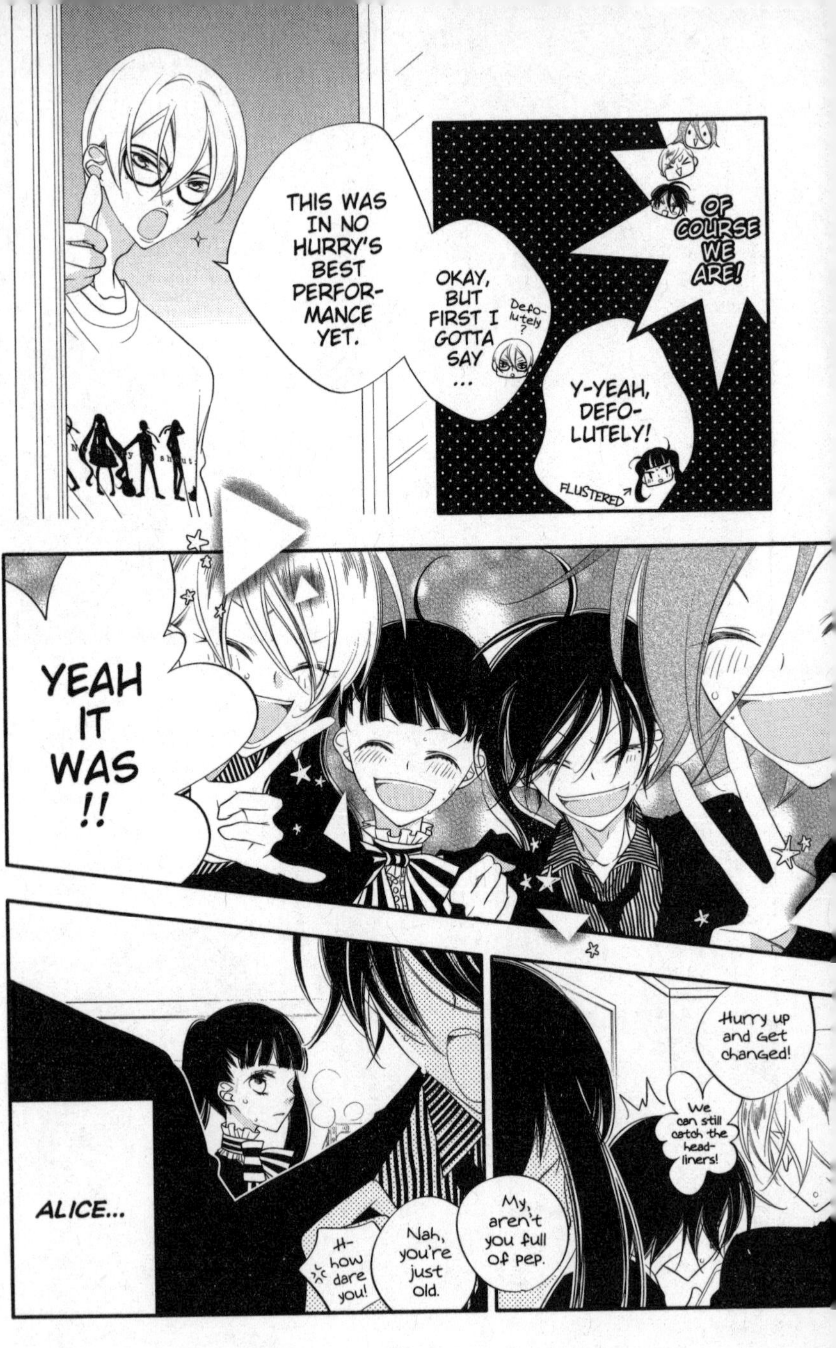
OF COURSE WE ARE!
Y-YEAH, DEFO-LUTELY!
FLUSTERED
OKAY, BUT FIRST I GOTTA SAY ...
Defo-lutely?
THIS WAS IN NO HURRY'S BEST PERFOR-MANCE YET.
YEAH IT WAS !!
Hurry up and get changed!
We can still catch the head-liners!
My, aren't you full of pep.
Nah, you're just old.
H-how dare you!
ALICE...

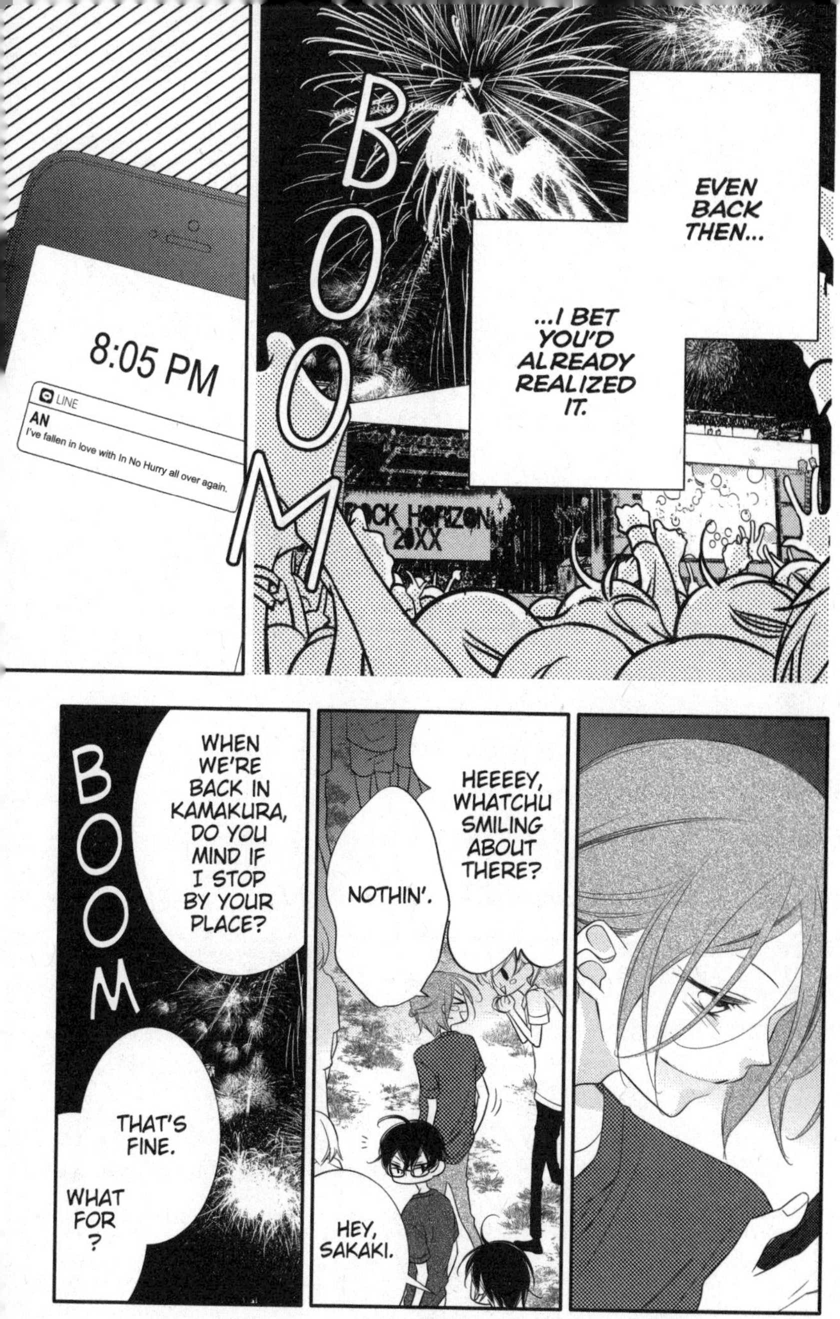
BOOM
EVEN BACK THEN...
...I BET YOU'D ALREADY REALIZED IT.
ROCK HORIZON 20XX
8:05 PM
LINE
AN
I've fallen in love with In No Hurry all over again.
HEEEEY, WHATCHU SMILING ABOUT THERE?
NOTHIN'.
HEY, SAKAKI.
WHEN WE'RE BACK IN KAMAKURA, DO YOU MIND IF I STOP BY YOUR PLACE?
BOOM
THAT'S FINE.
WHAT FOR?

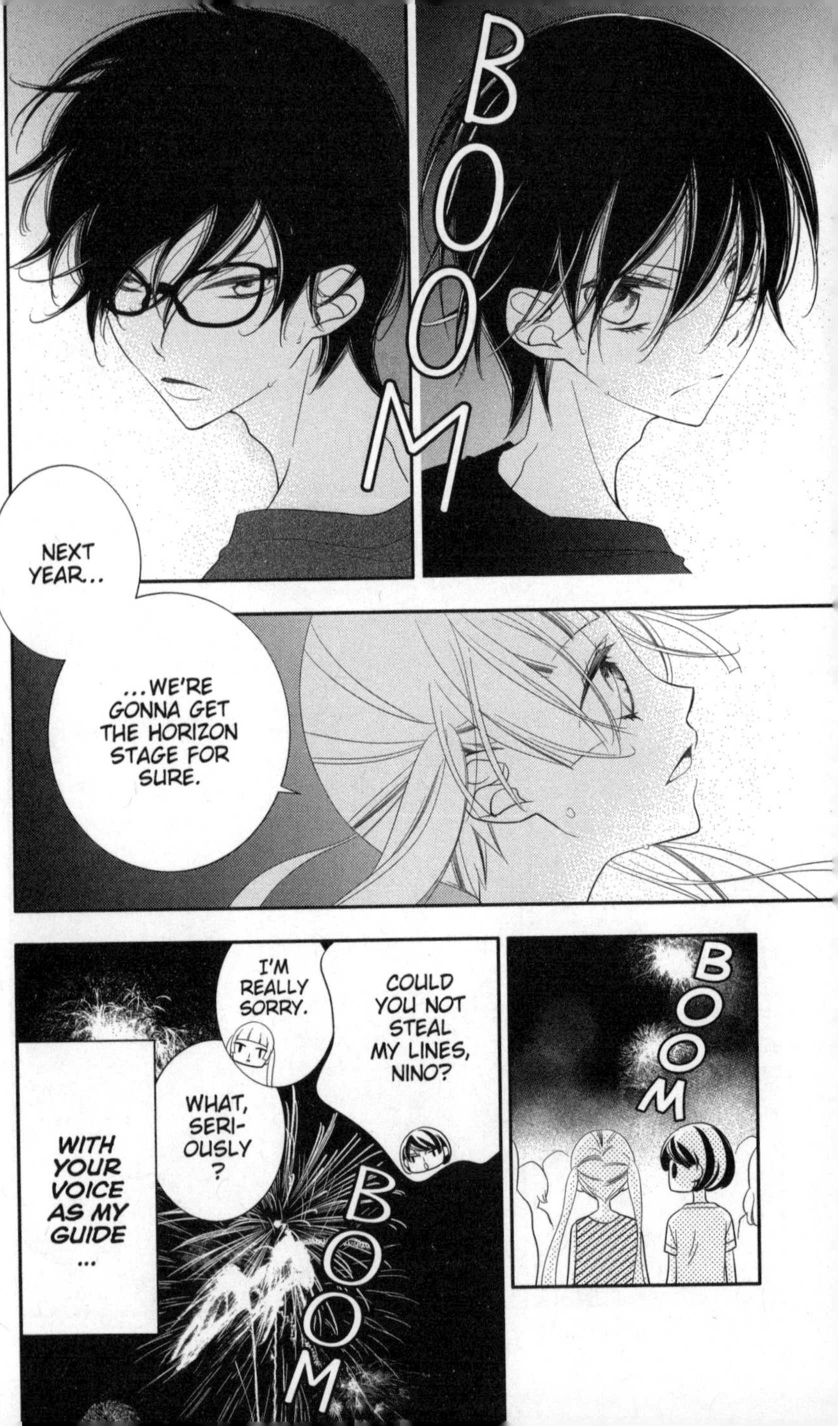
BOOM
NEXT YEAR...
...WE'RE GONNA GET THE HORIZON STAGE FOR SURE.
BOOM
COULD YOU NOT STEAL MY LINES, NINO?
I'M REALLY SORRY.
WHAT, SERIOUSLY?
BOOM
WITH YOUR VOICE AS MY GUIDE...

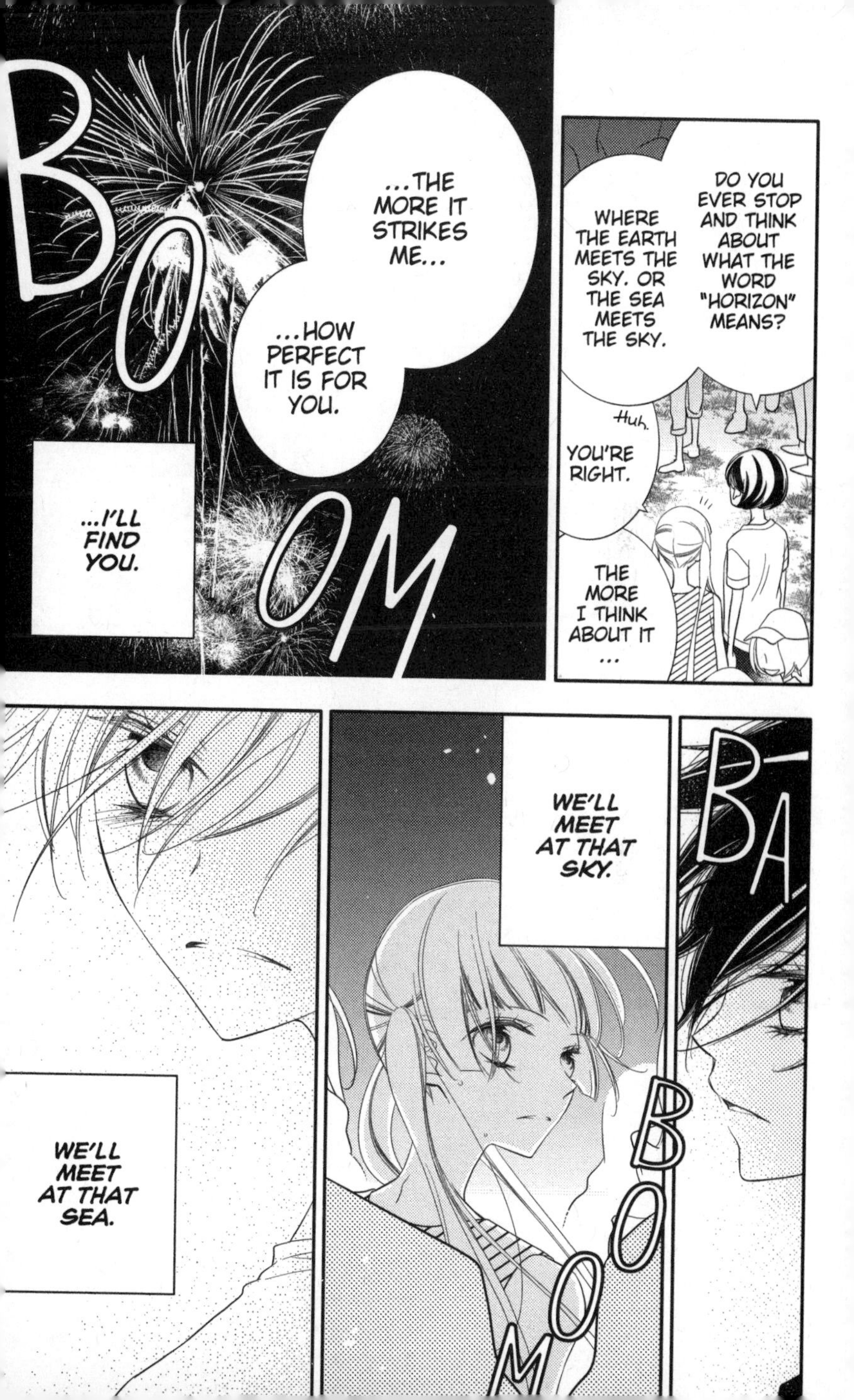
DO YOU EVER STOP AND THINK ABOUT WHAT THE WORD "HORIZON" MEANS?
WHERE THE EARTH MEETS THE SKY. OR THE SEA MEETS THE SKY.
Huh.
YOU'RE RIGHT.
THE MORE I THINK ABOUT IT ...
...THE MORE IT STRIKES ME...
...HOW PERFECT IT IS FOR YOU.
...I'LL FIND YOU.
BOOOM
BA-
WE'LL MEET AT THAT SKY.
BOOOM
WE'LL MEET AT THAT SEA.

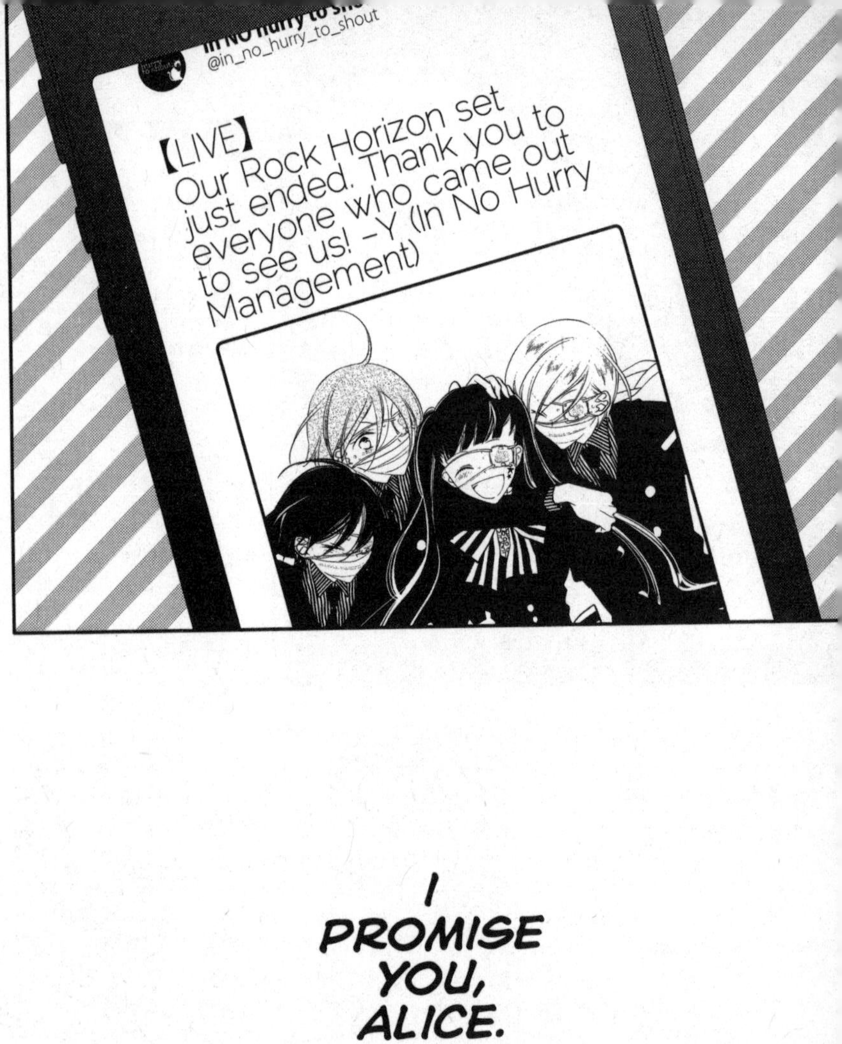
@in_no_hurry_to_shout
【LIVE】
Our Rock Horizon set just ended. Thank you to everyone who came out to see us! –Y (In No Hurry Management)
I PROMISE YOU, ALICE.

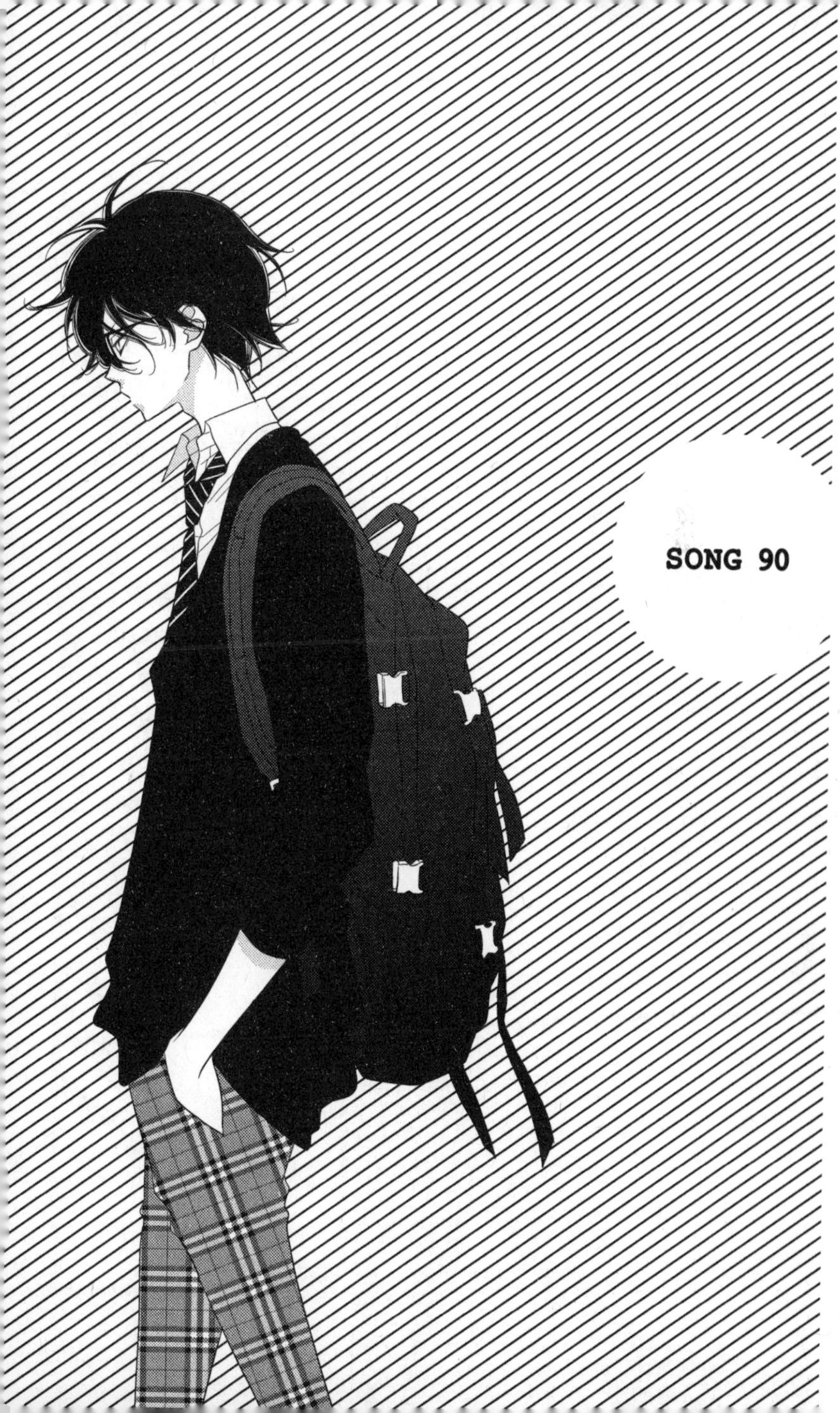
SONG 90

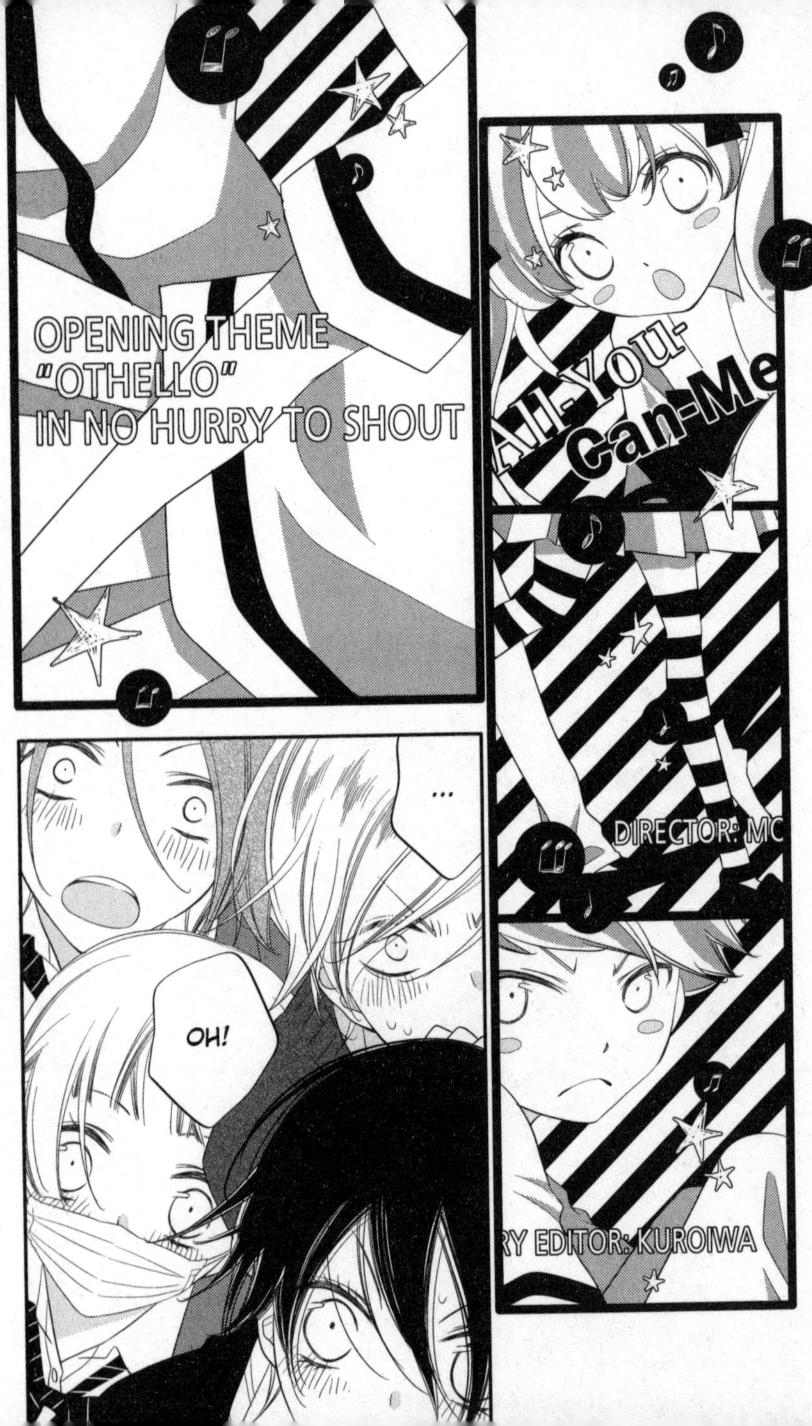
All-You-
Can-Me
DIRECTOR: MO
RY EDITOR: KUROIWA
OPENING THEME
"OTHELLO"
IN NO HURRY TO SHOUT
...
OH!

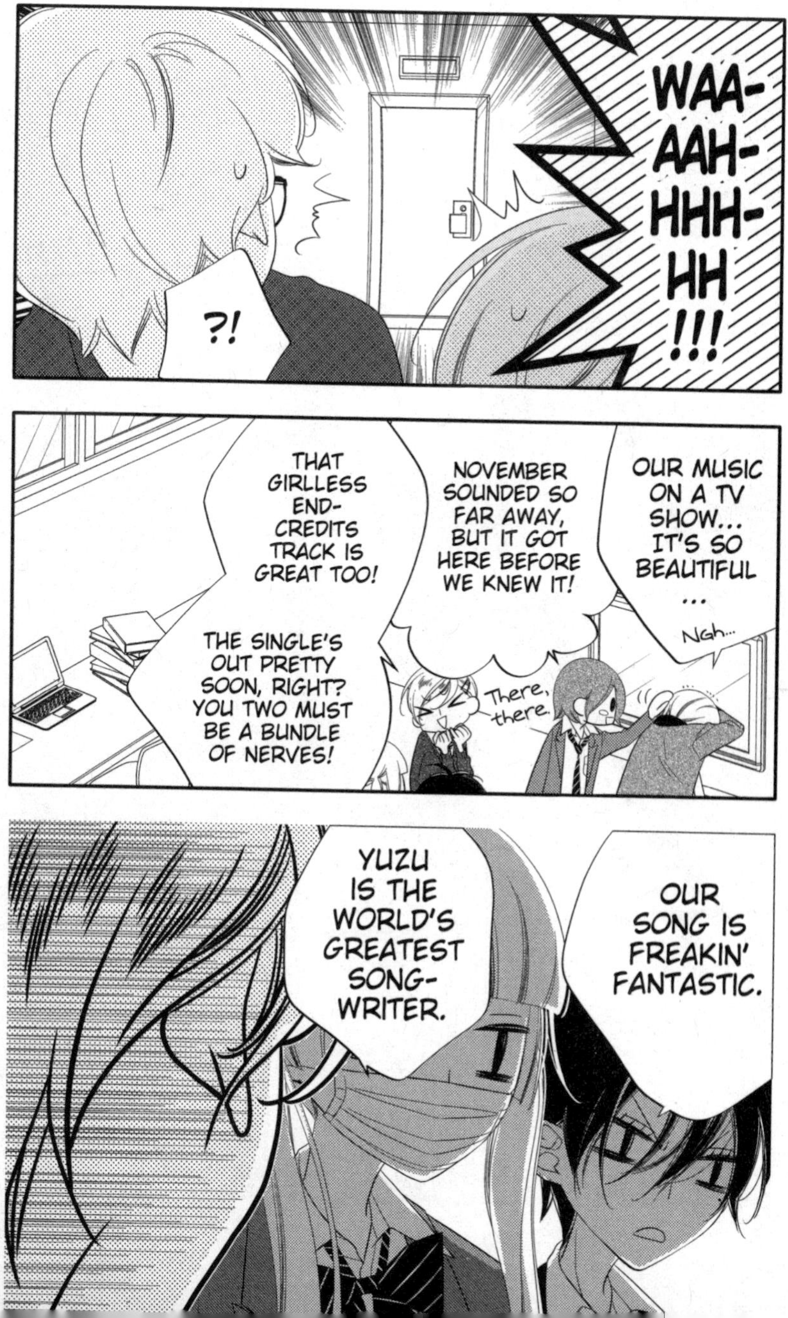
WAA-AAH-HHH-HH!!!
?!
OUR MUSIC ON A TV SHOW... IT'S SO BEAUTIFUL...
Ngh...
NOVEMBER SOUNDED SO FAR AWAY, BUT IT GOT HERE BEFORE WE KNEW IT!
There, there.
THAT GIRLLESS END-CREDITS TRACK IS GREAT TOO!
THE SINGLE'S OUT PRETTY SOON, RIGHT? YOU TWO MUST BE A BUNDLE OF NERVES!
OUR SONG IS FREAKIN' FANTASTIC.
YUZU IS THE WORLD'S GREATEST SONG-WRITER.

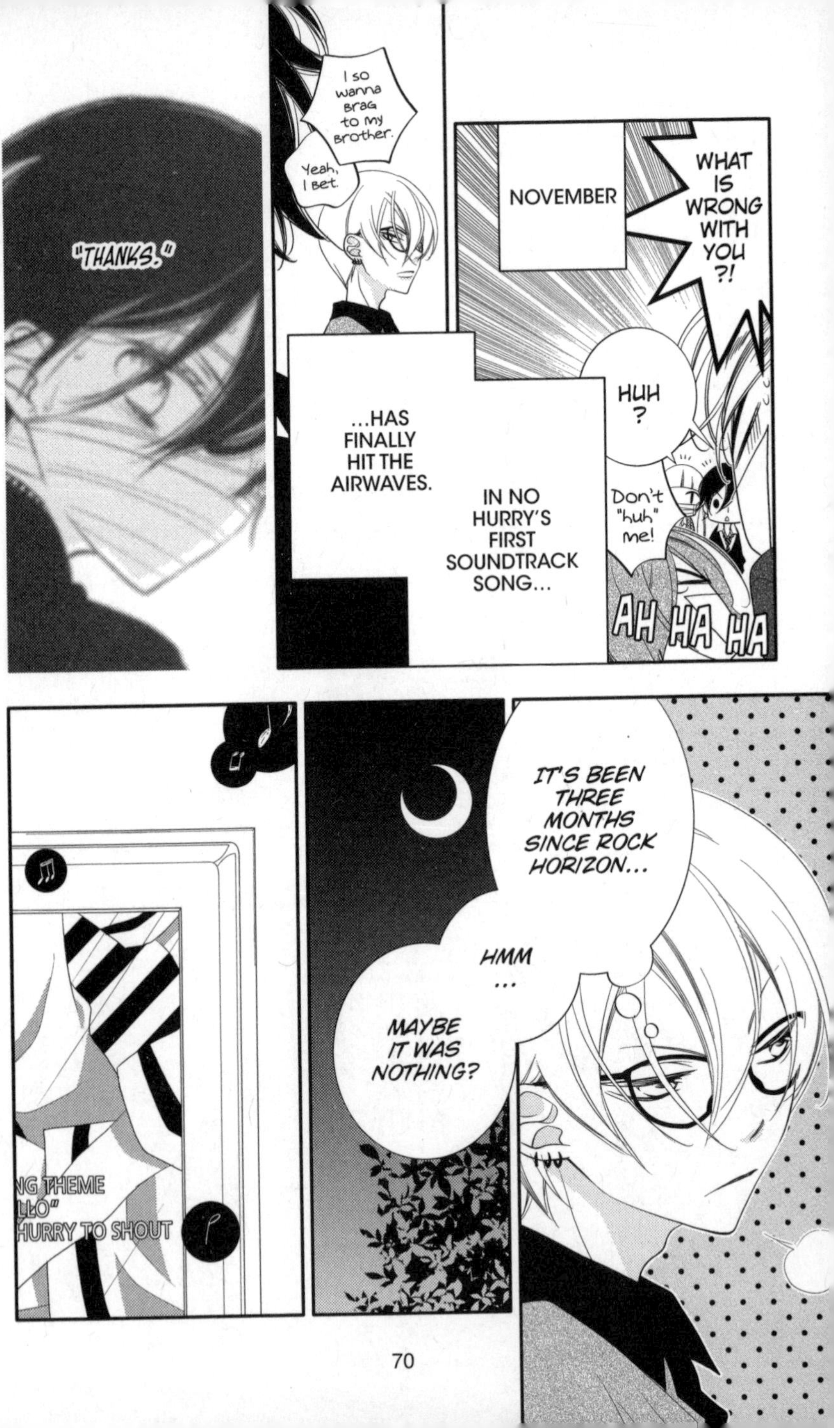
NOVEMBER
WHAT IS WRONG WITH YOU?!
HUH?
Don't "huh" me!
AH HA HA
I so wanna brag to my brother.
Yeah, I bet.
IN NO HURRY'S FIRST SOUNDTRACK SONG...
...HAS FINALLY HIT THE AIRWAVES.
"THANKS."
IT'S BEEN THREE MONTHS SINCE ROCK HORIZON...
HMM...
MAYBE IT WAS NOTHING?
NG THEME
LLO"
HURRY TO SHOUT

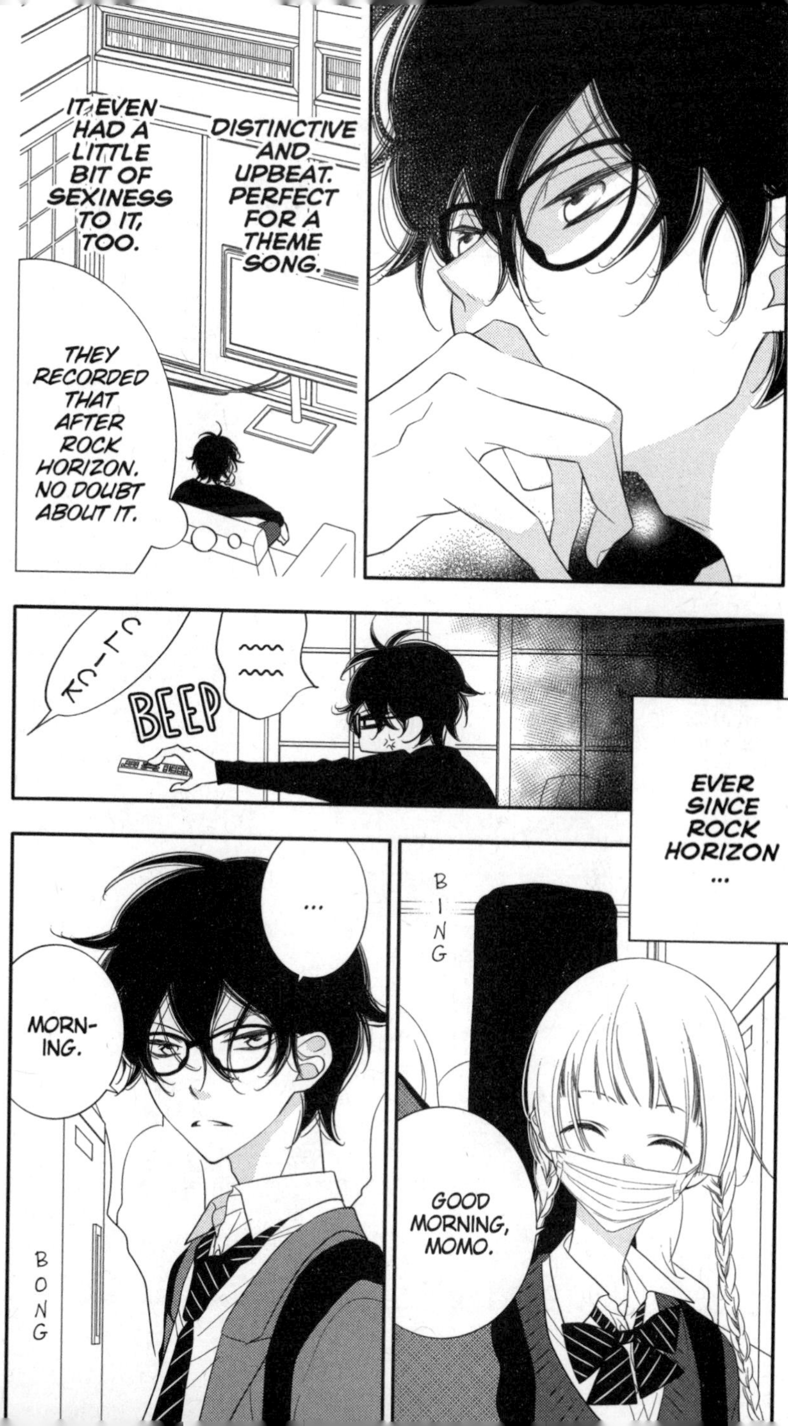

DISTINCTIVE AND UPBEAT. PERFECT FOR A THEME SONG.
IT EVEN HAD A LITTLE BIT OF SEXINESS TO IT, TOO.
THEY RECORDED THAT AFTER ROCK HORIZON. NO DOUBT ABOUT IT.
~~~ ~~~
BEEP
CLICK
EVER SINCE ROCK HORIZON...
BING
GOOD MORNING, MOMO.
...
MORNING.
BONG
~~~

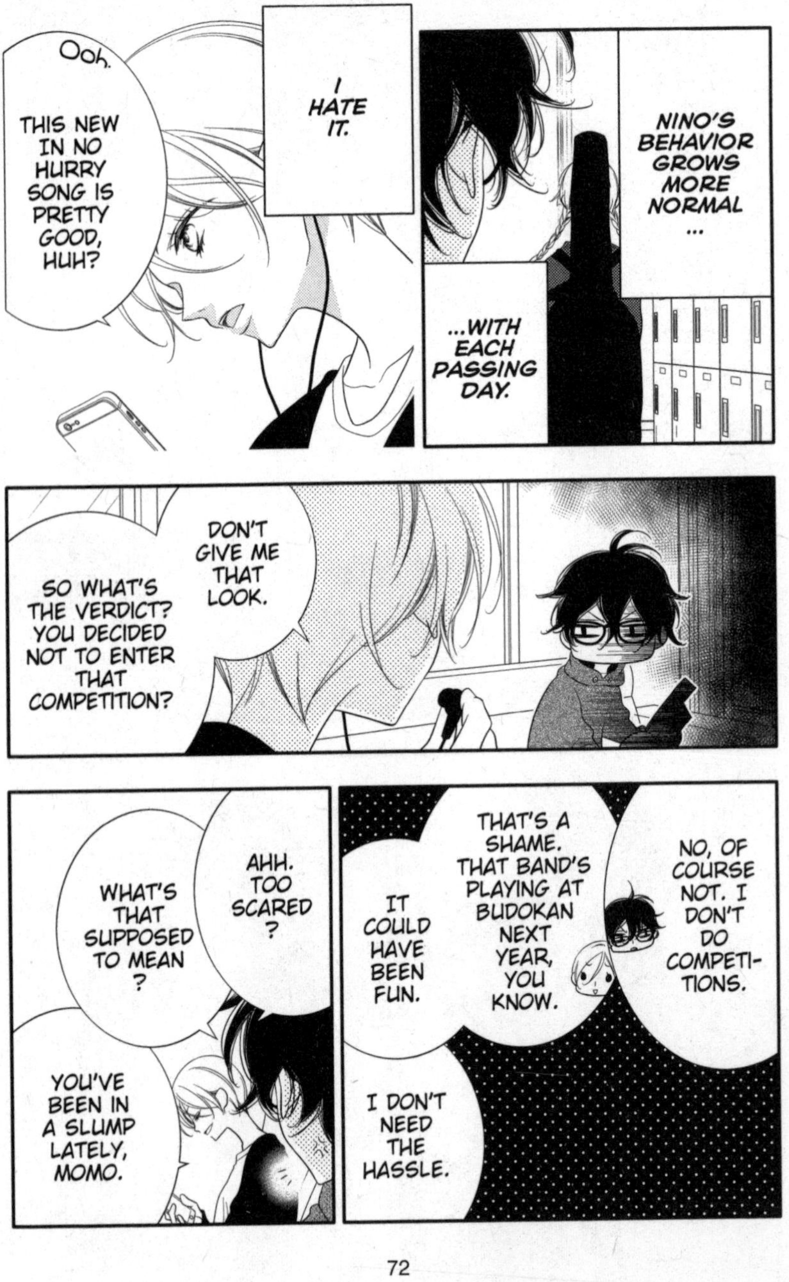
NINO'S BEHAVIOR GROWS MORE NORMAL...
...WITH EACH PASSING DAY.
I HATE IT.
Ooh.
THIS NEW IN NO HURRY SONG IS PRETTY GOOD, HUH?
DON'T GIVE ME THAT LOOK.
SO WHAT'S THE VERDICT? YOU DECIDED NOT TO ENTER THAT COMPETITION?
NO, OF COURSE NOT. I DON'T DO COMPETITIONS.
THAT'S A SHAME. THAT BAND'S PLAYING AT BUDOKAN NEXT YEAR, YOU KNOW.
IT COULD HAVE BEEN FUN.
I DON'T NEED THE HASSLE.
AHH. TOO SCARED?
WHAT'S THAT SUPPOSED TO MEAN?
YOU'VE BEEN IN A SLUMP LATELY, MOMO.

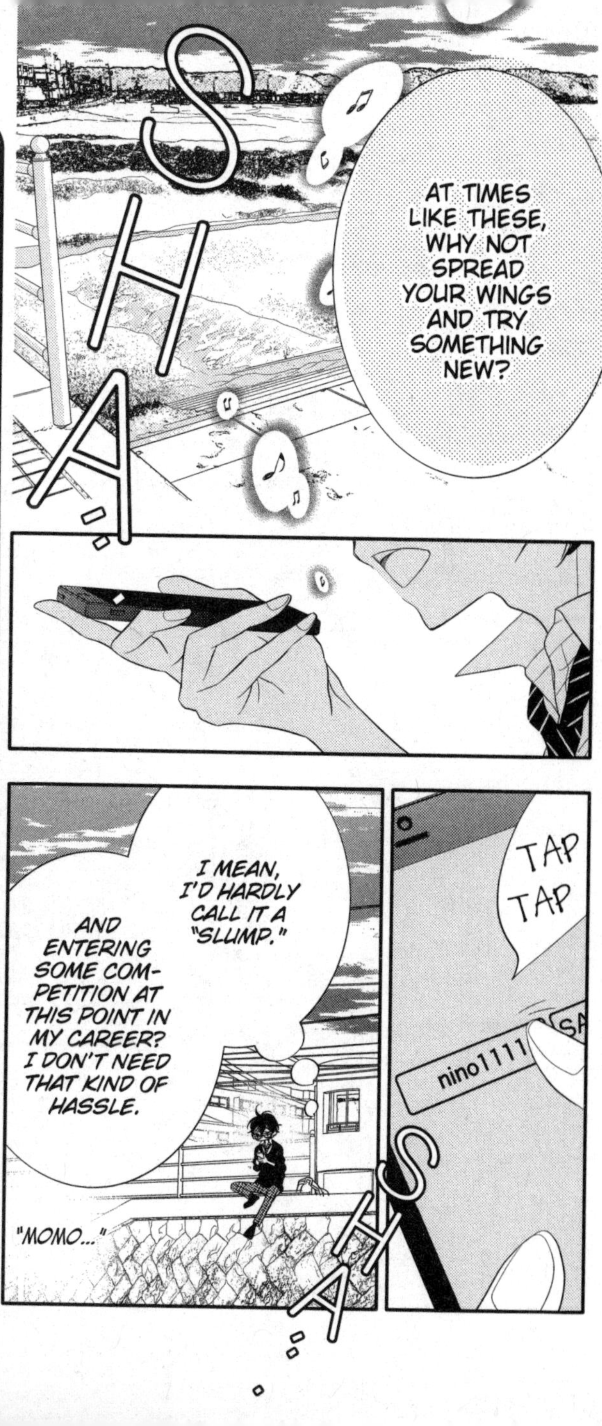
SHA
AT TIMES LIKE THESE, WHY NOT SPREAD YOUR WINGS AND TRY SOMETHING NEW?
TAP TAP
nino1111
SHA
I MEAN, I'D HARDLY CALL IT A "SLUMP."
AND ENTERING SOME COMPETITION AT THIS POINT IN MY CAREER? I DON'T NEED THAT KIND OF HASSLE.
"MOMO..."

3

When I was writing the last chapter of this volume, I went to the Tower Records store in Shibuya to gather materials.

The staff were very kind and helpful despite my being a nuisance on two of their busiest days (advance-purchase day and release day), and for that I am deeply grateful. They've been a great supporter of this manga all the way since volume 1, and they're still being amazing even now as we're nearing the end of our run!

(To be continued)

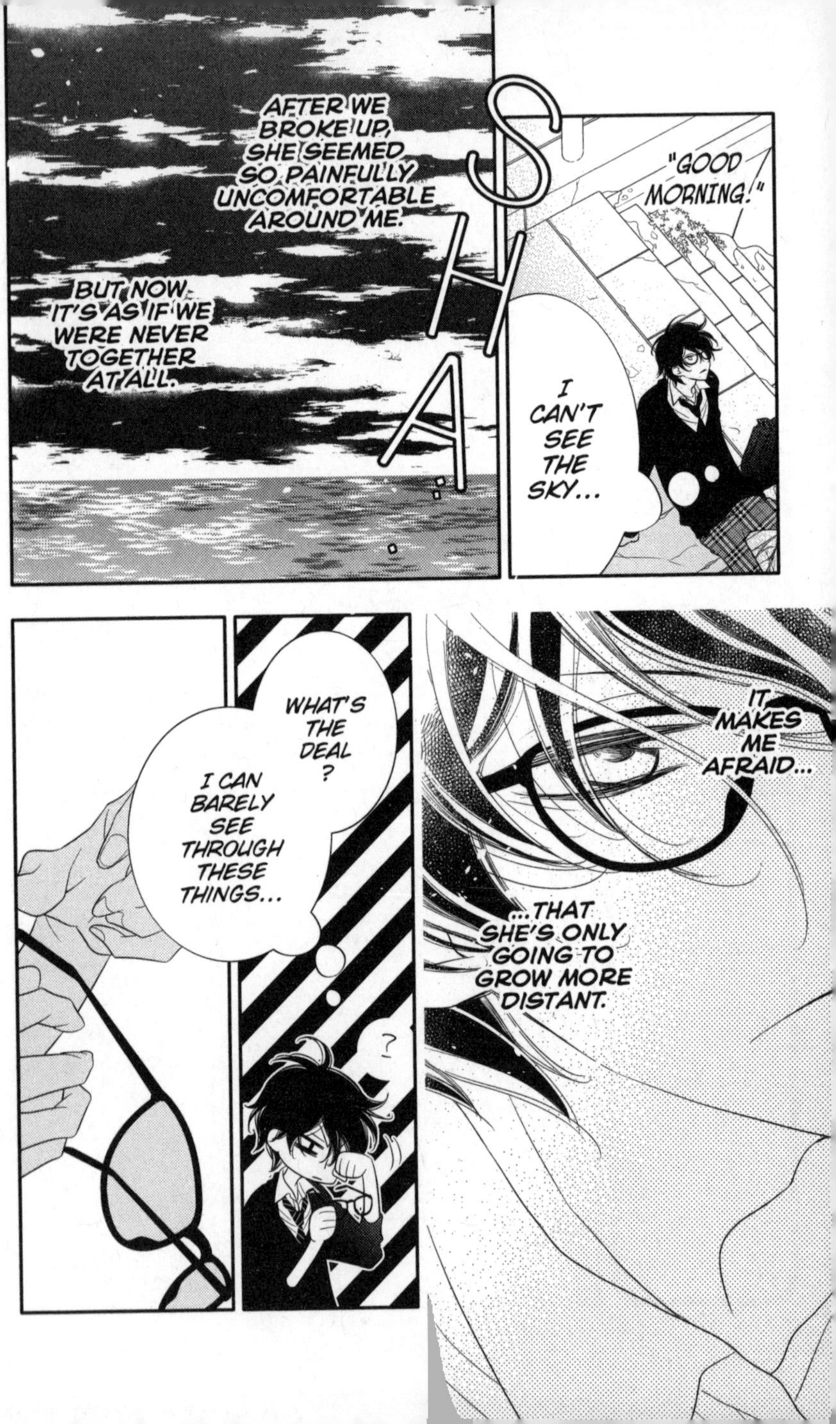
"GOOD MORNING!"
I CAN'T SEE THE SKY...
SHA
AFTER WE BROKE UP, SHE SEEMED SO PAINFULLY UNCOMFORTABLE AROUND ME.
BUT NOW IT'S AS IF WE WERE NEVER TOGETHER AT ALL.
IT MAKES ME AFRAID...
...THAT SHE'S ONLY GOING TO GROW MORE DISTANT.
WHAT'S THE DEAL?
I CAN BARELY SEE THROUGH THESE THINGS...
?

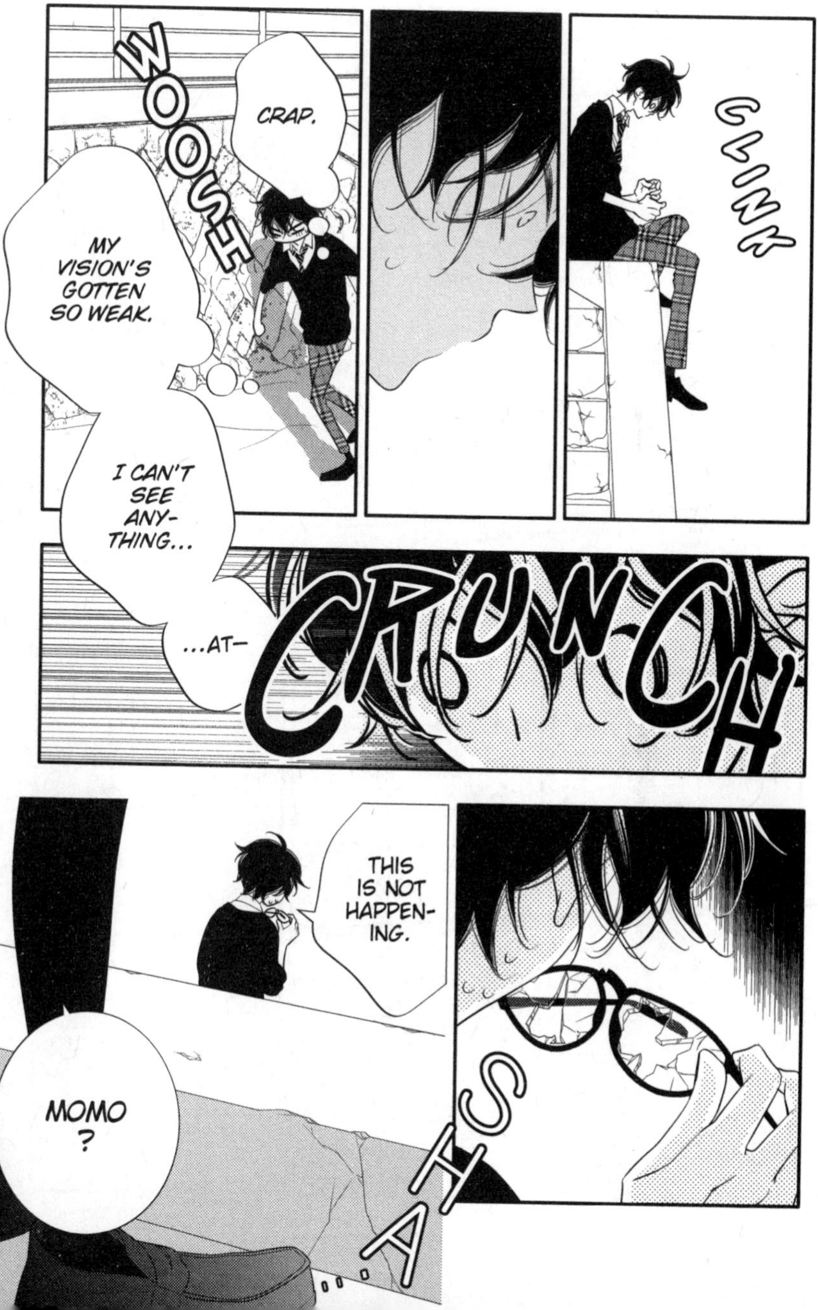
CLINK
WOOSH
CRAP.
MY VISION'S GOTTEN SO WEAK.
I CAN'T SEE ANY-THING...
...AT—
CRUNCH
SHA...
THIS IS NOT HAPPEN-ING.
MOMO?

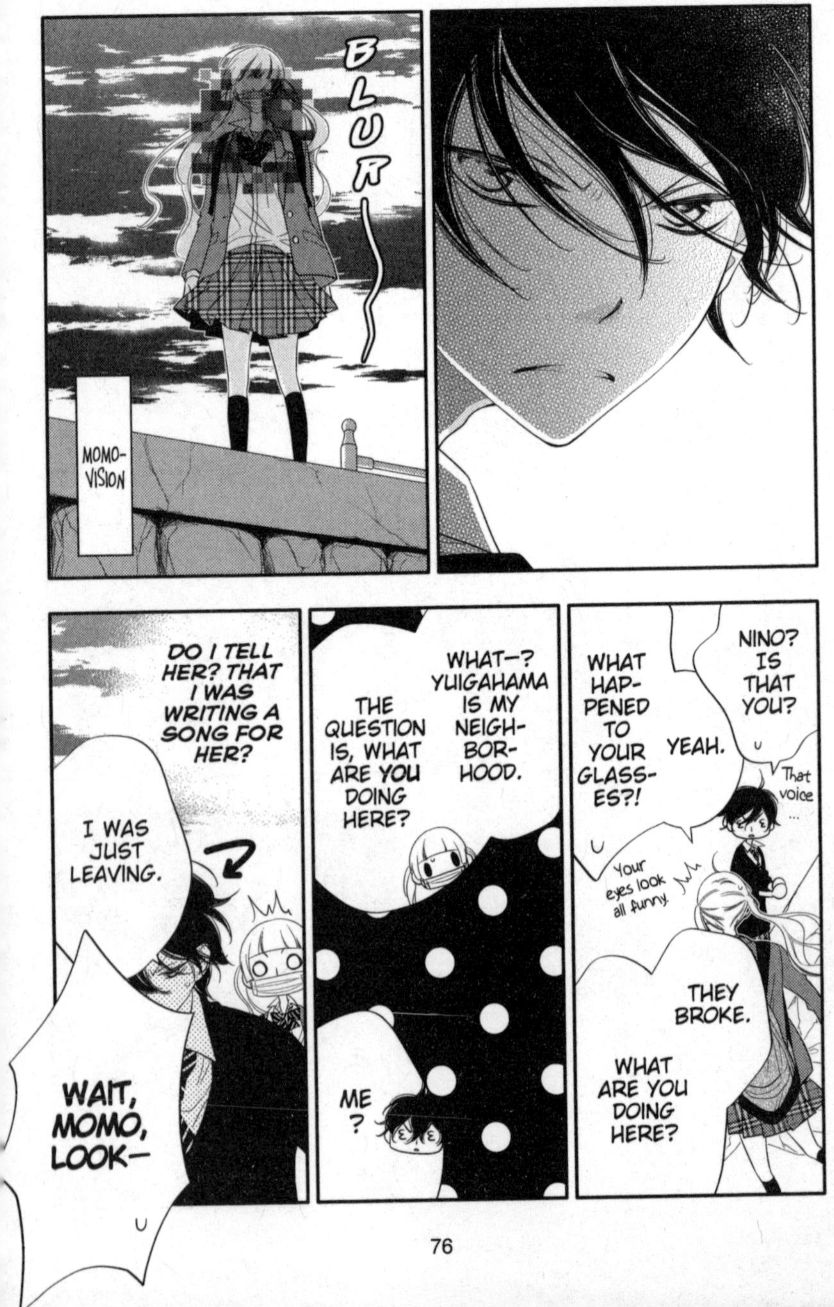
BLUR~
MOMO-VISION
NINO? IS THAT YOU?
That voice...
YEAH.
WHAT HAPPENED TO YOUR GLASSES?!
Your eyes look all funny.
THEY BROKE.
WHAT ARE YOU DOING HERE?
WHAT—? YUIGAHAMA IS MY NEIGHBORHOOD.
THE QUESTION IS, WHAT ARE YOU DOING HERE?
ME?
DO I TELL HER? THAT I WAS WRITING A SONG FOR HER?
I WAS JUST LEAVING.
WAIT, MOMO, LOOK—

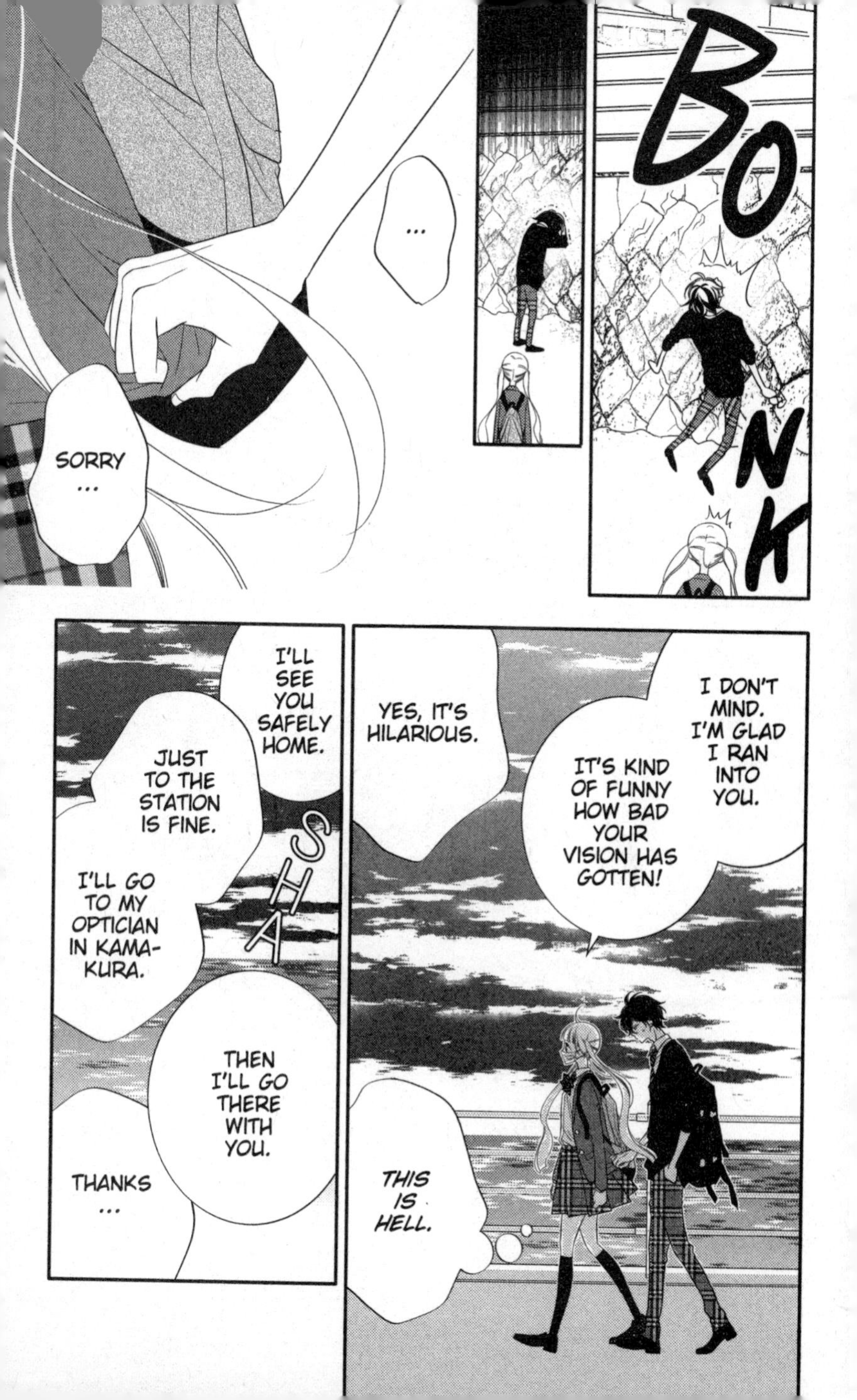
BONK
...
SORRY ...
I DON'T MIND. I'M GLAD I RAN INTO YOU.
IT'S KIND OF FUNNY HOW BAD YOUR VISION HAS GOTTEN!
YES, IT'S HILARIOUS.
THIS IS HELL.
I'LL SEE YOU SAFELY HOME.
JUST TO THE STATION IS FINE.
SHA
I'LL GO TO MY OPTICIAN IN KAMA-KURA.
THEN I'LL GO THERE WITH YOU.
THANKS ...

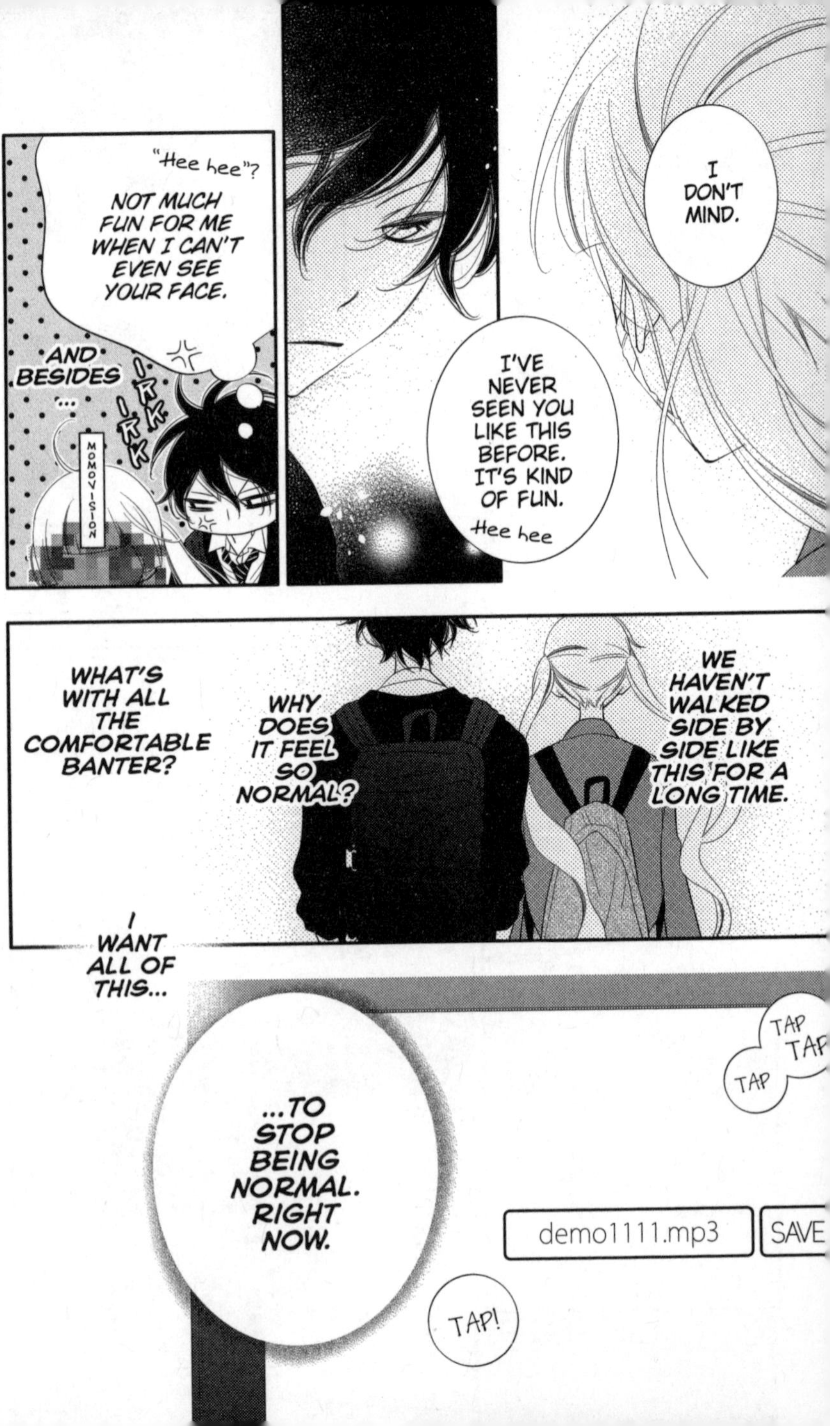
I DON'T MIND.
I'VE NEVER SEEN YOU LIKE THIS BEFORE. IT'S KIND OF FUN.
Hee hee
"Hee hee"?
NOT MUCH FUN FOR ME WHEN I CAN'T EVEN SEE YOUR FACE.
AND BESIDES ...
IRK IRK
MOMOVISION
WE HAVEN'T WALKED SIDE BY SIDE LIKE THIS FOR A LONG TIME.
WHY DOES IT FEEL SO NORMAL?
WHAT'S WITH ALL THE COMFORTABLE BANTER?
TAP TAP
I WANT ALL OF THIS...
...TO STOP BEING NORMAL. RIGHT NOW.
demo1111.mp3
SAVE
TAP!

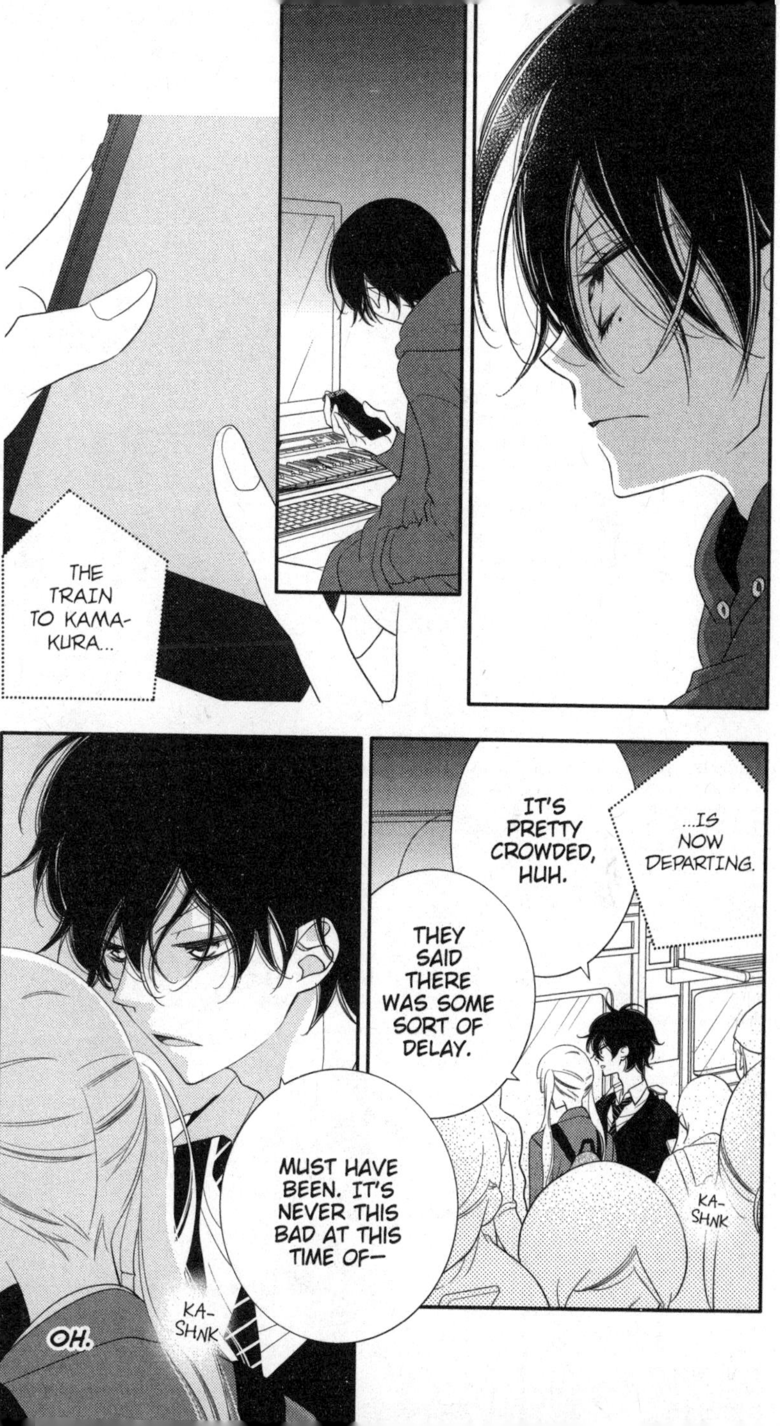
THE TRAIN TO KAMA-KURA...
...IS NOW DEPARTING.
IT'S PRETTY CROWDED, HUH.
THEY SAID THERE WAS SOME SORT OF DELAY.
KA-SHNK
MUST HAVE BEEN. IT'S NEVER THIS BAD AT THIS TIME OF—
KA-SHNK
OH.

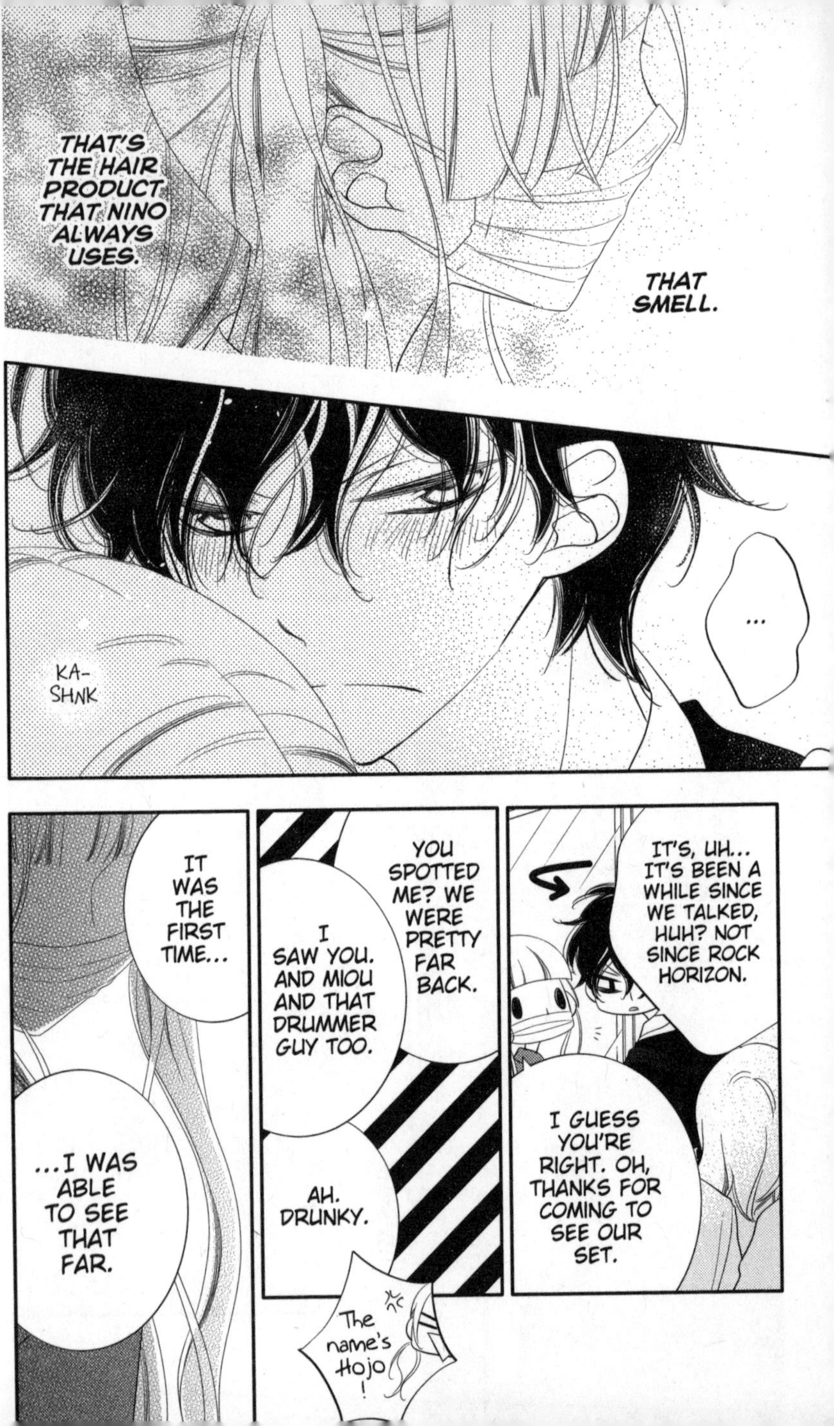
THAT SMELL.
THAT'S THE HAIR PRODUCT THAT NINO ALWAYS USES.
...
KA-SHNK
IT'S, UH... IT'S BEEN A WHILE SINCE WE TALKED, HUH? NOT SINCE ROCK HORIZON.
I GUESS YOU'RE RIGHT. OH, THANKS FOR COMING TO SEE OUR SET.
YOU SPOTTED ME? WE WERE PRETTY FAR BACK.
I SAW YOU. AND MIOU AND THAT DRUMMER GUY TOO.
AH. DRUNKY.
The name's Hojo!
IT WAS THE FIRST TIME...
...I WAS ABLE TO SEE THAT FAR.

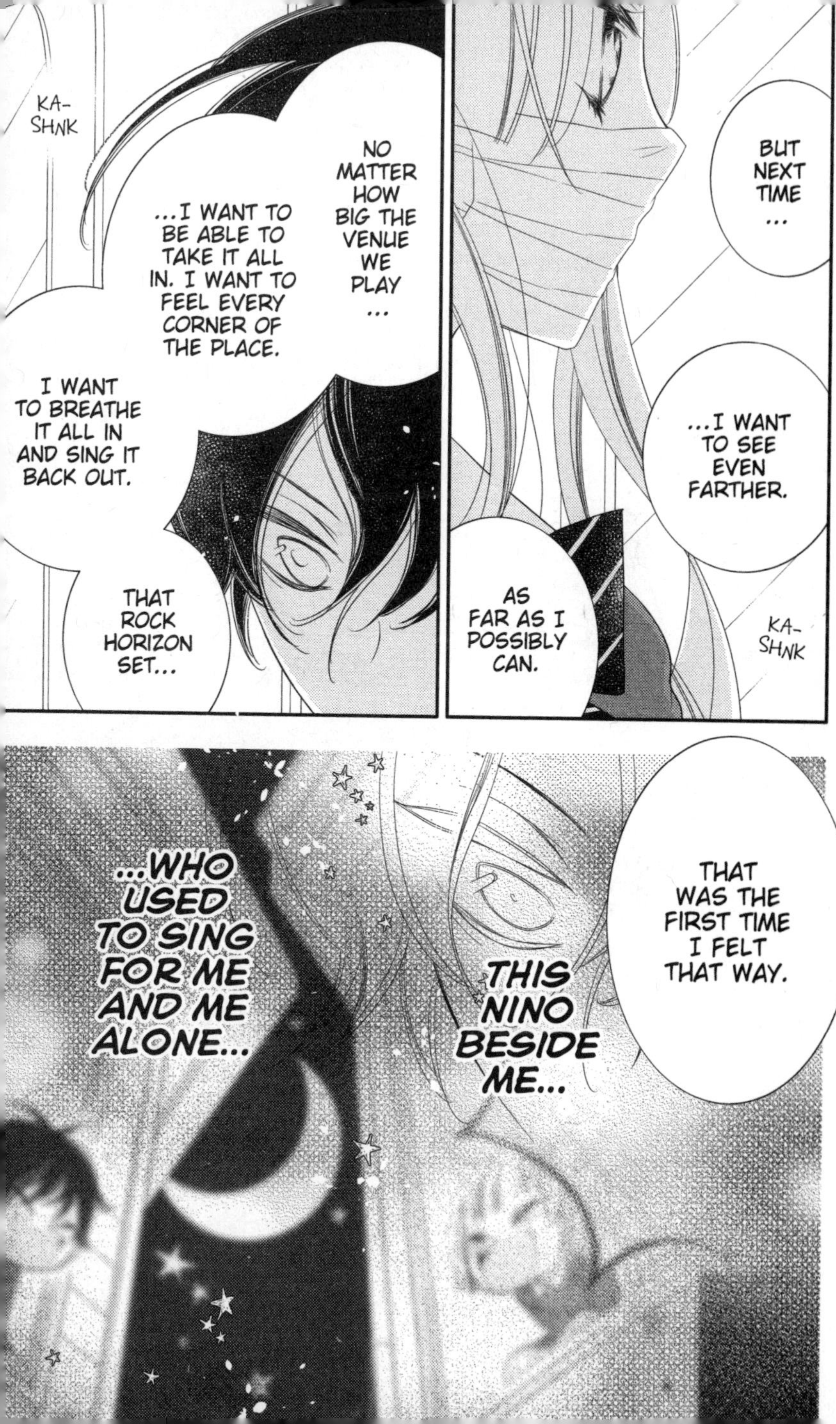
BUT NEXT TIME...
...I WANT TO SEE EVEN FARTHER.
AS FAR AS I POSSIBLY CAN.
KA-SHNK
NO MATTER HOW BIG THE VENUE WE PLAY...
...I WANT TO BE ABLE TO TAKE IT ALL IN. I WANT TO FEEL EVERY CORNER OF THE PLACE.
KA-SHNK
I WANT TO BREATHE IT ALL IN AND SING IT BACK OUT.
THAT ROCK HORIZON SET...
THAT WAS THE FIRST TIME I FELT THAT WAY.
THIS NINO BESIDE ME...
...WHO USED TO SING FOR ME AND ME ALONE...

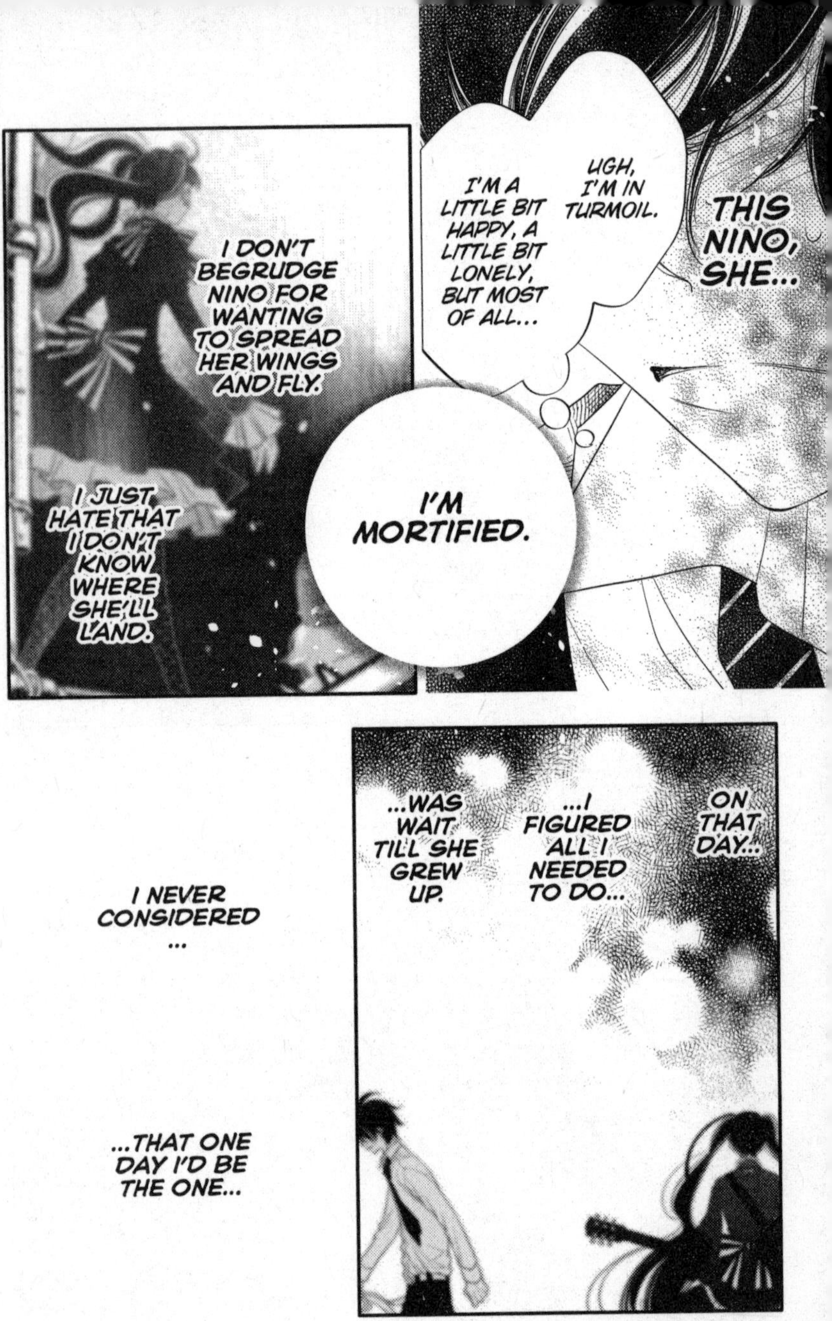
THIS NINO, SHE...
UGH, I'M IN TURMOIL.
I'M A LITTLE BIT HAPPY, A LITTLE BIT LONELY, BUT MOST OF ALL...
I'M MORTIFIED.
I DON'T BEGRUDGE NINO FOR WANTING TO SPREAD HER WINGS AND FLY.
I JUST HATE THAT I DON'T KNOW WHERE SHE'LL LAND.
ON THAT DAY...
...I FIGURED ALL I NEEDED TO DO...
...WAS WAIT TILL SHE GREW UP.
I NEVER CONSIDERED ...
...THAT ONE DAY I'D BE THE ONE...

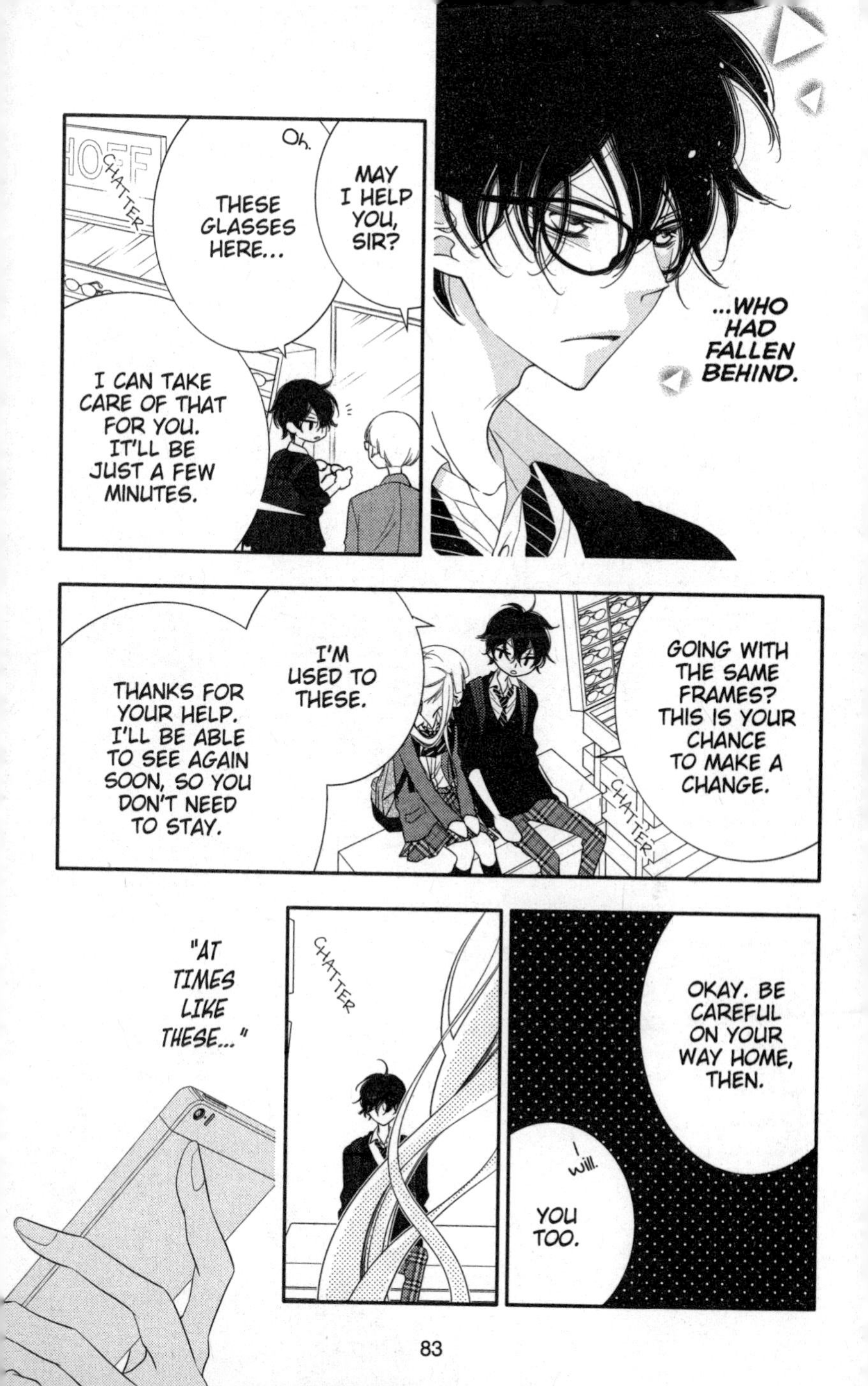
...WHO HAD FALLEN BEHIND.
MAY I HELP YOU, SIR?
Oh.
THESE GLASSES HERE...
CHATTER
I CAN TAKE CARE OF THAT FOR YOU. IT'LL BE JUST A FEW MINUTES.
GOING WITH THE SAME FRAMES? THIS IS YOUR CHANCE TO MAKE A CHANGE.
CHATTER
I'M USED TO THESE.
THANKS FOR YOUR HELP. I'LL BE ABLE TO SEE AGAIN SOON, SO YOU DON'T NEED TO STAY.
OKAY. BE CAREFUL ON YOUR WAY HOME, THEN.
I will.
YOU TOO.
CHATTER
"AT TIMES LIKE THESE..."

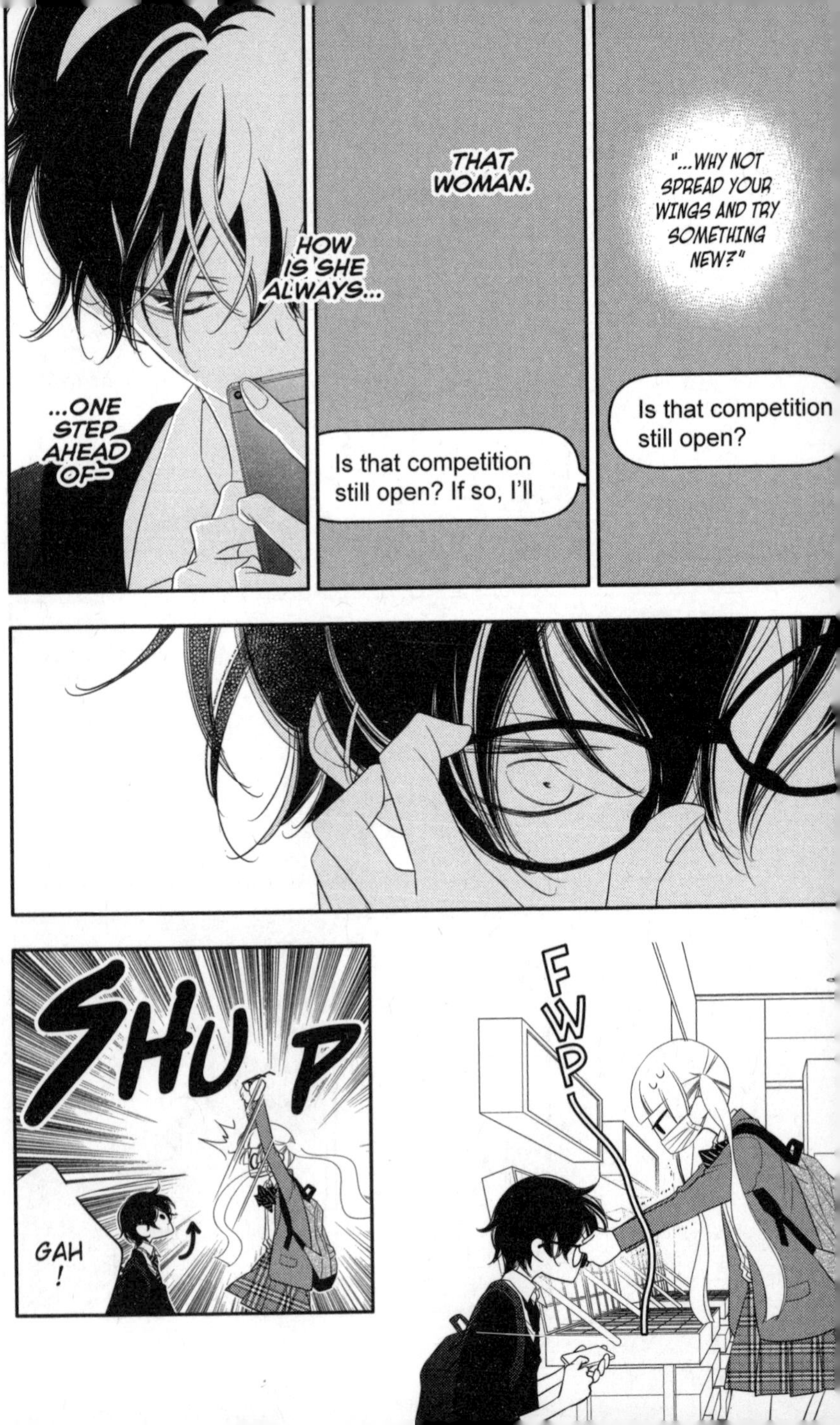
"...WHY NOT SPREAD YOUR WINGS AND TRY SOMETHING NEW?"
Is that competition still open?
THAT WOMAN.
Is that competition still open? If so, I'll
HOW IS SHE ALWAYS...
...ONE STEP AHEAD OF—
FWP
SHUP
GAH!

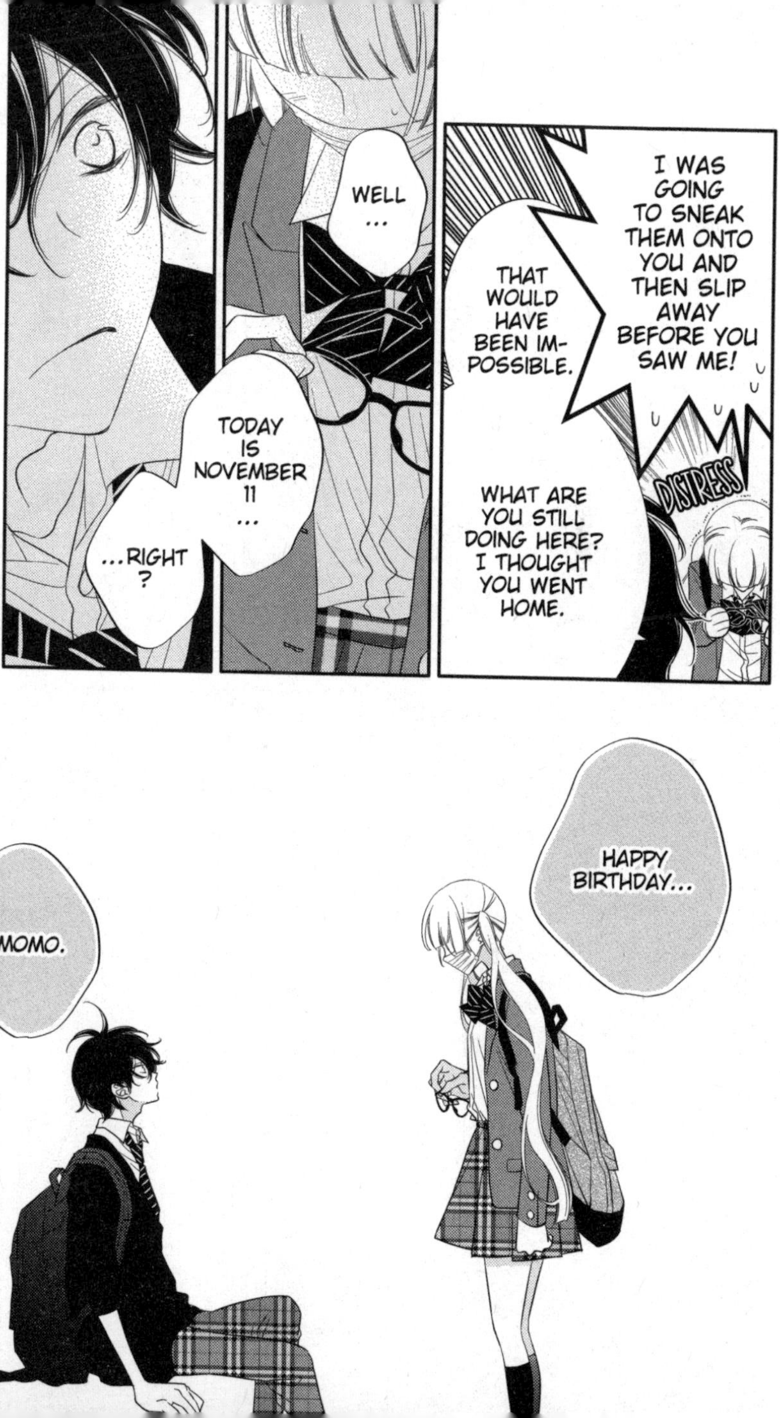

I WAS GOING TO SNEAK THEM ONTO YOU AND THEN SLIP AWAY BEFORE YOU SAW ME!
THAT WOULD HAVE BEEN IM- POSSIBLE.
DISTRESS
WHAT ARE YOU STILL DOING HERE? I THOUGHT YOU WENT HOME.
WELL...
TODAY IS NOVEMBER 11...
...RIGHT?
HAPPY BIRTHDAY...
...MOMO.

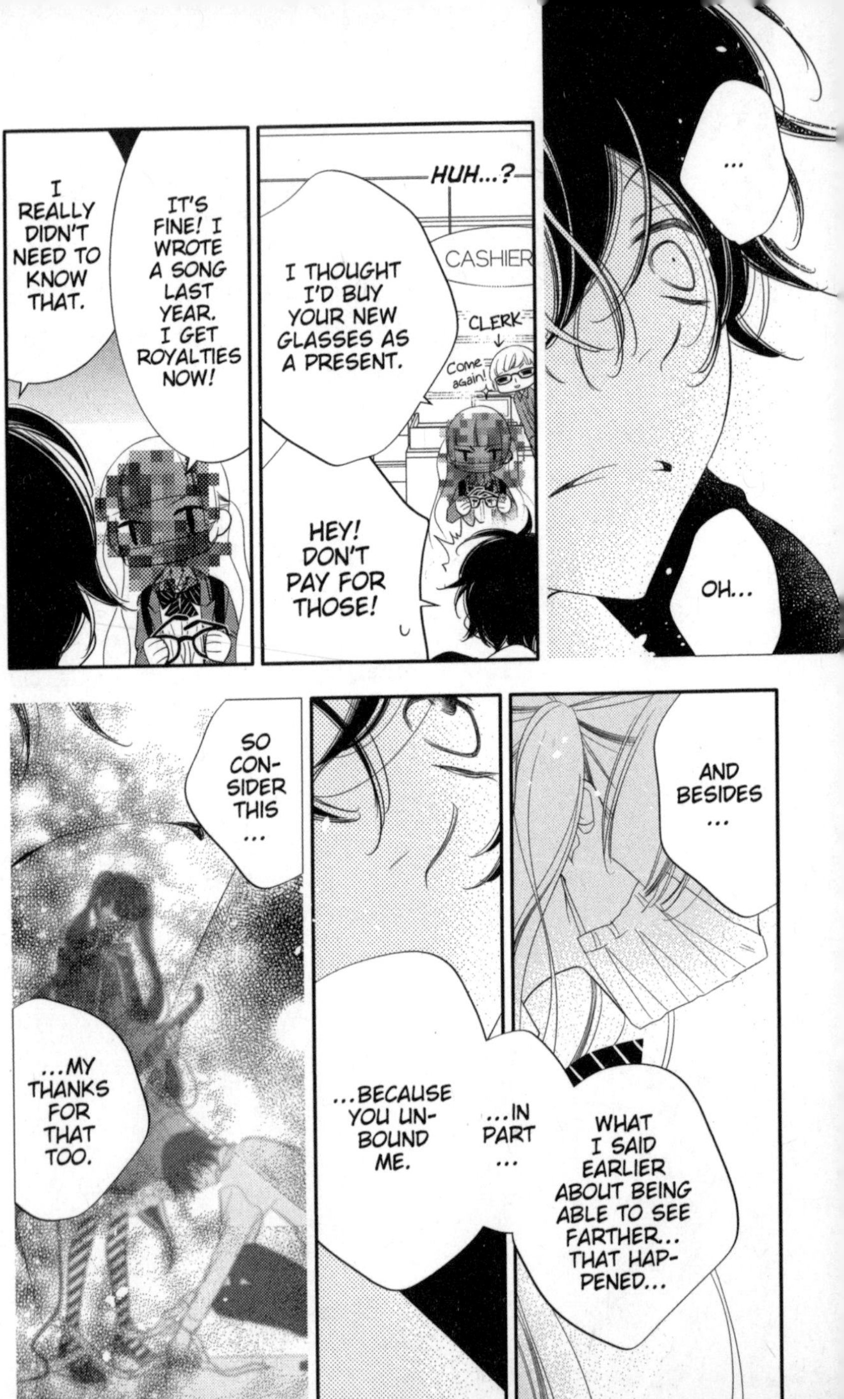
...
OH...
HUH...?
CASHIER
I THOUGHT I'D BUY YOUR NEW GLASSES AS A PRESENT.
CLERK
Come again!
HEY! DON'T PAY FOR THOSE!
IT'S FINE! I WROTE A SONG LAST YEAR. I GET ROYALTIES NOW!
I REALLY DIDN'T NEED TO KNOW THAT.
AND BESIDES...
WHAT I SAID EARLIER ABOUT BEING ABLE TO SEE FARTHER... THAT HAP-PENED...
...IN PART...
...BECAUSE YOU UN-BOUND ME.
SO CON-SIDER THIS...
...MY THANKS FOR THAT TOO.

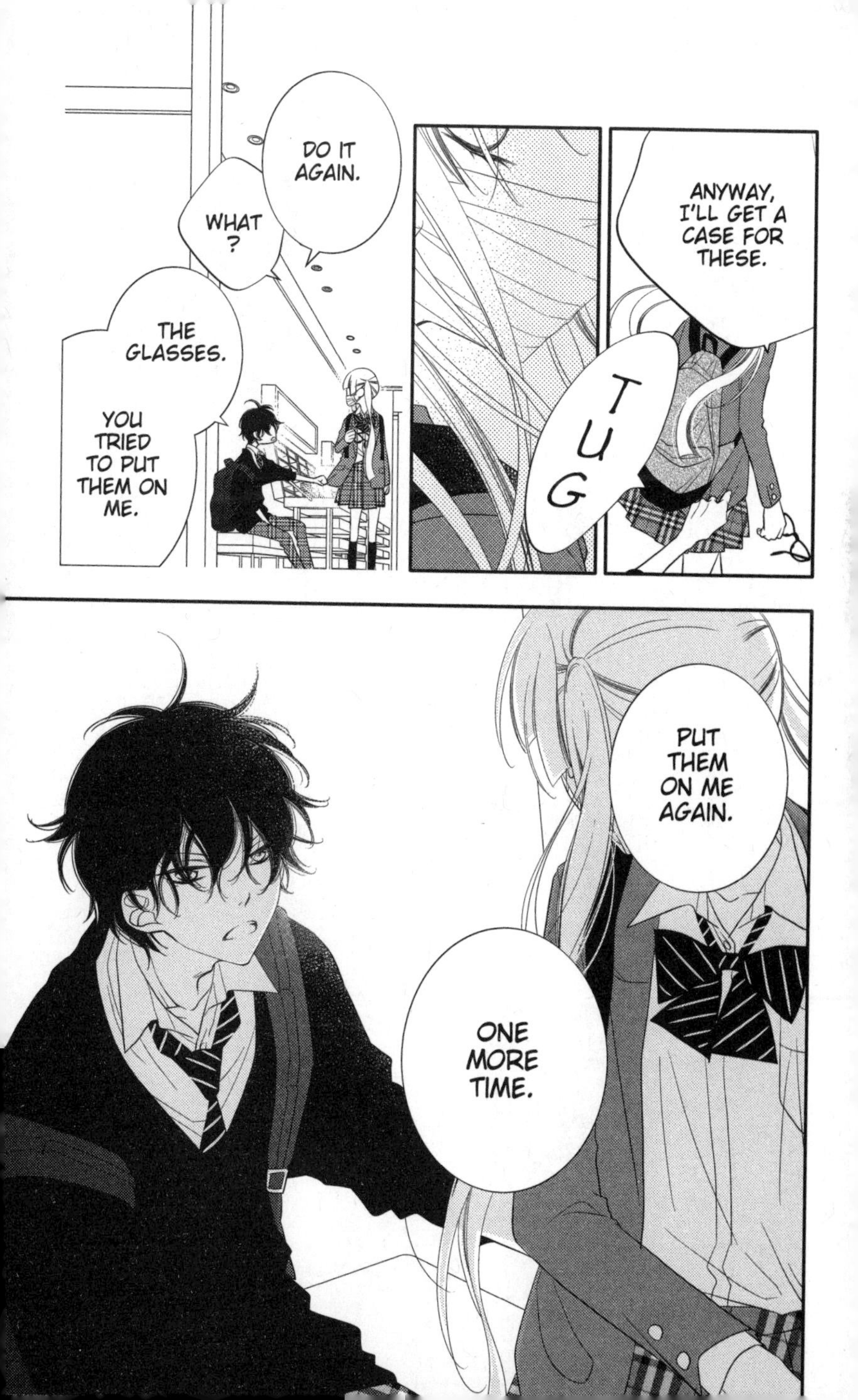
ANYWAY, I'LL GET A CASE FOR THESE.
TUG
DO IT AGAIN.
WHAT?
THE GLASSES.
YOU TRIED TO PUT THEM ON ME.
PUT THEM ON ME AGAIN.
ONE MORE TIME.

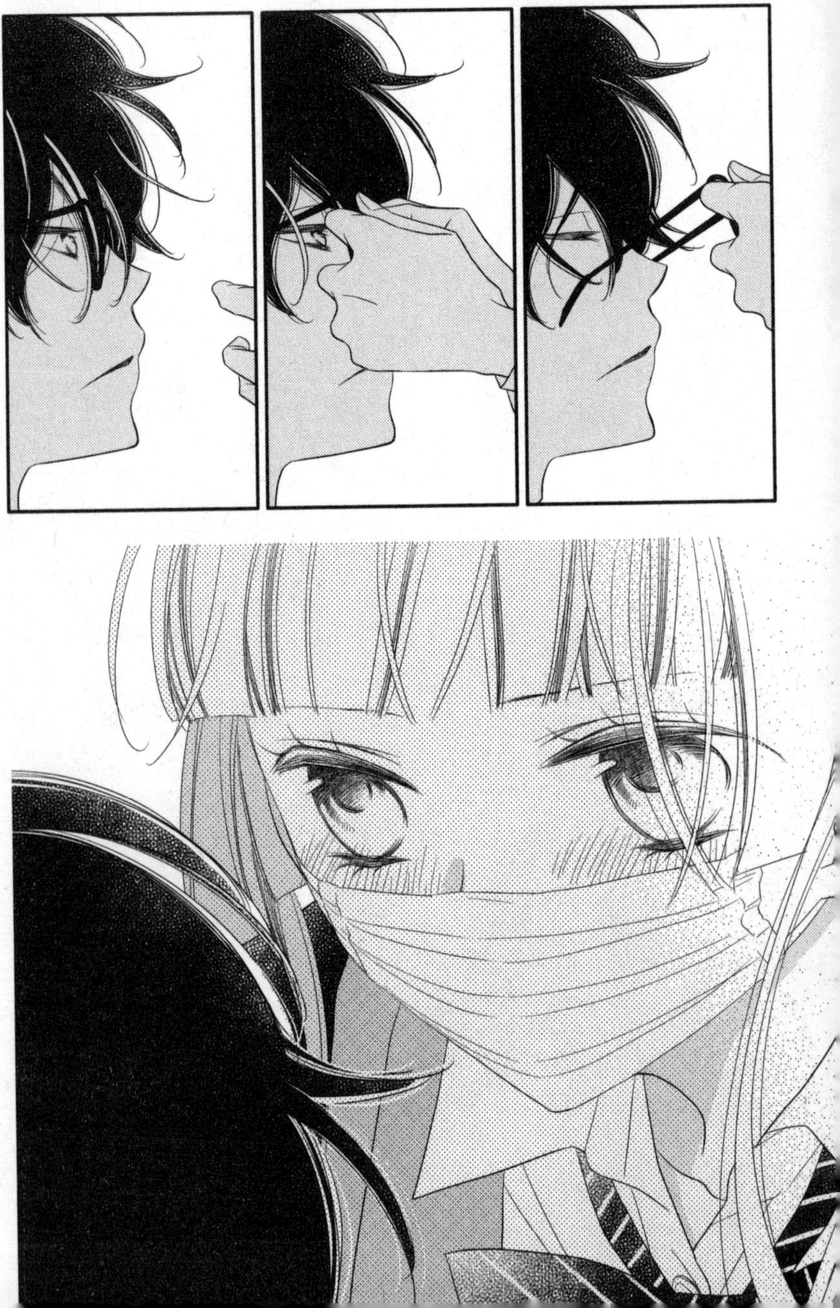

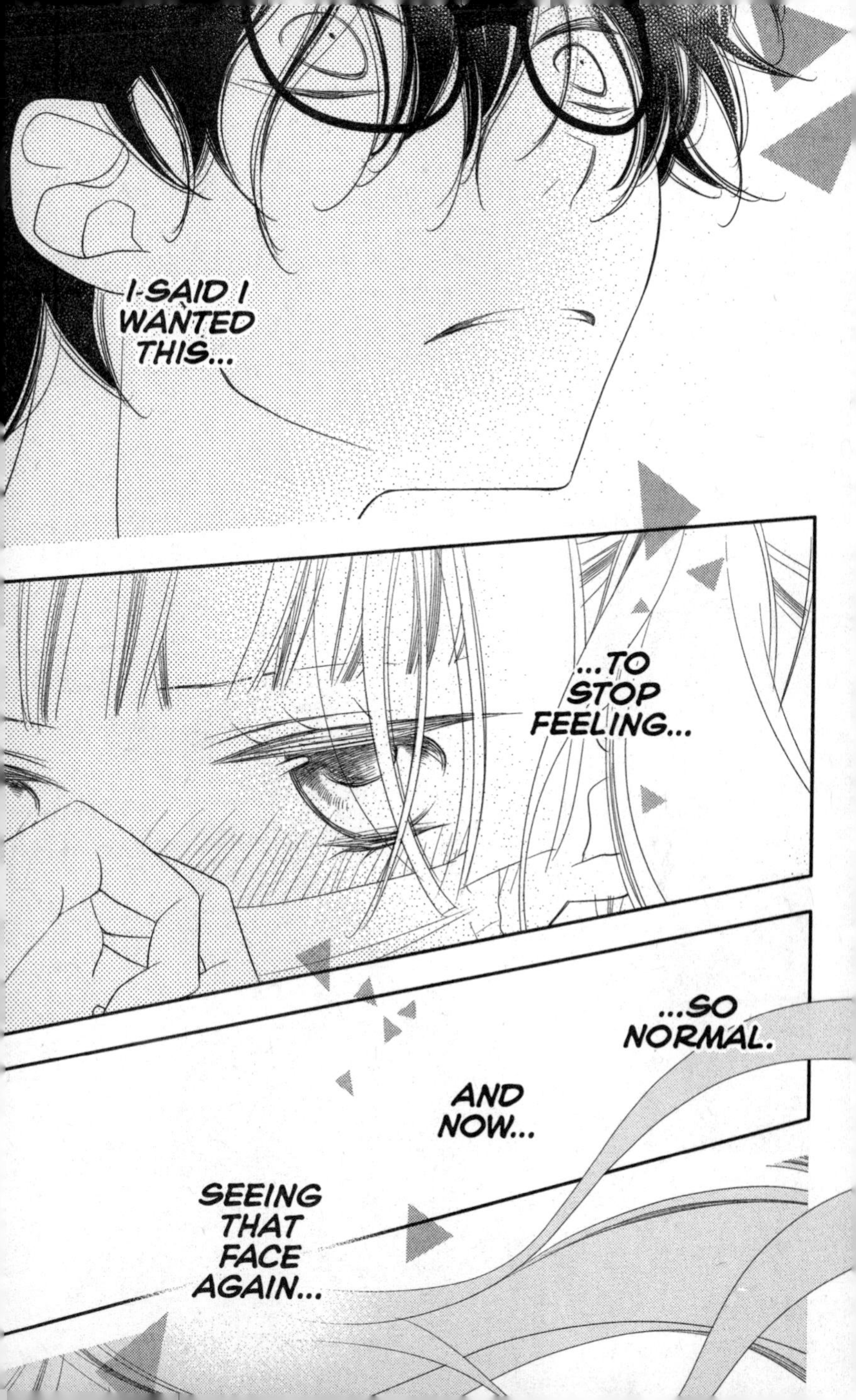
I-SAID I WANTED THIS...
...TO STOP FEELING...
...SO NORMAL.
AND NOW...
SEEING THAT FACE AGAIN...

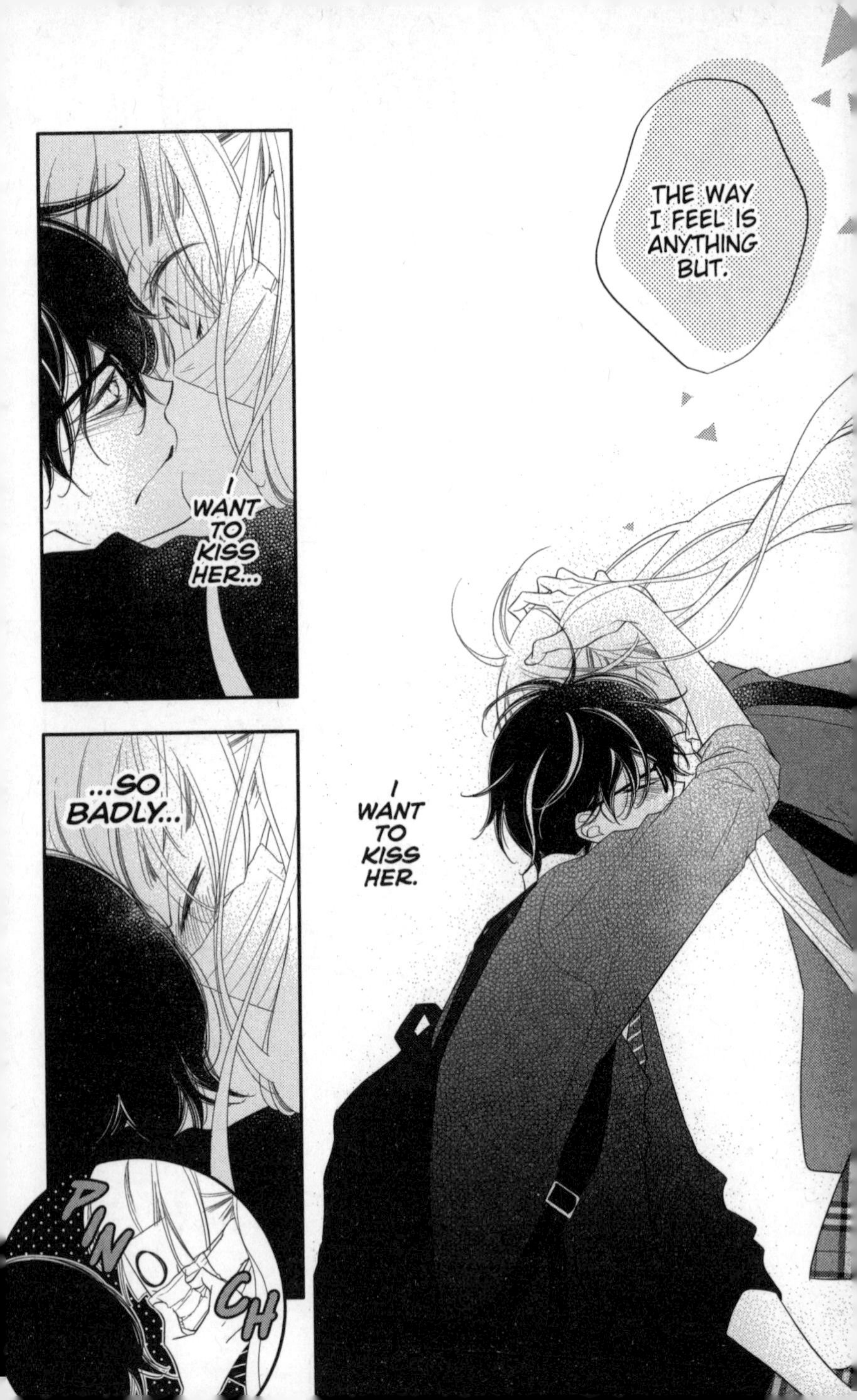
THE WAY I FEEL IS ANYTHING BUT.
I WANT TO KISS HER.
I WANT TO KISS HER...
...SO BADLY...
PINCH

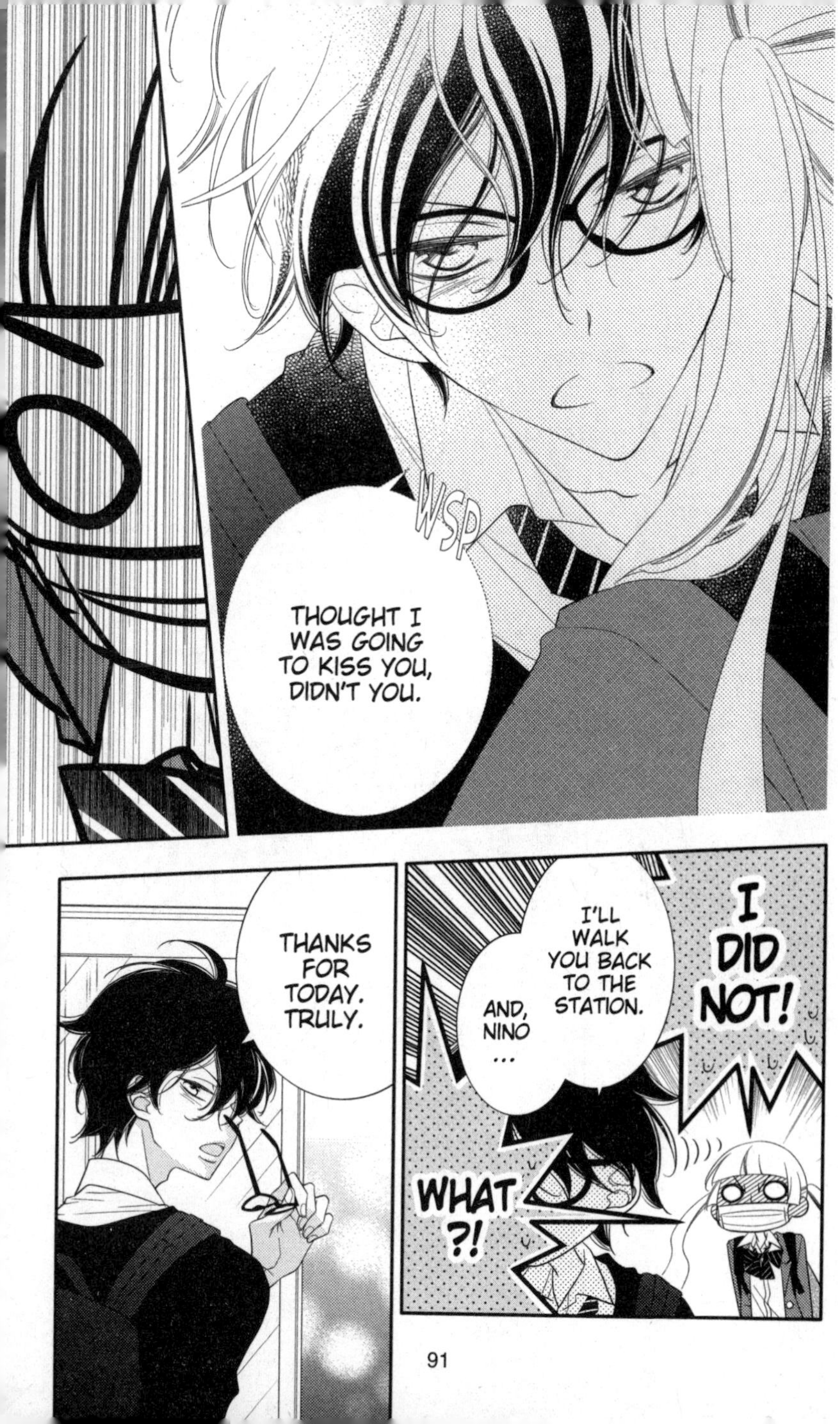
WSP
THOUGHT I WAS GOING TO KISS YOU, DIDN'T YOU.
I DID NOT!
I'LL WALK YOU BACK TO THE STATION.
AND, NINO ...
WHAT ?!
THANKS FOR TODAY. TRULY.

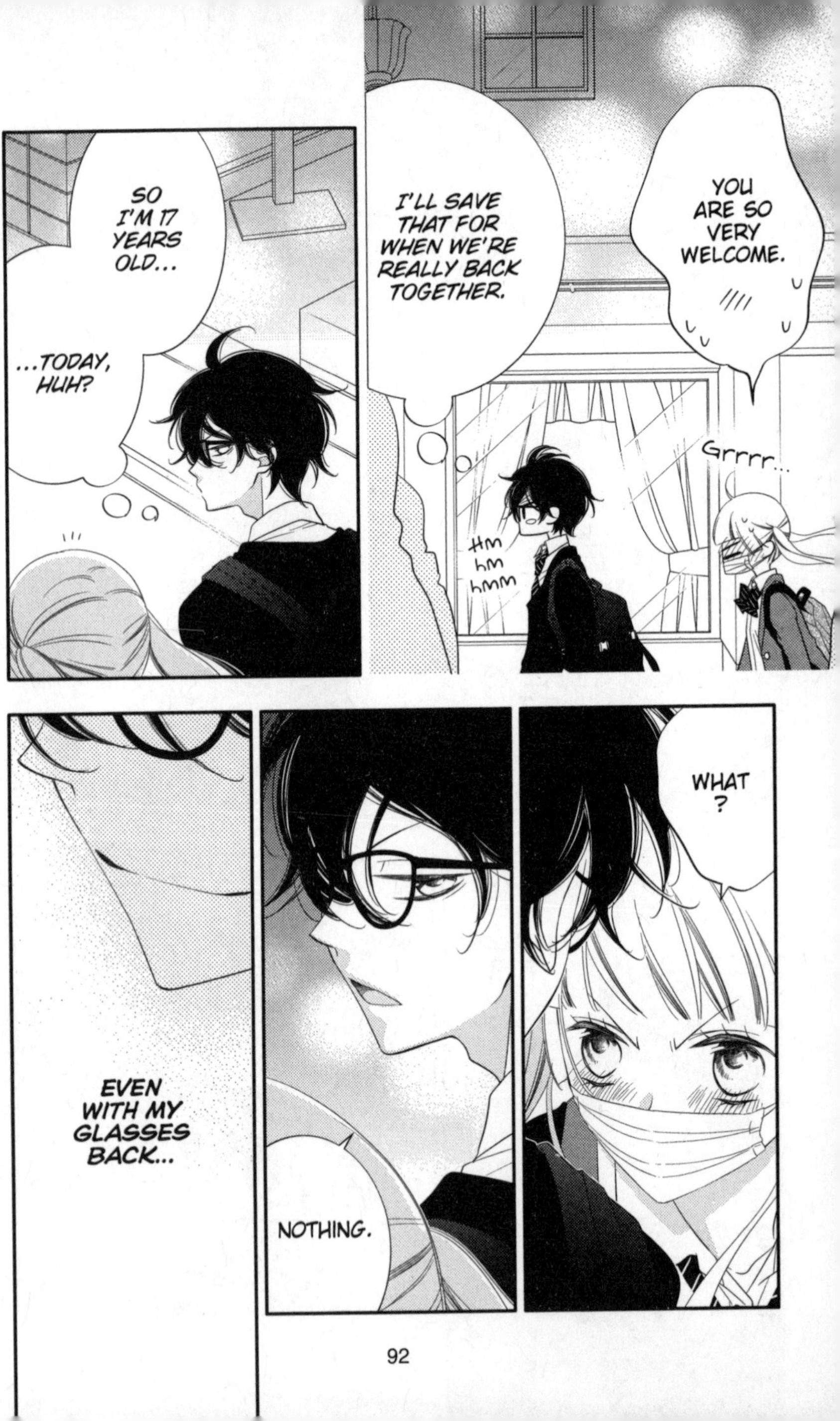
YOU ARE SO VERY WELCOME.
I'LL SAVE THAT FOR WHEN WE'RE REALLY BACK TOGETHER.
Grrrr...
Hm hm hmm
SO I'M 17 YEARS OLD...
...TODAY, HUH?
WHAT?
NOTHING.
EVEN WITH MY GLASSES BACK...

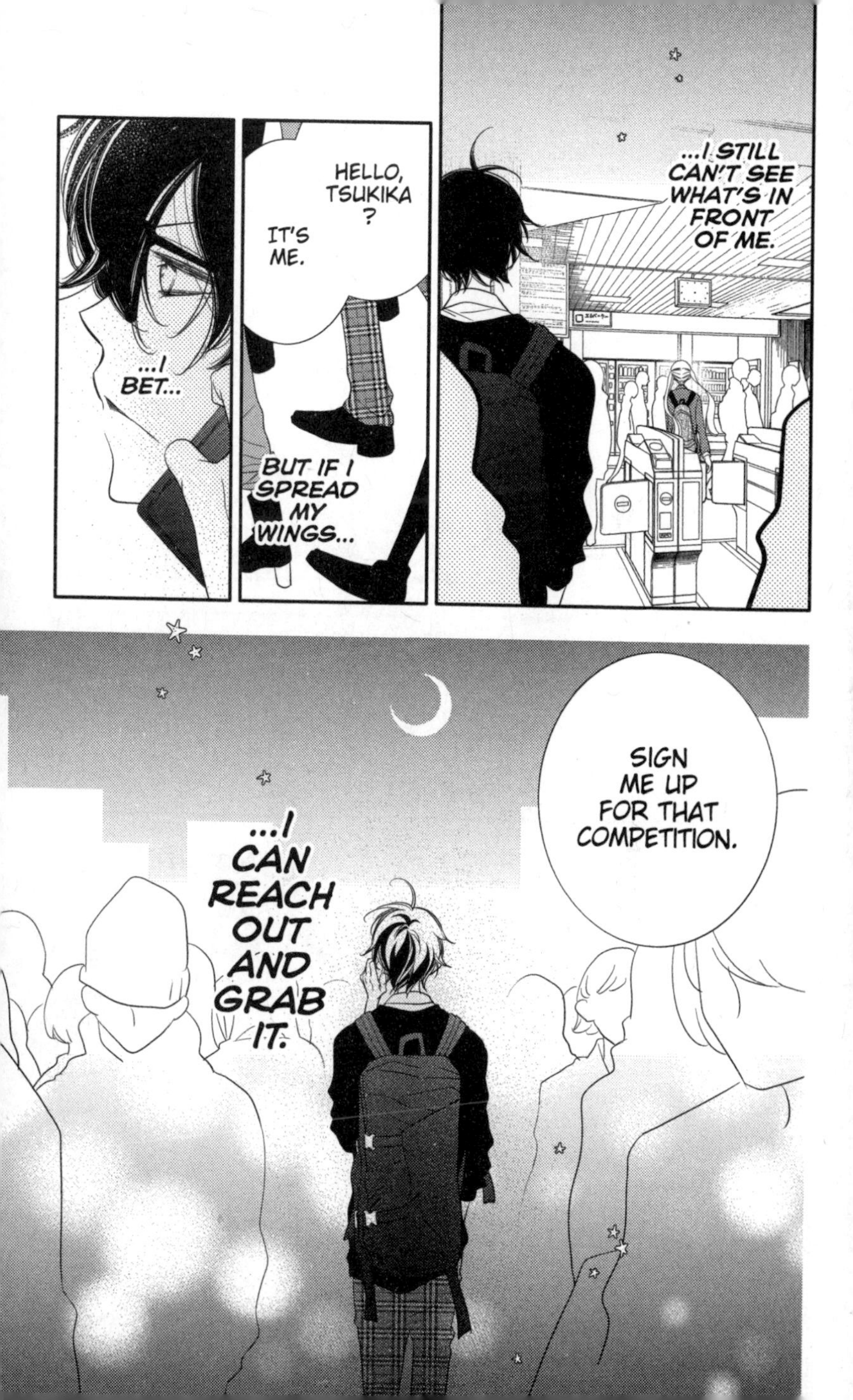
...I STILL CAN'T SEE WHAT'S IN FRONT OF ME.
HELLO, TSUKIKA?
IT'S ME.
BUT IF I SPREAD MY WINGS...
...I BET...
SIGN ME UP FOR THAT COMPETITION.
...I CAN REACH OUT AND GRAB IT.

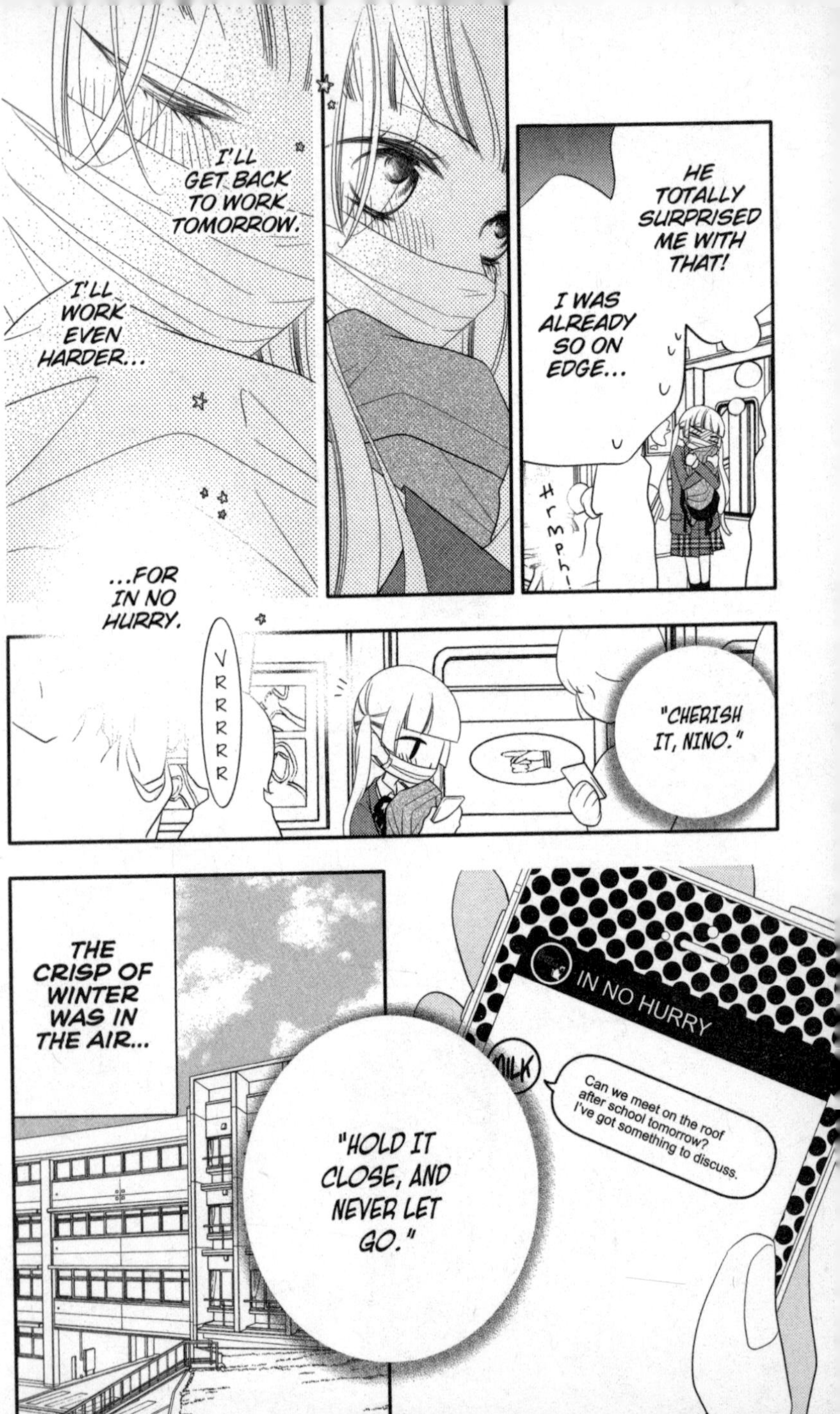
HE TOTALLY SURPRISED ME WITH THAT!
I WAS ALREADY SO ON EDGE...
Hrmph!
I'LL GET BACK TO WORK TOMORROW.
I'LL WORK EVEN HARDER...
...FOR IN NO HURRY.
"CHERISH IT, NINO."
VRRRRR
IN NO HURRY
MILK
Can we meet on the roof after school tomorrow? I've got something to discuss.
"HOLD IT CLOSE, AND NEVER LET GO."
THE CRISP OF WINTER WAS IN THE AIR...

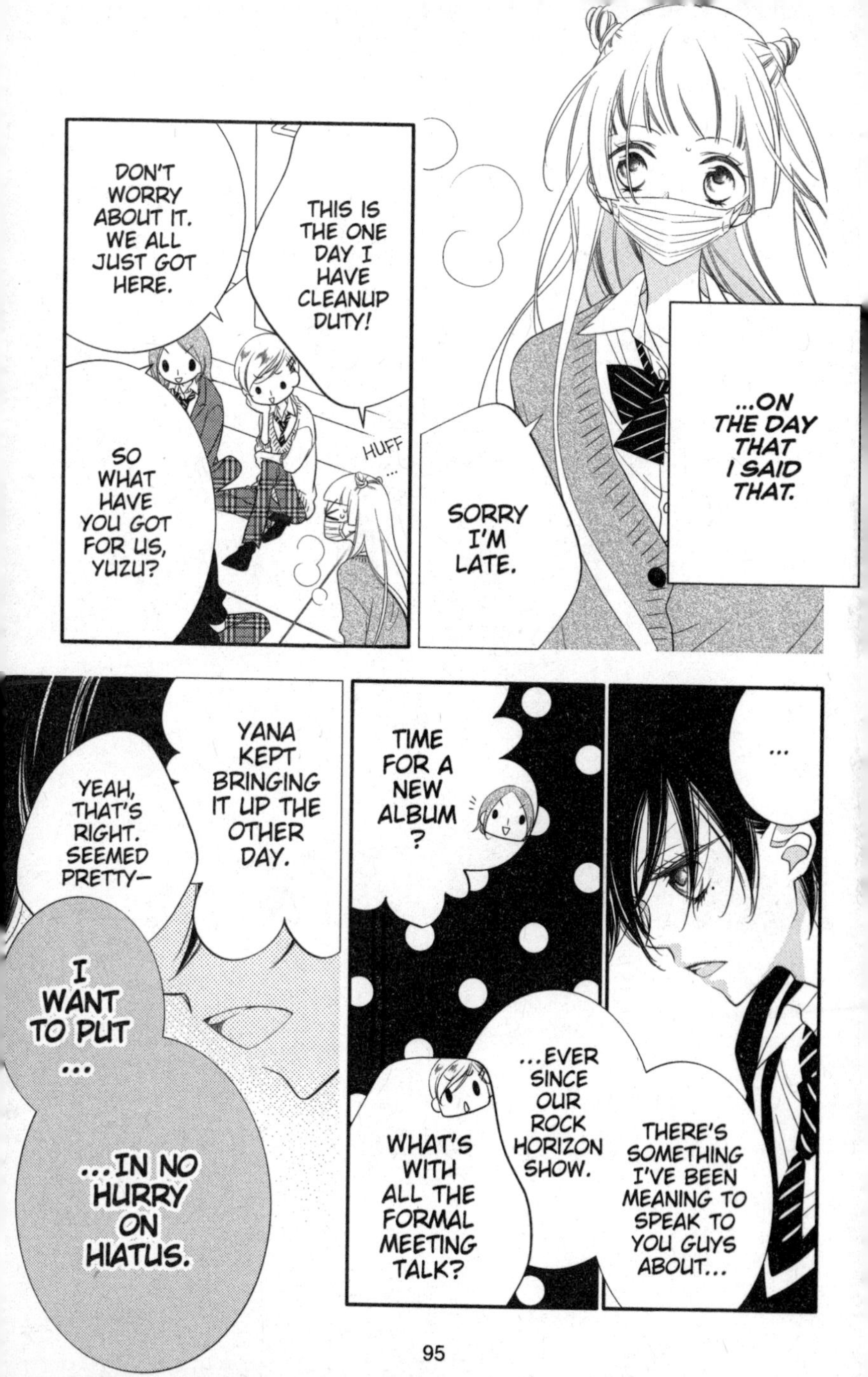
...ON THE DAY THAT I SAID THAT.
SORRY I'M LATE.
THIS IS THE ONE DAY I HAVE CLEANUP DUTY!
DON'T WORRY ABOUT IT. WE ALL JUST GOT HERE.
HUFF ...
SO WHAT HAVE YOU GOT FOR US, YUZU?
...
THERE'S SOMETHING I'VE BEEN MEANING TO SPEAK TO YOU GUYS ABOUT...
TIME FOR A NEW ALBUM?
...EVER SINCE OUR ROCK HORIZON SHOW.
WHAT'S WITH ALL THE FORMAL MEETING TALK?
YANA KEPT BRINGING IT UP THE OTHER DAY.
YEAH, THAT'S RIGHT. SEEMED PRETTY—
I WANT TO PUT ...
...IN NO HURRY ON HIATUS.

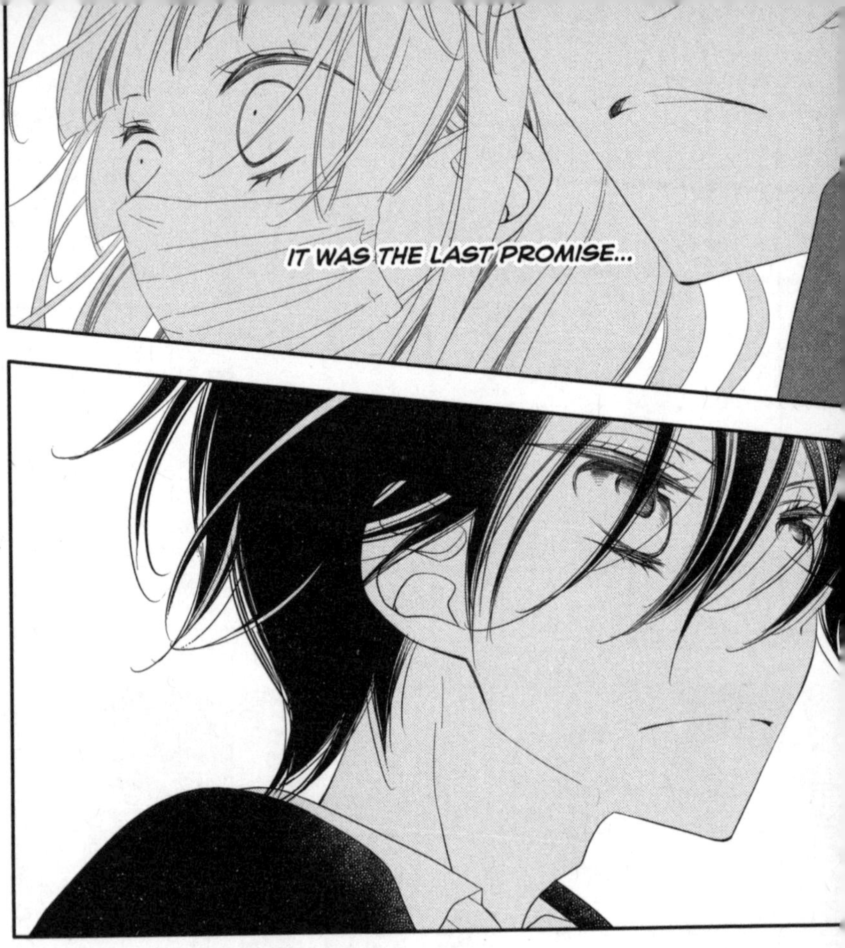
IT WAS THE LAST PROMISE...

...I EVER MADE TO YOU.

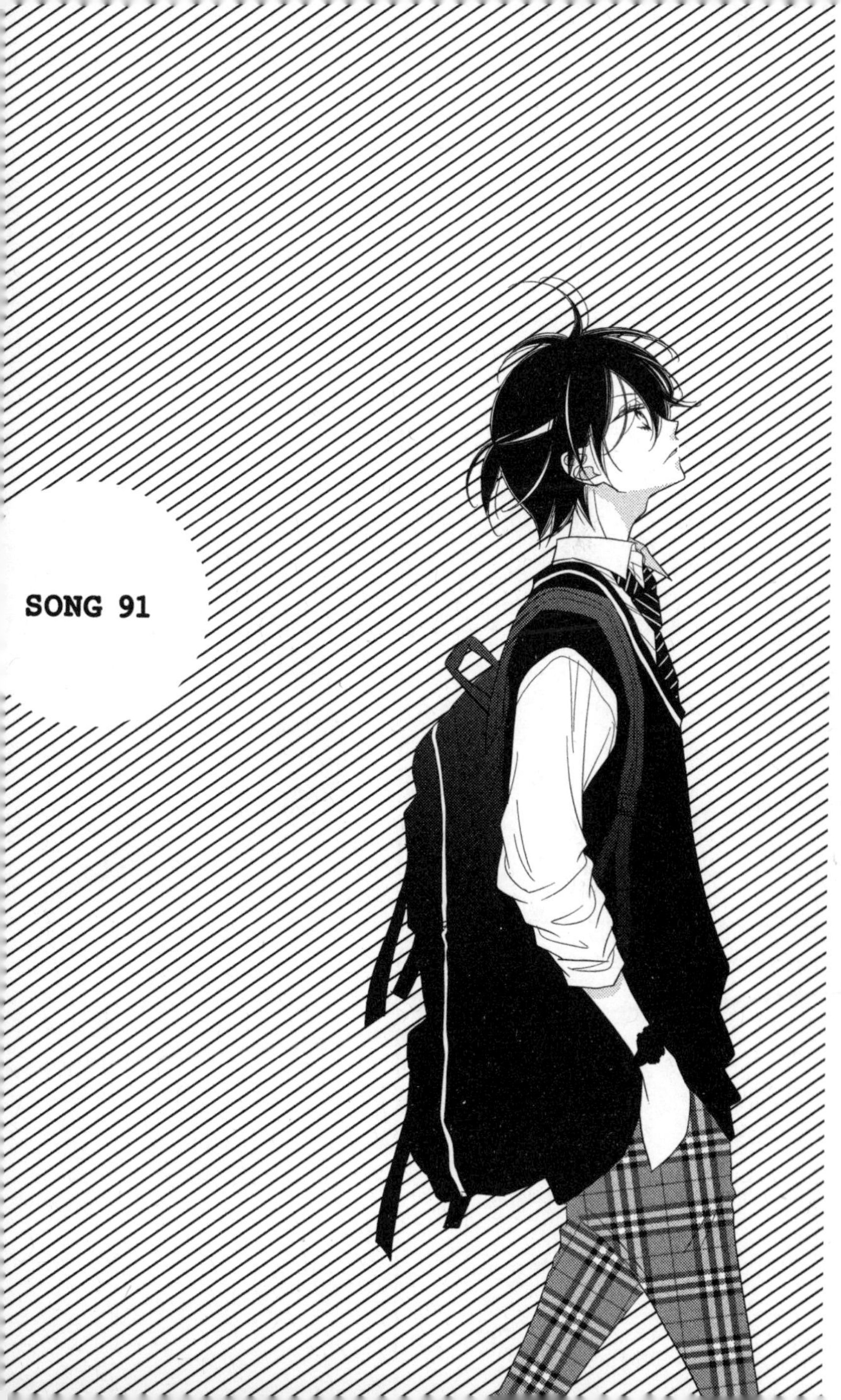
SONG 91

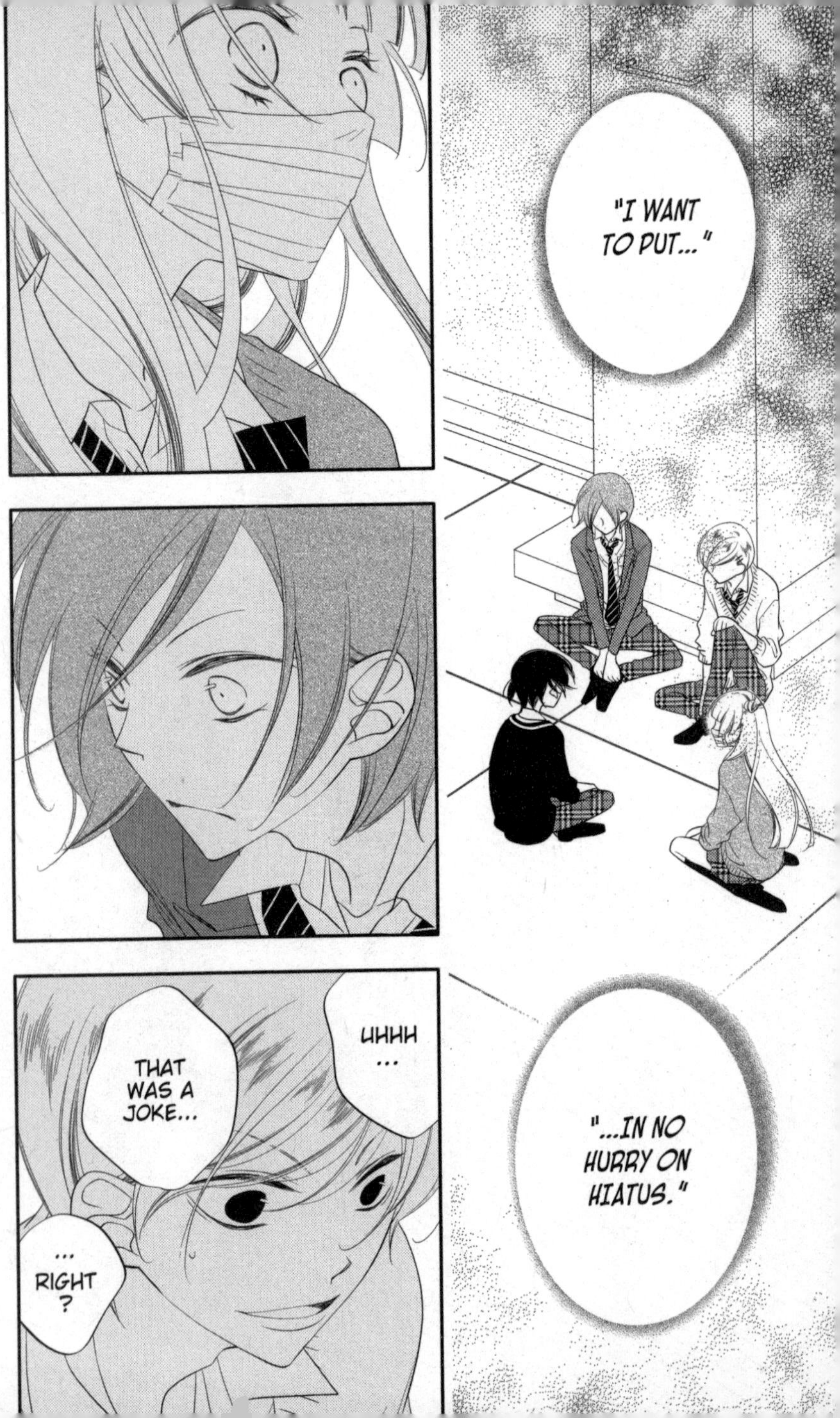
"I WANT TO PUT..."
"...IN NO HURRY ON HIATUS."
UHHH ...
THAT WAS A JOKE...
... RIGHT ?

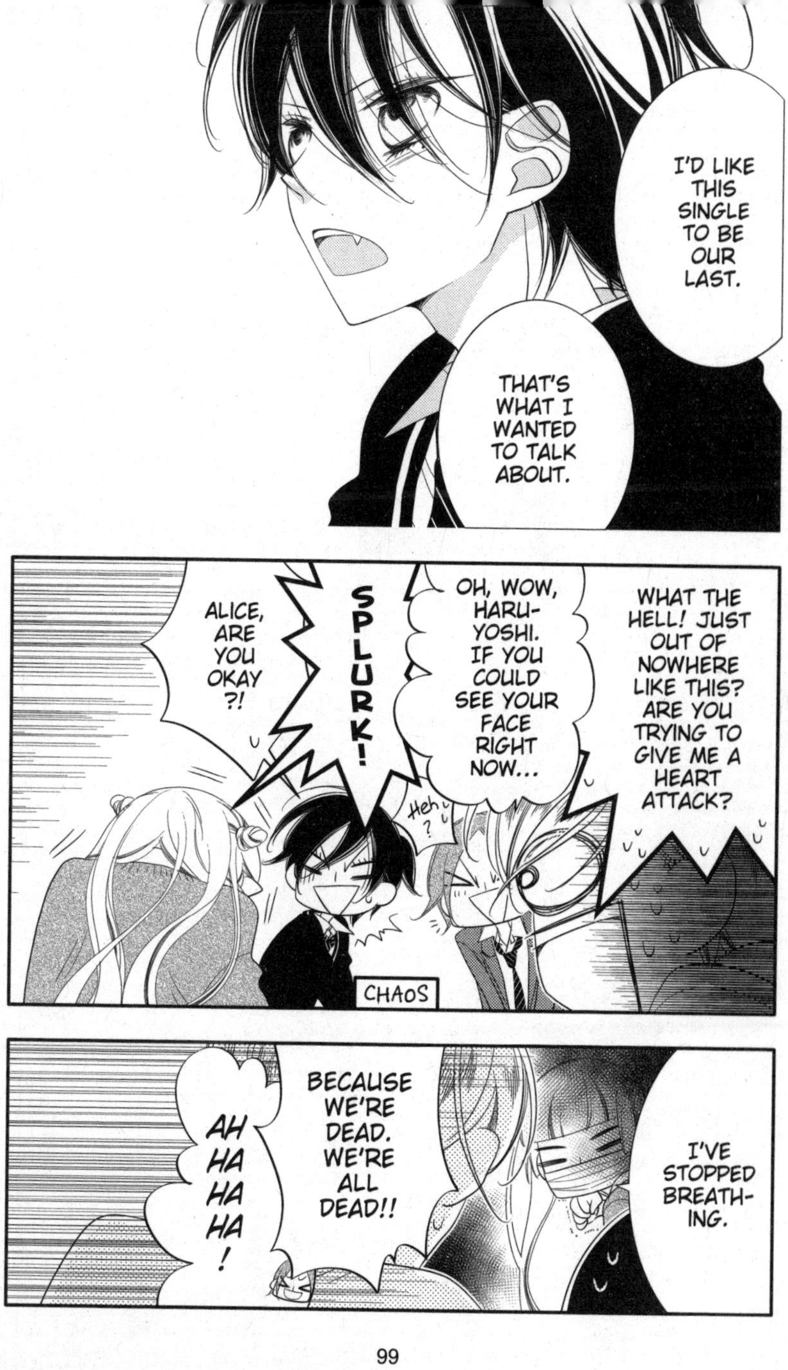

I'D LIKE THIS SINGLE TO BE OUR LAST.
THAT'S WHAT I WANTED TO TALK ABOUT.
WHAT THE HELL! JUST OUT OF NOWHERE LIKE THIS? ARE YOU TRYING TO GIVE ME A HEART ATTACK?
OH, WOW, HARUYOSHI. IF YOU COULD SEE YOUR FACE RIGHT NOW...
SPLURK!
ALICE, ARE YOU OKAY?!
Heh?
CHAOS
I'VE STOPPED BREATHING.
BECAUSE WE'RE DEAD. WE'RE ALL DEAD!!
AH HA HA HA!

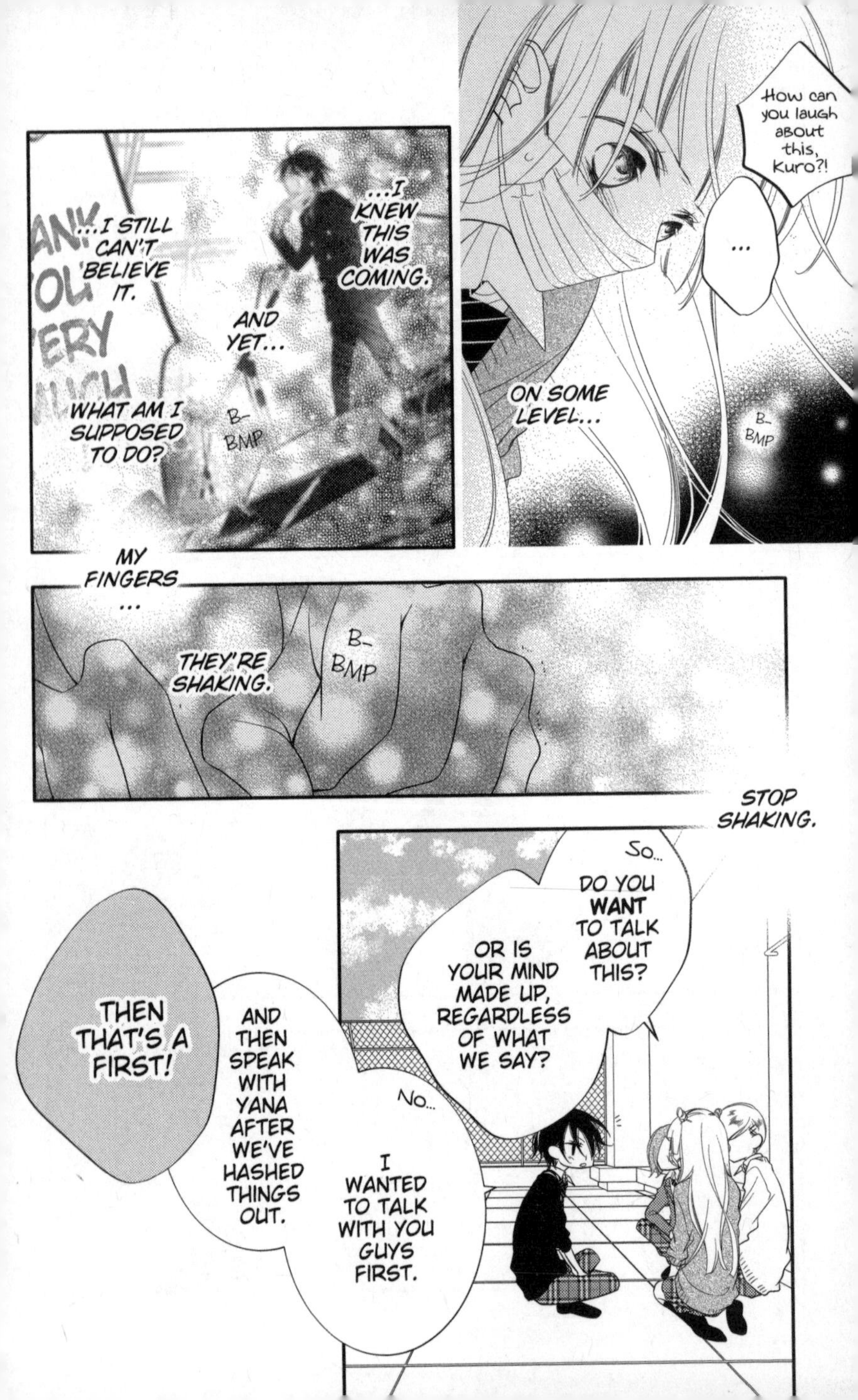
How can you laugh about this, Kuro?!
...
ON SOME LEVEL...
B-BMP
...I KNEW THIS WAS COMING.
AND YET...
...I STILL CAN'T BELIEVE IT.
WHAT AM I SUPPOSED TO DO?
B-BMP
MY FINGERS...
THEY'RE SHAKING.
B-BMP
STOP SHAKING.
So... DO YOU WANT TO TALK ABOUT THIS?
OR IS YOUR MIND MADE UP, REGARDLESS OF WHAT WE SAY?
No...
I WANTED TO TALK WITH YOU GUYS FIRST.
AND THEN SPEAK WITH YANA AFTER WE'VE HASHED THINGS OUT.
THEN THAT'S A FIRST!

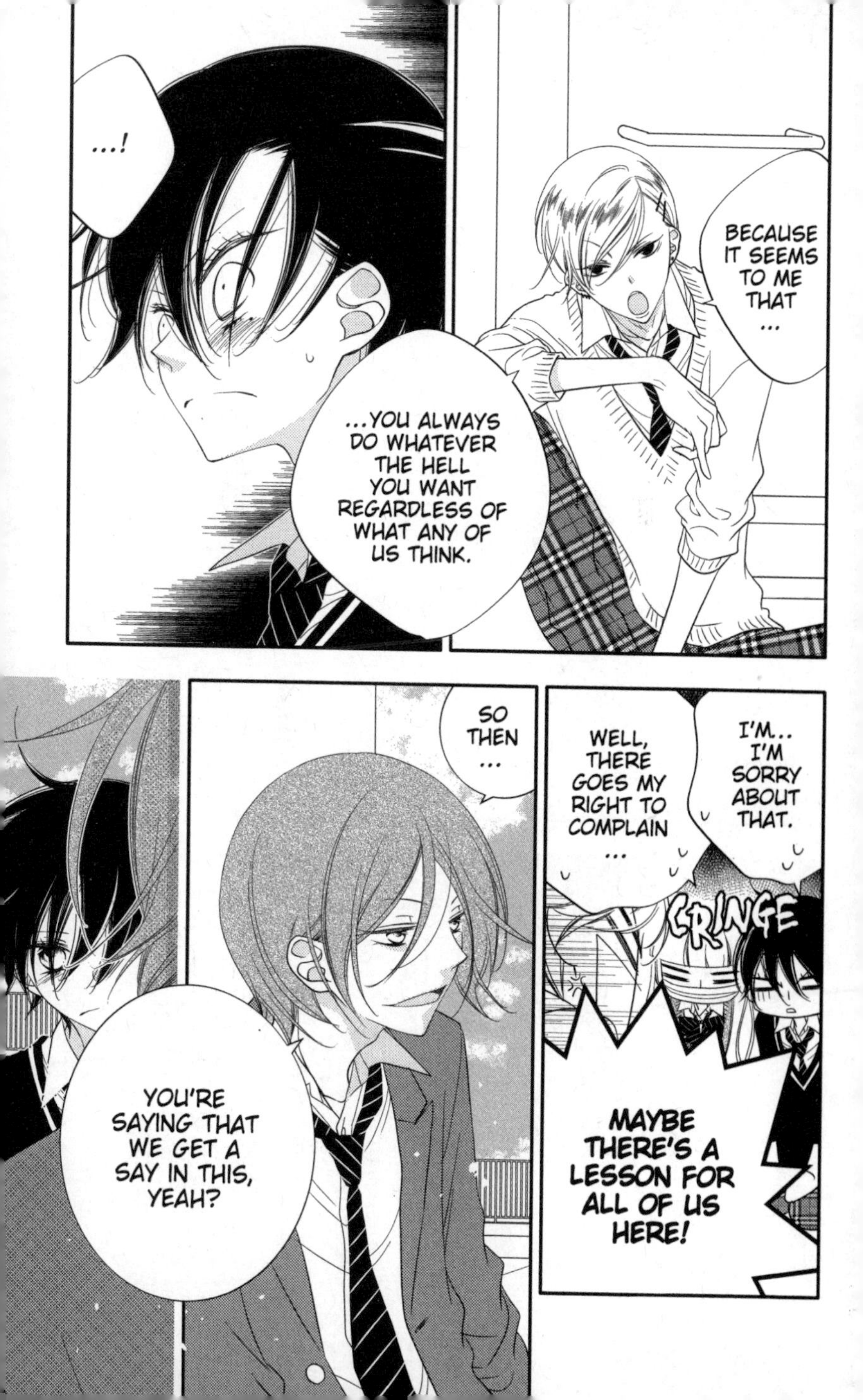
BECAUSE IT SEEMS TO ME THAT ...
...YOU ALWAYS DO WHATEVER THE HELL YOU WANT REGARDLESS OF WHAT ANY OF US THINK.
...!
I'M.. I'M SORRY ABOUT THAT.
WELL, THERE GOES MY RIGHT TO COMPLAIN ...
CRINGE
MAYBE THERE'S A LESSON FOR ALL OF US HERE!
SO THEN ...
YOU'RE SAYING THAT WE GET A SAY IN THIS, YEAH?

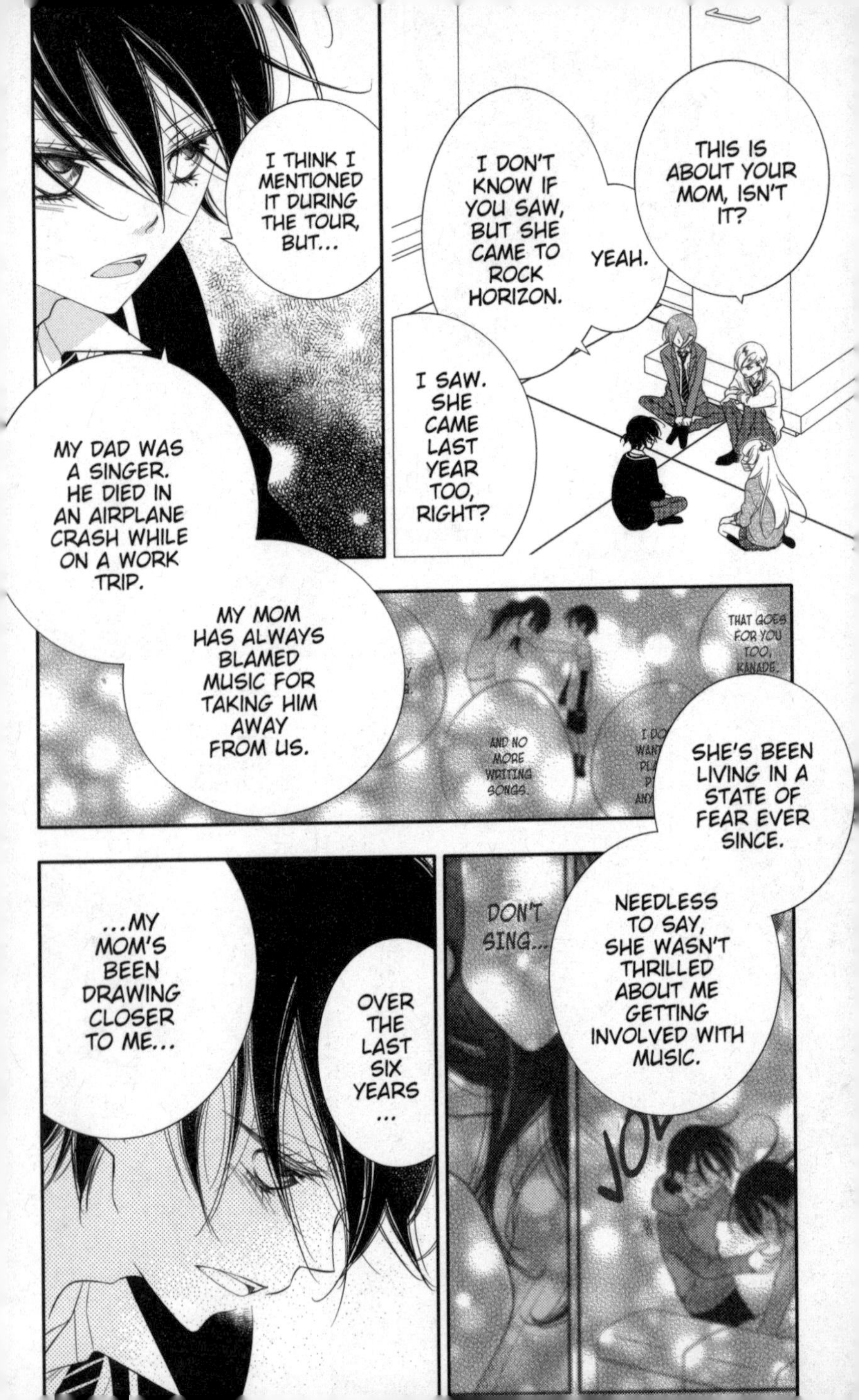
THIS IS ABOUT YOUR MOM, ISN'T IT?
YEAH.
I DON'T KNOW IF YOU SAW, BUT SHE CAME TO ROCK HORIZON.
I SAW. SHE CAME LAST YEAR TOO, RIGHT?
I THINK I MENTIONED IT DURING THE TOUR, BUT...
MY DAD WAS A SINGER. HE DIED IN AN AIRPLANE CRASH WHILE ON A WORK TRIP.
THAT GOES FOR YOU TOO, KANADE.
AND NO MORE WRITING SONGS.
MY MOM HAS ALWAYS BLAMED MUSIC FOR TAKING HIM AWAY FROM US.
SHE'S BEEN LIVING IN A STATE OF FEAR EVER SINCE.
DON'T SING...
NEEDLESS TO SAY, SHE WASN'T THRILLED ABOUT ME GETTING INVOLVED WITH MUSIC.
OVER THE LAST SIX YEARS...
...MY MOM'S BEEN DRAWING CLOSER TO ME...

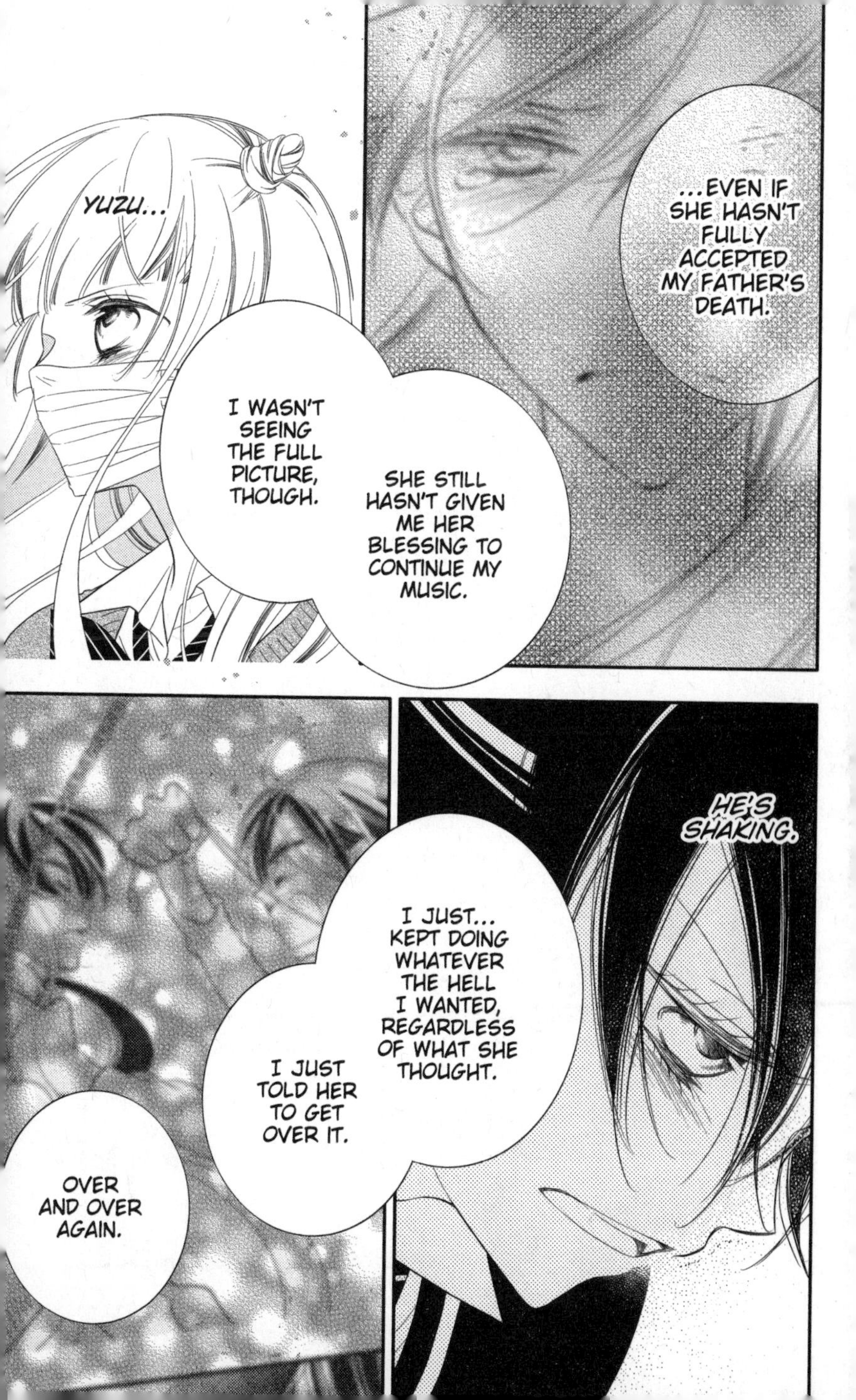
...EVEN IF SHE HASN'T FULLY ACCEPTED MY FATHER'S DEATH.
YUZU...
I WASN'T SEEING THE FULL PICTURE, THOUGH.
SHE STILL HASN'T GIVEN ME HER BLESSING TO CONTINUE MY MUSIC.
HE'S SHAKING.
I JUST... KEPT DOING WHATEVER THE HELL I WANTED, REGARDLESS OF WHAT SHE THOUGHT.
I JUST TOLD HER TO GET OVER IT.
OVER AND OVER AGAIN.

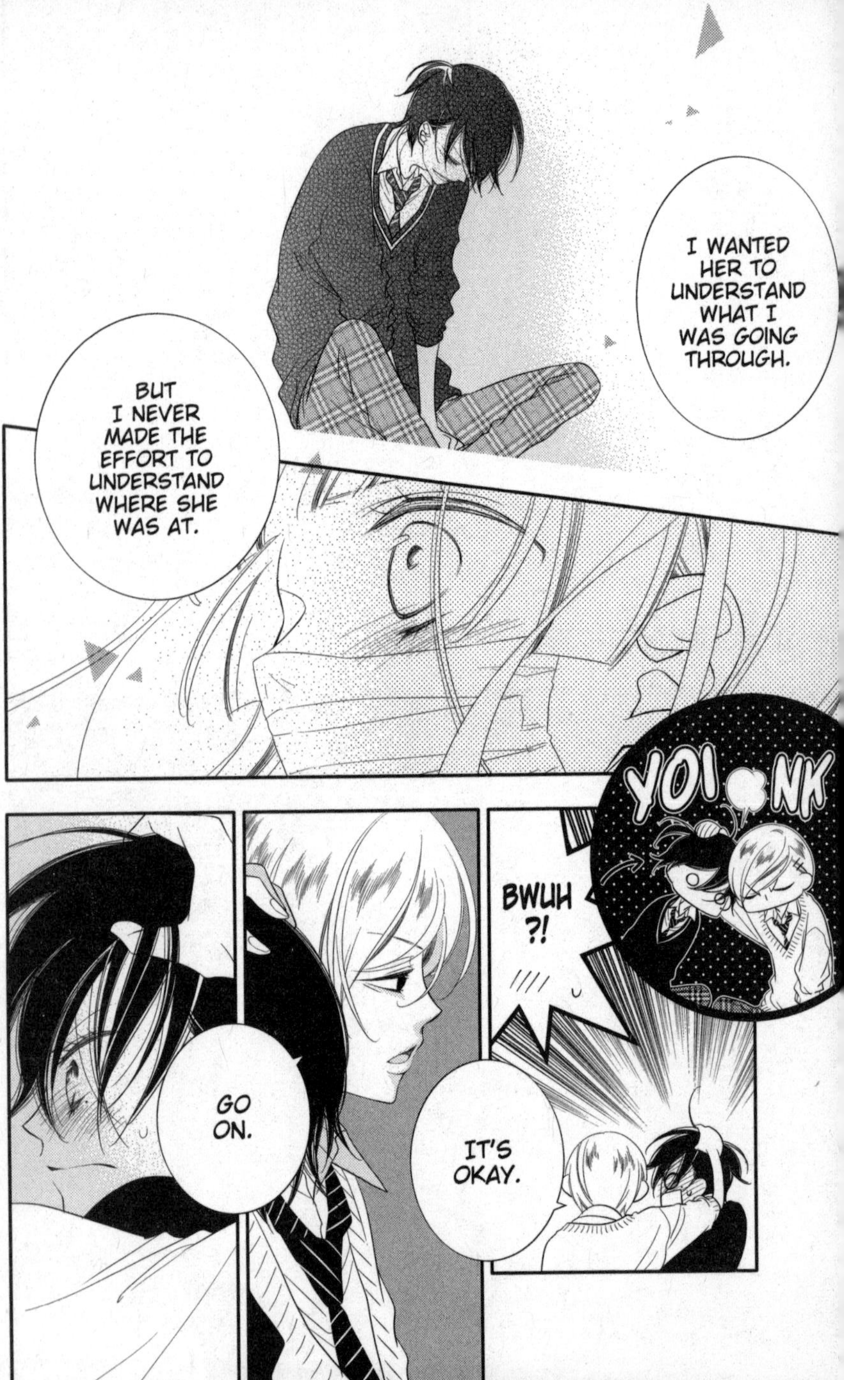
I WANTED HER TO UNDERSTAND WHAT I WAS GOING THROUGH.
BUT I NEVER MADE THE EFFORT TO UNDERSTAND WHERE SHE WAS AT.
YOI●NK
BWUH ?!
IT'S OKAY.
GO ON.

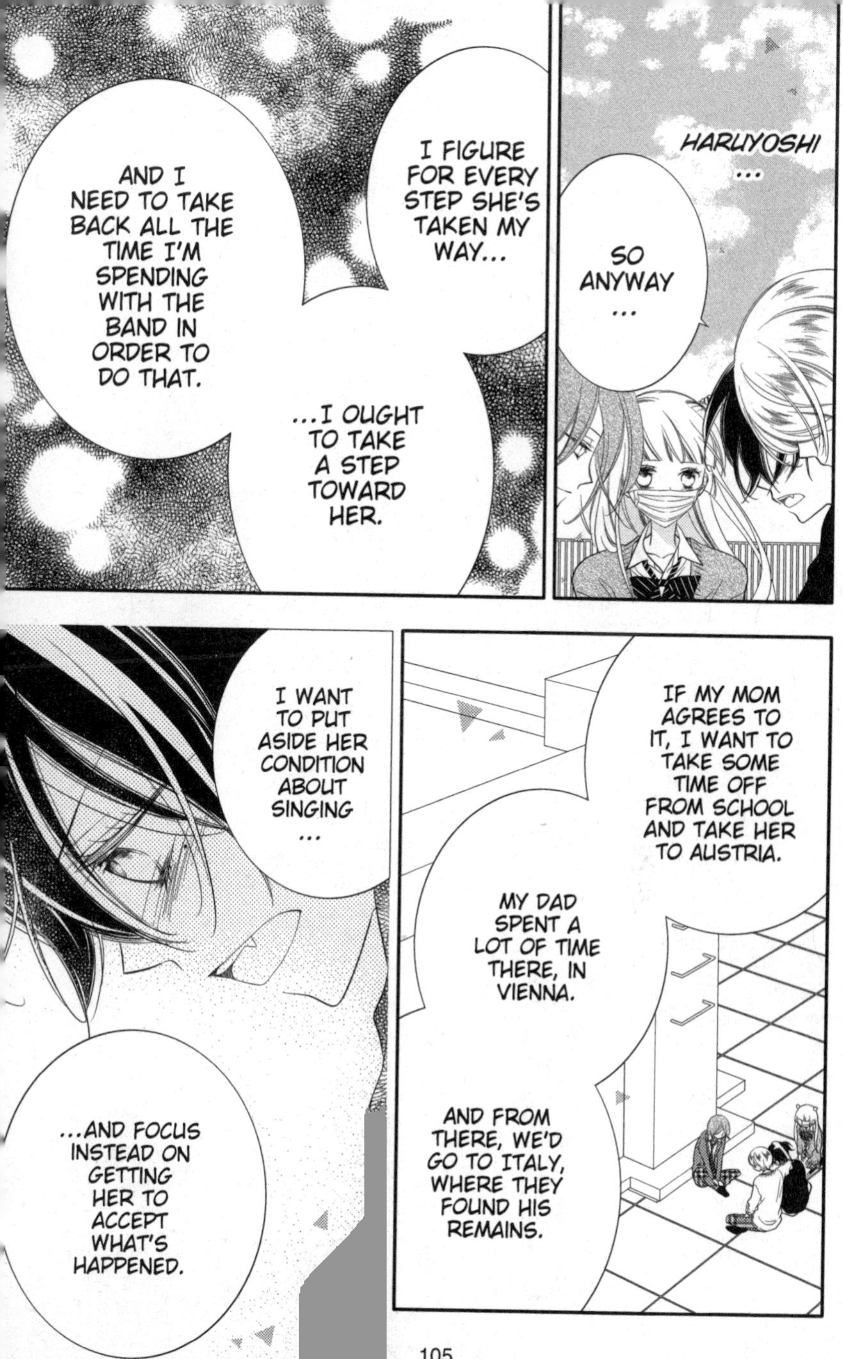
HARUYOSHI
...
SO ANYWAY
...
I FIGURE FOR EVERY STEP SHE'S TAKEN MY WAY...
...I OUGHT TO TAKE A STEP TOWARD HER.
AND I NEED TO TAKE BACK ALL THE TIME I'M SPENDING WITH THE BAND IN ORDER TO DO THAT.
IF MY MOM AGREES TO IT, I WANT TO TAKE SOME TIME OFF FROM SCHOOL AND TAKE HER TO AUSTRIA.
MY DAD SPENT A LOT OF TIME THERE, IN VIENNA.
AND FROM THERE, WE'D GO TO ITALY, WHERE THEY FOUND HIS REMAINS.
I WANT TO PUT ASIDE HER CONDITION ABOUT SINGING
...
...AND FOCUS INSTEAD ON GETTING HER TO ACCEPT WHAT'S HAPPENED.

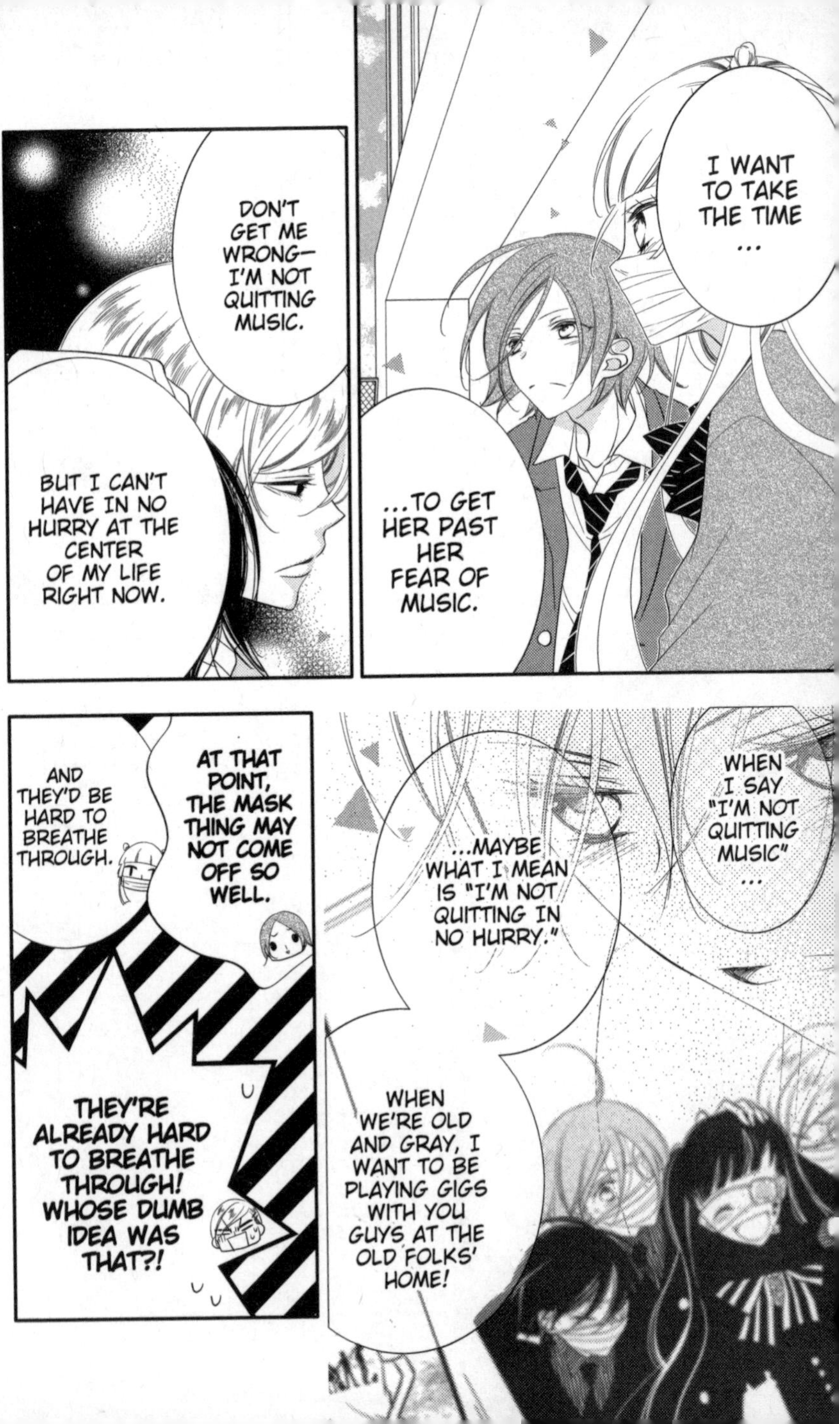

I WANT TO TAKE THE TIME ...
...TO GET HER PAST HER FEAR OF MUSIC.
DON'T GET ME WRONG— I'M NOT QUITTING MUSIC.
BUT I CAN'T HAVE IN NO HURRY AT THE CENTER OF MY LIFE RIGHT NOW.
WHEN I SAY "I'M NOT QUITTING MUSIC" ...
...MAYBE WHAT I MEAN IS "I'M NOT QUITTING IN NO HURRY."
WHEN WE'RE OLD AND GRAY, I WANT TO BE PLAYING GIGS WITH YOU GUYS AT THE OLD FOLKS' HOME!
AT THAT POINT, THE MASK THING MAY NOT COME OFF SO WELL.
AND THEY'D BE HARD TO BREATHE THROUGH.
THEY'RE ALREADY HARD TO BREATHE THROUGH! WHOSE DUMB IDEA WAS THAT?!

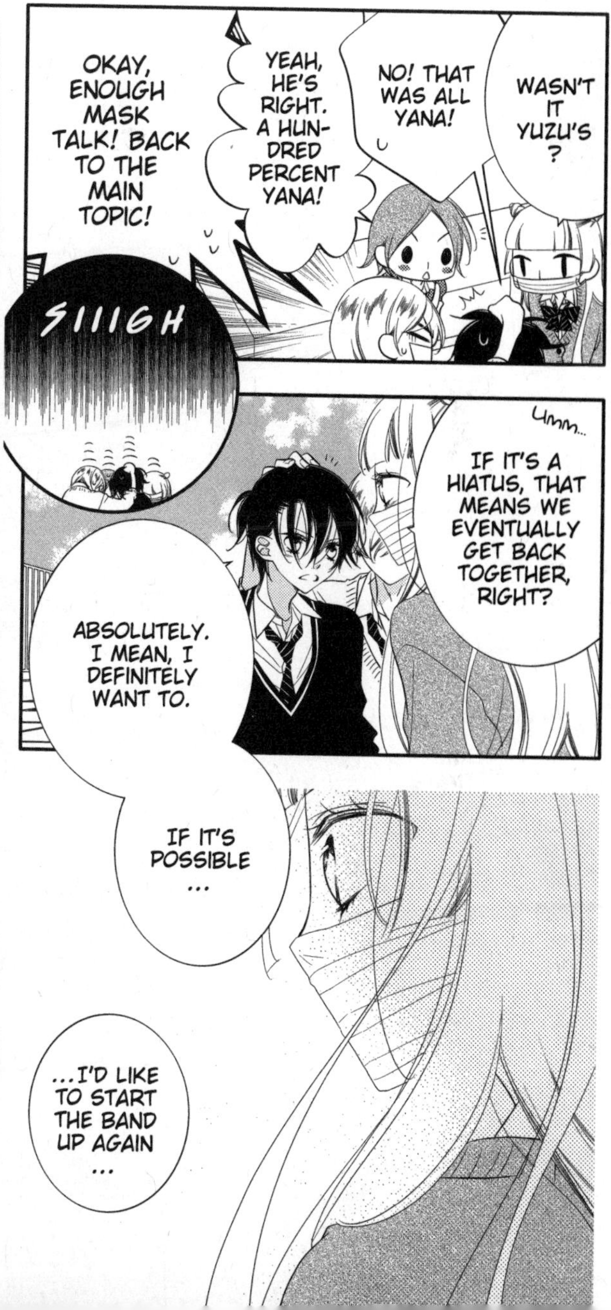
WASN'T IT YUZU'S?
NO! THAT WAS ALL YANA!
YEAH, HE'S RIGHT. A HUN-DRED PERCENT YANA!
OKAY, ENOUGH MASK TALK! BACK TO THE MAIN TOPIC!
SIIIGH
Umm...
IF IT'S A HIATUS, THAT MEANS WE EVENTUALLY GET BACK TOGETHER, RIGHT?
ABSOLUTELY. I MEAN, I DEFINITELY WANT TO.
IF IT'S POSSIBLE...
...I'D LIKE TO START THE BAND UP AGAIN...

4

I have such deep feelings of gratitude about this. To everyone at the Tower Records in Shibuya, thank you!

Working on this manga has taken me to so many places I never imagined I would be able to go. And I don't just mean that physically, but professionally and psychologically as well. And whenever I think about all the opportunities it has given me, you, the reader, are always foremost in my heart. Thank you so much.

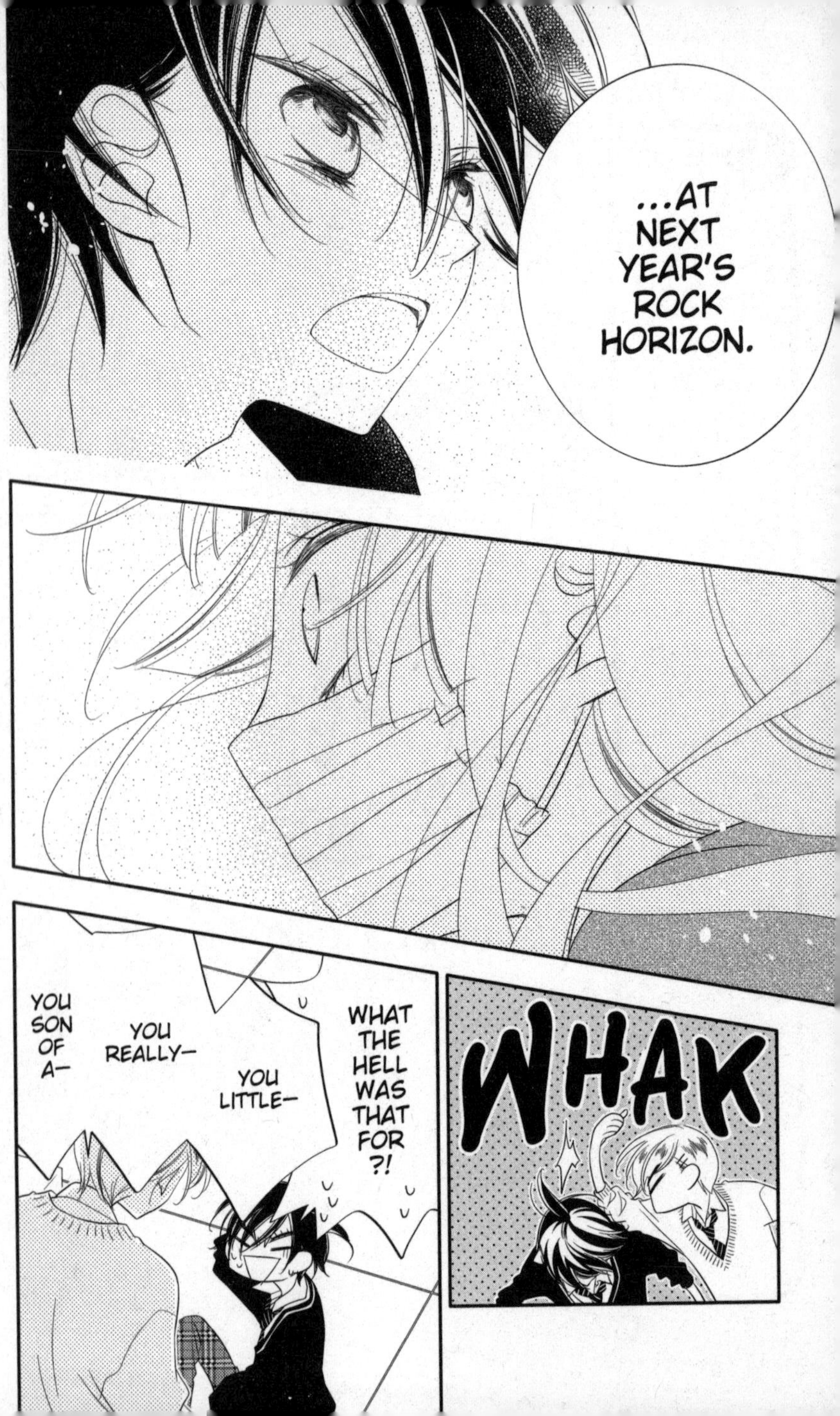
...AT NEXT YEAR'S ROCK HORIZON.
WHAK
WHAT THE HELL WAS THAT FOR?!
YOU LITTLE—
YOU REALLY—
YOU SON OF A—

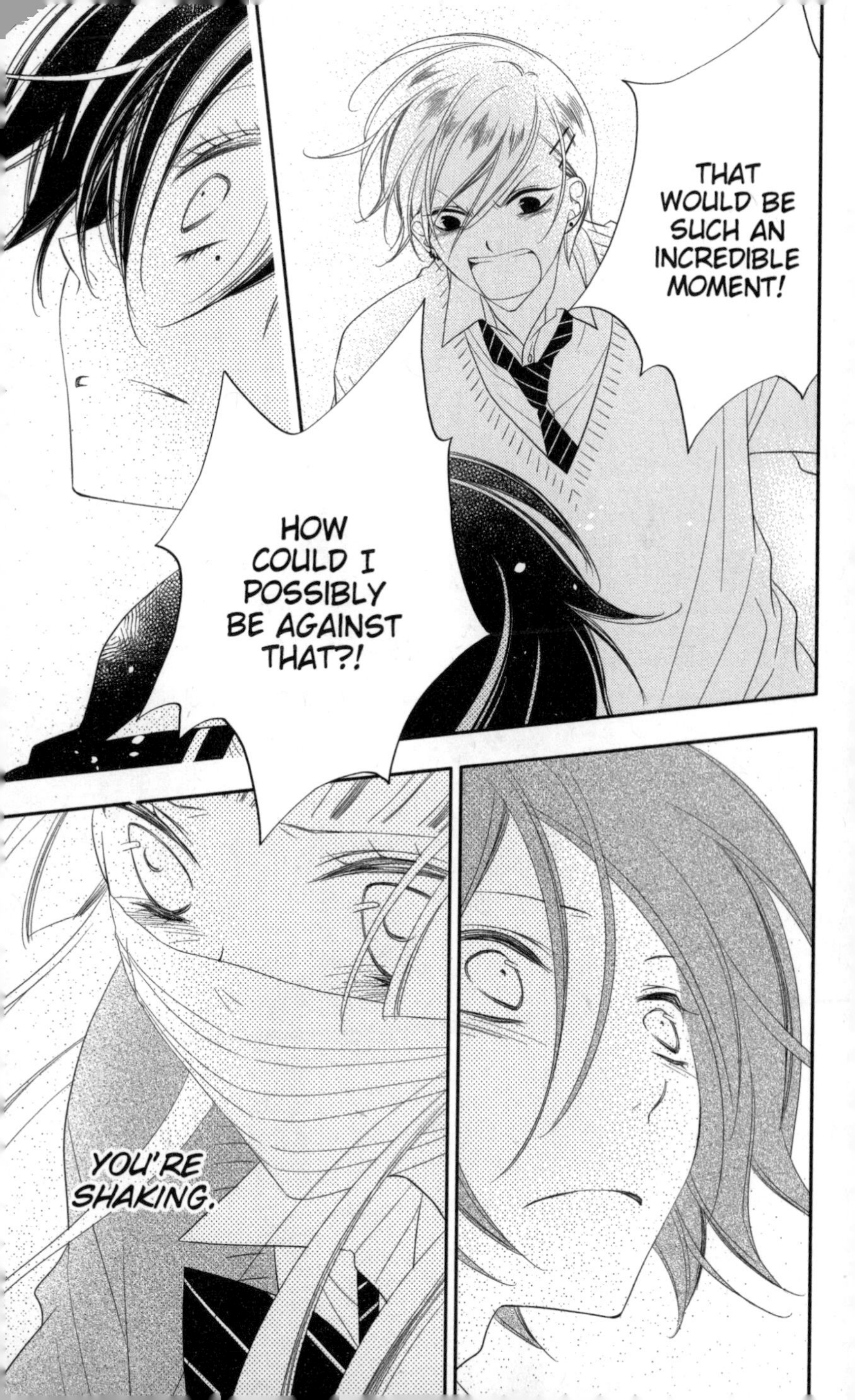
THAT WOULD BE SUCH AN INCREDIBLE MOMENT!
HOW COULD I POSSIBLY BE AGAINST THAT?!
YOU'RE SHAKING.

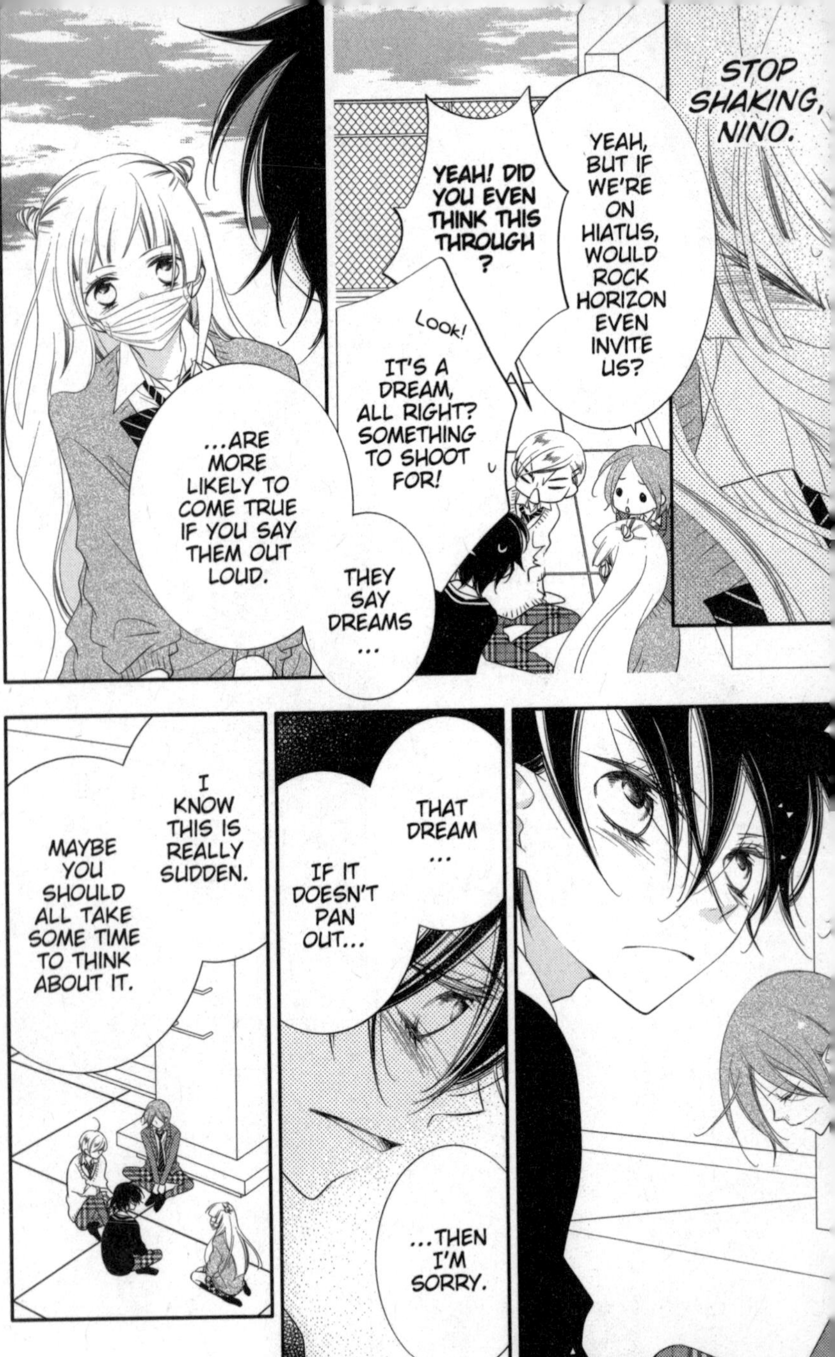
STOP SHAKING, NINO.
YEAH, BUT IF WE'RE ON HIATUS, WOULD ROCK HORIZON EVEN INVITE US?
YEAH! DID YOU EVEN THINK THIS THROUGH?
LOOK!
IT'S A DREAM, ALL RIGHT? SOMETHING TO SHOOT FOR!
THEY SAY DREAMS...
...ARE MORE LIKELY TO COME TRUE IF YOU SAY THEM OUT LOUD.
THAT DREAM...
IF IT DOESN'T PAN OUT...
...THEN I'M SORRY.
I KNOW THIS IS REALLY SUDDEN.
MAYBE YOU SHOULD ALL TAKE SOME TIME TO THINK ABOUT IT.

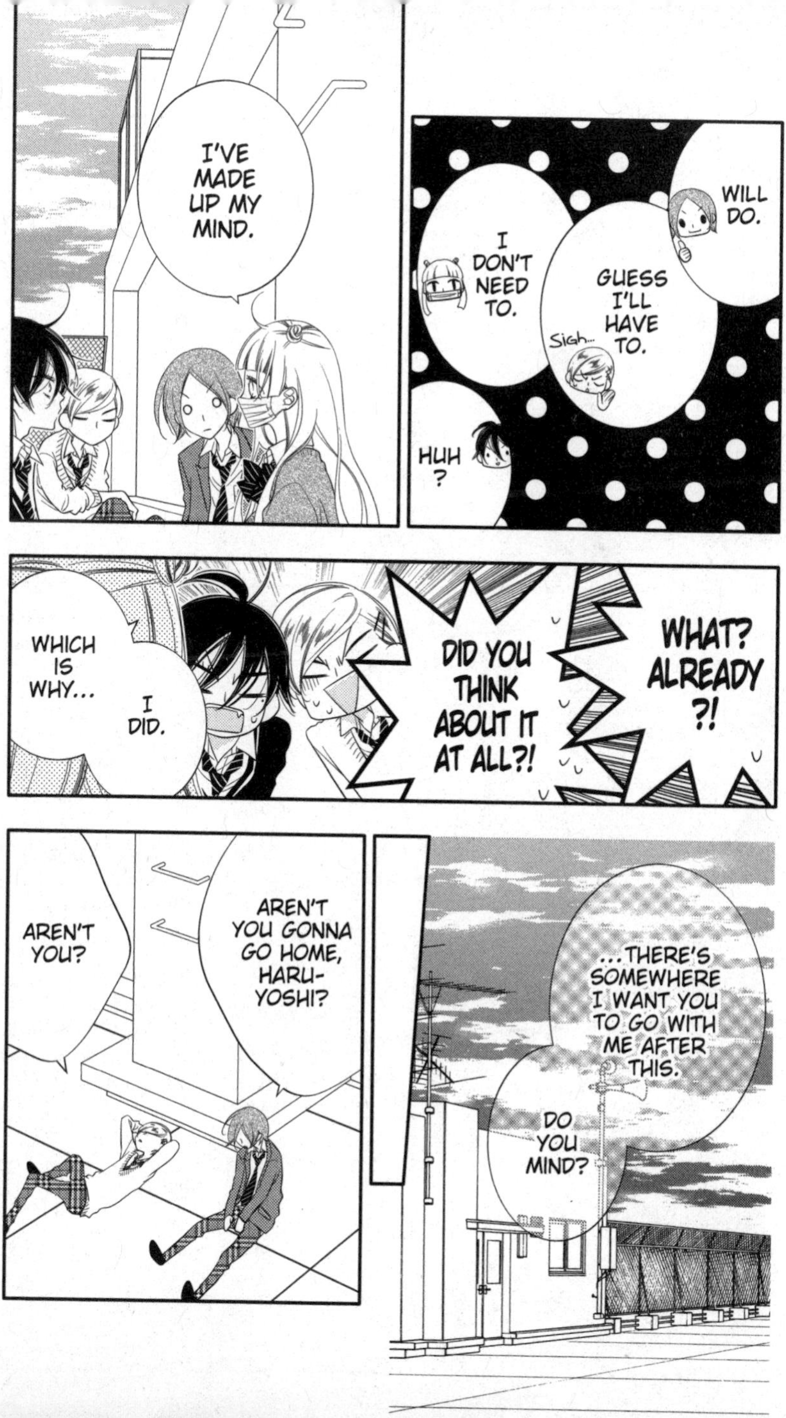
WILL DO.
GUESS I'LL HAVE TO.
Sigh...
I DON'T NEED TO.
HUH?
I'VE MADE UP MY MIND.
WHAT? ALREADY?!
DID YOU THINK ABOUT IT AT ALL?!
I DID.
WHICH IS WHY...
...THERE'S SOMEWHERE I WANT YOU TO GO WITH ME AFTER THIS.
DO YOU MIND?
AREN'T YOU GONNA GO HOME, HARU-YOSHI?
AREN'T YOU?

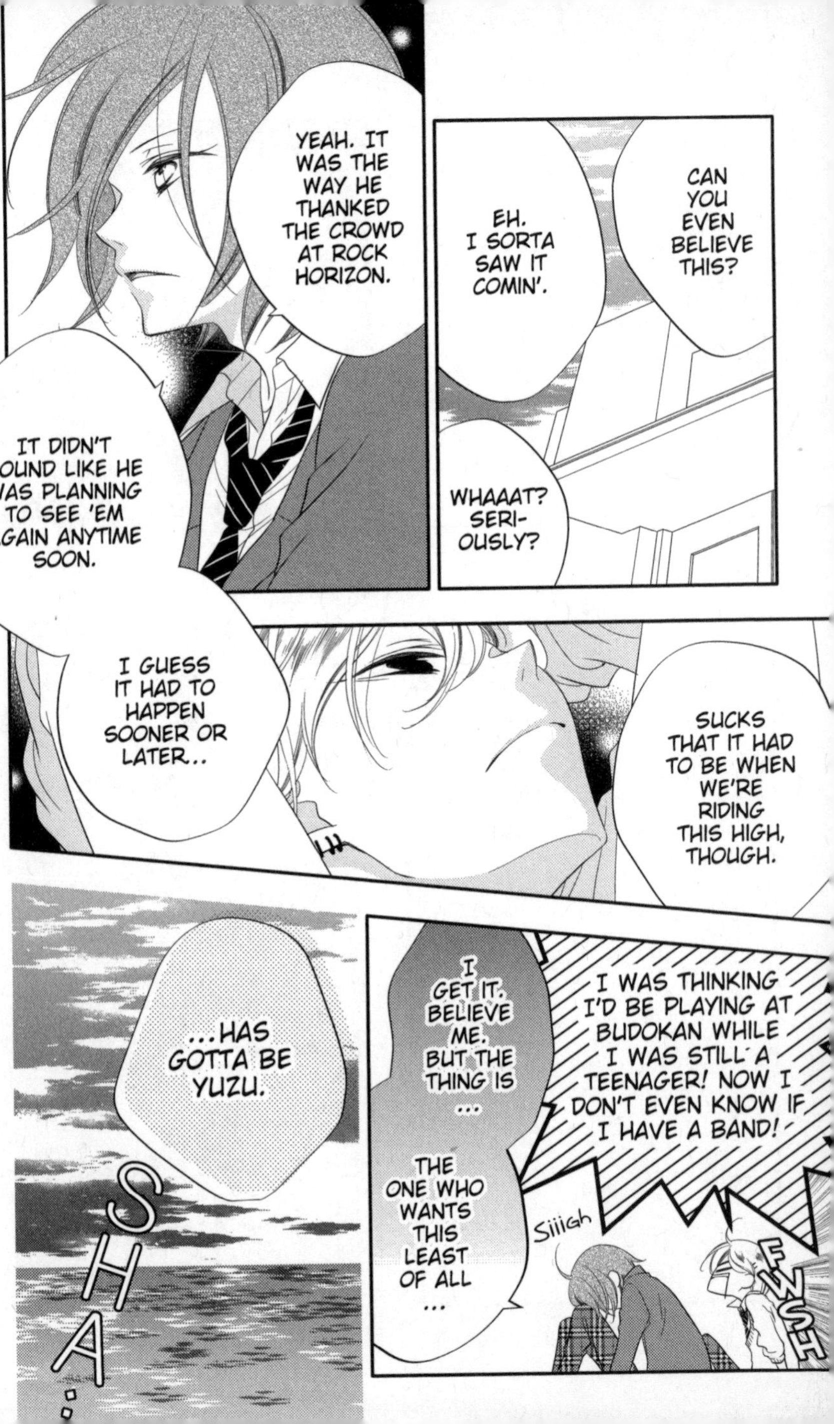
CAN YOU EVEN BELIEVE THIS?
EH. I SORTA SAW IT COMIN'.
WHAAAT? SERI-OUSLY?
YEAH. IT WAS THE WAY HE THANKED THE CROWD AT ROCK HORIZON.
IT DIDN'T SOUND LIKE HE WAS PLANNING TO SEE 'EM AGAIN ANYTIME SOON.
SUCKS THAT IT HAD TO BE WHEN WE'RE RIDING THIS HIGH, THOUGH.
I GUESS IT HAD TO HAPPEN SOONER OR LATER...
I WAS THINKING I'D BE PLAYING AT BUDOKAN WHILE I WAS STILL A TEENAGER! NOW I DON'T EVEN KNOW IF I HAVE A BAND!
FWSH
Siiigh
I GET IT. BELIEVE ME. BUT THE THING IS ...
THE ONE WHO WANTS THIS LEAST OF ALL ...
...HAS GOTTA BE YUZU.
SHA..

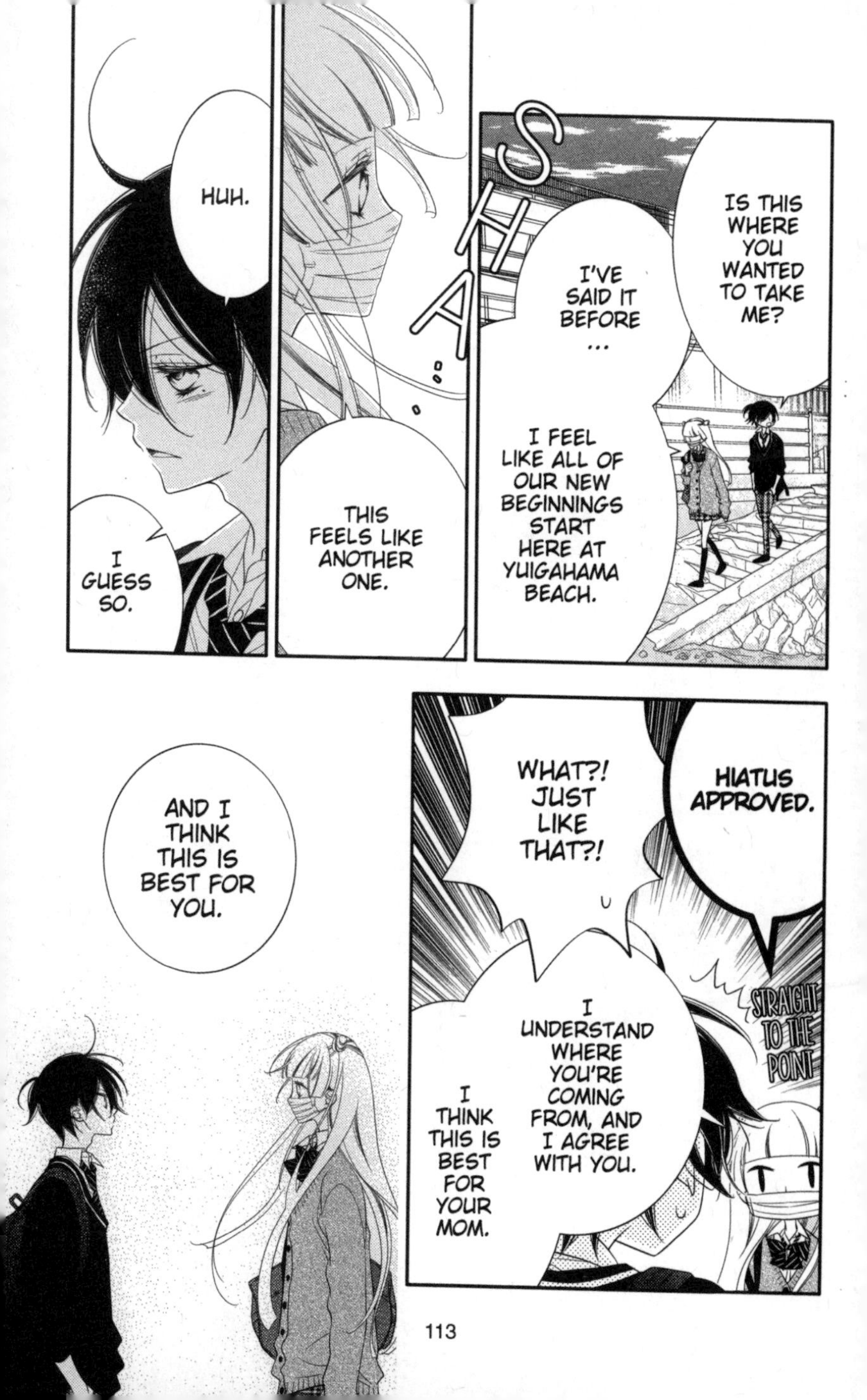
IS THIS WHERE YOU WANTED TO TAKE ME?
I'VE SAID IT BEFORE ...
I FEEL LIKE ALL OF OUR NEW BEGINNINGS START HERE AT YUIGAHAMA BEACH.
SHA
THIS FEELS LIKE ANOTHER ONE.
HUH.
I GUESS SO.
HIATUS APPROVED.
WHAT?! JUST LIKE THAT?!
STRAIGHT TO THE POINT
I UNDERSTAND WHERE YOU'RE COMING FROM, AND I AGREE WITH YOU.
I THINK THIS IS BEST FOR YOUR MOM.
AND I THINK THIS IS BEST FOR YOU.

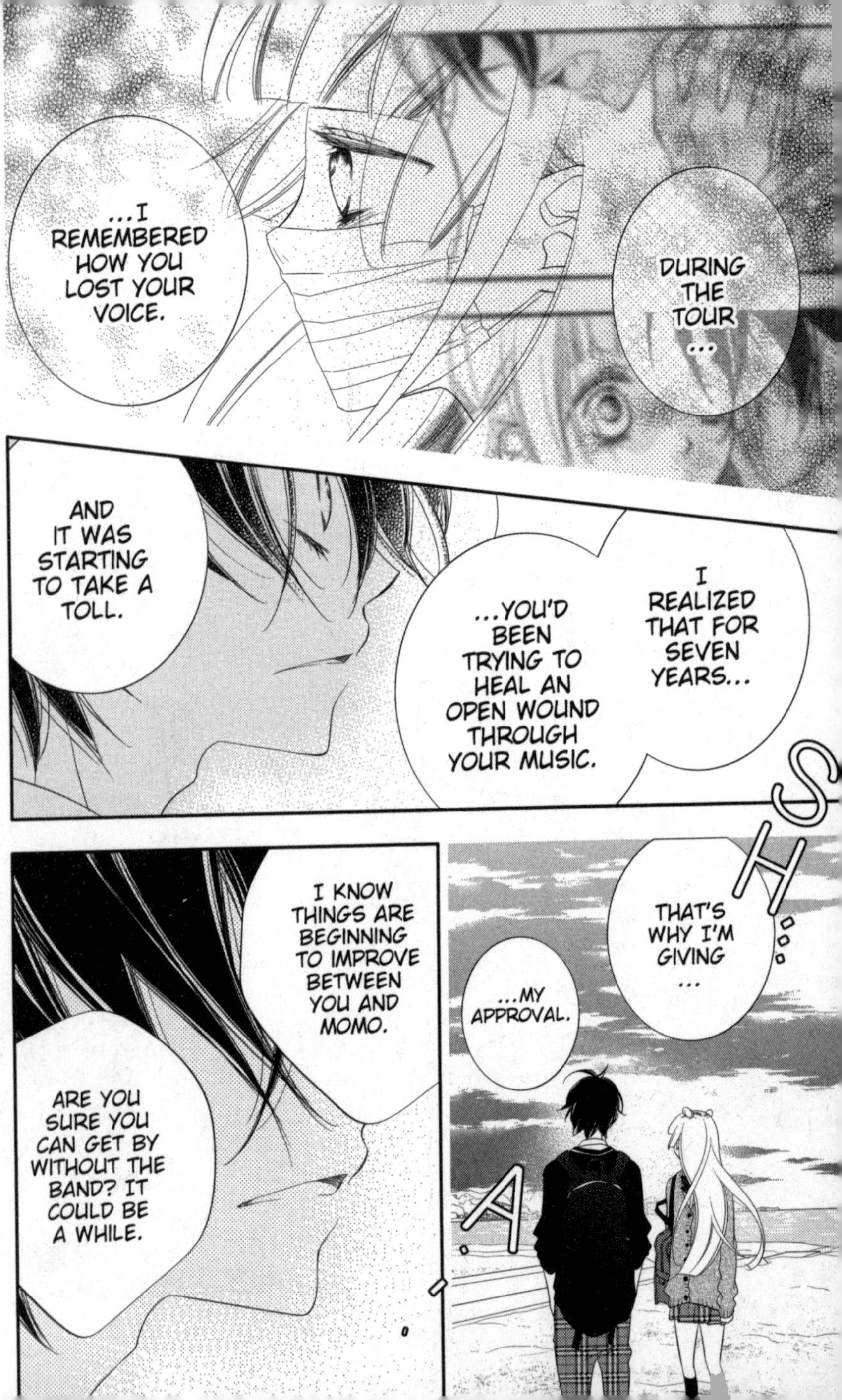
DURING THE TOUR...
...I REMEMBERED HOW YOU LOST YOUR VOICE.
I REALIZED THAT FOR SEVEN YEARS...
...YOU'D BEEN TRYING TO HEAL AN OPEN WOUND THROUGH YOUR MUSIC.
AND IT WAS STARTING TO TAKE A TOLL.
SH...
THAT'S WHY I'M GIVING...
...MY APPROVAL.
A
I KNOW THINGS ARE BEGINNING TO IMPROVE BETWEEN YOU AND MOMO.
ARE YOU SURE YOU CAN GET BY WITHOUT THE BAND? IT COULD BE A WHILE.

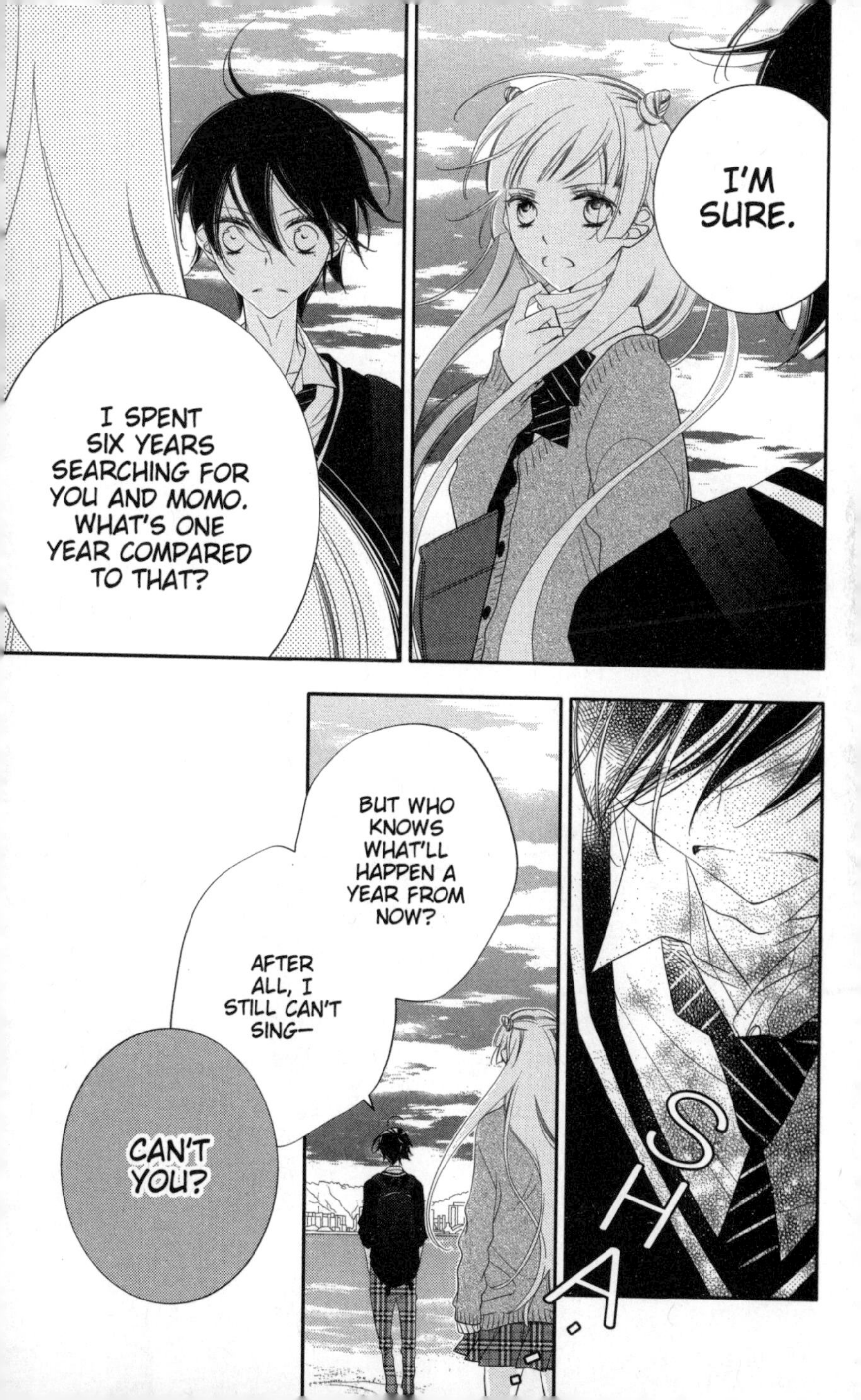
I'M SURE.
I SPENT SIX YEARS SEARCHING FOR YOU AND MOMO. WHAT'S ONE YEAR COMPARED TO THAT?
SHA
BUT WHO KNOWS WHAT'LL HAPPEN A YEAR FROM NOW?
AFTER ALL, I STILL CAN'T SING—
CAN'T YOU?

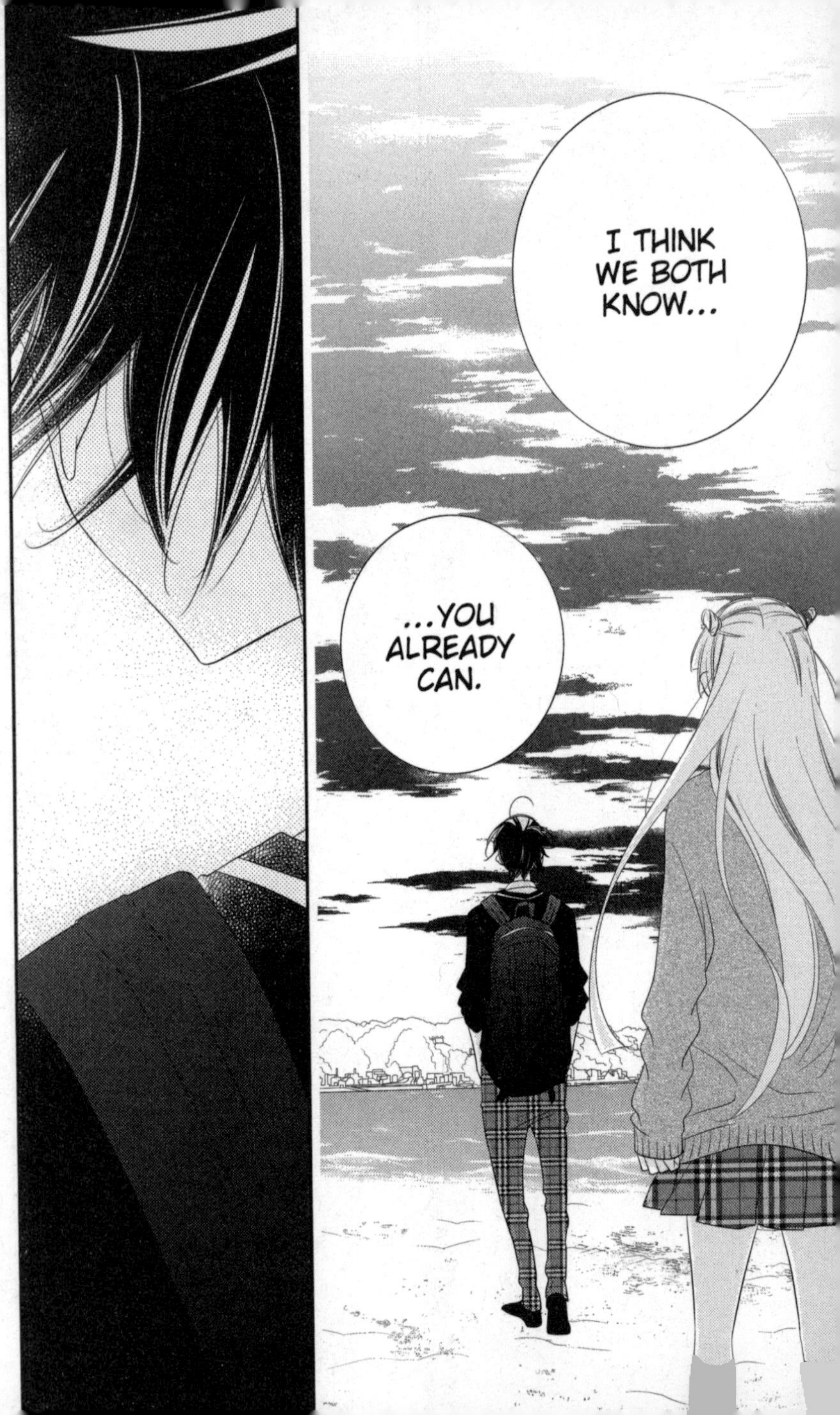
I THINK WE BOTH KNOW...
...YOU ALREADY CAN.

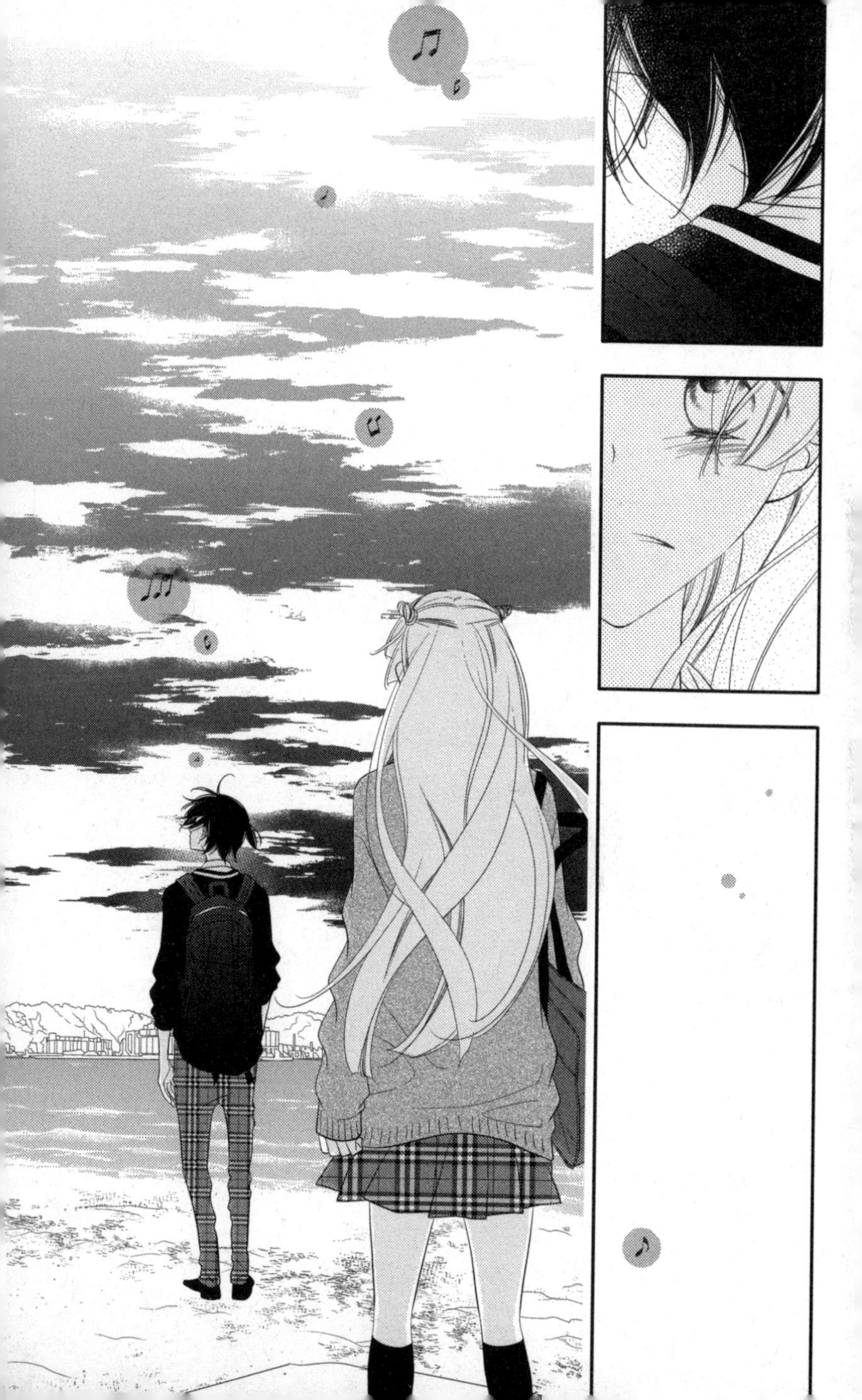

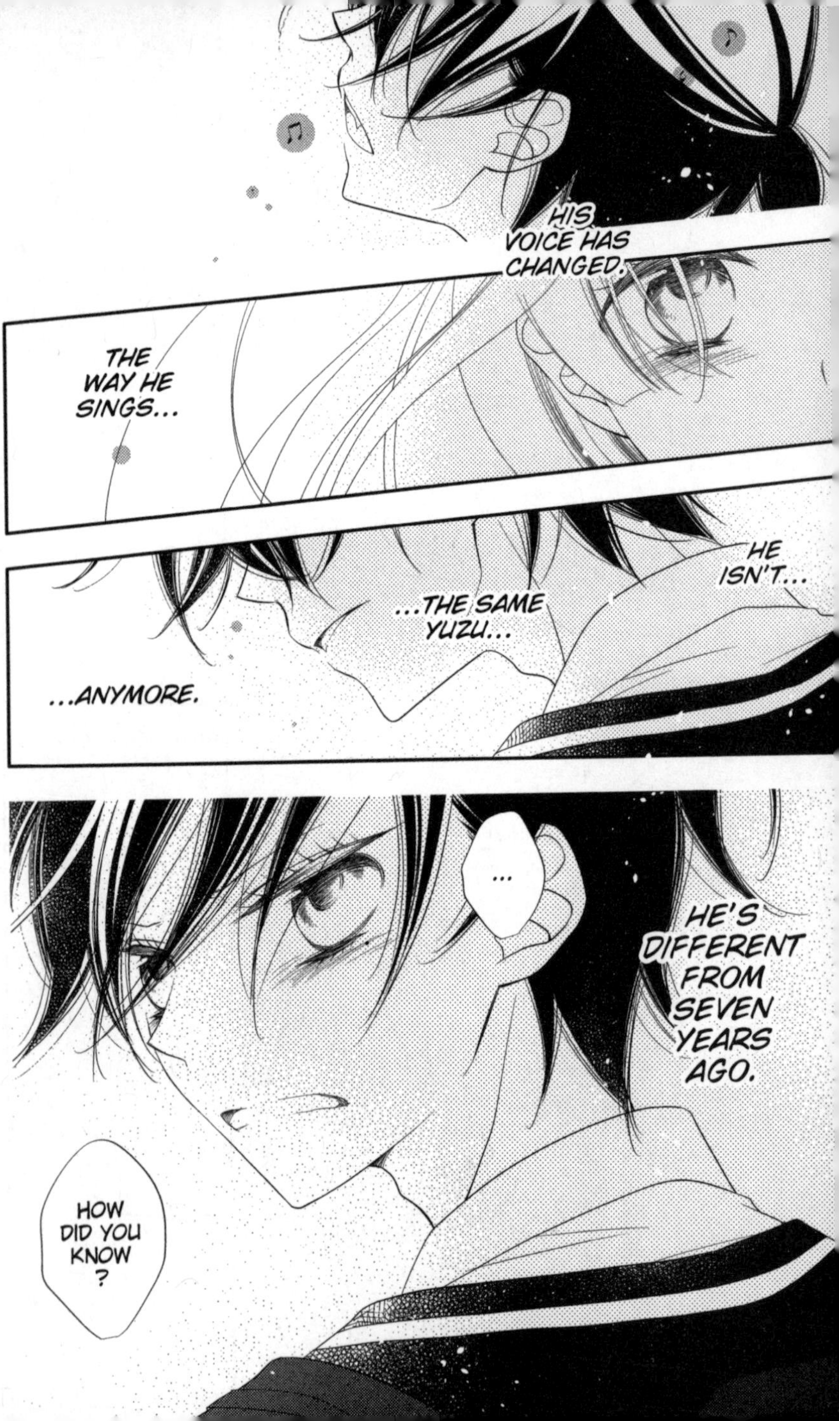
HIS VOICE HAS CHANGED.
THE WAY HE SINGS...
HE ISN'T...
...THE SAME YUZU...
...ANYMORE.
...
HE'S DIFFERENT FROM SEVEN YEARS AGO.
HOW DID YOU KNOW?

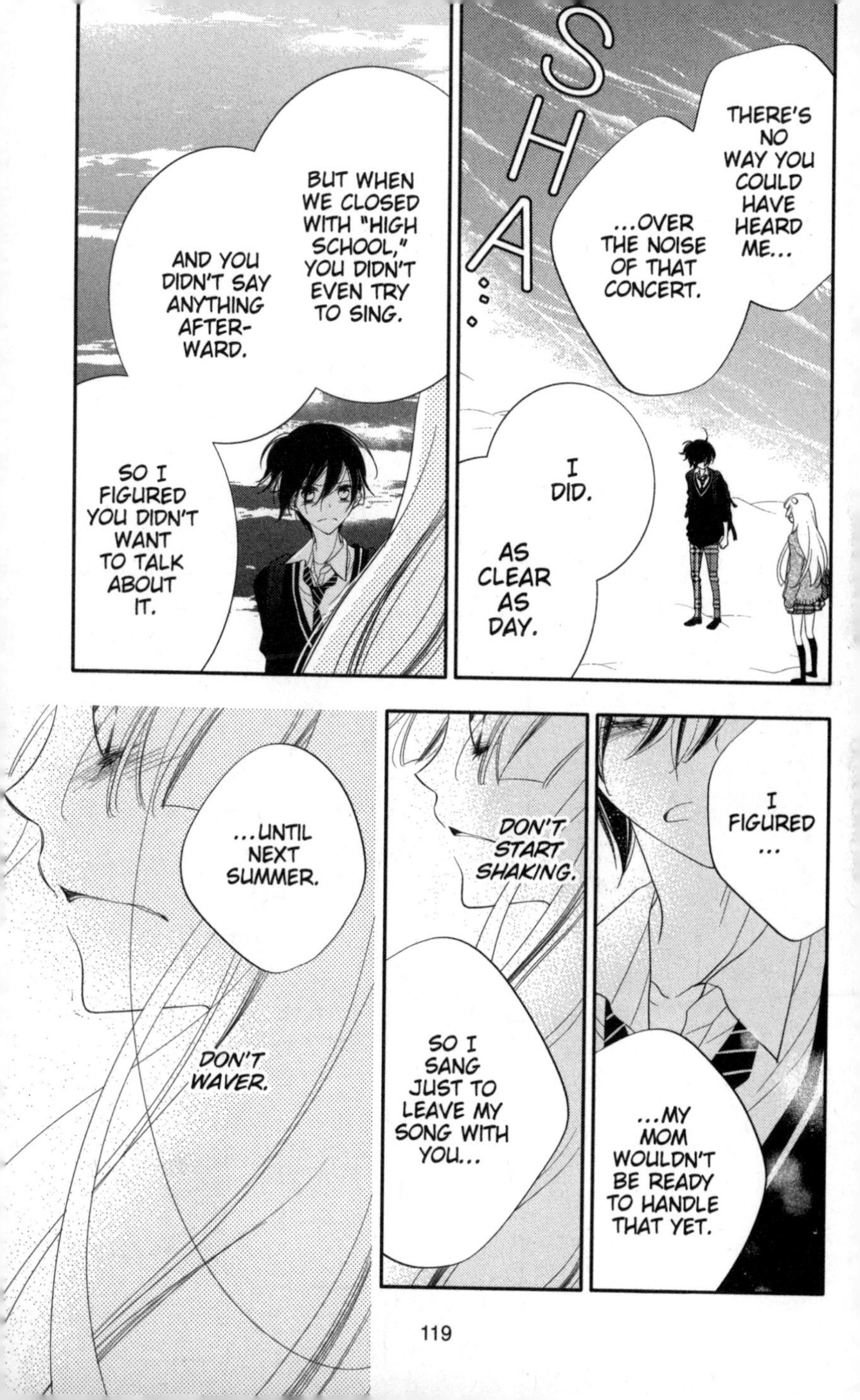
SHA...
THERE'S NO WAY YOU COULD HAVE HEARD ME...
...OVER THE NOISE OF THAT CONCERT.
I DID.
AS CLEAR AS DAY.
BUT WHEN WE CLOSED WITH "HIGH SCHOOL," YOU DIDN'T EVEN TRY TO SING.
AND YOU DIDN'T SAY ANYTHING AFTER-WARD.
SO I FIGURED YOU DIDN'T WANT TO TALK ABOUT IT.
I FIGURED...
...MY MOM WOULDN'T BE READY TO HANDLE THAT YET.
DON'T START SHAKING.
SO I SANG JUST TO LEAVE MY SONG WITH YOU...
...UNTIL NEXT SUMMER.
DON'T WAVER.

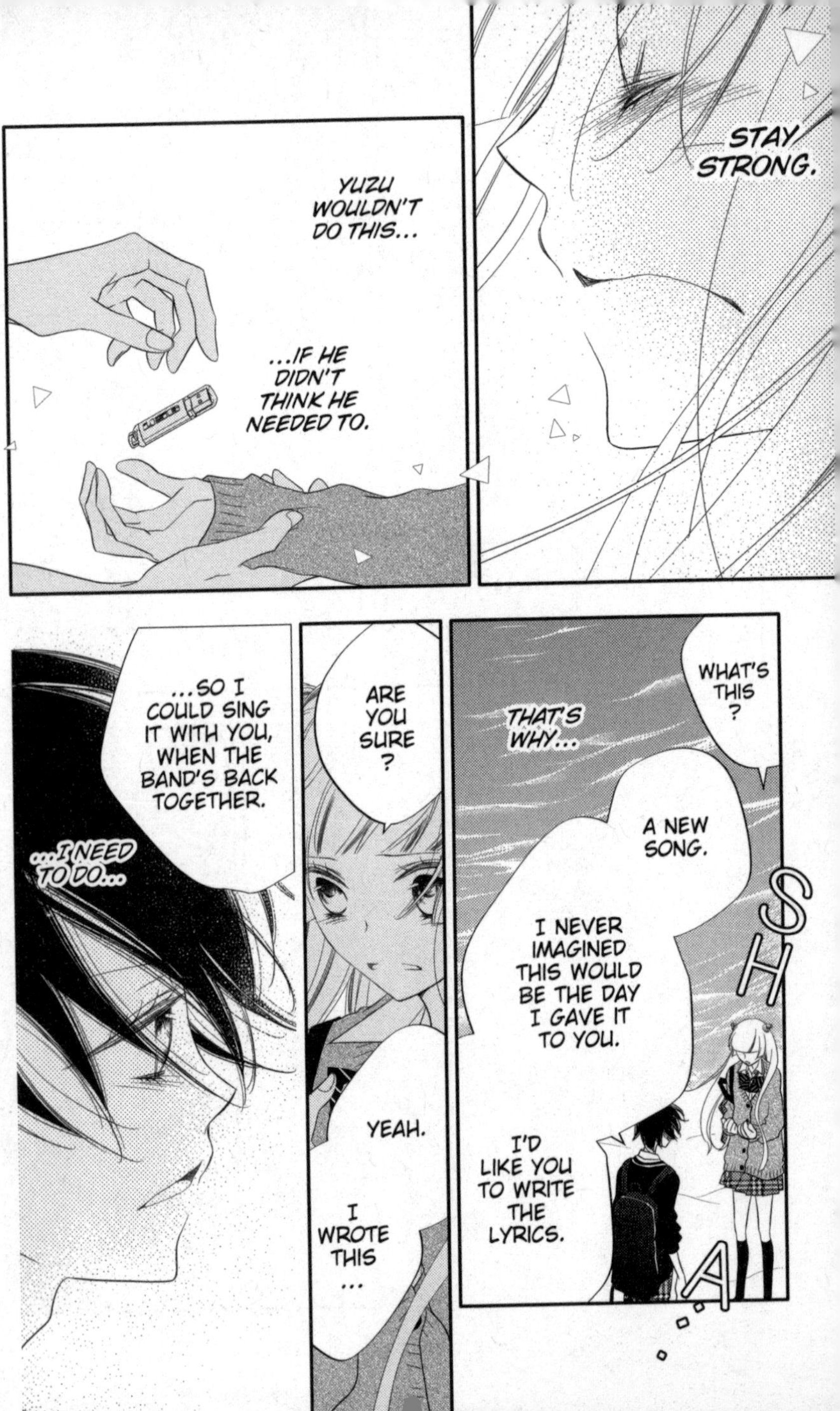
STAY STRONG.
YUZU WOULDN'T DO THIS...
...IF HE DIDN'T THINK HE NEEDED TO.
WHAT'S THIS?
THAT'S WHY...
A NEW SONG.
I NEVER IMAGINED THIS WOULD BE THE DAY I GAVE IT TO YOU.
I'D LIKE YOU TO WRITE THE LYRICS.
SHA
ARE YOU SURE?
YEAH.
I WROTE THIS...
...SO I COULD SING IT WITH YOU, WHEN THE BAND'S BACK TOGETHER.
...I NEED TO DO...

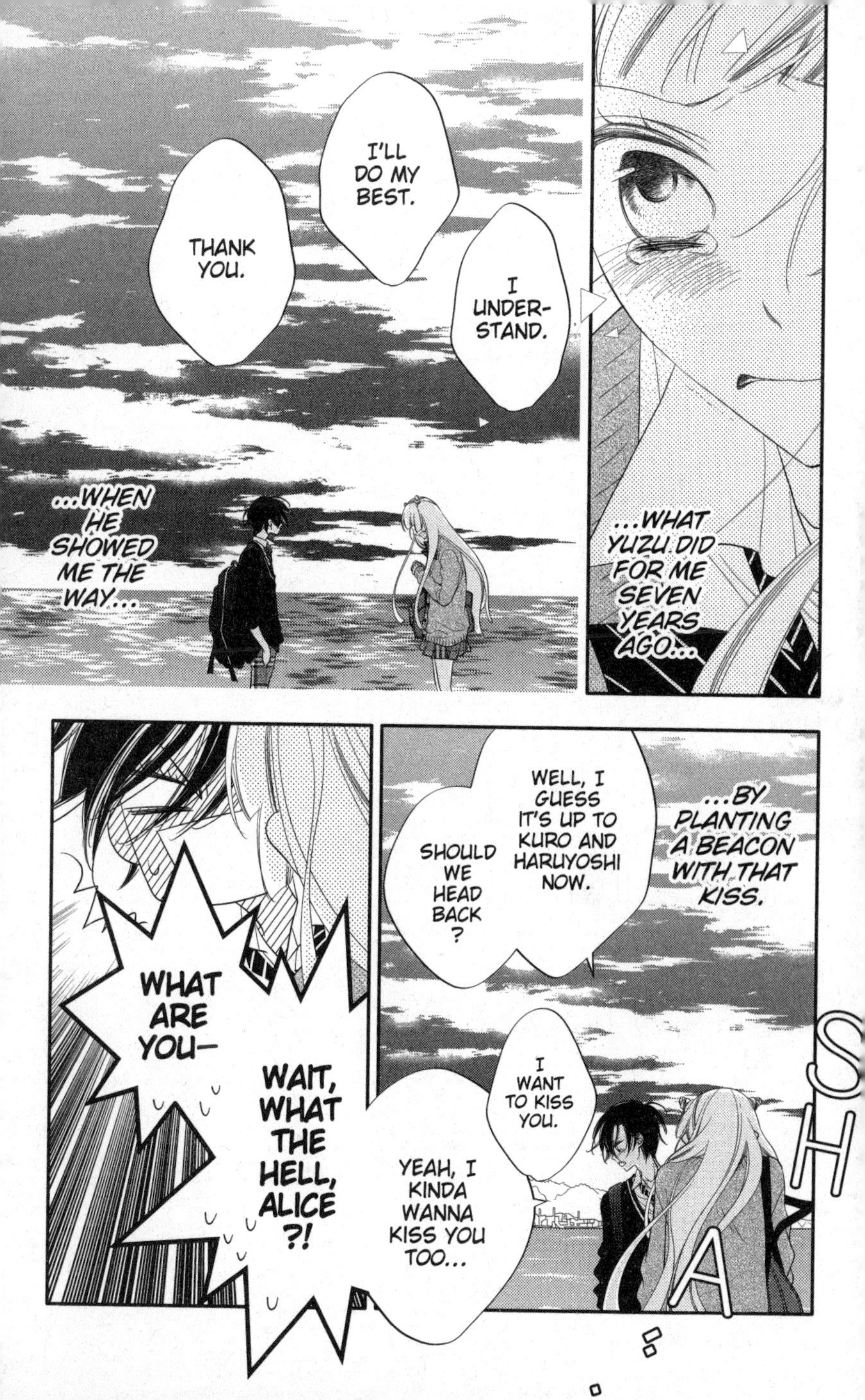
...WHAT YUZU DID FOR ME SEVEN YEARS AGO...
I UNDERSTAND.
I'LL DO MY BEST.
THANK YOU.
...WHEN HE SHOWED ME THE WAY...
...BY PLANTING A BEACON WITH THAT KISS.
WELL, I GUESS IT'S UP TO KURO AND HARUYOSHI NOW.
SHOULD WE HEAD BACK?
I WANT TO KISS YOU.
YEAH, I KINDA WANNA KISS YOU TOO...
SHA
WHAT ARE YOU—
WAIT, WHAT THE HELL, ALICE?!

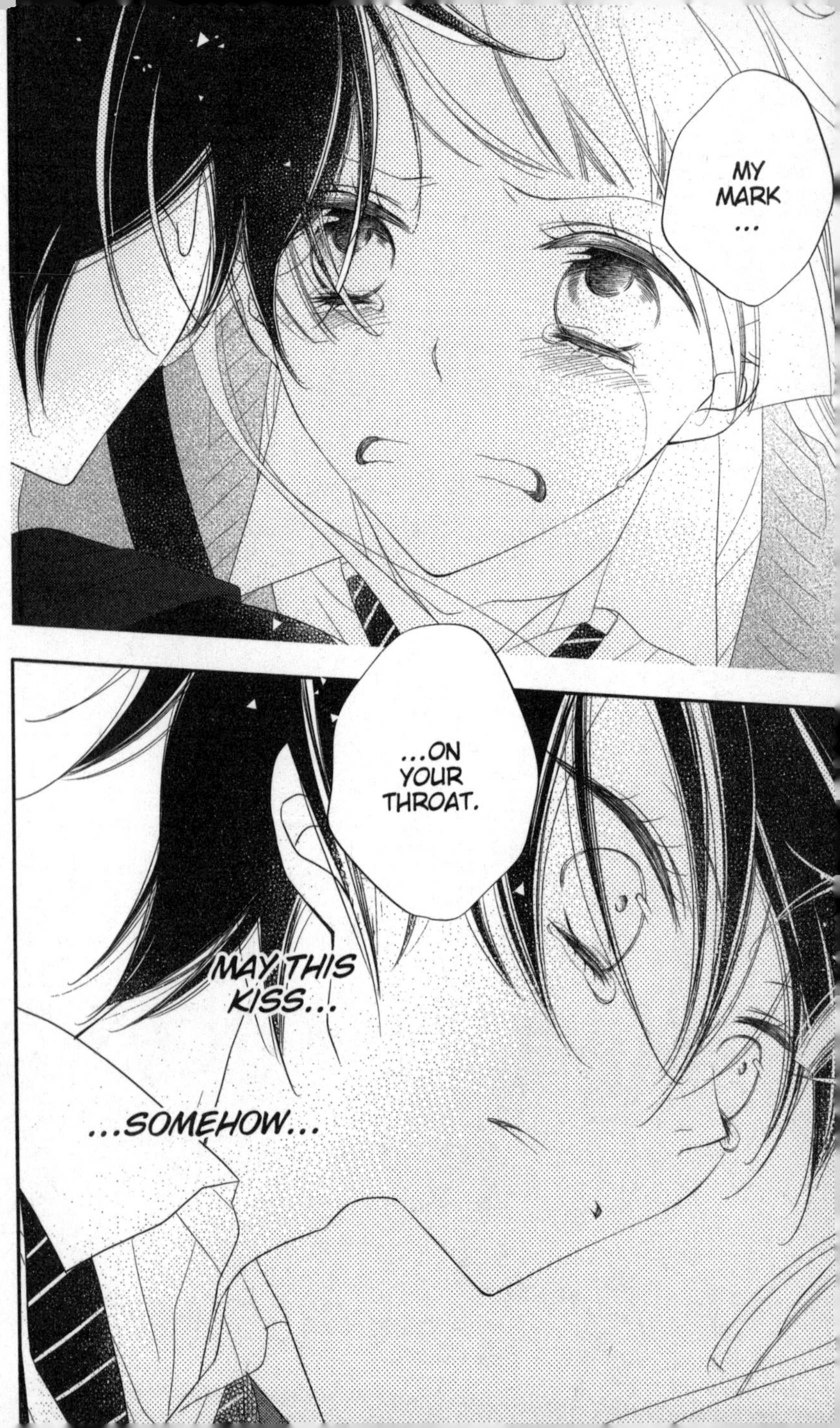
MY MARK ...
...ON YOUR THROAT.
MAY THIS KISS...
...SOMEHOW...

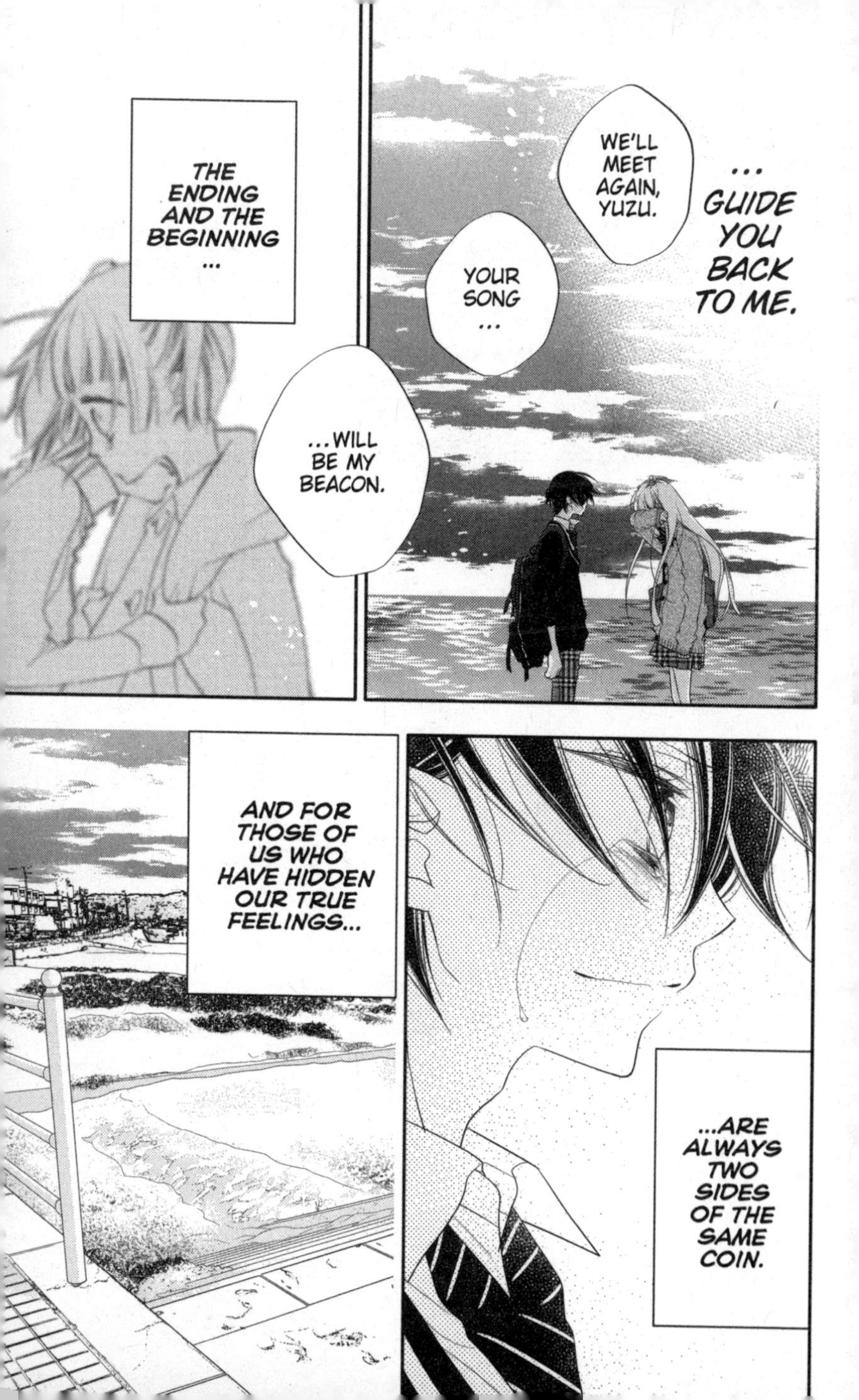
...GUIDE YOU BACK TO ME.
WE'LL MEET AGAIN, YUZU.
YOUR SONG ...
...WILL BE MY BEACON.
THE ENDING AND THE BEGINNING ...
AND FOR THOSE OF US WHO HAVE HIDDEN OUR TRUE FEELINGS...
...ARE ALWAYS TWO SIDES OF THE SAME COIN.

...IT WON'T BE LONG...

...BEFORE WE MEET AGAIN.

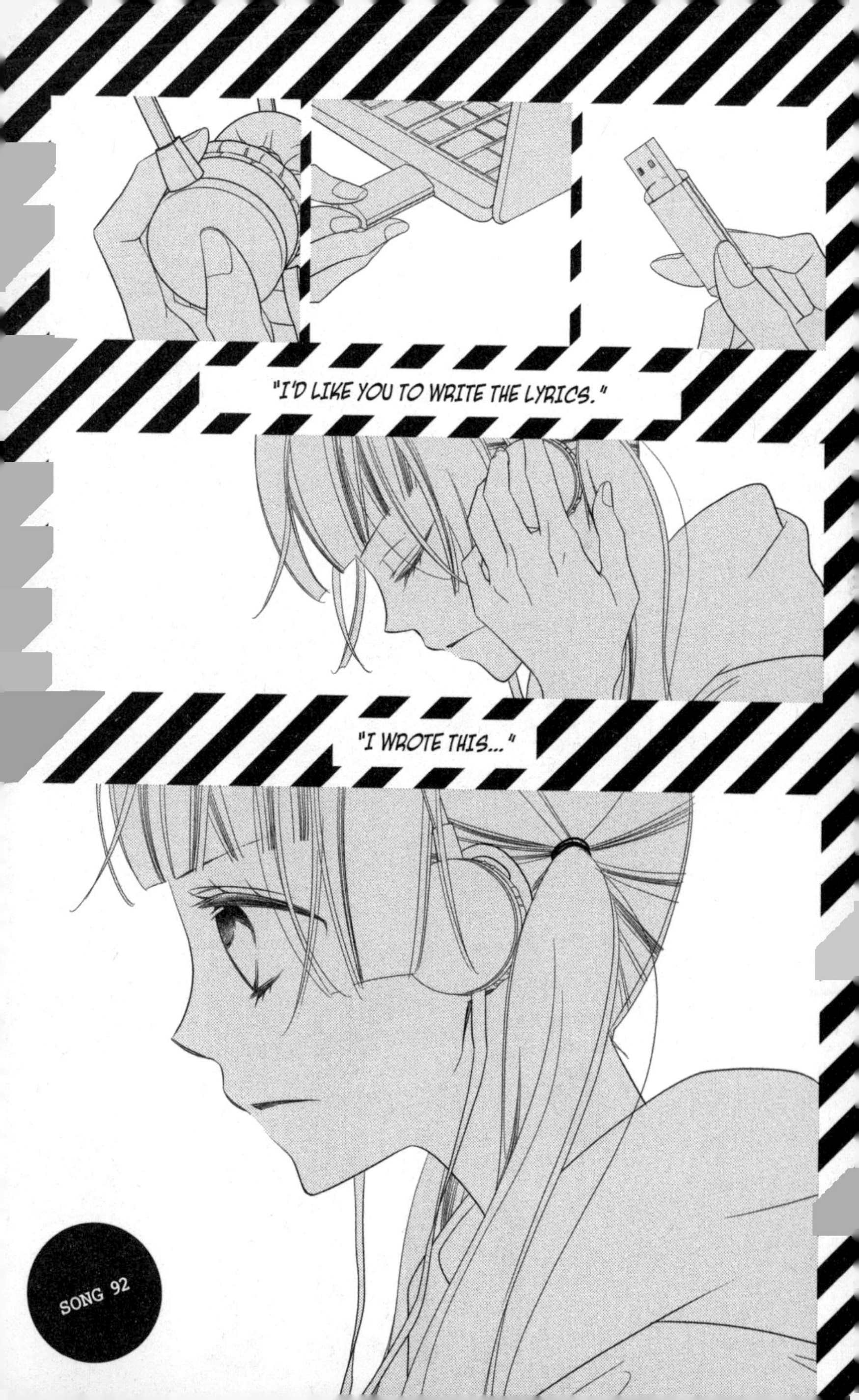
"I'D LIKE YOU TO WRITE THE LYRICS."
"I WROTE THIS..."
SONG 92

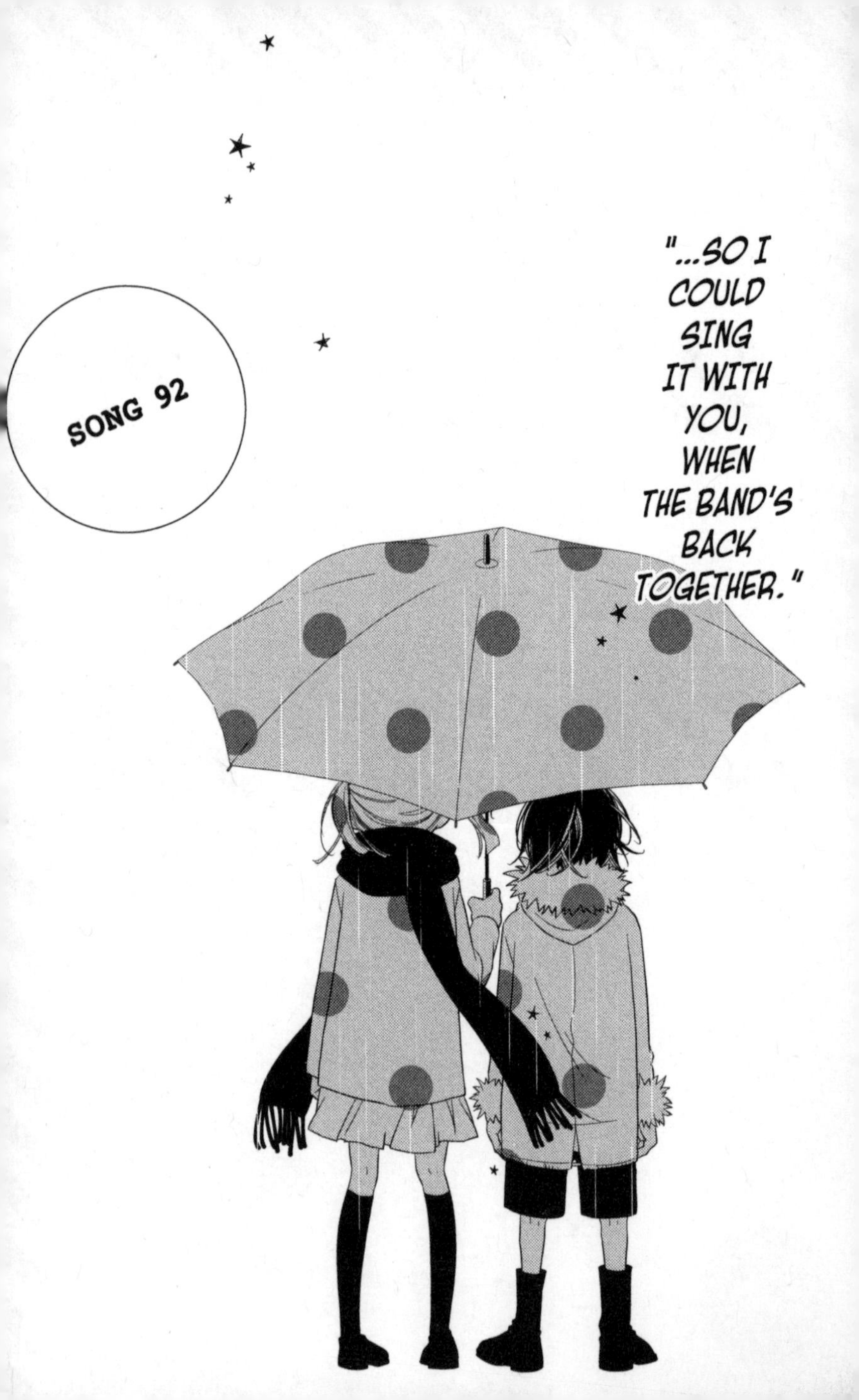
"...SO I COULD SING IT WITH YOU, WHEN THE BAND'S BACK TOGETHER."
SONG 92

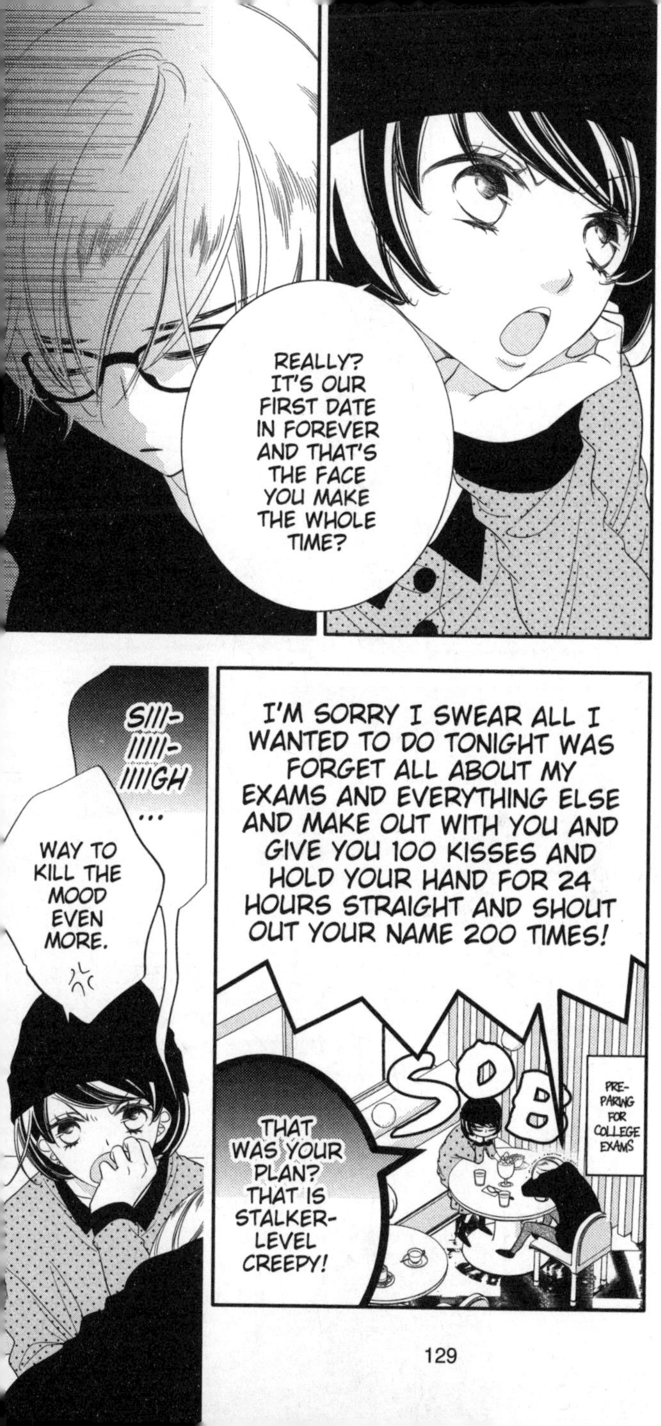
REALLY? IT'S OUR FIRST DATE IN FOREVER AND THAT'S THE FACE YOU MAKE THE WHOLE TIME?
I'M SORRY I SWEAR ALL I WANTED TO DO TONIGHT WAS FORGET ALL ABOUT MY EXAMS AND EVERYTHING ELSE AND MAKE OUT WITH YOU AND GIVE YOU 100 KISSES AND HOLD YOUR HAND FOR 24 HOURS STRAIGHT AND SHOUT OUT YOUR NAME 200 TIMES!
SOB
PRE-PARING FOR COLLEGE EXAMS
THAT WAS YOUR PLAN? THAT IS STALKER-LEVEL CREEPY!
SIII-IIIII-IIIIGH...
WAY TO KILL THE MOOD EVEN MORE.

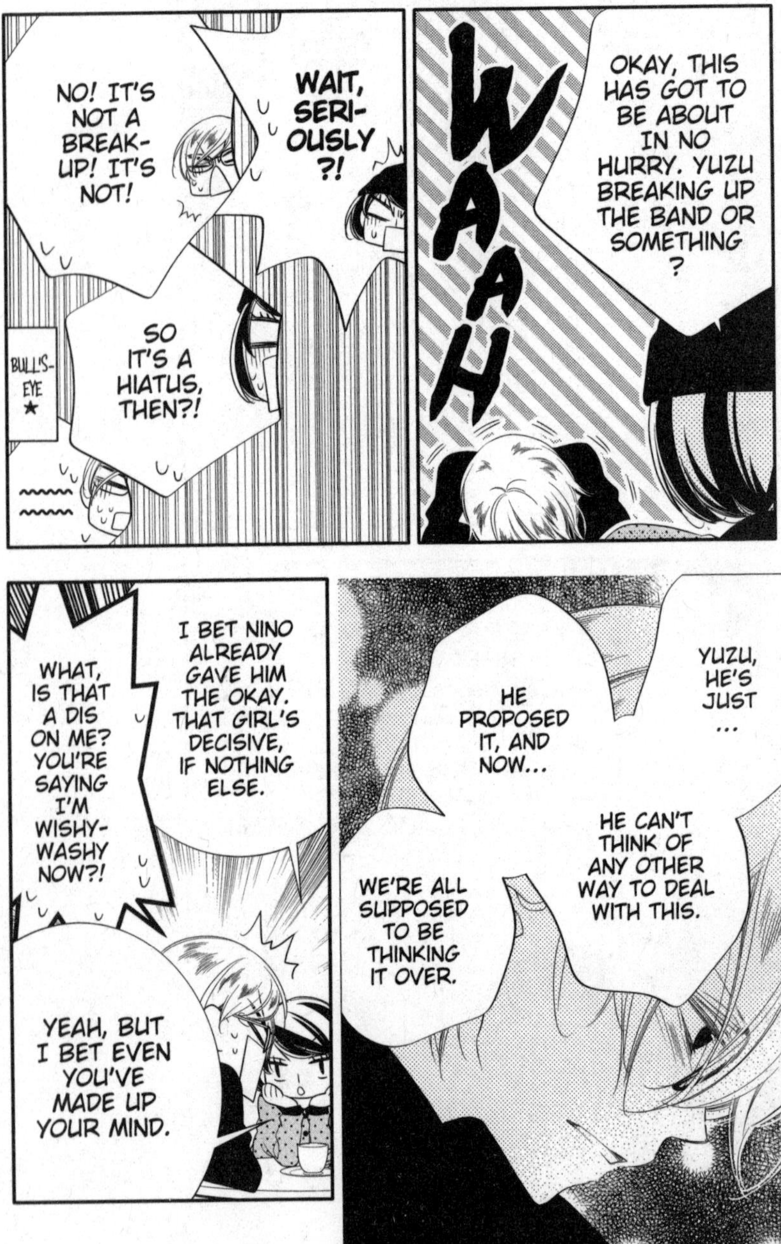
WAAH
OKAY, THIS HAS GOT TO BE ABOUT IN NO HURRY. YUZU BREAKING UP THE BAND OR SOMETHING?
WAIT, SERIOUSLY?!
NO! IT'S NOT A BREAK-UP! IT'S NOT!
SO IT'S A HIATUS, THEN?!
BULL'S-EYE ★
YUZU, HE'S JUST...
HE PROPOSED IT, AND NOW...
HE CAN'T THINK OF ANY OTHER WAY TO DEAL WITH THIS.
WE'RE ALL SUPPOSED TO BE THINKING IT OVER.
I BET NINO ALREADY GAVE HIM THE OKAY. THAT GIRL'S DECISIVE, IF NOTHING ELSE.
WHAT, IS THAT A DIS ON ME? YOU'RE SAYING I'M WISHY-WASHY NOW?!
YEAH, BUT I BET EVEN YOU'VE MADE UP YOUR MIND.

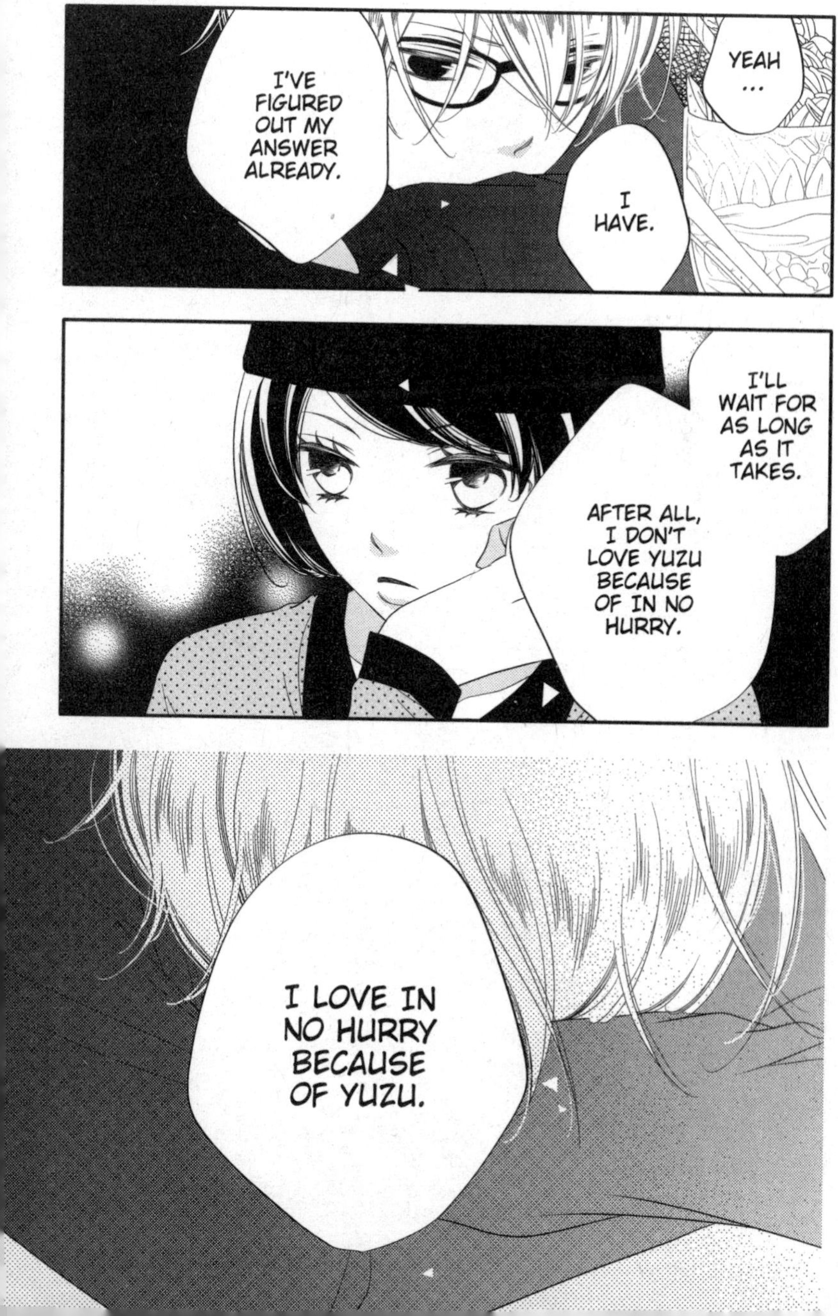
YEAH ...
I HAVE.
I'VE FIGURED OUT MY ANSWER ALREADY.
I'LL WAIT FOR AS LONG AS IT TAKES.
AFTER ALL, I DON'T LOVE YUZU BECAUSE OF IN NO HURRY.
I LOVE IN NO HURRY BECAUSE OF YUZU.

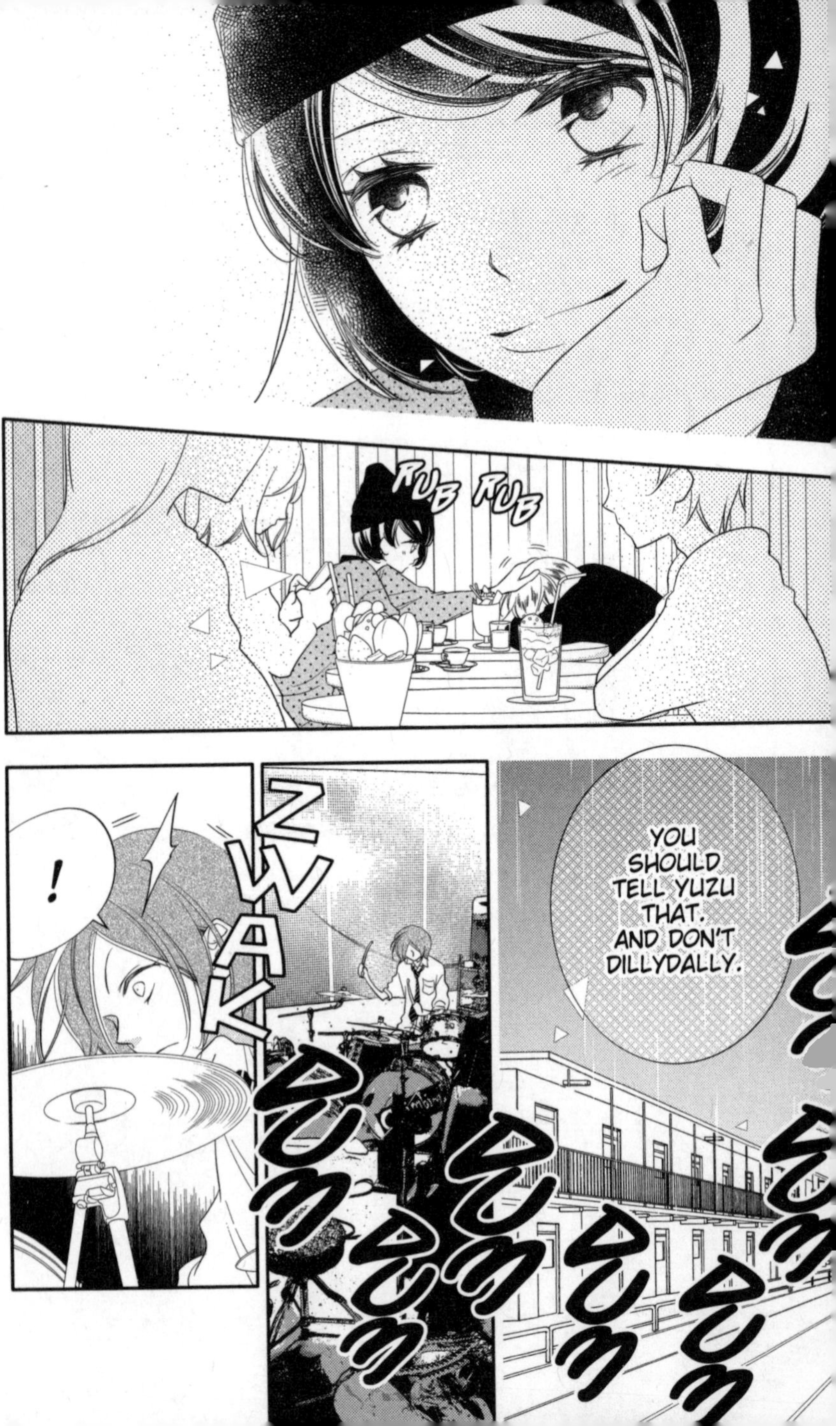
RUB RUB
YOU SHOULD TELL YUZU THAT. AND DON'T DILLYDALLY.
DUM DUM DUM
DUM DUM DUM
ZWAK
DUM DUM DUM
!

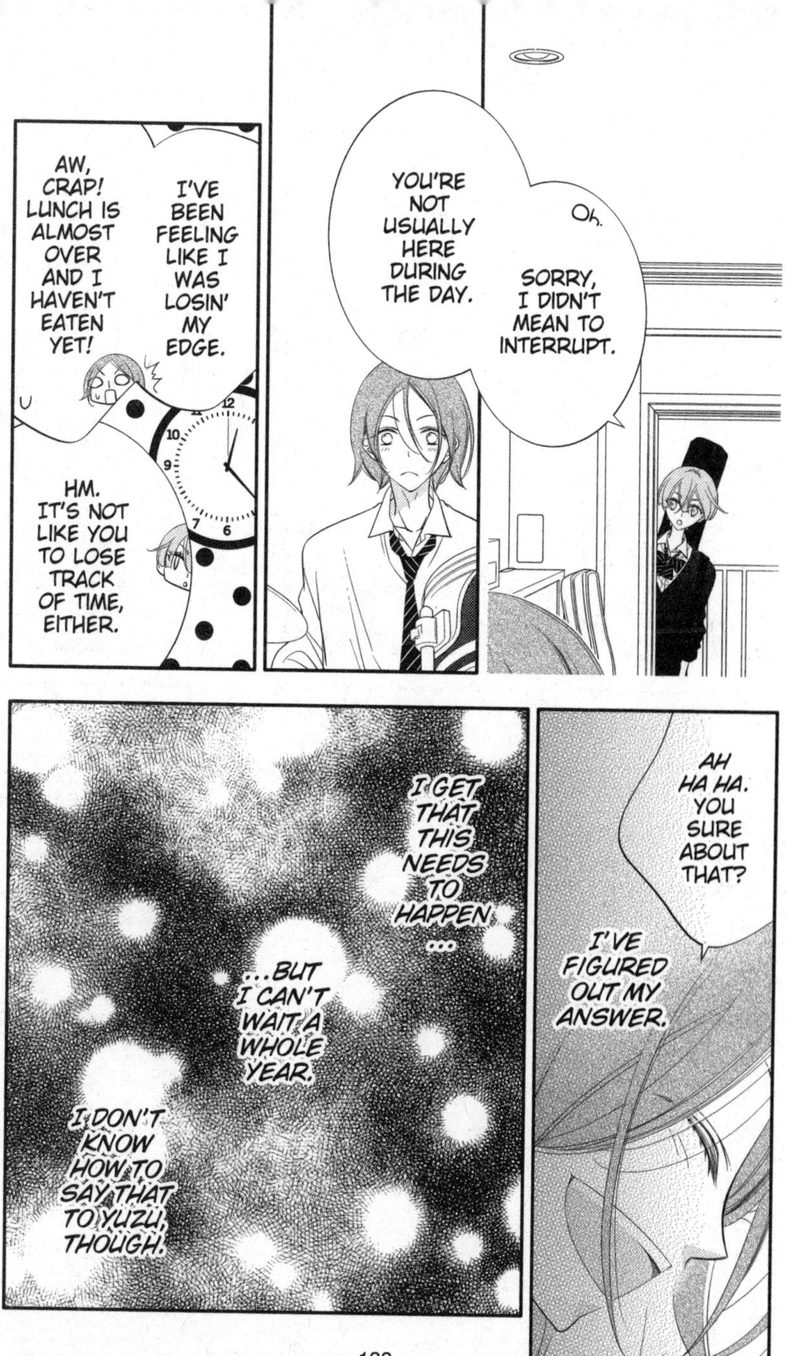
Oh.
SORRY, I DIDN'T MEAN TO INTERRUPT.
YOU'RE NOT USUALLY HERE DURING THE DAY.
I'VE BEEN FEELING LIKE I WAS LOSIN' MY EDGE.
AW, CRAP! LUNCH IS ALMOST OVER AND I HAVEN'T EATEN YET!
HM. IT'S NOT LIKE YOU TO LOSE TRACK OF TIME, EITHER.
AH HA HA. YOU SURE ABOUT THAT?
I'VE FIGURED OUT MY ANSWER.
I GET THAT THIS NEEDS TO HAPPEN...
...BUT I CAN'T WAIT A WHOLE YEAR.
I DON'T KNOW HOW TO SAY THAT TO YUZU, THOUGH.

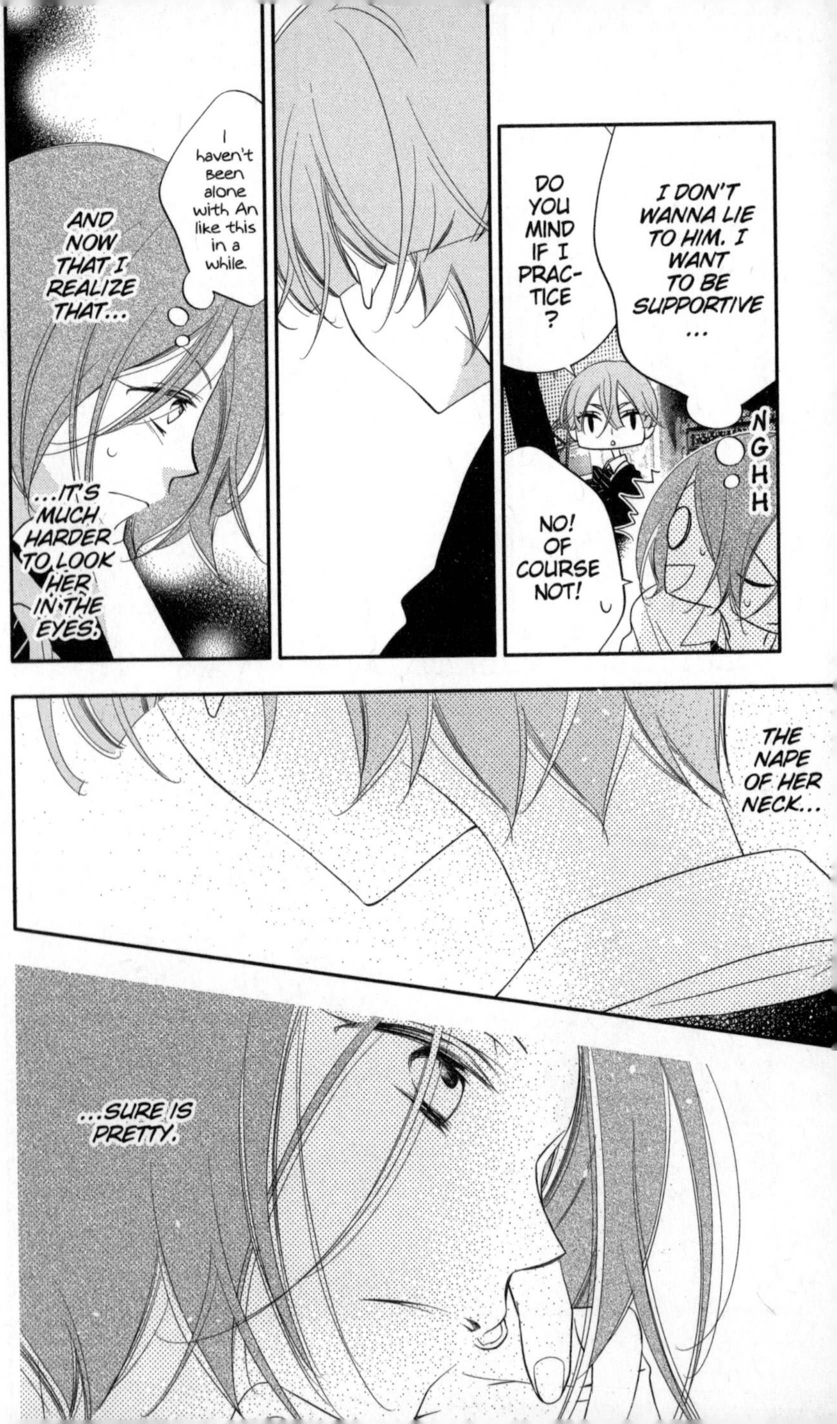
I DON'T WANNA LIE TO HIM. I WANT TO BE SUPPORTIVE...
DO YOU MIND IF I PRAC-TICE?
NGHH
NO! OF COURSE NOT!
I haven't been alone with An like this in a while.
AND NOW THAT I REALIZE THAT...
...IT'S MUCH HARDER TO LOOK HER IN THE EYES.
THE NAPE OF HER NECK...
...SURE IS PRETTY.

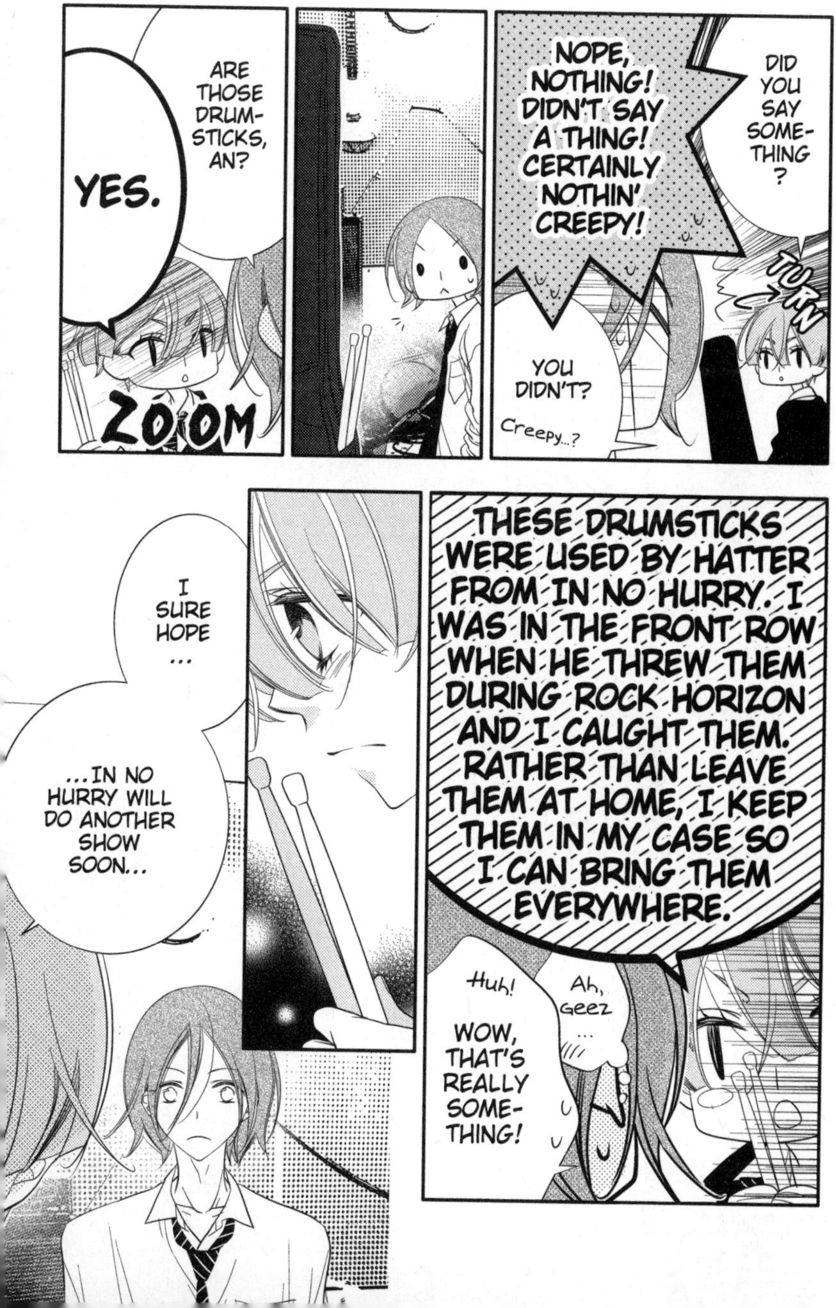
DID YOU SAY SOME-THING?
TURN
NOPE, NOTHING! DIDN'T SAY A THING! CERTAINLY NOTHIN' CREEPY!
YOU DIDN'T?
Creepy...?
ARE THOSE DRUM-STICKS, AN?
YES.
ZOOM
THESE DRUMSTICKS WERE USED BY HATTER FROM IN NO HURRY. I WAS IN THE FRONT ROW WHEN HE THREW THEM DURING ROCK HORIZON AND I CAUGHT THEM. RATHER THAN LEAVE THEM AT HOME, I KEEP THEM IN MY CASE SO I CAN BRING THEM EVERYWHERE.
Huh!
Ah, Geez...
WOW, THAT'S REALLY SOME-THING!
I SURE HOPE...
...IN NO HURRY WILL DO ANOTHER SHOW SOON...

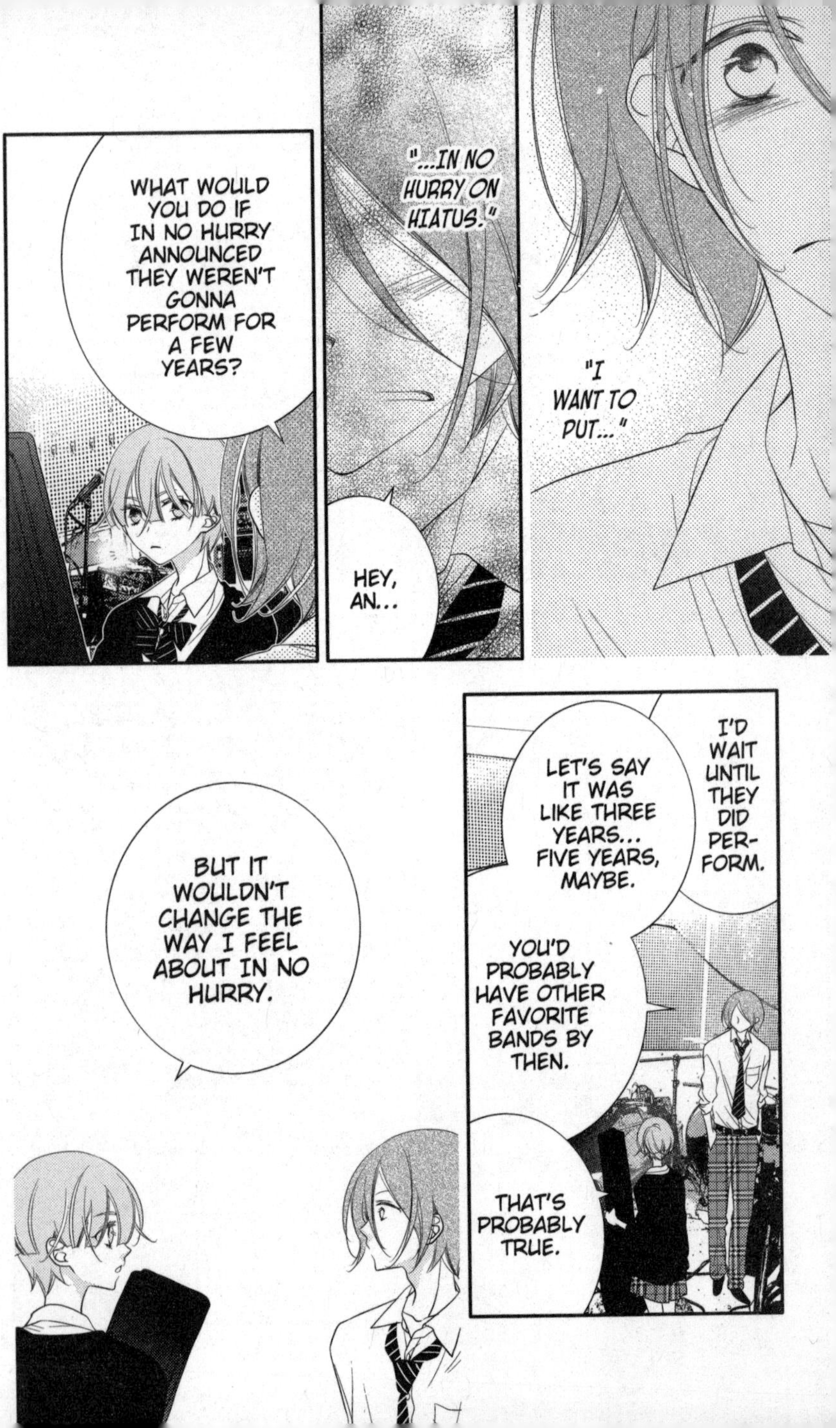
"I WANT TO PUT..."
"...IN NO HURRY ON HIATUS."
HEY, AN...
WHAT WOULD YOU DO IF IN NO HURRY ANNOUNCED THEY WEREN'T GONNA PERFORM FOR A FEW YEARS?
I'D WAIT UNTIL THEY DID PER-FORM.
LET'S SAY IT WAS LIKE THREE YEARS... FIVE YEARS, MAYBE.
YOU'D PROBABLY HAVE OTHER FAVORITE BANDS BY THEN.
THAT'S PROBABLY TRUE.
BUT IT WOULDN'T CHANGE THE WAY I FEEL ABOUT IN NO HURRY.

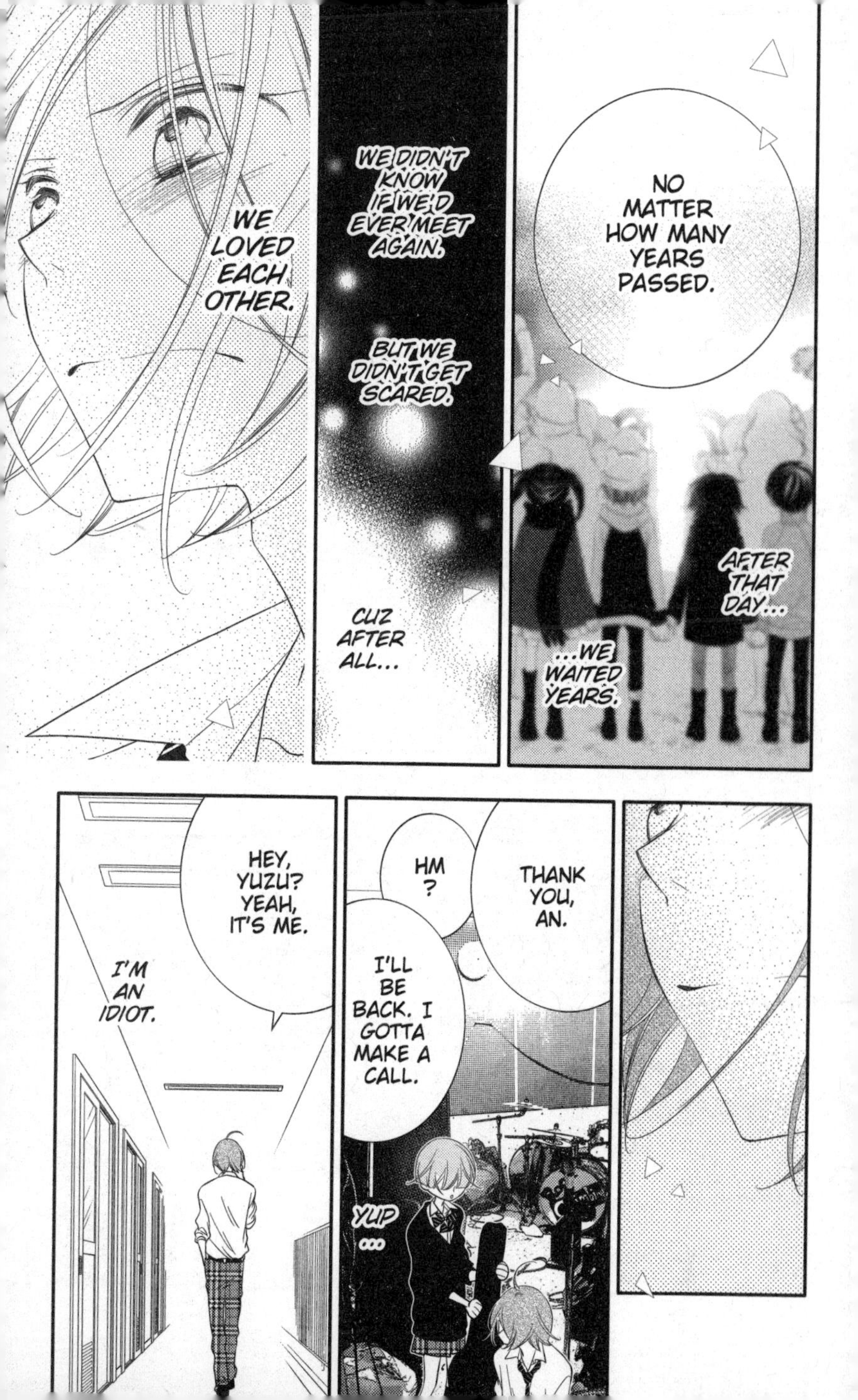
NO MATTER HOW MANY YEARS PASSED.
AFTER THAT DAY...
...WE WAITED YEARS.
WE DIDN'T KNOW IF WE'D EVER MEET AGAIN.
BUT WE DIDN'T GET SCARED.
CUZ AFTER ALL...
WE LOVED EACH OTHER.
THANK YOU, AN.
HM?
I'LL BE BACK. I GOTTA MAKE A CALL.
YUP...
HEY, YUZU? YEAH, IT'S ME.
I'M AN IDIOT.

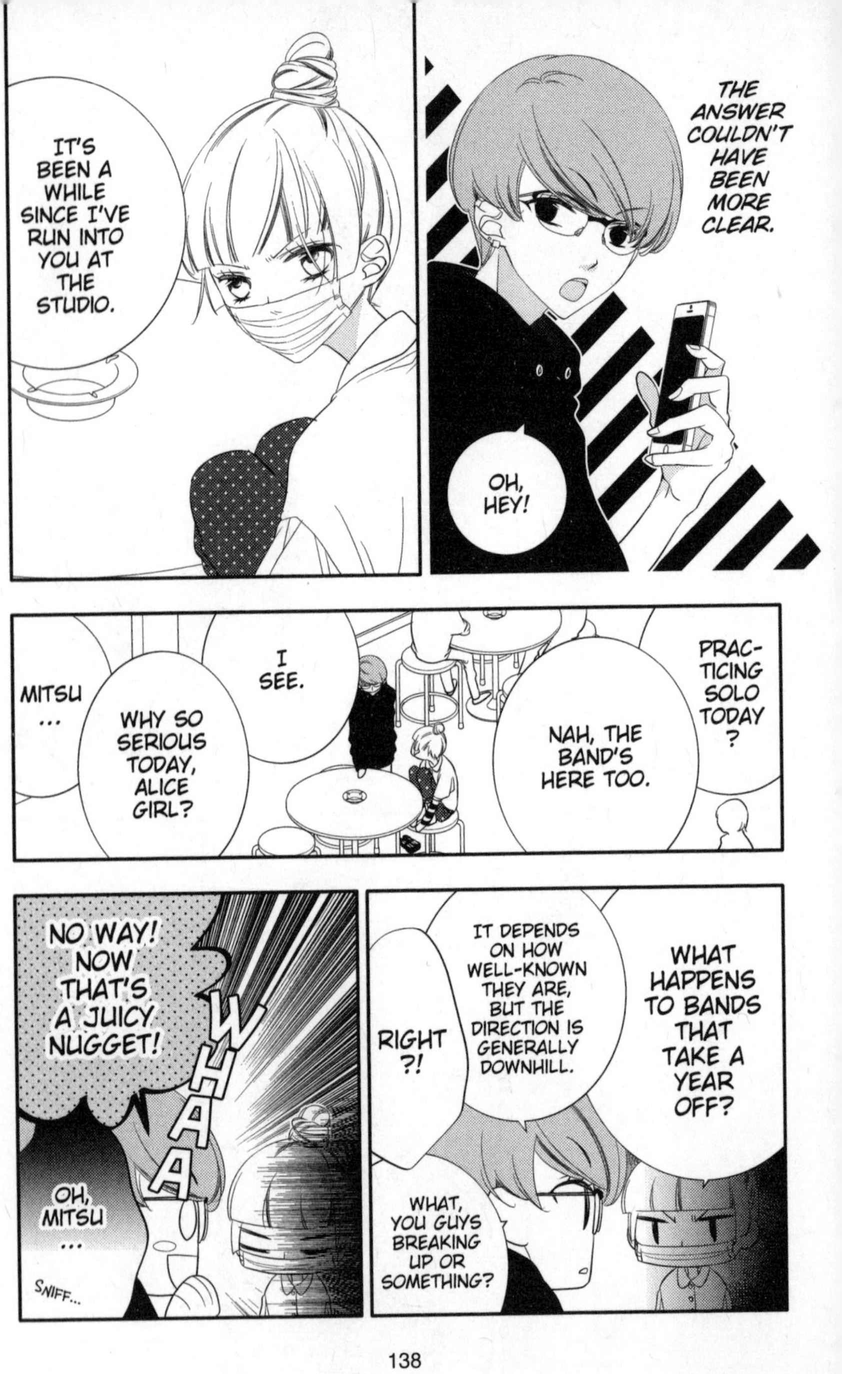
THE ANSWER COULDN'T HAVE BEEN MORE CLEAR.
OH, HEY!
IT'S BEEN A WHILE SINCE I'VE RUN INTO YOU AT THE STUDIO.
PRAC-TICING SOLO TODAY?
NAH, THE BAND'S HERE TOO.
I SEE.
WHY SO SERIOUS TODAY, ALICE GIRL?
MITSU...
WHAT HAPPENS TO BANDS THAT TAKE A YEAR OFF?
IT DEPENDS ON HOW WELL-KNOWN THEY ARE, BUT THE DIRECTION IS GENERALLY DOWNHILL.
RIGHT?!
WHAT, YOU GUYS BREAKING UP OR SOMETHING?
NO WAY! NOW THAT'S A JUICY NUGGET!
WHHAAA
OH, MITSU...
SNIFF...

WELL, IF YOU DO PLAN TO REGROUP ONE DAY, YOU NEED TO PRESERVE YOUR MOMENTUM.
PRE-SERVE MOMEN-TUM...
TRICKY THING ABOUT MOMENTUM, THOUGH.
IF YOU JUST TRY TO MAINTAIN IT, YOU'LL ONLY SLOW THE DECLINE.
IT'S LIKE DRIVING UP A HILL. YOU GOTTA ACCELERATE JUST TO KEEP MOVING.
BUILD MOMENTUM... ACCELER-ATE UP THE HILL...
YOU GOT IT.
THAT SOUNDS HARD...
WHAT ARE YOU TALKING ABOUT?

5

Readers of the magazine and my Instagram followers already know this, but *Anonymous Noise* will be drawing to a close over the next year.

The final chapter is expected to run in the magazine just a few months from now. It's really been hitting me hard as I've been writing the final chapters, and that was especially true with chapter 91 in this volume. If you have the time, I'd love for you to reread chapter 1 with that chapter in mind!

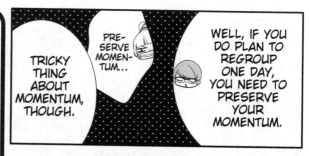

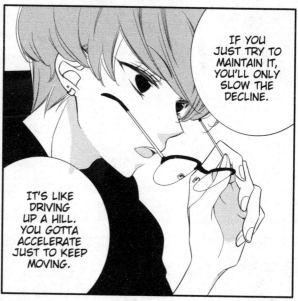

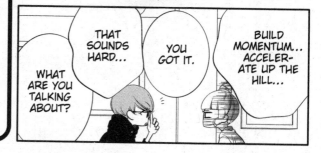

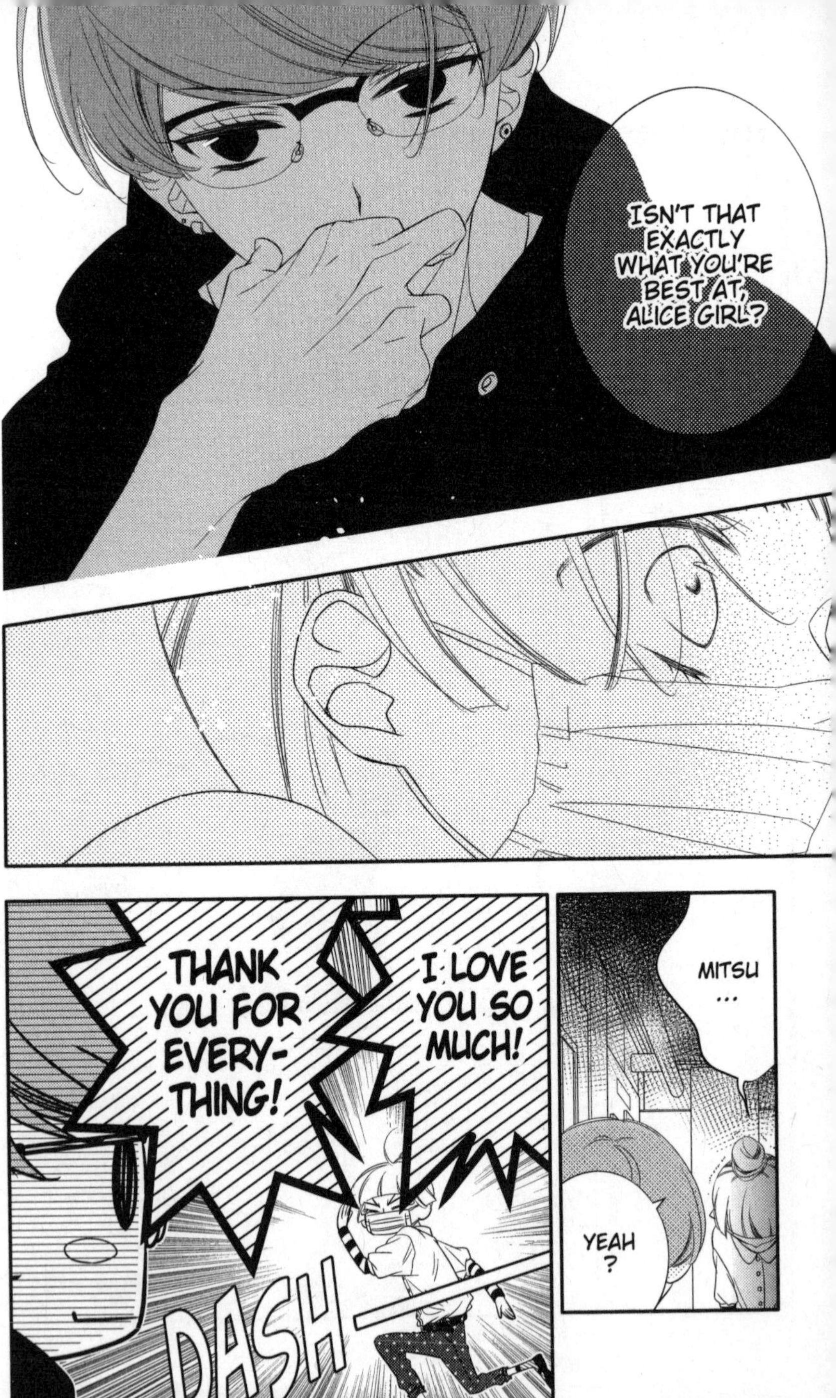
ISN'T THAT EXACTLY WHAT YOU'RE BEST AT, ALICE GIRL?
MITSU...
YEAH?
I LOVE YOU SO MUCH!
THANK YOU FOR EVERY-THING!
DASH

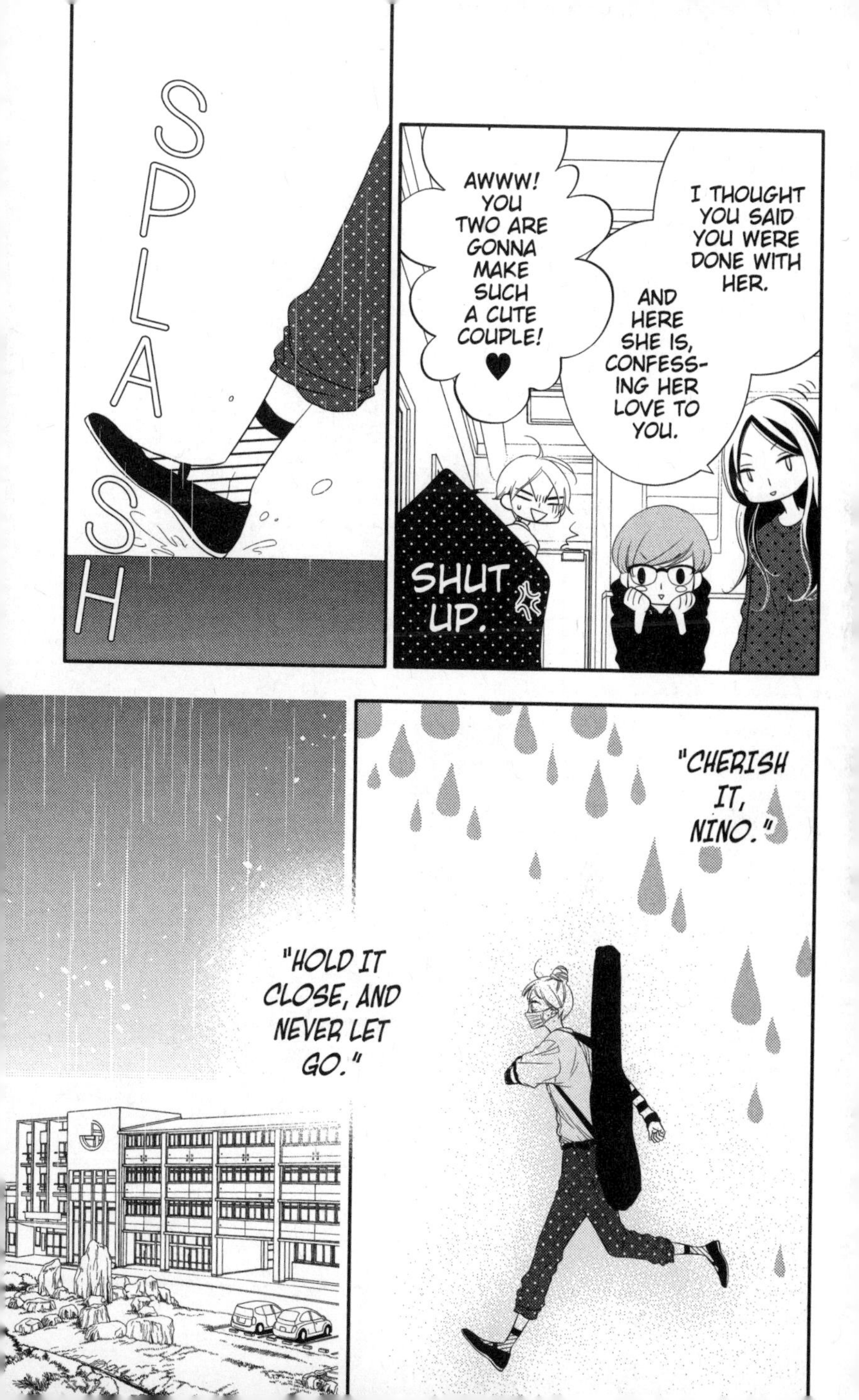
I THOUGHT YOU SAID YOU WERE DONE WITH HER.
AND HERE SHE IS, CONFESSING HER LOVE TO YOU.
AWWW! YOU TWO ARE GONNA MAKE SUCH A CUTE COUPLE! ♥
SHUT UP.
SPLASH
"CHERISH IT, NINO."
"HOLD IT CLOSE, AND NEVER LET GO."

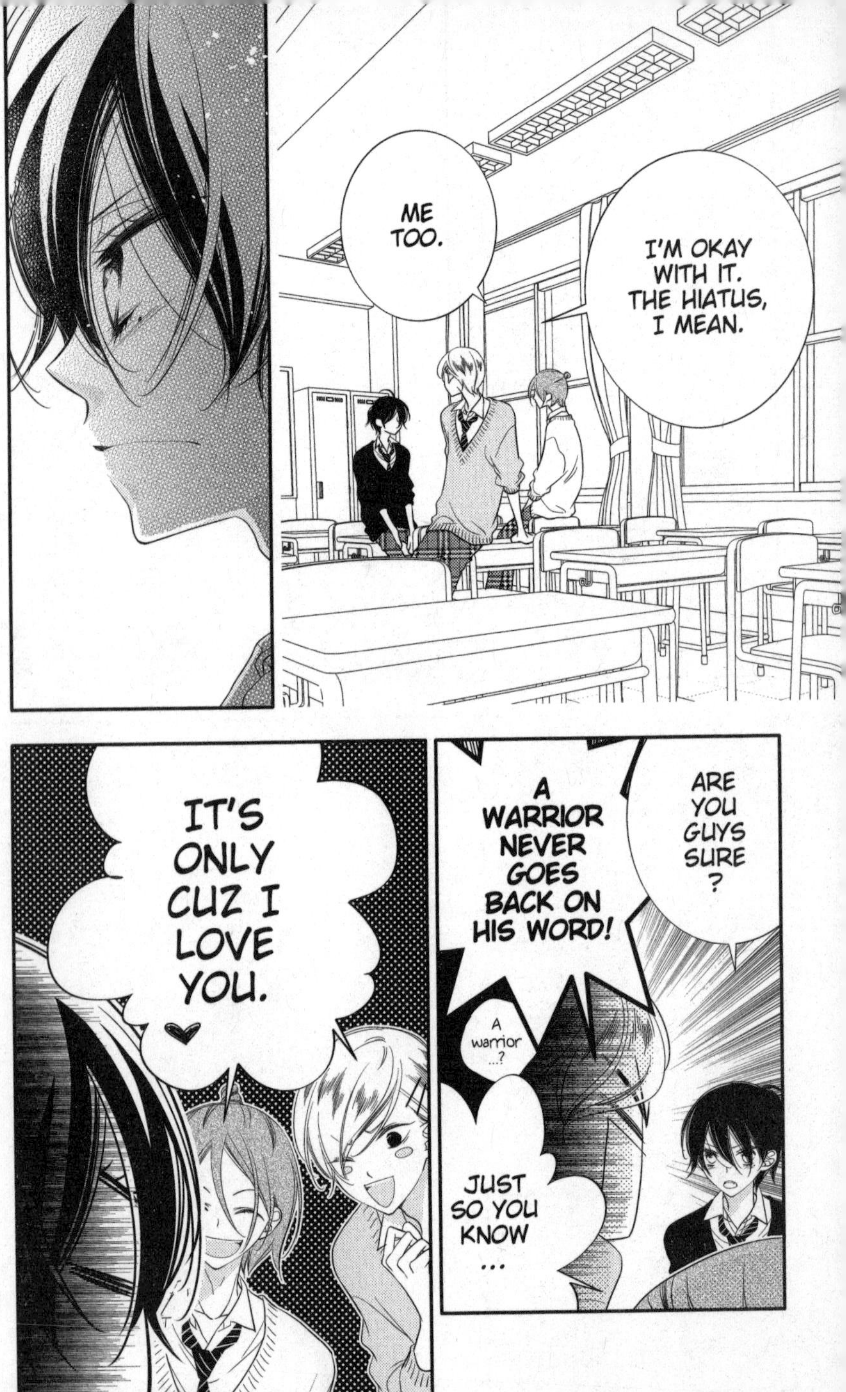
I'M OKAY WITH IT. THE HIATUS, I MEAN.
ME TOO.
ARE YOU GUYS SURE?
A WARRIOR NEVER GOES BACK ON HIS WORD!
A warrior...?
JUST SO YOU KNOW...
IT'S ONLY CUZ I LOVE YOU. ❤

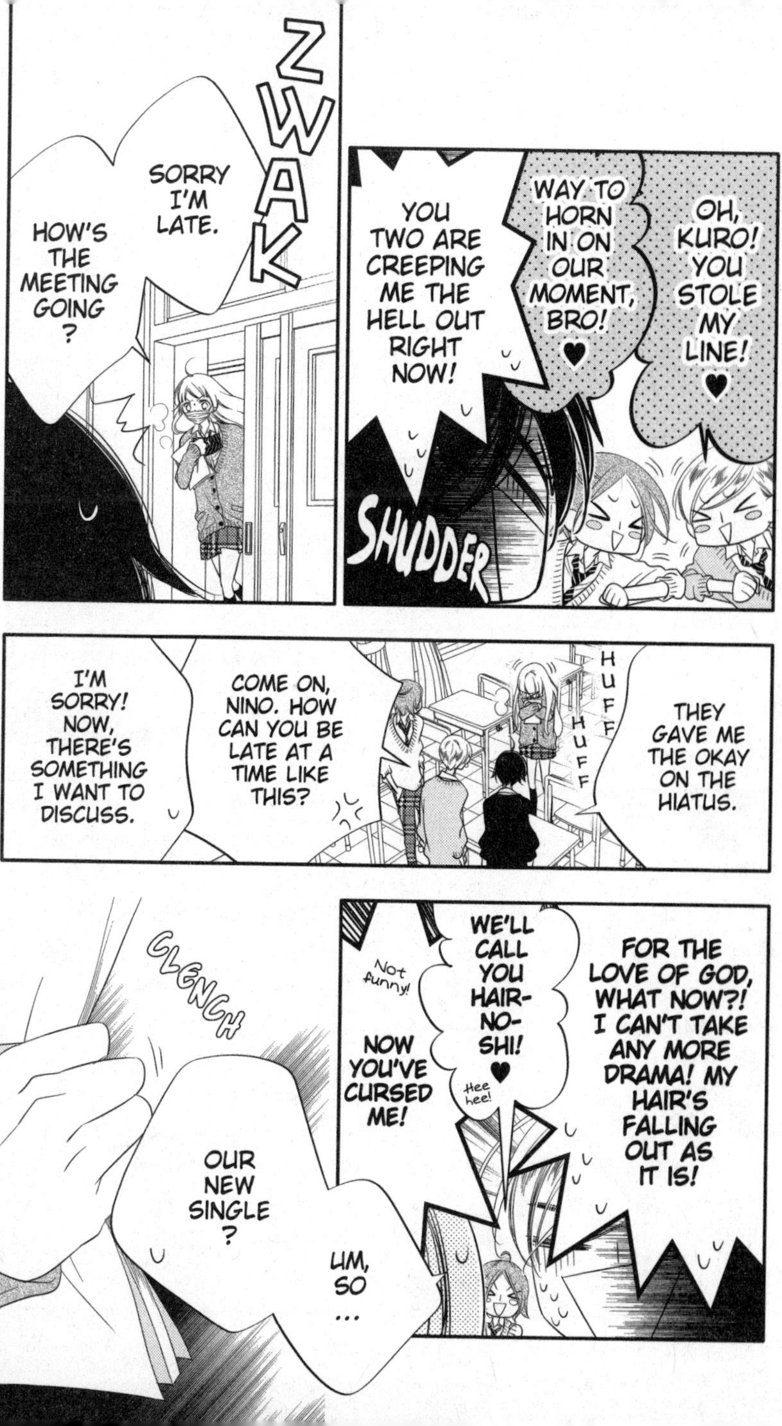
OH, KURO! YOU STOLE MY LINE! ♥
WAY TO HORN IN ON OUR MOMENT, BRO! ♥
YOU TWO ARE CREEPING ME THE HELL OUT RIGHT NOW!
SHUDDER
ZWAK
SORRY I'M LATE.
HOW'S THE MEETING GOING?
THEY GAVE ME THE OKAY ON THE HIATUS.
HUFF HUFF
COME ON, NINO. HOW CAN YOU BE LATE AT A TIME LIKE THIS?
I'M SORRY! NOW, THERE'S SOMETHING I WANT TO DISCUSS.
FOR THE LOVE OF GOD, WHAT NOW?! I CAN'T TAKE ANY MORE DRAMA! MY HAIR'S FALLING OUT AS IT IS!
WE'LL CALL YOU HAIR-NO-SHI! ♥
Hee hee!
Not funny!
NOW YOU'VE CURSED ME!
CLENCH
UM, SO ...
OUR NEW SINGLE?

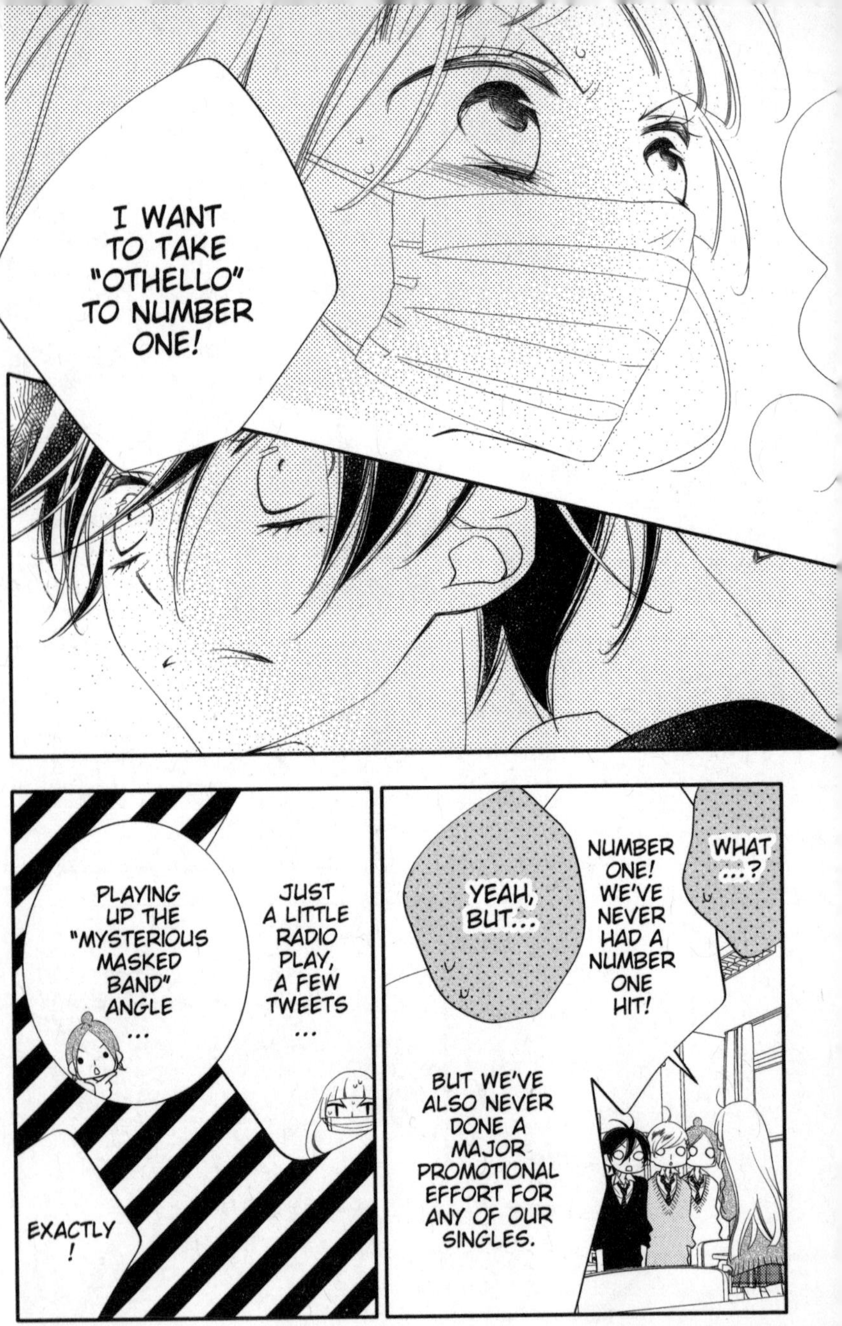
I WANT TO TAKE "OTHELLO" TO NUMBER ONE!
WHAT ...?
NUMBER ONE! WE'VE NEVER HAD A NUMBER ONE HIT!
YEAH, BUT...
BUT WE'VE ALSO NEVER DONE A MAJOR PROMOTIONAL EFFORT FOR ANY OF OUR SINGLES.
JUST A LITTLE RADIO PLAY, A FEW TWEETS ...
PLAYING UP THE "MYSTERIOUS MASKED BAND" ANGLE ...
EXACTLY!

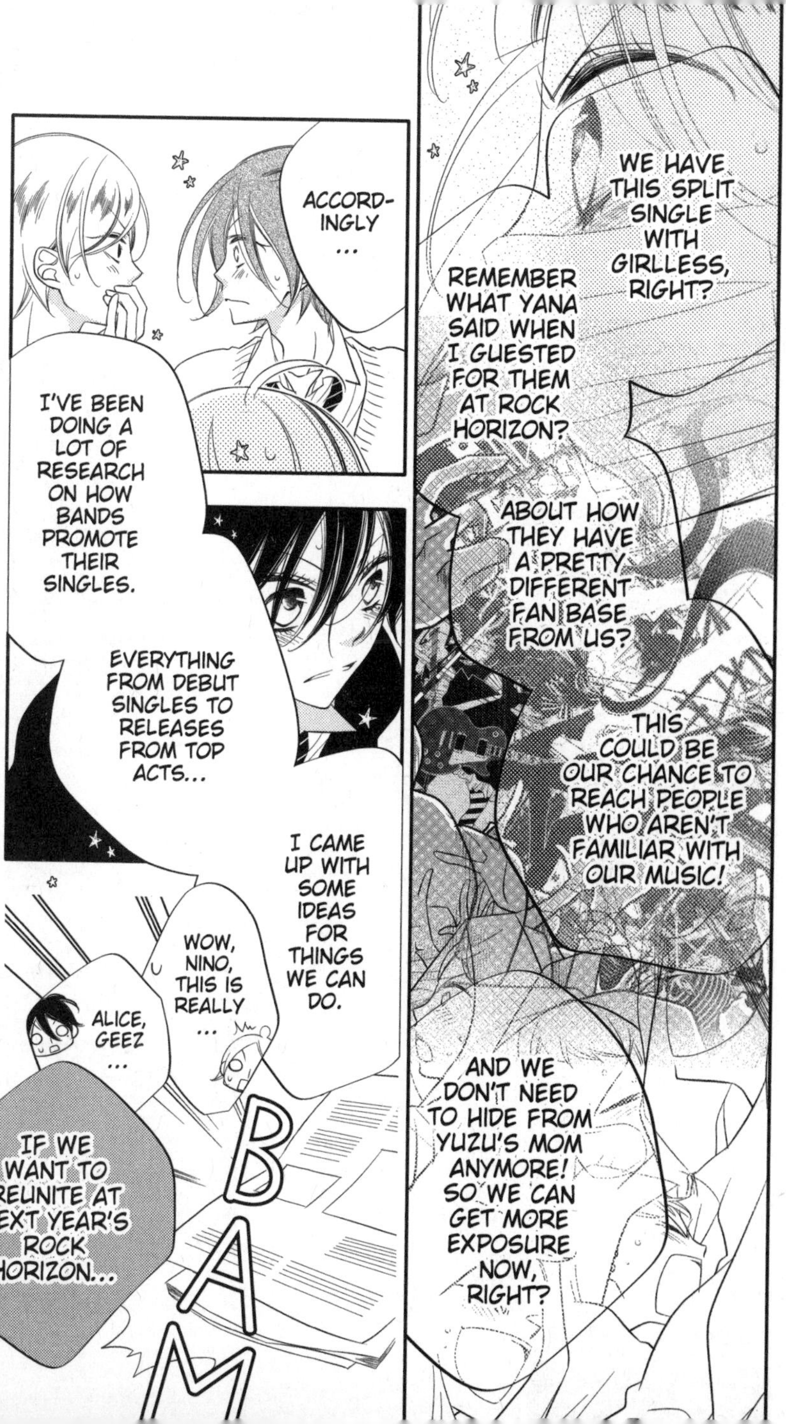
WE HAVE THIS SPLIT SINGLE WITH GIRLLESS, RIGHT?
REMEMBER WHAT YANA SAID WHEN I GUESTED FOR THEM AT ROCK HORIZON?
ABOUT HOW THEY HAVE A PRETTY DIFFERENT FAN BASE FROM US?
THIS COULD BE OUR CHANCE TO REACH PEOPLE WHO AREN'T FAMILIAR WITH OUR MUSIC!
AND WE DON'T NEED TO HIDE FROM YUZU'S MOM ANYMORE! SO WE CAN GET MORE EXPOSURE NOW, RIGHT?
ACCORD-INGLY ...
I'VE BEEN DOING A LOT OF RESEARCH ON HOW BANDS PROMOTE THEIR SINGLES.
EVERYTHING FROM DEBUT SINGLES TO RELEASES FROM TOP ACTS...
I CAME UP WITH SOME IDEAS FOR THINGS WE CAN DO.
WOW, NINO, THIS IS REALLY ...
ALICE, GEEZ ...
IF WE WANT TO REUNITE AT NEXT YEAR'S ROCK HORIZON...
BAM

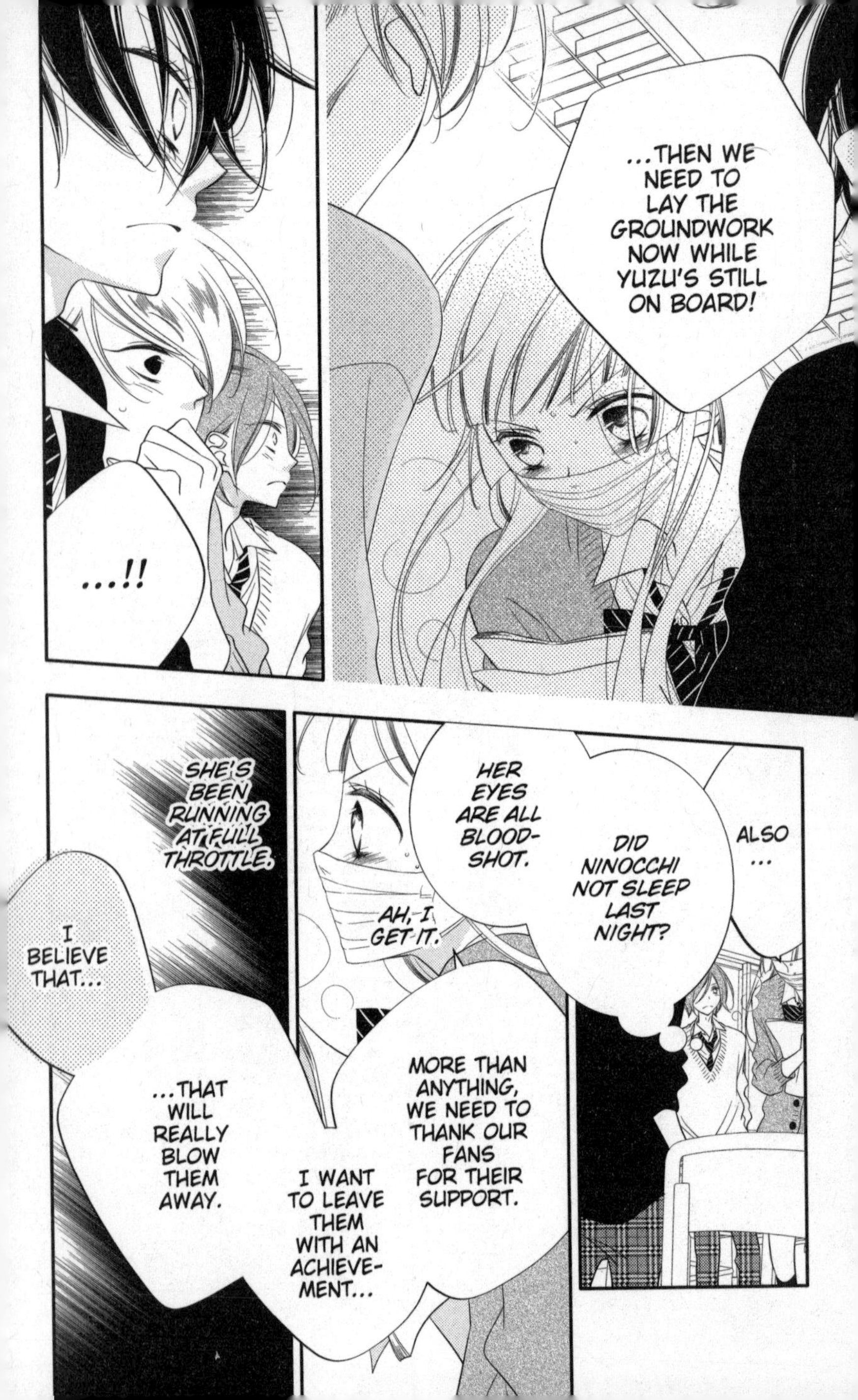
...THEN WE NEED TO LAY THE GROUNDWORK NOW WHILE YUZU'S STILL ON BOARD!
...!!
ALSO ...
DID NINOCCHI NOT SLEEP LAST NIGHT?
HER EYES ARE ALL BLOOD-SHOT.
AH, I GET IT.
MORE THAN ANYTHING, WE NEED TO THANK OUR FANS FOR THEIR SUPPORT.
I WANT TO LEAVE THEM WITH AN ACHIEVE-MENT...
...THAT WILL REALLY BLOW THEM AWAY.
SHE'S BEEN RUNNING AT FULL THROTTLE.
I BELIEVE THAT...

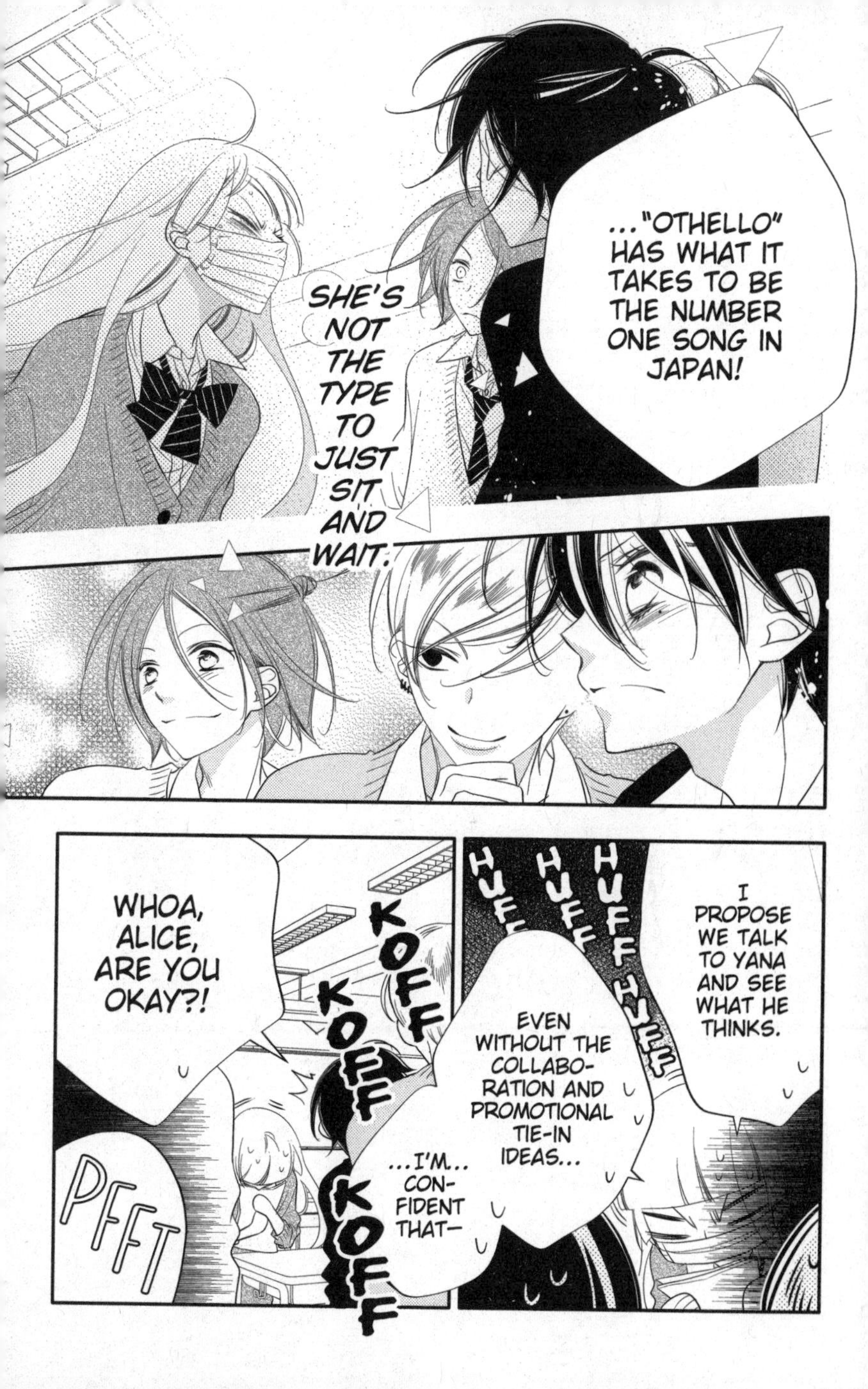
..."OTHELLO" HAS WHAT IT TAKES TO BE THE NUMBER ONE SONG IN JAPAN!
SHE'S NOT THE TYPE TO JUST SIT AND WAIT.
HUFF HUFF HUFF HUFF
I PROPOSE WE TALK TO YANA AND SEE WHAT HE THINKS.
EVEN WITHOUT THE COLLABO-RATION AND PROMOTIONAL TIE-IN IDEAS...
...I'M... CON-FIDENT THAT—
KOFF KOFF KOFF KOFF
WHOA, ALICE, ARE YOU OKAY?!
PFFT

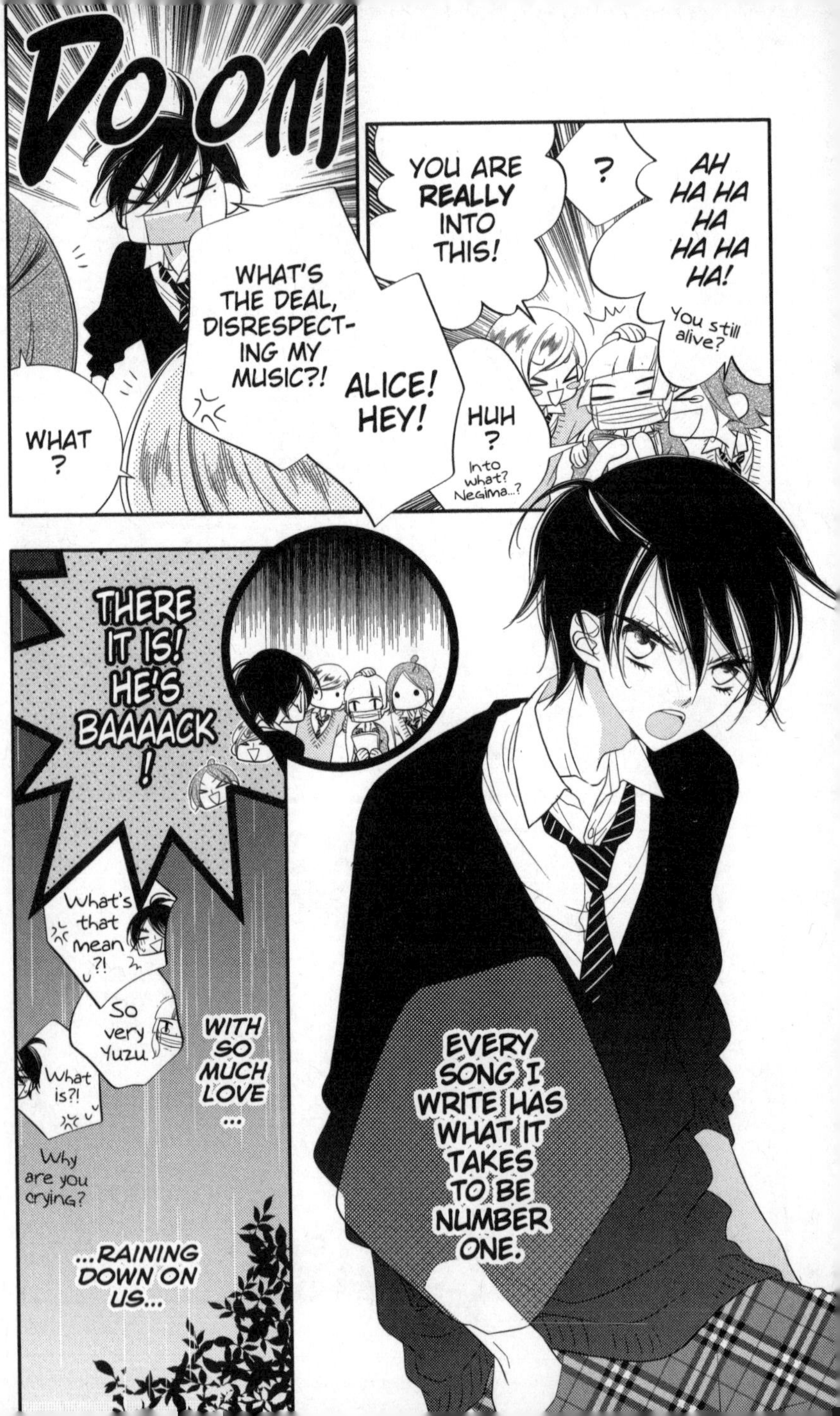
AH HA HA HA HA HA HA!
You still alive?
?
YOU ARE REALLY INTO THIS!
HUH? Into what? Negima...?
DOOM
ALICE! HEY!
WHAT'S THE DEAL, DISRESPECTING MY MUSIC?!
WHAT?
EVERY SONG I WRITE HAS WHAT IT TAKES TO BE NUMBER ONE.
THERE IT IS! HE'S BAAAACK!
What's that mean?!
So very Yuzu.
What is?!
Why are you crying?
WITH SO MUCH LOVE...
...RAINING DOWN ON US...

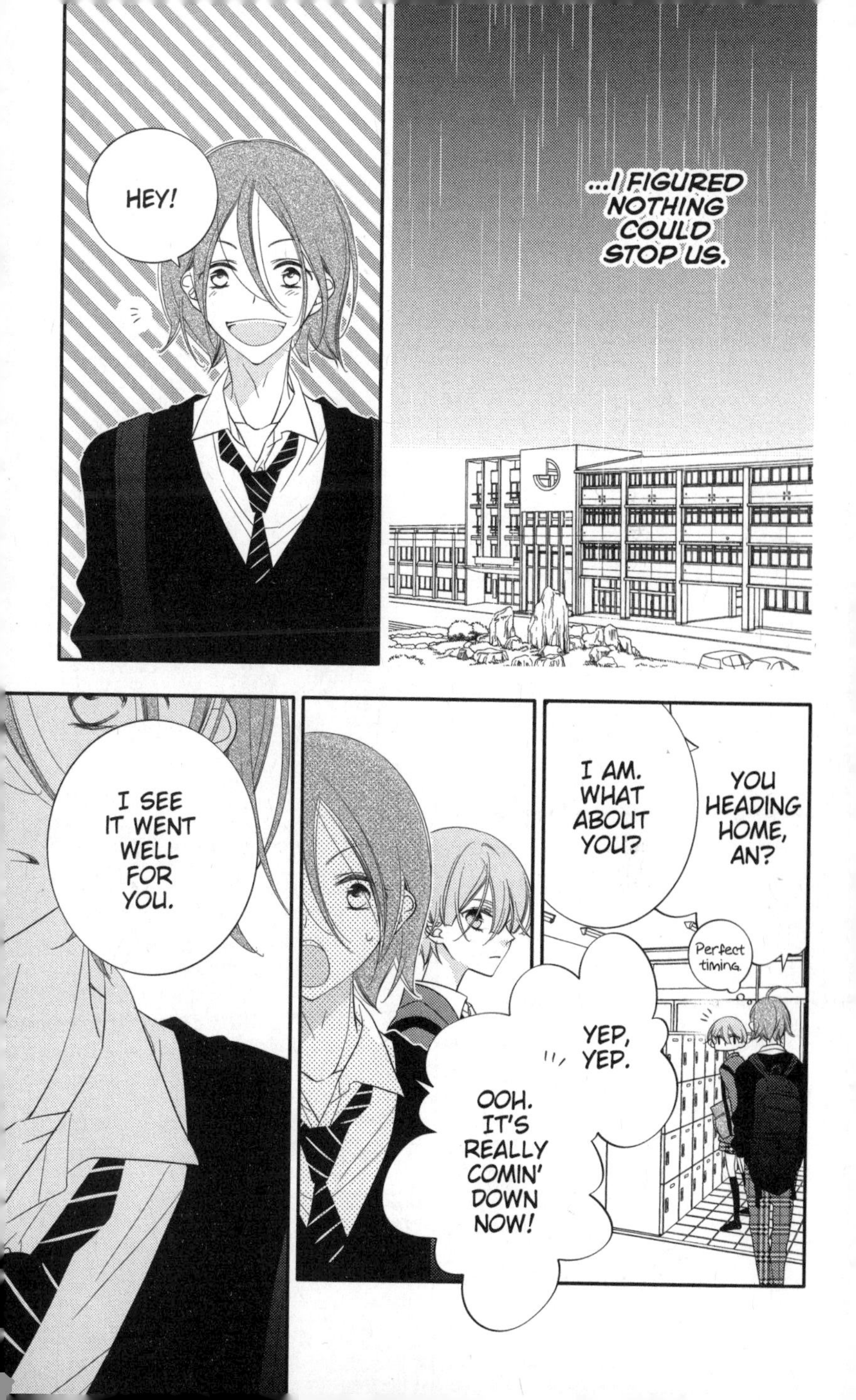
...I FIGURED NOTHING COULD STOP US.
HEY!
YOU HEADING HOME, AN?
I AM. WHAT ABOUT YOU?
Perfect timing.
YEP, YEP.
OOH. IT'S REALLY COMIN' DOWN NOW!
I SEE IT WENT WELL FOR YOU.

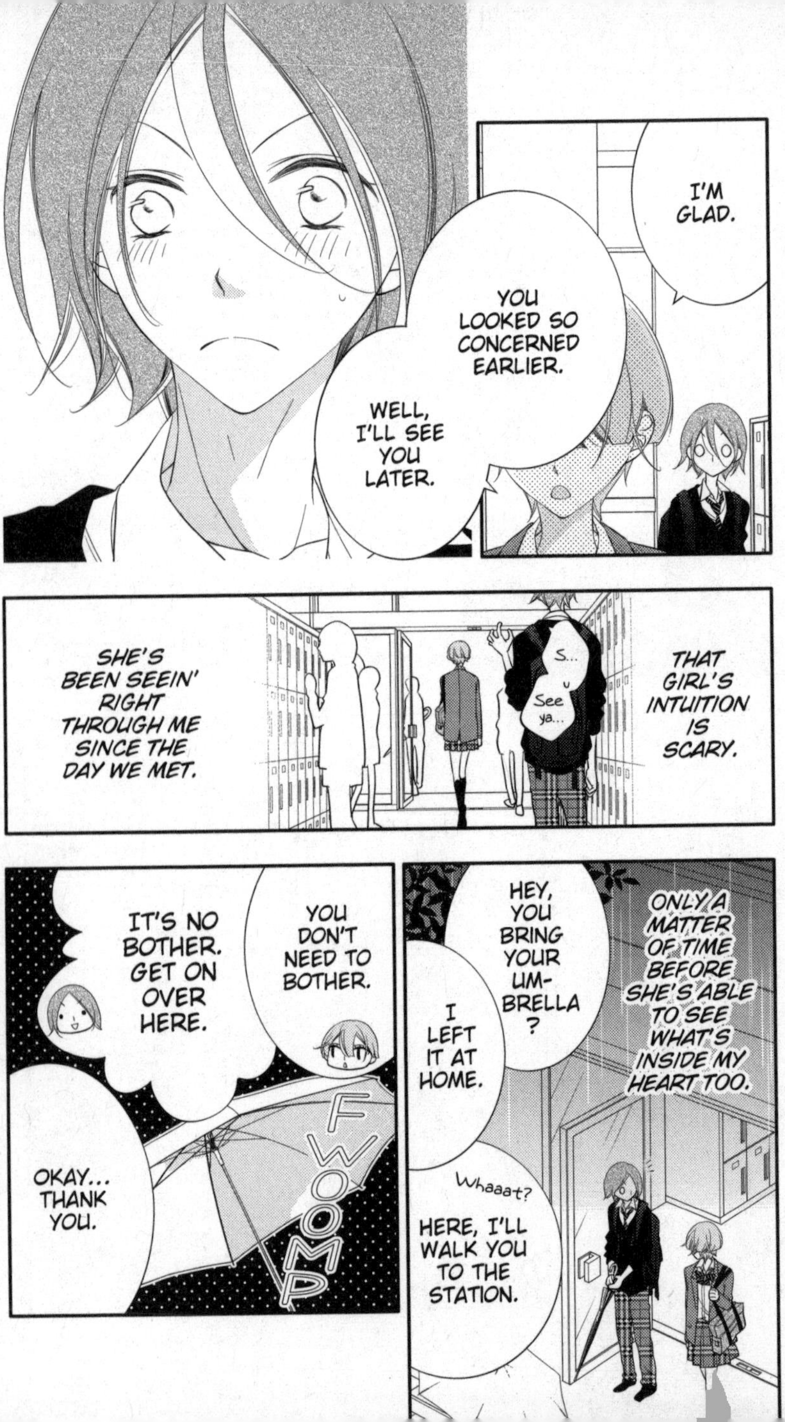
I'M GLAD.
YOU LOOKED SO CONCERNED EARLIER.
WELL, I'LL SEE YOU LATER.
THAT GIRL'S INTUITION IS SCARY.
S... See ya...
SHE'S BEEN SEEIN' RIGHT THROUGH ME SINCE THE DAY WE MET.
ONLY A MATTER OF TIME BEFORE SHE'S ABLE TO SEE WHAT'S INSIDE MY HEART TOO.
HEY, YOU BRING YOUR UM-BRELLA?
I LEFT IT AT HOME.
Whaaat?
HERE, I'LL WALK YOU TO THE STATION.
YOU DON'T NEED TO BOTHER.
IT'S NO BOTHER. GET ON OVER HERE.
FWOOMP
OKAY... THANK YOU.

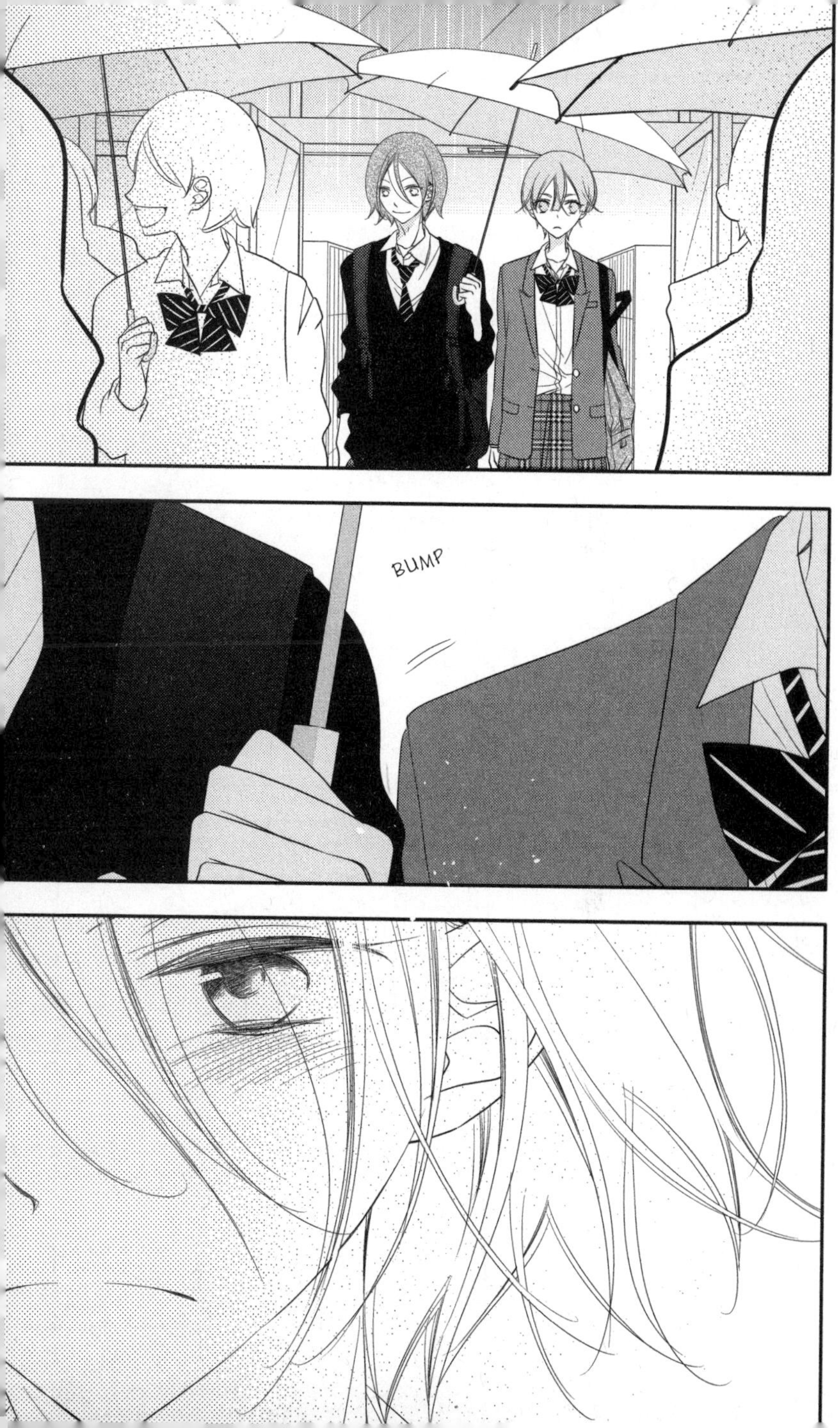
BUMP

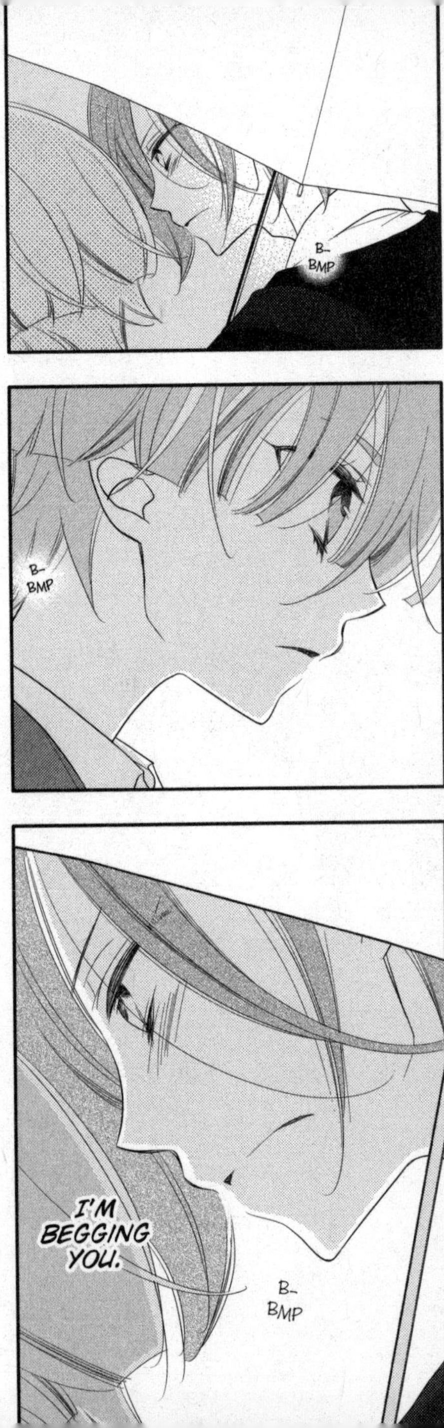
B-
BMP
B-
BMP
I'M
BEGGING
YOU.
B-
BMP

DON'T
SEE
THROUGH
THIS.

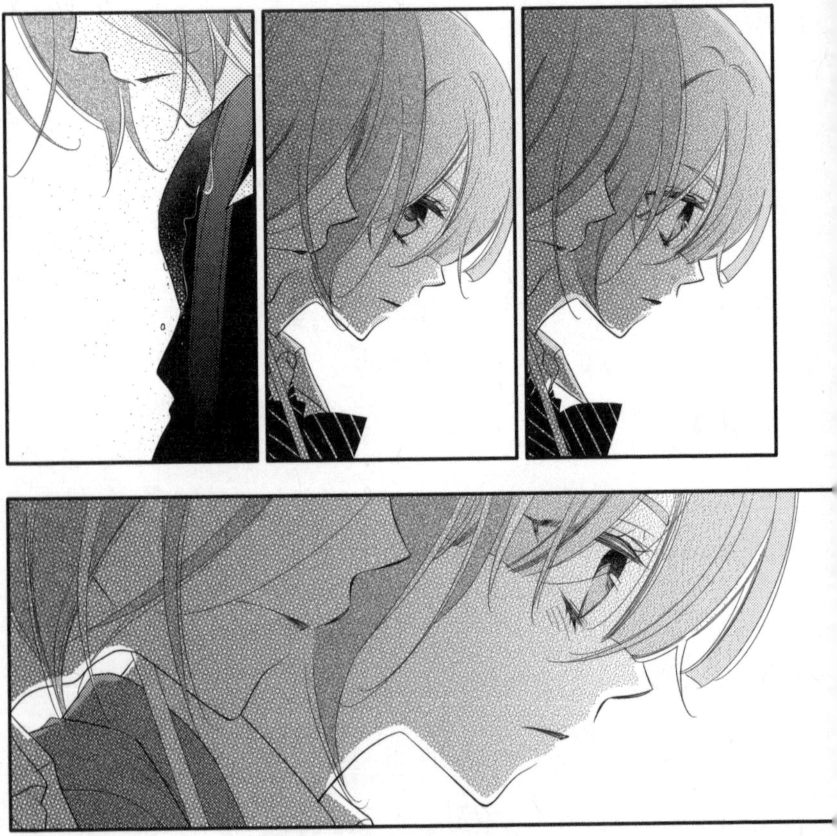

MY LOVE
FOR YOU...

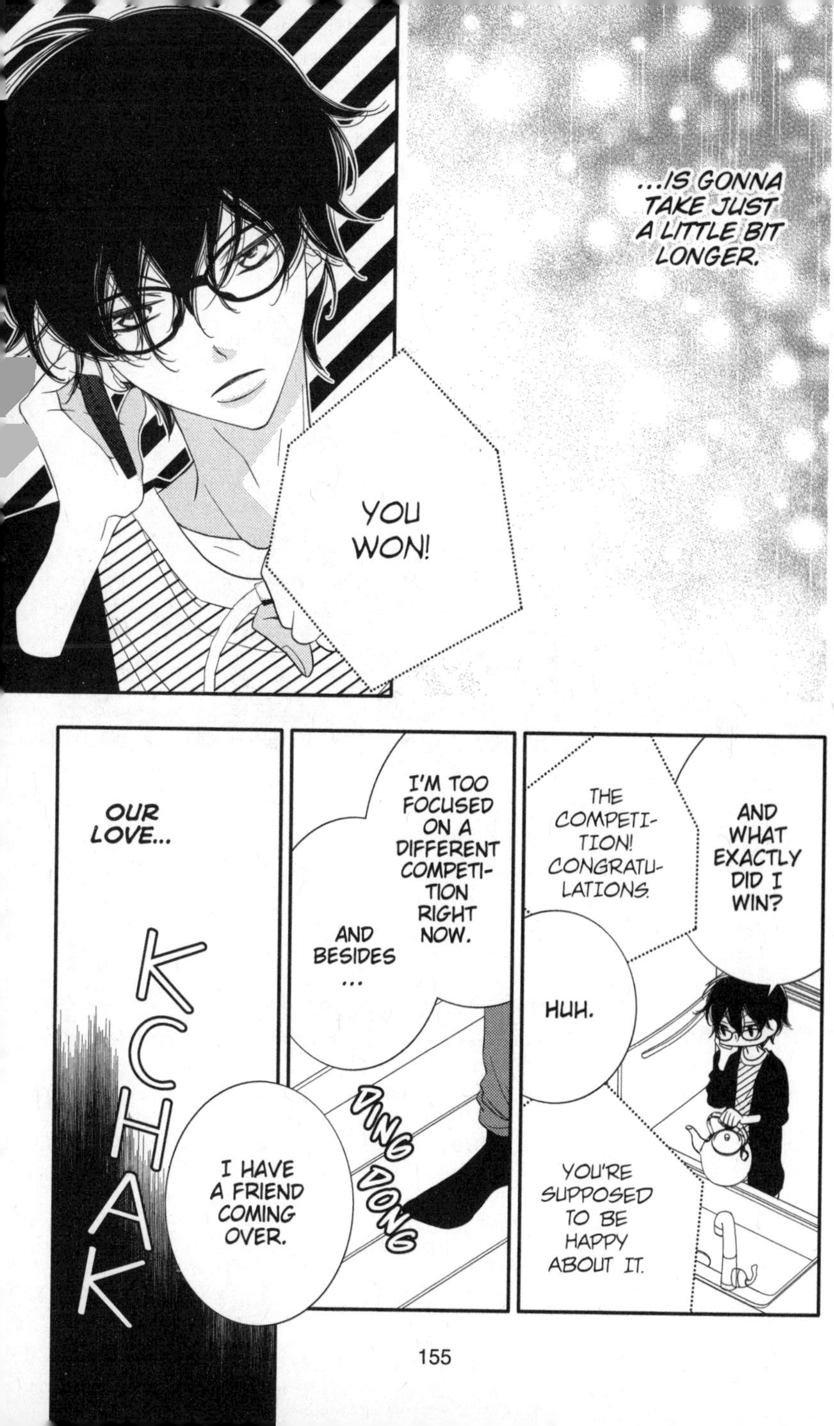
...IS GONNA TAKE JUST A LITTLE BIT LONGER.
YOU WON!
AND WHAT EXACTLY DID I WIN?
THE COMPETITION! CONGRATULATIONS.
HUH.
YOU'RE SUPPOSED TO BE HAPPY ABOUT IT.
I'M TOO FOCUSED ON A DIFFERENT COMPETITION RIGHT NOW.
AND BESIDES...
DING DONG
I HAVE A FRIEND COMING OVER.
OUR LOVE...
KCHAK

...IS GONNA TAKE JUST
A LITTLE BIT LONGER.

SONG 93

MY HUNCHES ARE NEVER WRONG.

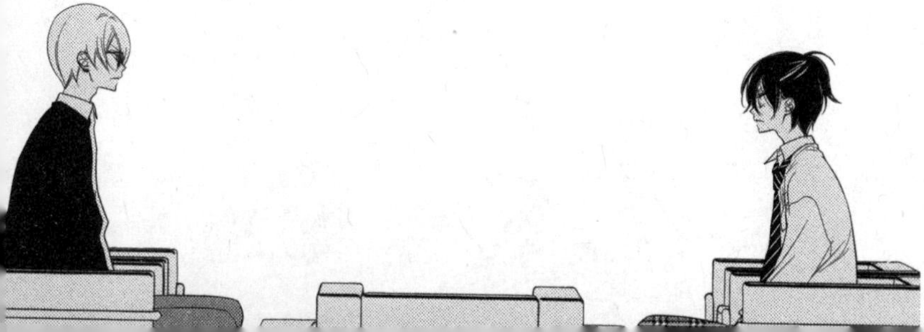

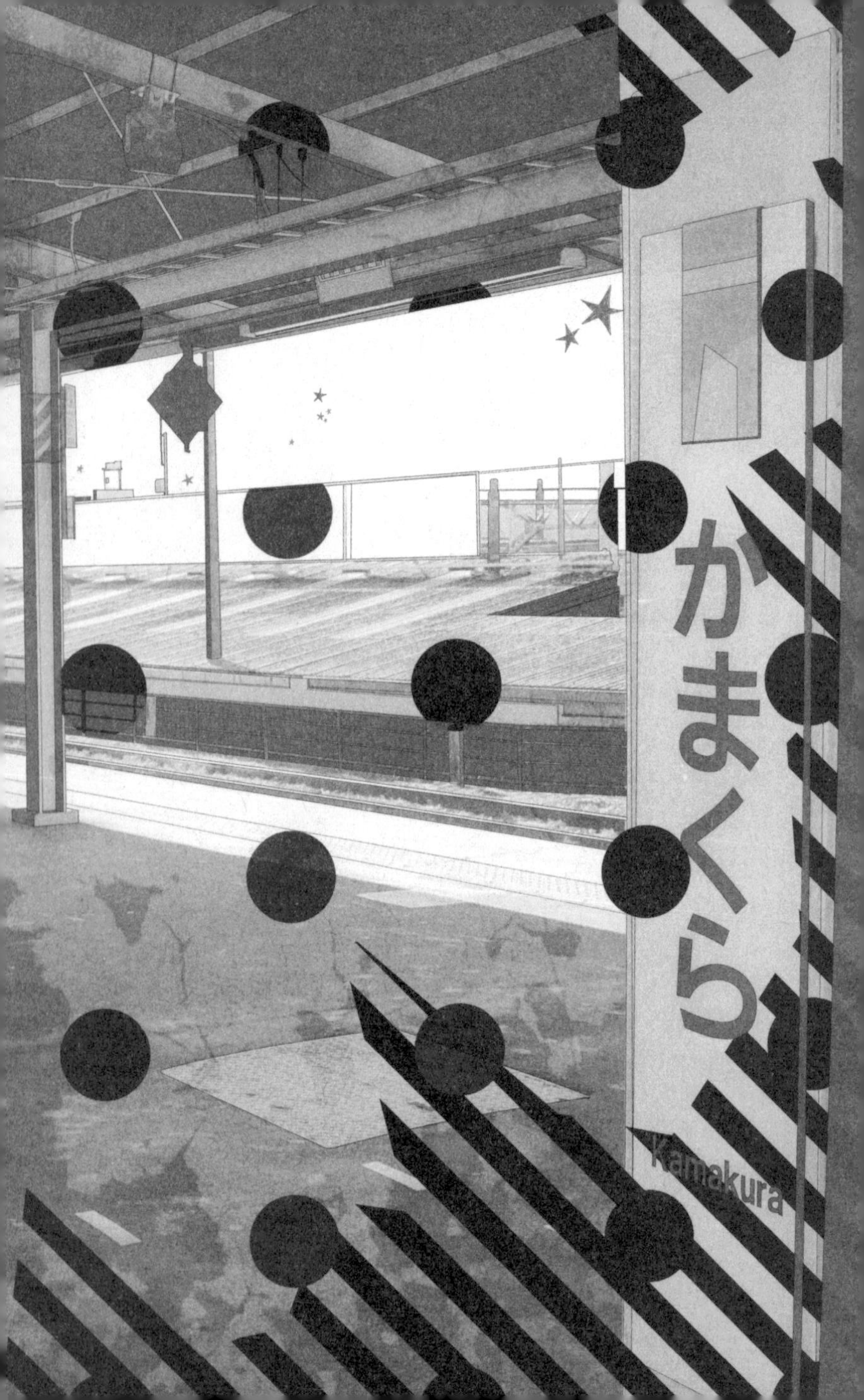
かまくら
Kamakura

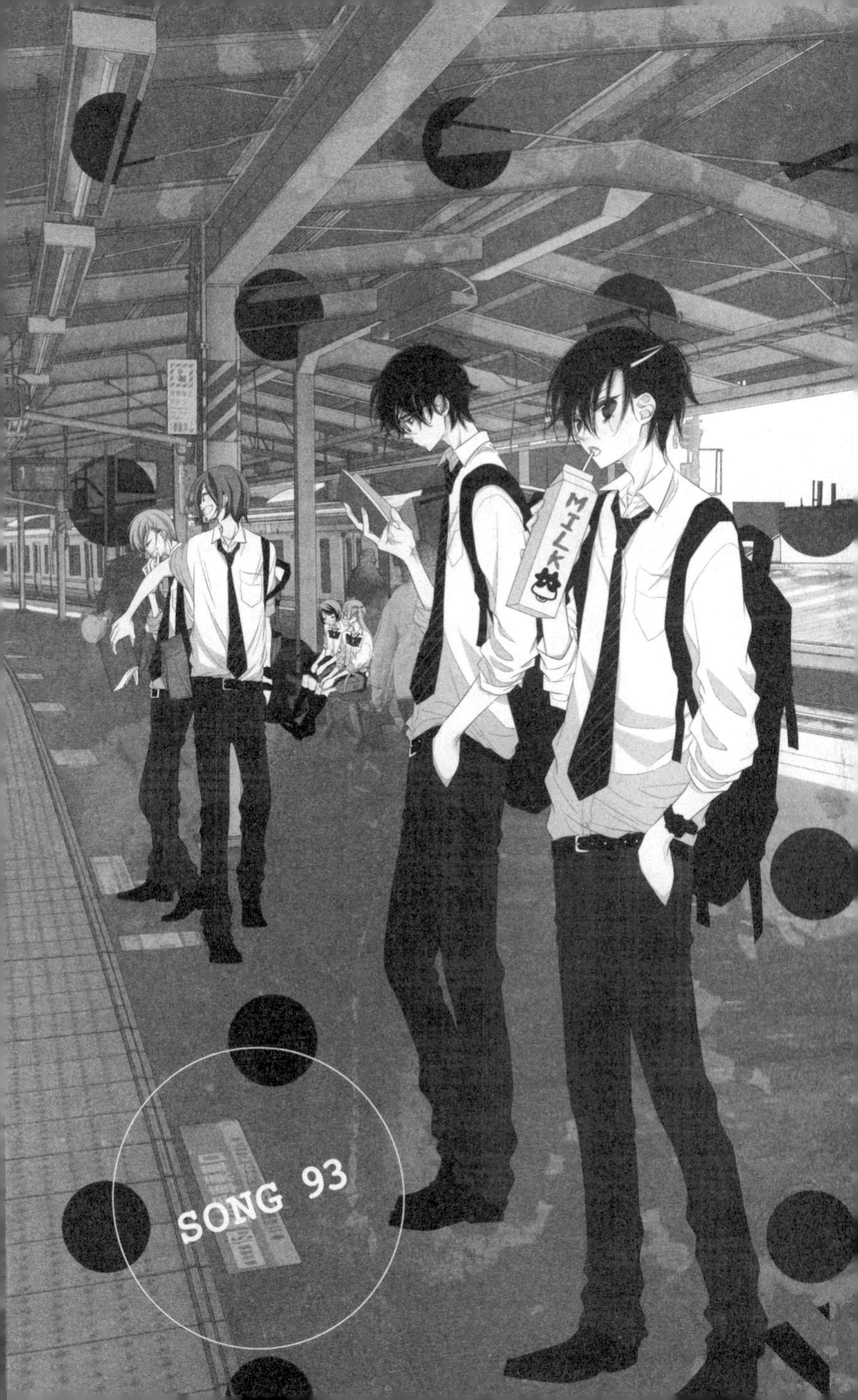
MILK
SONG 93

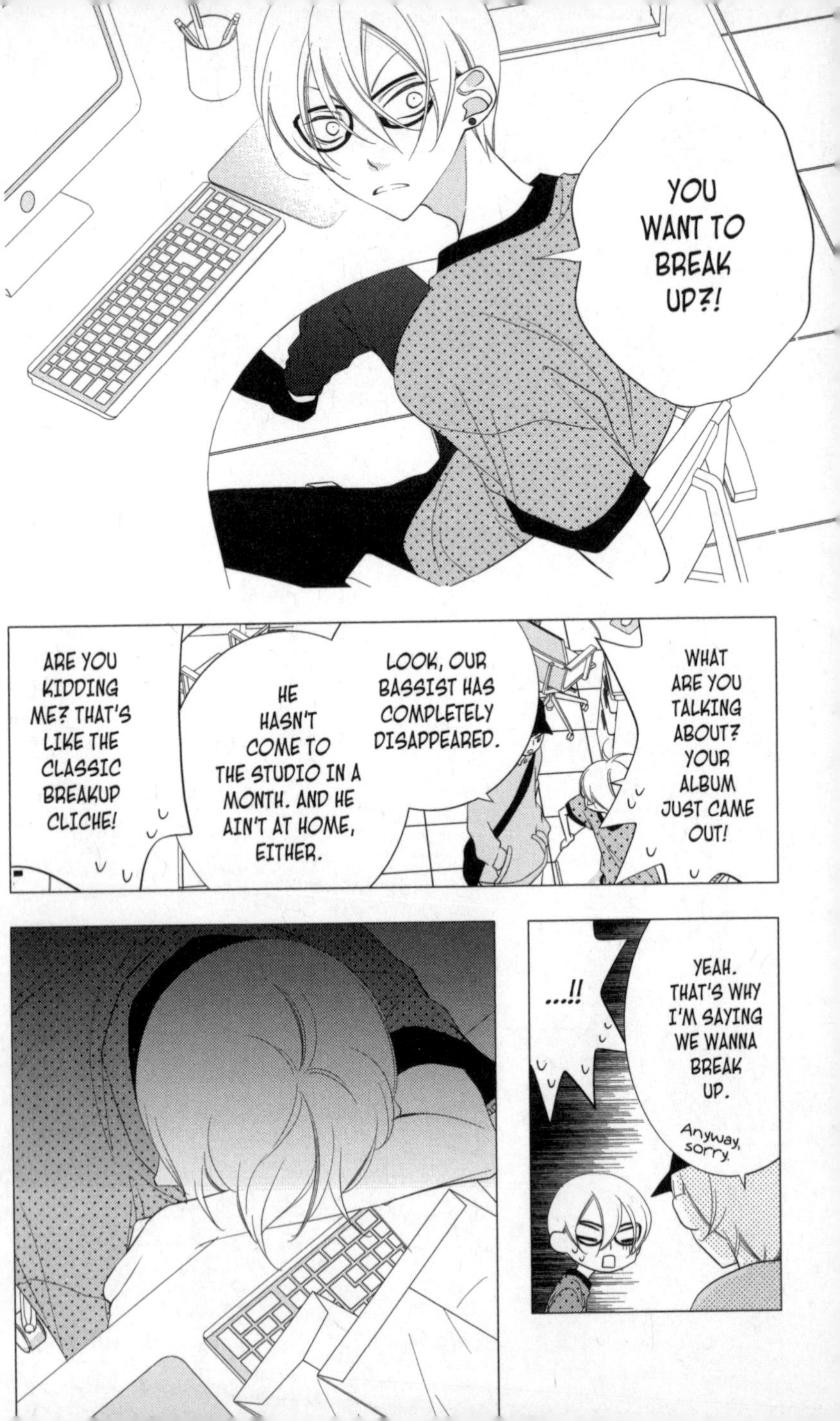
YOU WANT TO BREAK UP?!
WHAT ARE YOU TALKING ABOUT? YOUR ALBUM JUST CAME OUT!
LOOK, OUR BASSIST HAS COMPLETELY DISAPPEARED.
HE HASN'T COME TO THE STUDIO IN A MONTH. AND HE AIN'T AT HOME, EITHER.
ARE YOU KIDDING ME? THAT'S LIKE THE CLASSIC BREAKUP CLICHE!
YEAH. THAT'S WHY I'M SAYING WE WANNA BREAK UP.
Anyway, sorry.
...!!

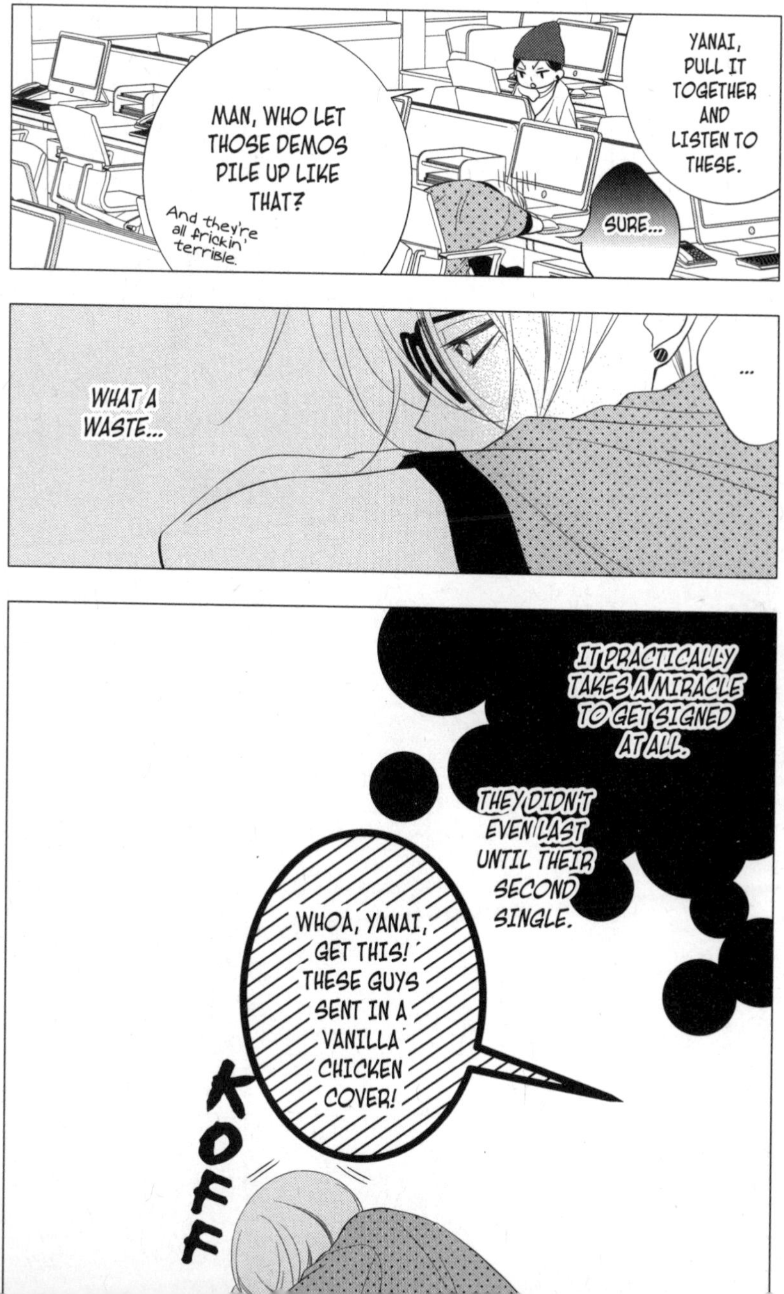
YANAI, PULL IT TOGETHER AND LISTEN TO THESE.
SURE...
MAN, WHO LET THOSE DEMOS PILE UP LIKE THAT?
And they're all frickin' terrible.
...
WHAT A WASTE...
IT PRACTICALLY TAKES A MIRACLE TO GET SIGNED AT ALL.
THEY DIDN'T EVEN LAST UNTIL THEIR SECOND SINGLE.
WHOA, YANAI, GET THIS! THESE GUYS SENT IN A VANILLA CHICKEN COVER!
KOFF

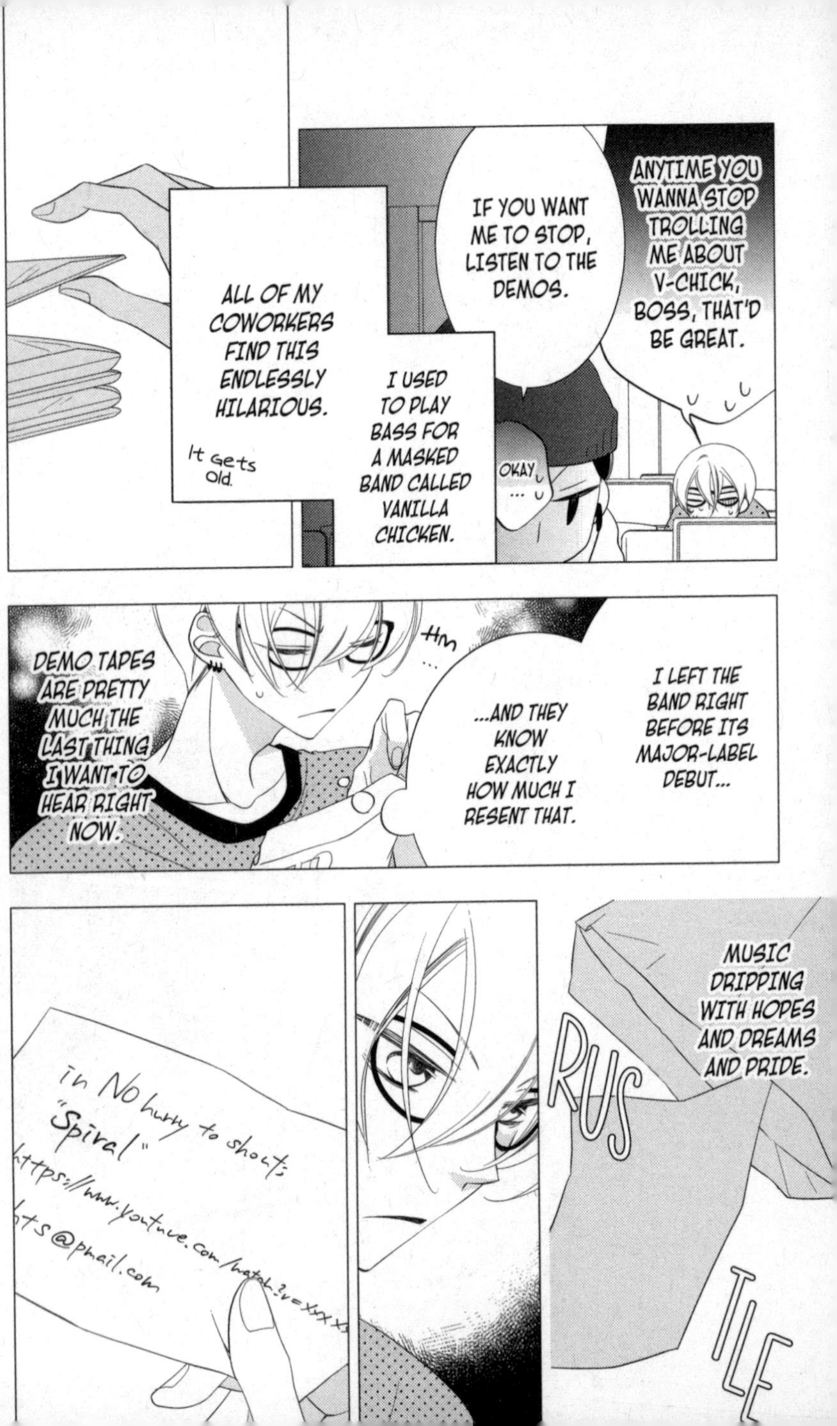
ANYTIME YOU WANNA STOP TROLLING ME ABOUT V-CHICK, BOSS, THAT'D BE GREAT.
IF YOU WANT ME TO STOP, LISTEN TO THE DEMOS.
OKAY ...
I USED TO PLAY BASS FOR A MASKED BAND CALLED VANILLA CHICKEN.
ALL OF MY COWORKERS FIND THIS ENDLESSLY HILARIOUS.
It gets old.
I LEFT THE BAND RIGHT BEFORE ITS MAJOR-LABEL DEBUT...
...AND THEY KNOW EXACTLY HOW MUCH I RESENT THAT.
Hm ...
DEMO TAPES ARE PRETTY MUCH THE LAST THING I WANT TO HEAR RIGHT NOW.
MUSIC DRIPPING WITH HOPES AND DREAMS AND PRIDE.
RUSTLE
in No hurry to shout;
"Spiral"
https://www.youtuve.com/watch?v=xxxx
hts@pmail.com

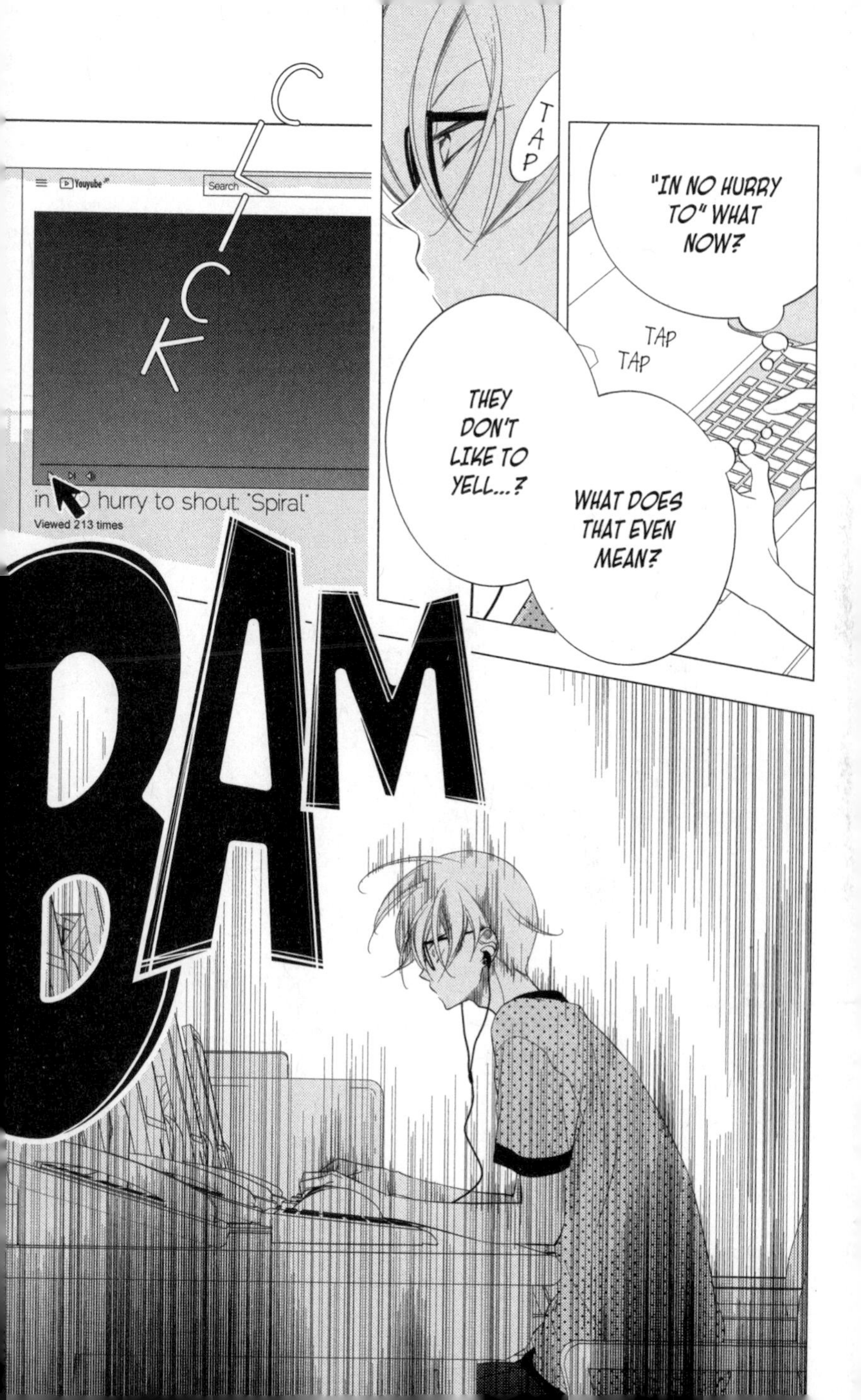
"IN NO HURRY TO" WHAT NOW?
TAP TAP
THEY DON'T LIKE TO YELL...?
WHAT DOES THAT EVEN MEAN?
TAP
Youyube
Search
CLICK
in NO hurry to shout: "Spiral"
Viewed 213 times
BAM

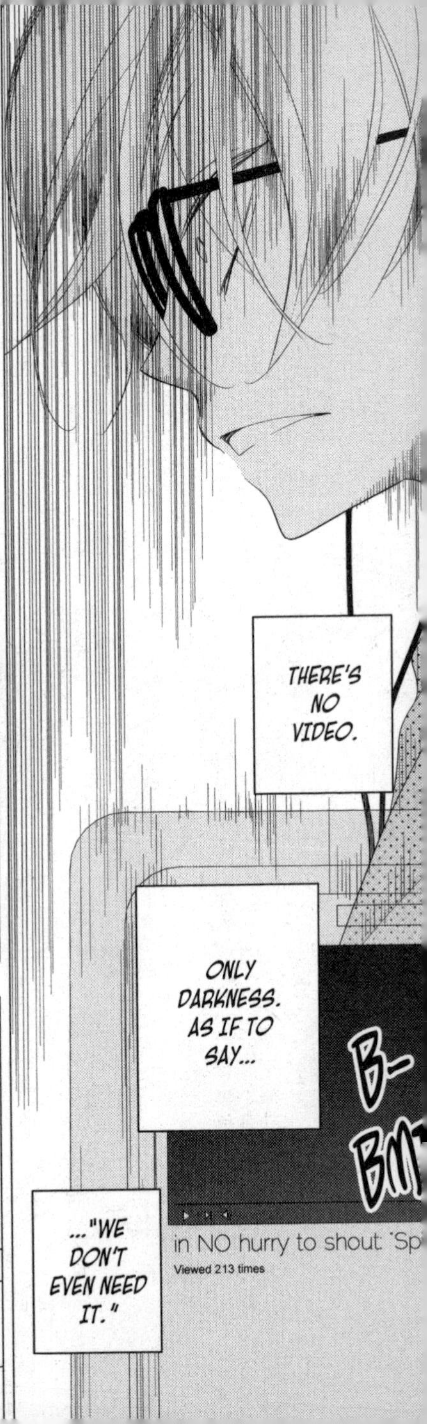
THERE'S NO VIDEO.
ONLY DARKNESS. AS IF TO SAY...
B-
in NO hurry to shout:
Viewed 213 times
..."WE DON'T EVEN NEED IT."
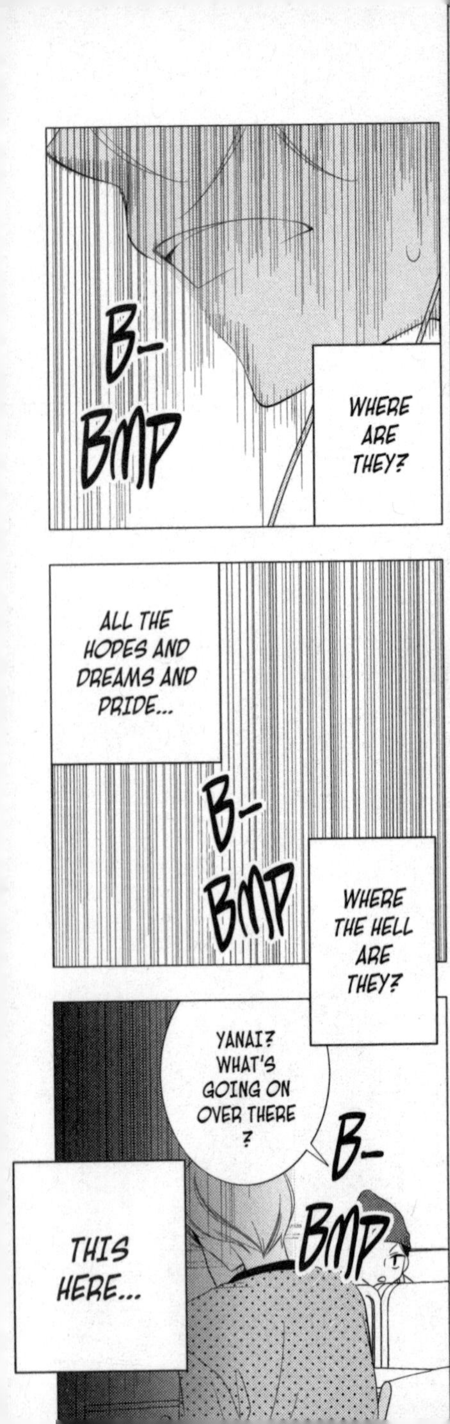
WHERE ARE THEY?
B-BMP
ALL THE HOPES AND DREAMS AND PRIDE...
B-BMP
WHERE THE HELL ARE THEY?
YANAI? WHAT'S GOING ON OVER THERE?
B-BMP
THIS HERE...

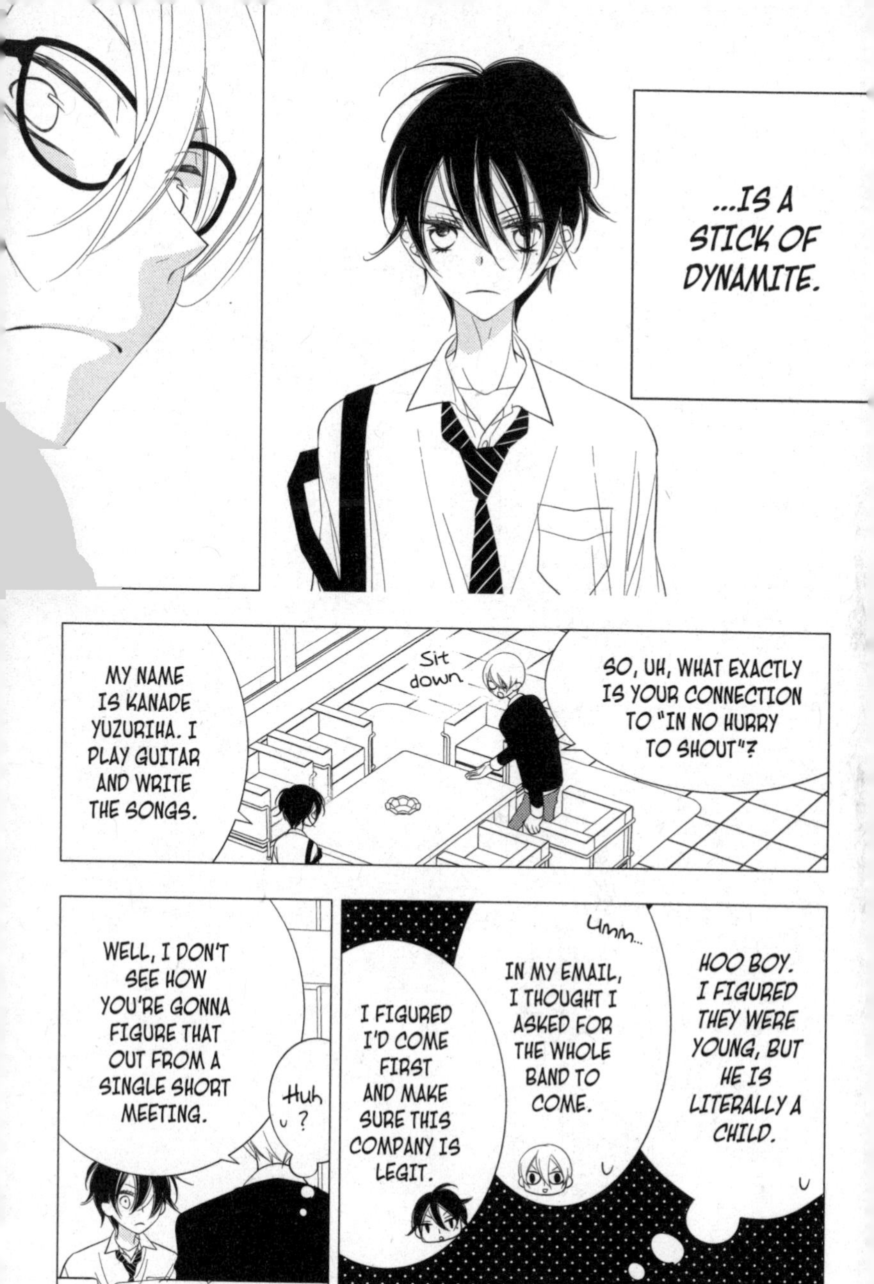
...IS A STICK OF DYNAMITE.
SO, UH, WHAT EXACTLY IS YOUR CONNECTION TO "IN NO HURRY TO SHOUT"?
Sit down
MY NAME IS KANADE YUZURIHA. I PLAY GUITAR AND WRITE THE SONGS.
HOO BOY. I FIGURED THEY WERE YOUNG, BUT HE IS LITERALLY A CHILD.
Umm...
IN MY EMAIL, I THOUGHT I ASKED FOR THE WHOLE BAND TO COME.
I FIGURED I'D COME FIRST AND MAKE SURE THIS COMPANY IS LEGIT.
Huh?
WELL, I DON'T SEE HOW YOU'RE GONNA FIGURE THAT OUT FROM A SINGLE SHORT MEETING.

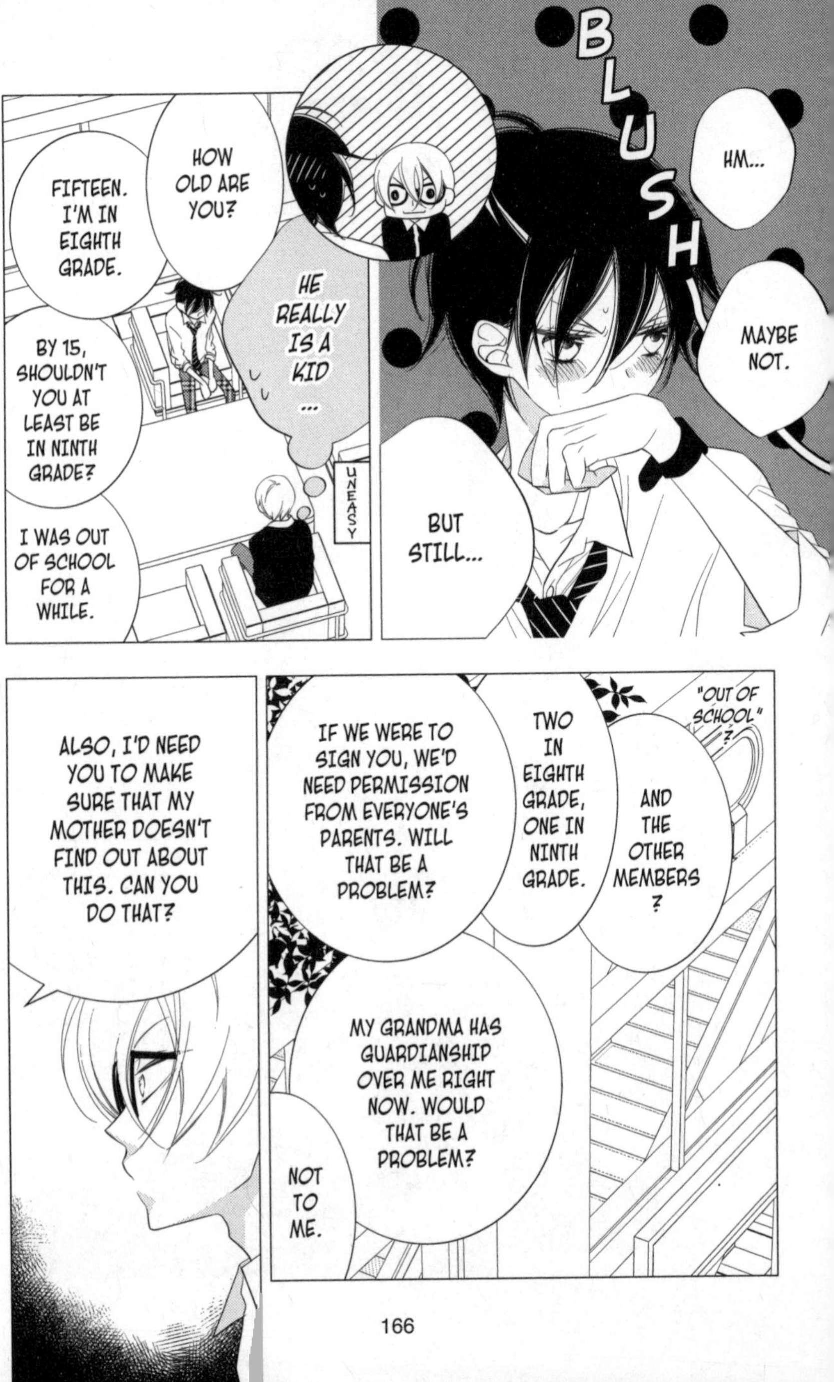
BLUSH
HM...
MAYBE NOT.
BUT STILL...
HOW OLD ARE YOU?
FIFTEEN. I'M IN EIGHTH GRADE.
HE REALLY IS A KID...
UNEASY
BY 15, SHOULDN'T YOU AT LEAST BE IN NINTH GRADE?
I WAS OUT OF SCHOOL FOR A WHILE.
"OUT OF SCHOOL"?
AND THE OTHER MEMBERS?
TWO IN EIGHTH GRADE, ONE IN NINTH GRADE.
IF WE WERE TO SIGN YOU, WE'D NEED PERMISSION FROM EVERYONE'S PARENTS. WILL THAT BE A PROBLEM?
MY GRANDMA HAS GUARDIANSHIP OVER ME RIGHT NOW. WOULD THAT BE A PROBLEM?
NOT TO ME.
ALSO, I'D NEED YOU TO MAKE SURE THAT MY MOTHER DOESN'T FIND OUT ABOUT THIS. CAN YOU DO THAT?

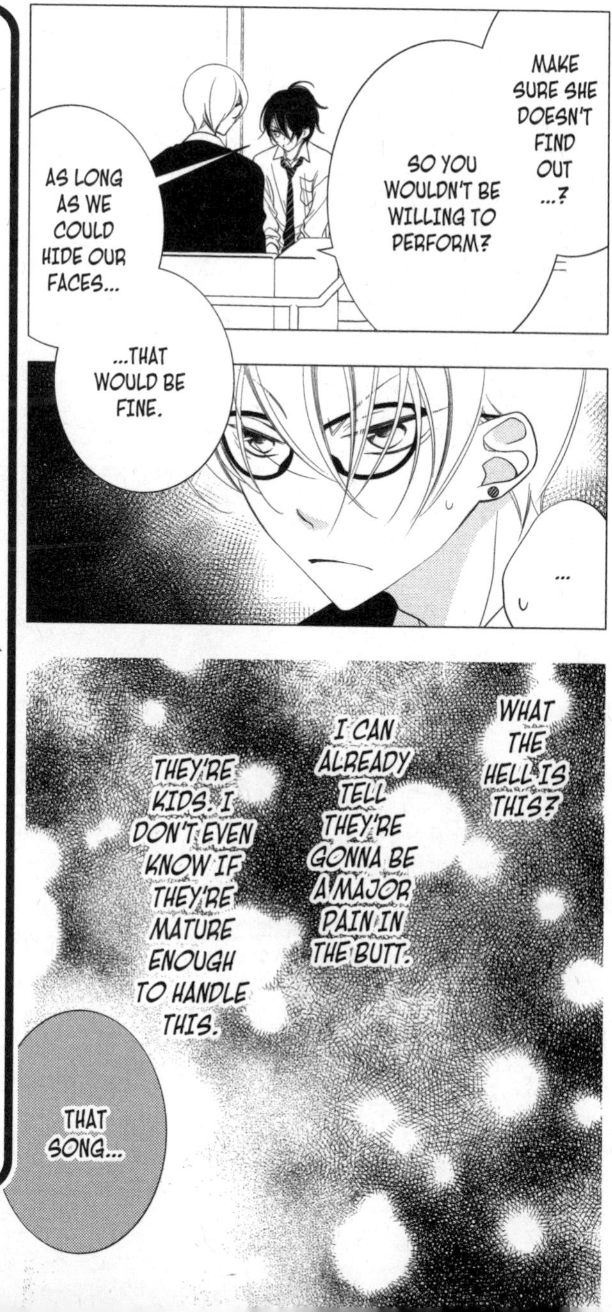
MAKE SURE SHE DOESN'T FIND OUT ...?
SO YOU WOULDN'T BE WILLING TO PERFORM?
AS LONG AS WE COULD HIDE OUR FACES...
...THAT WOULD BE FINE.
...
WHAT THE HELL IS THIS?
I CAN ALREADY TELL THEY'RE GONNA BE A MAJOR PAIN IN THE BUTT.
THEY'RE KIDS. I DON'T EVEN KNOW IF THEY'RE MATURE ENOUGH TO HANDLE THIS.
THAT SONG...

6

Well, that about wraps it up for volume 16. *Phew*, it looks like I'm gonna make my deadline in time after all. That's a relief!

What did you think of this volume? I can't wait to hear your impressions! I hope we can meet again in volume 17!

[SPECIAL THANKS]
MOSAGE
TAKAYUKI NAGASHIMA
IKUMI ISHIGAKI
AYAKA TOKUSHIGE
KENJU NORO
MY FAMILY
MY FRIENDS
AND YOU!!

Ryoko Fukuyama
c/o Anonymous Noise Editor
VIZ Media
P.O. Box 77010
San Francisco, CA 94107

HP http://ryoconet/
@ryocoryocoryoco
https://www.instagram.com/ryocofukuyama/

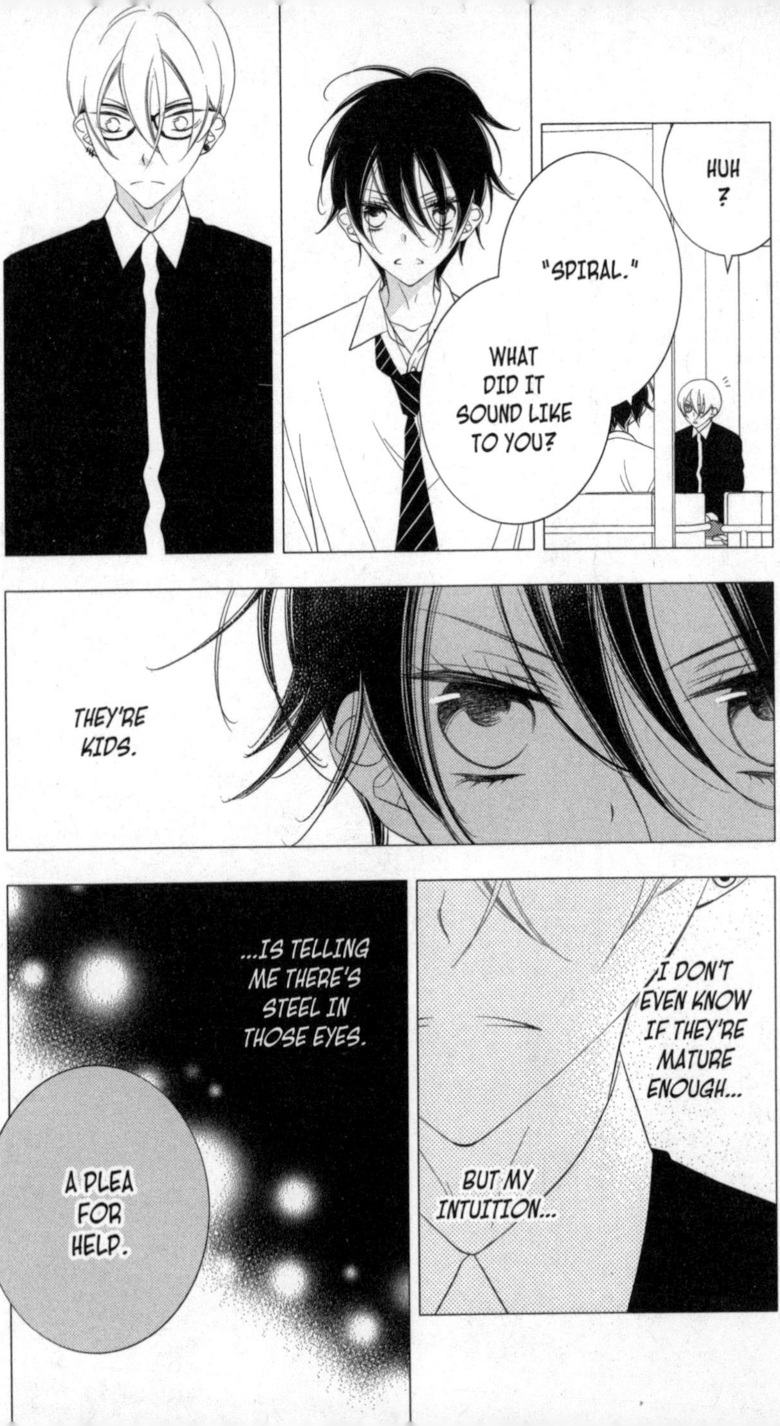
HUH?
"SPIRAL."
WHAT DID IT SOUND LIKE TO YOU?
THEY'RE KIDS.
I DON'T EVEN KNOW IF THEY'RE MATURE ENOUGH...
BUT MY INTUITION...
...IS TELLING ME THERE'S STEEL IN THOSE EYES.
A PLEA FOR HELP.

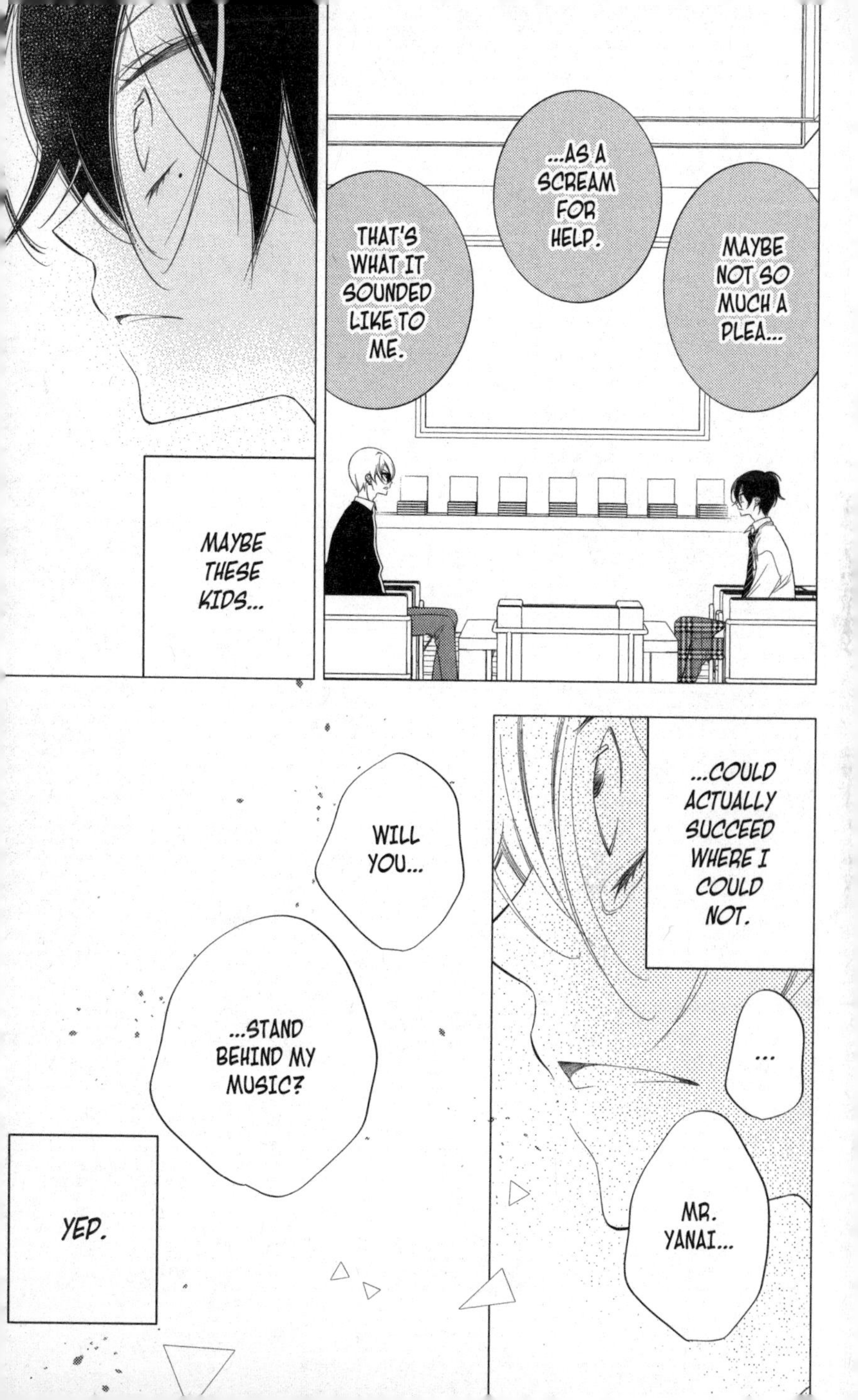
MAYBE NOT SO MUCH A PLEA...
...AS A SCREAM FOR HELP.
THAT'S WHAT IT SOUNDED LIKE TO ME.
MAYBE THESE KIDS...
...COULD ACTUALLY SUCCEED WHERE I COULD NOT.
...
MR. YANAI...
WILL YOU...
...STAND BEHIND MY MUSIC?
YEP.

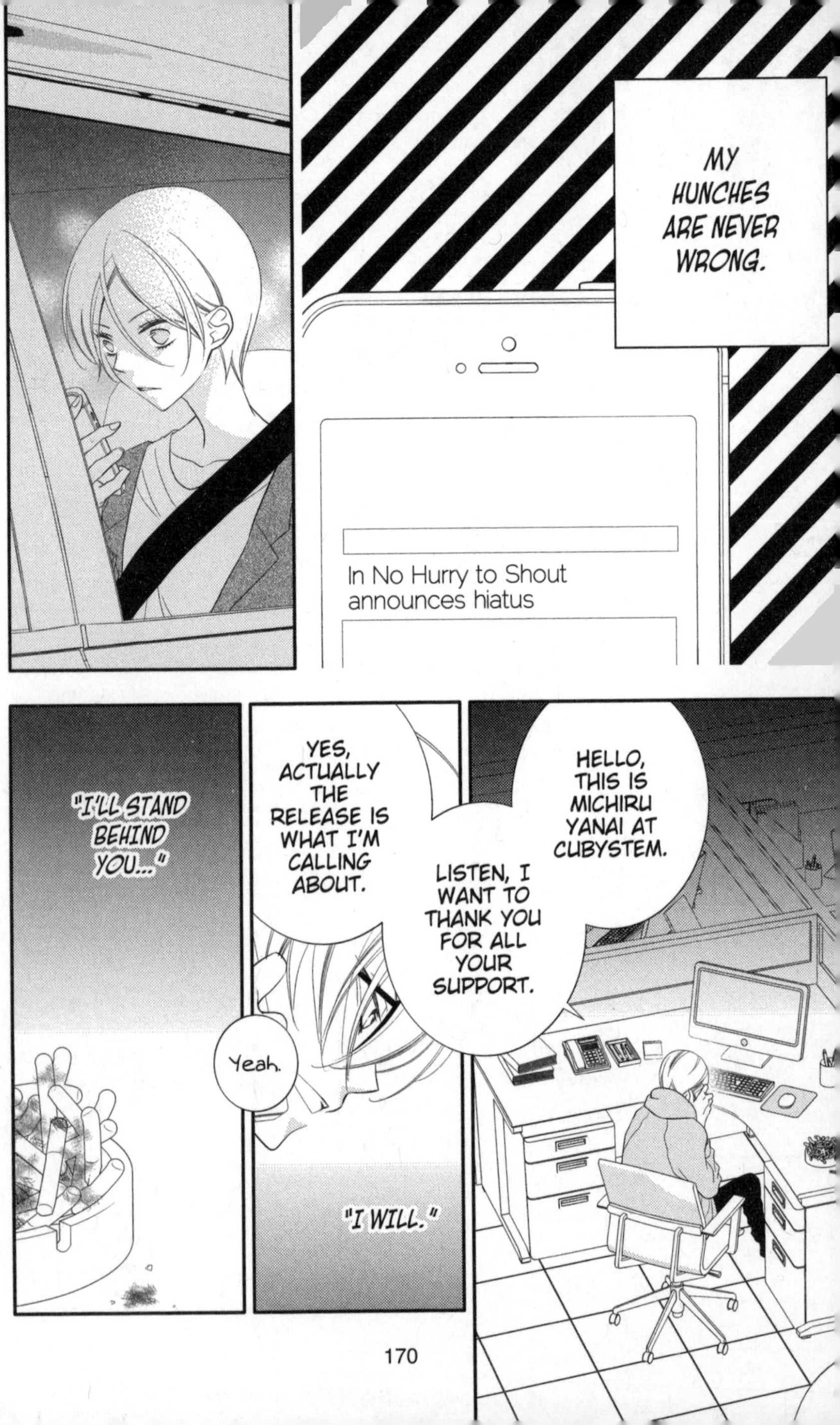
MY HUNCHES ARE NEVER WRONG.
In No Hurry to Shout announces hiatus
HELLO, THIS IS MICHIRU YANAI AT CUBYSTEM.
LISTEN, I WANT TO THANK YOU FOR ALL YOUR SUPPORT.
YES, ACTUALLY THE RELEASE IS WHAT I'M CALLING ABOUT.
Yeah.
"I WILL."
"I'LL STAND BEHIND YOU..."

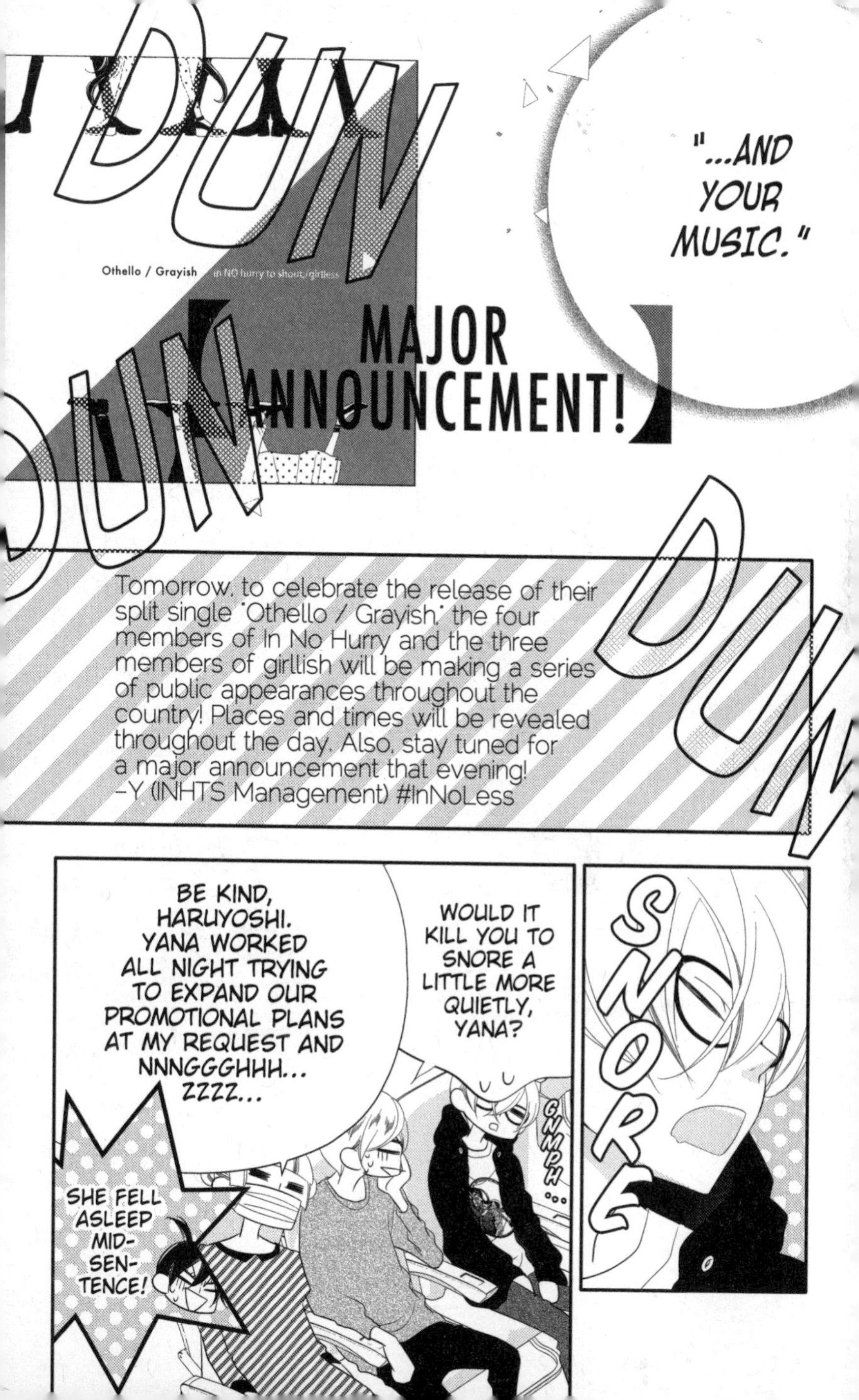
"...AND YOUR MUSIC."
DUN DUN
Othello / Grayish
in NO hurry to shout/girlless
MAJOR ANNOUNCEMENT!
DUN DUN
Tomorrow, to celebrate the release of their split single "Othello / Grayish," the four members of In No Hurry and the three members of girllish will be making a series of public appearances throughout the country! Places and times will be revealed throughout the day. Also, stay tuned for a major announcement that evening! –Y (INHTS Management) #InNoLess
DUN DUN
SNORE
WOULD IT KILL YOU TO SNORE A LITTLE MORE QUIETLY, YANA?
BE KIND, HARUYOSHI. YANA WORKED ALL NIGHT TRYING TO EXPAND OUR PROMOTIONAL PLANS AT MY REQUEST AND NNNGGGHHH... ZZZZ...
GNMPH...
SHE FELL ASLEEP MID-SENTENCE!

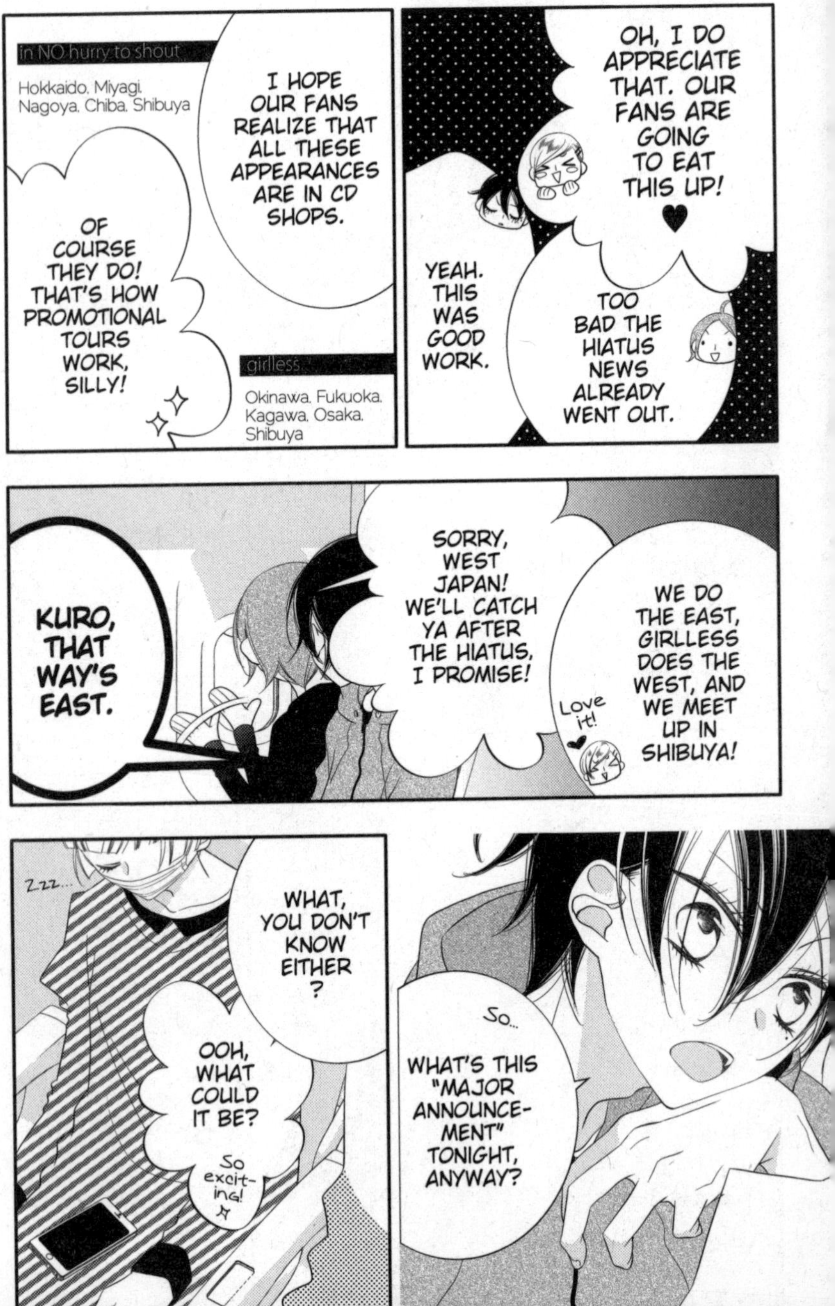
OH, I DO APPRECIATE THAT. OUR FANS ARE GOING TO EAT THIS UP! ♥
YEAH. THIS WAS GOOD WORK.
TOO BAD THE HIATUS NEWS ALREADY WENT OUT.
I HOPE OUR FANS REALIZE THAT ALL THESE APPEARANCES ARE IN CD SHOPS.
in NO hurry to shout
Hokkaido. Miyagi. Nagoya. Chiba. Shibuya
OF COURSE THEY DO! THAT'S HOW PROMOTIONAL TOURS WORK, SILLY!
girlless
Okinawa. Fukuoka. Kagawa. Osaka. Shibuya
WE DO THE EAST, GIRLLESS DOES THE WEST, AND WE MEET UP IN SHIBUYA!
Love it!
SORRY, WEST JAPAN! WE'LL CATCH YA AFTER THE HIATUS, I PROMISE!
KURO, THAT WAY'S EAST.
So...
WHAT'S THIS "MAJOR ANNOUNCEMENT" TONIGHT, ANYWAY?
WHAT, YOU DON'T KNOW EITHER?
Zzz...
OOH, WHAT COULD IT BE?
So exciting!

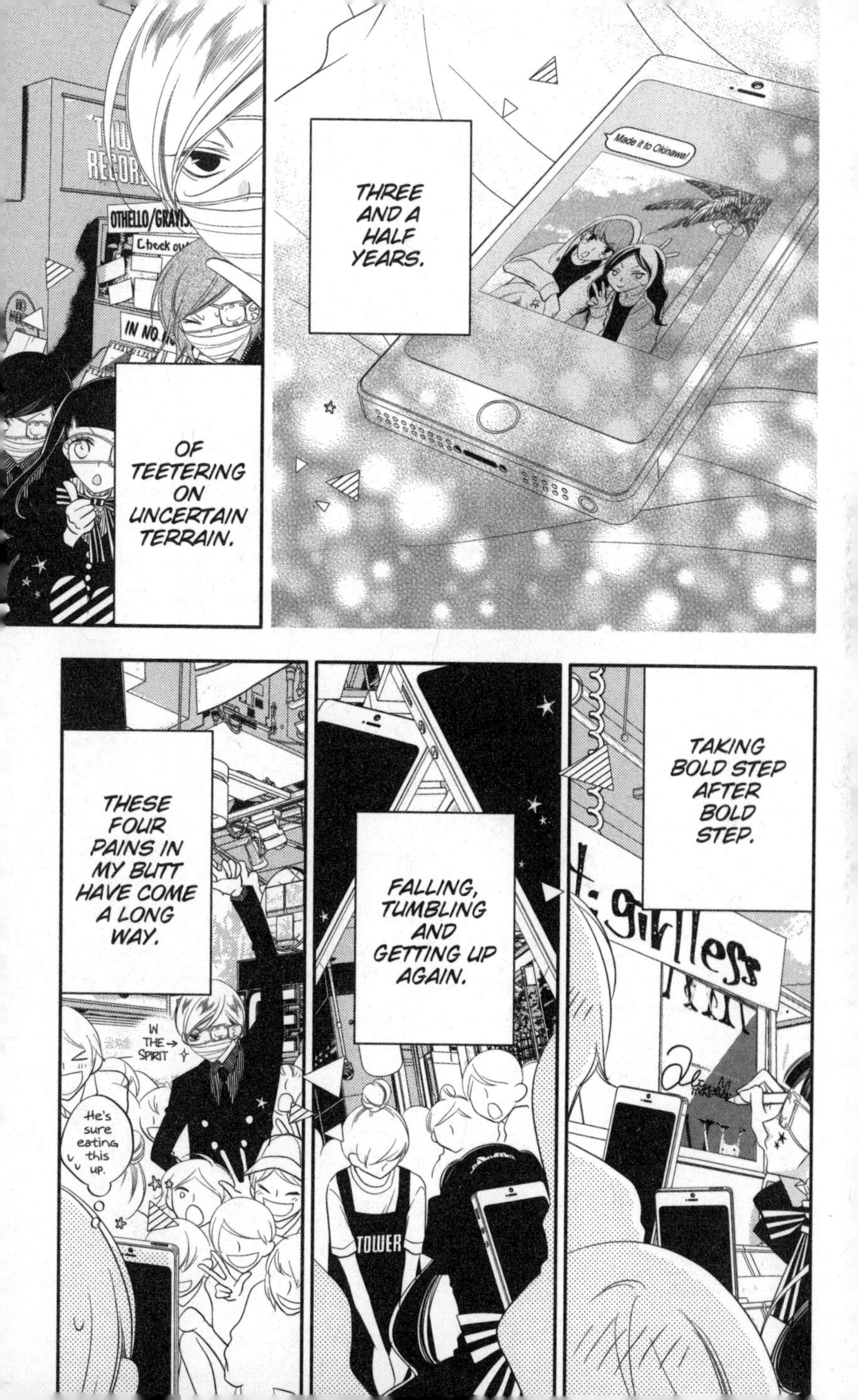

Made it to Okinawa!
THREE AND A HALF YEARS.
OTHELLO/GRAVIS
Check out
IN NO
OF TEETERING ON UNCERTAIN TERRAIN.
TAKING BOLD STEP AFTER BOLD STEP.
FALLING, TUMBLING AND GETTING UP AGAIN.
TOWER
THESE FOUR PAINS IN MY BUTT HAVE COME A LONG WAY.
IN THE SPIRIT
He's sure eating this up.

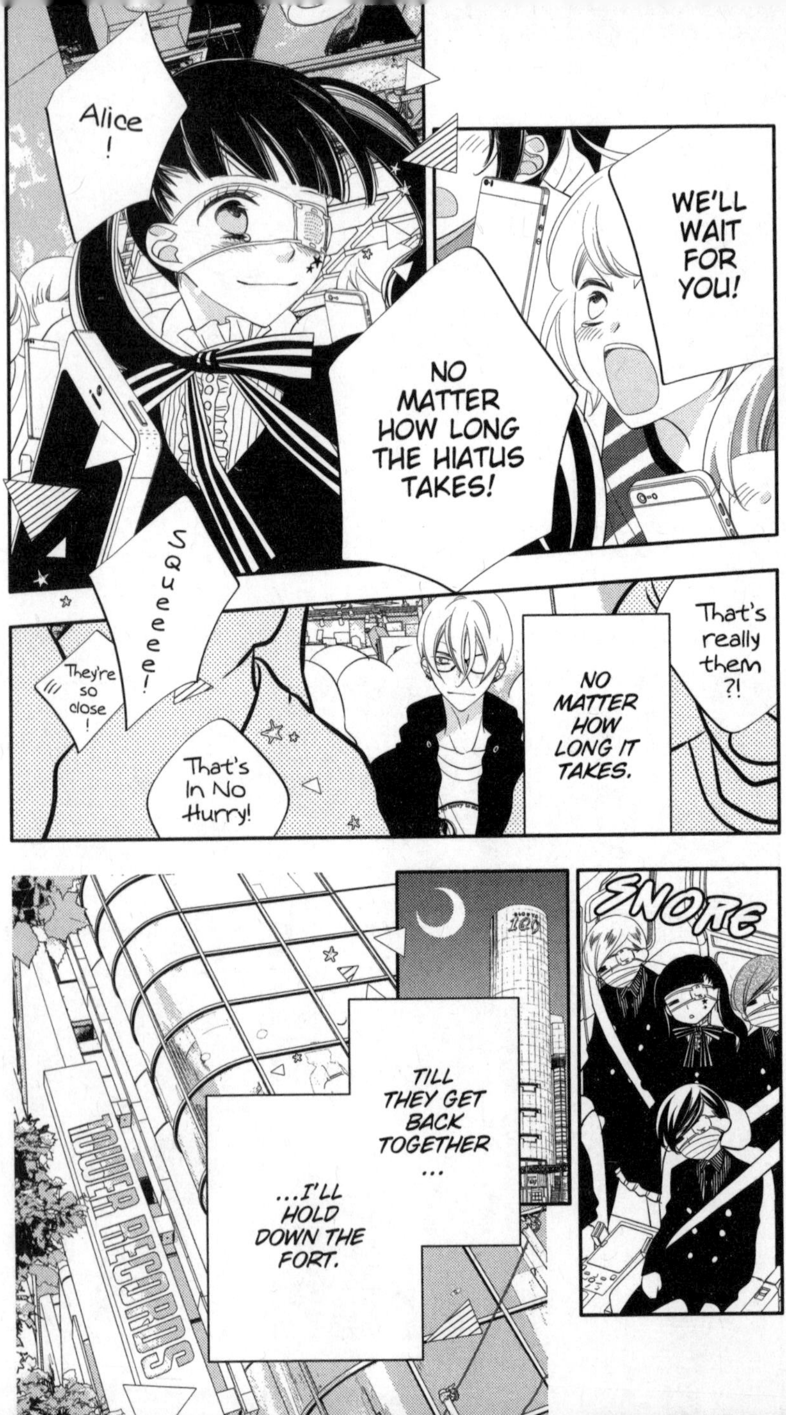
WE'LL WAIT FOR YOU!
NO MATTER HOW LONG THE HIATUS TAKES!
Alice!
Squeeeee!
That's really them?!
NO MATTER HOW LONG IT TAKES.
That's In No Hurry!
They're so close!
SNORE
109
TILL THEY GET BACK TOGETHER ...
...I'LL HOLD DOWN THE FORT.
TOWER RECORDS

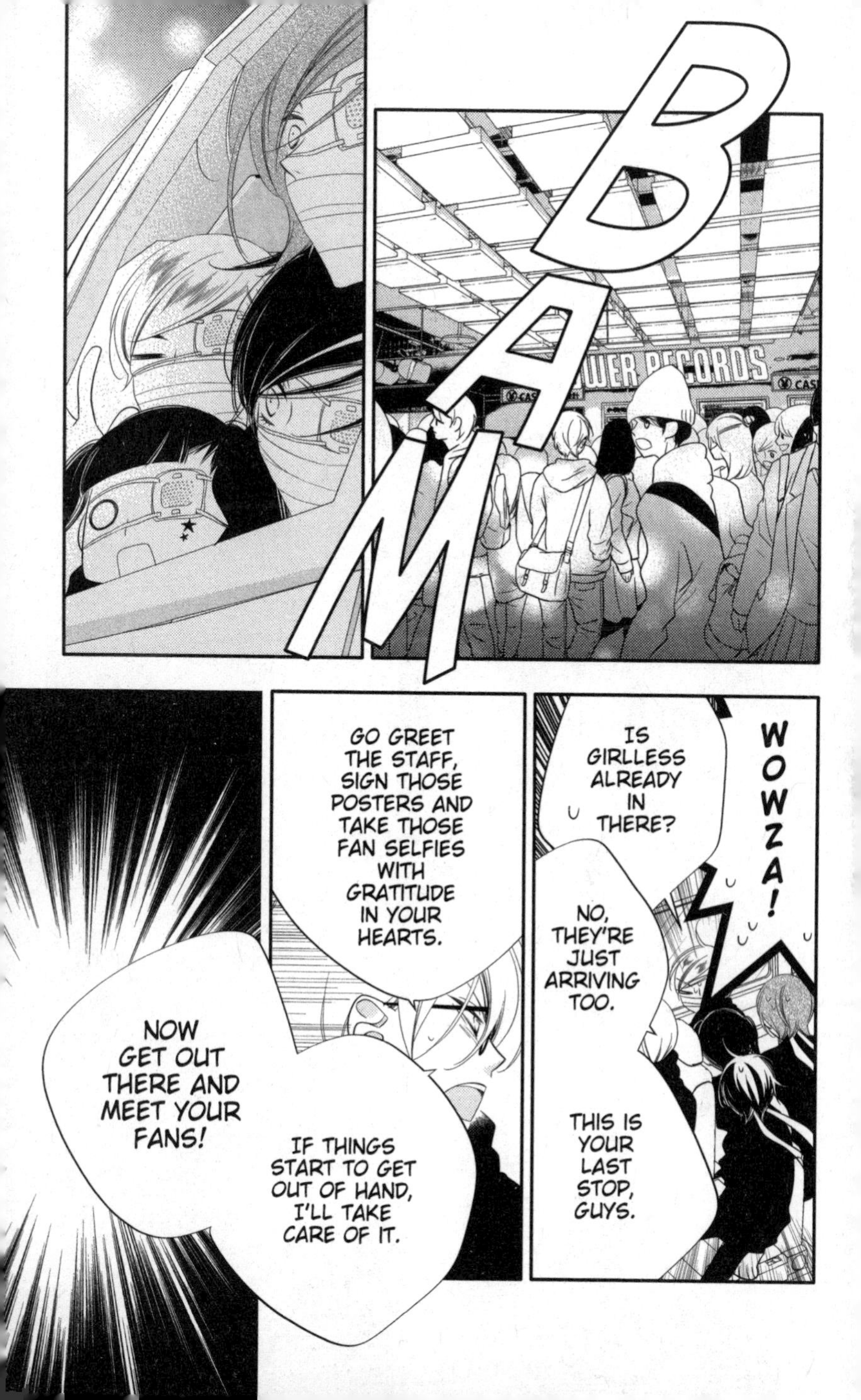
BAM
WOWZA!
IS GIRLLESS ALREADY IN THERE?
NO, THEY'RE JUST ARRIVING TOO.
THIS IS YOUR LAST STOP, GUYS.
GO GREET THE STAFF, SIGN THOSE POSTERS AND TAKE THOSE FAN SELFIES WITH GRATITUDE IN YOUR HEARTS.
IF THINGS START TO GET OUT OF HAND, I'LL TAKE CARE OF IT.
NOW GET OUT THERE AND MEET YOUR FANS!

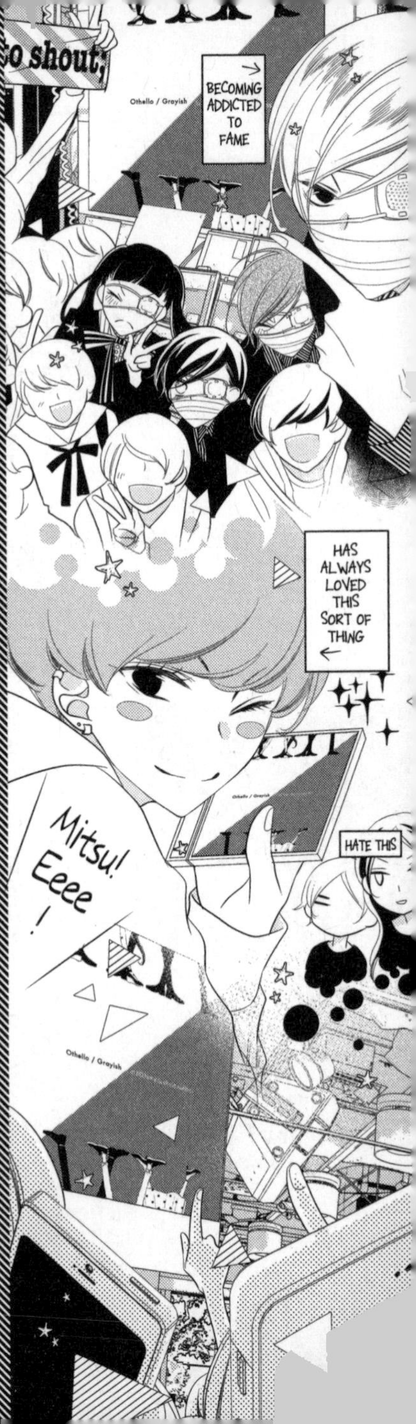
to shout;
Othello / Grayish
BECOMING ADDICTED TO FAME
HAS ALWAYS LOVED THIS SORT OF THING
Mitsu! Eeee!
HATE THIS
Othello / Grayish

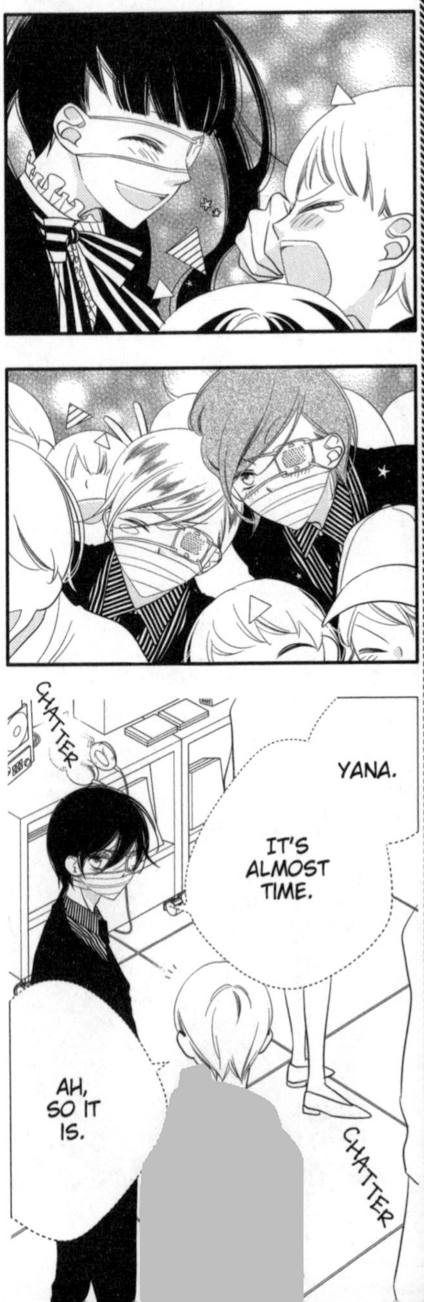
YANA.
IT'S ALMOST TIME.
CHATTER
AH, SO IT IS.
CHATTER

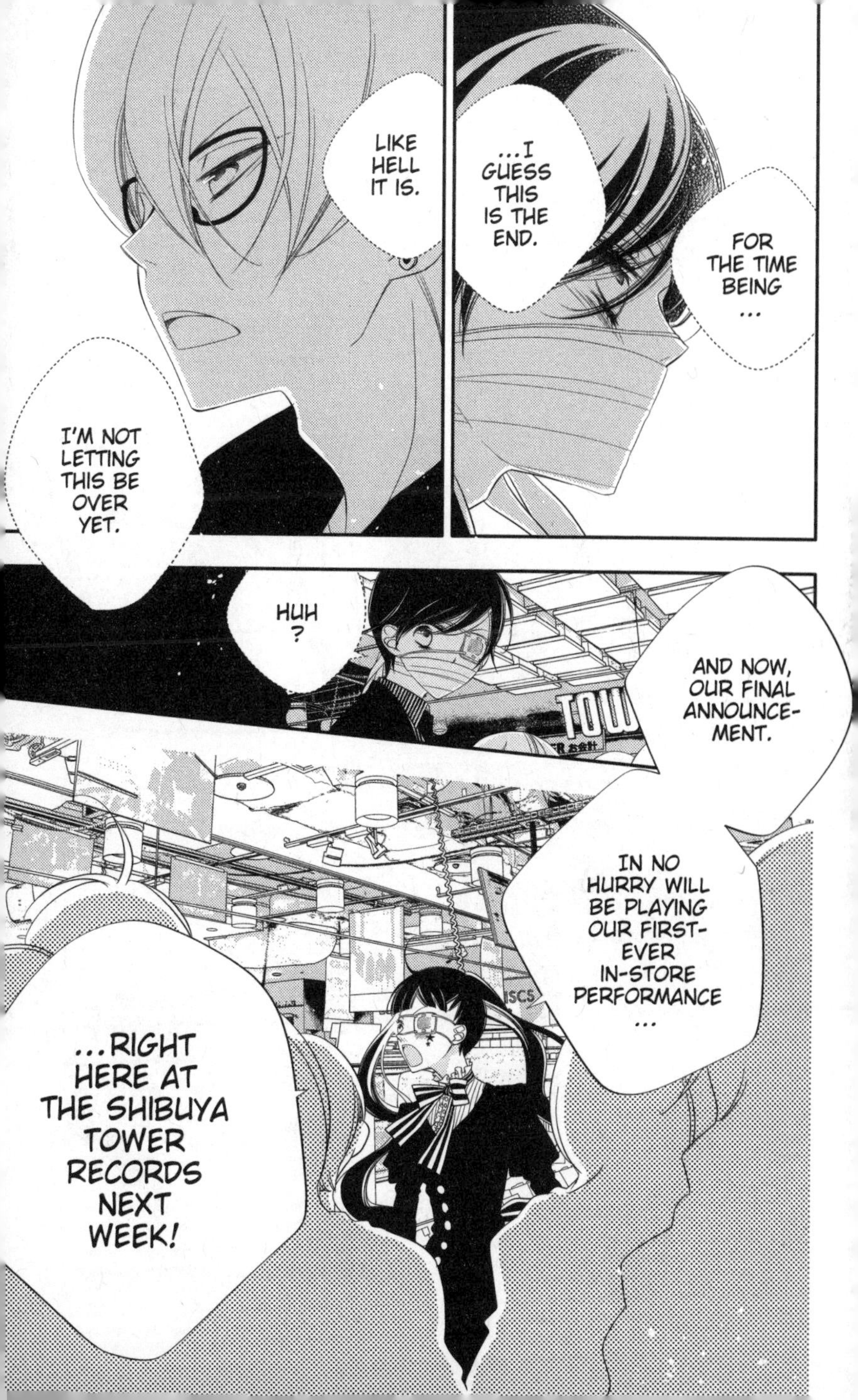
FOR THE TIME BEING ...
...I GUESS THIS IS THE END.
LIKE HELL IT IS.
I'M NOT LETTING THIS BE OVER YET.
AND NOW, OUR FINAL ANNOUNCE-MENT.
HUH ?
IN NO HURRY WILL BE PLAYING OUR FIRST-EVER IN-STORE PERFORMANCE ...
...RIGHT HERE AT THE SHIBUYA TOWER RECORDS NEXT WEEK!

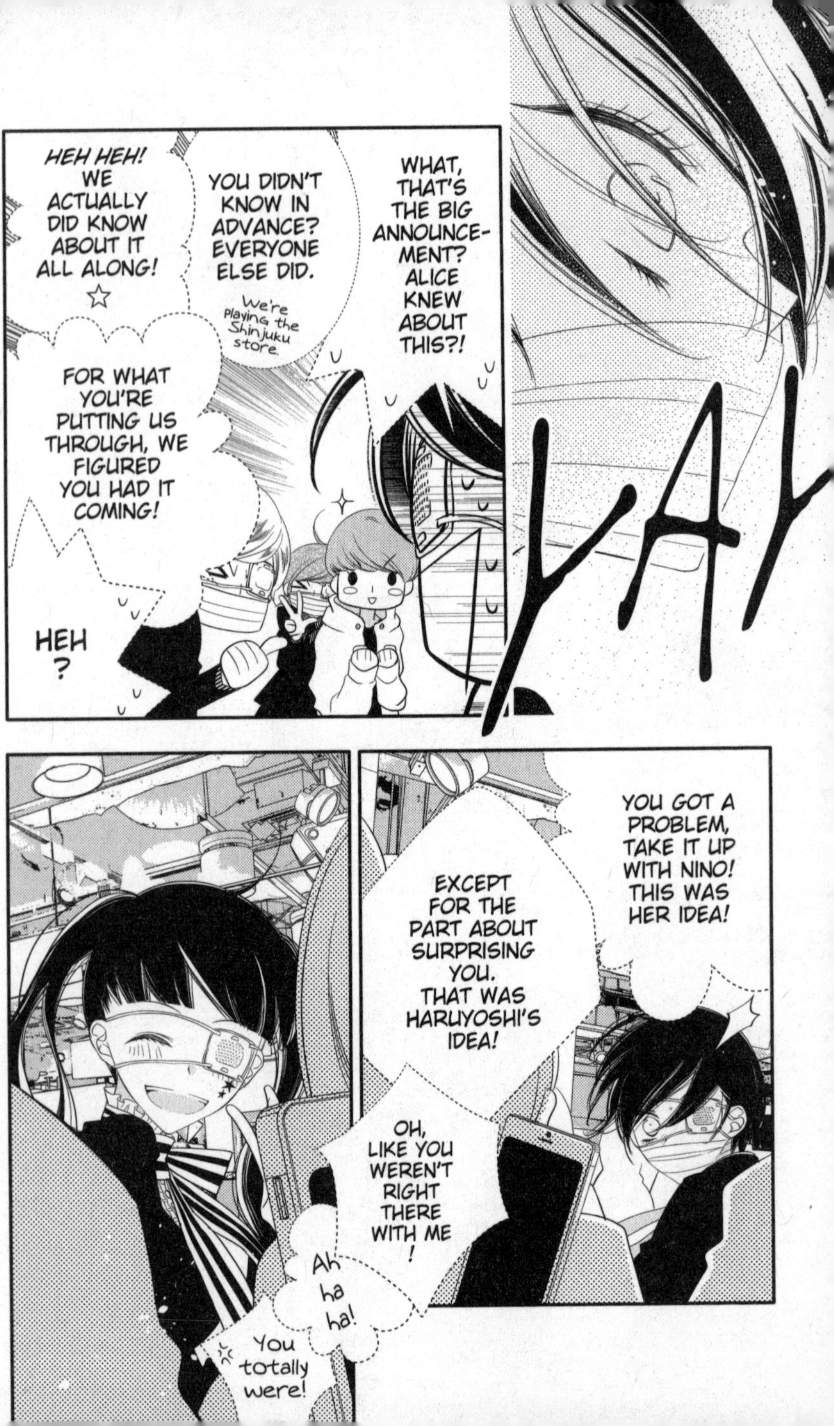
YAY
WHAT, THAT'S THE BIG ANNOUNCEMENT? ALICE KNEW ABOUT THIS?!
YOU DIDN'T KNOW IN ADVANCE? EVERYONE ELSE DID.
We're playing the Shinjuku store.
HEH HEH! WE ACTUALLY DID KNOW ABOUT IT ALL ALONG! ☆
FOR WHAT YOU'RE PUTTING US THROUGH, WE FIGURED YOU HAD IT COMING!
HEH?
YOU GOT A PROBLEM, TAKE IT UP WITH NINO! THIS WAS HER IDEA!
EXCEPT FOR THE PART ABOUT SURPRISING YOU. THAT WAS HARUYOSHI'S IDEA!
OH, LIKE YOU WEREN'T RIGHT THERE WITH ME!
Ah ha ha!
You totally were!

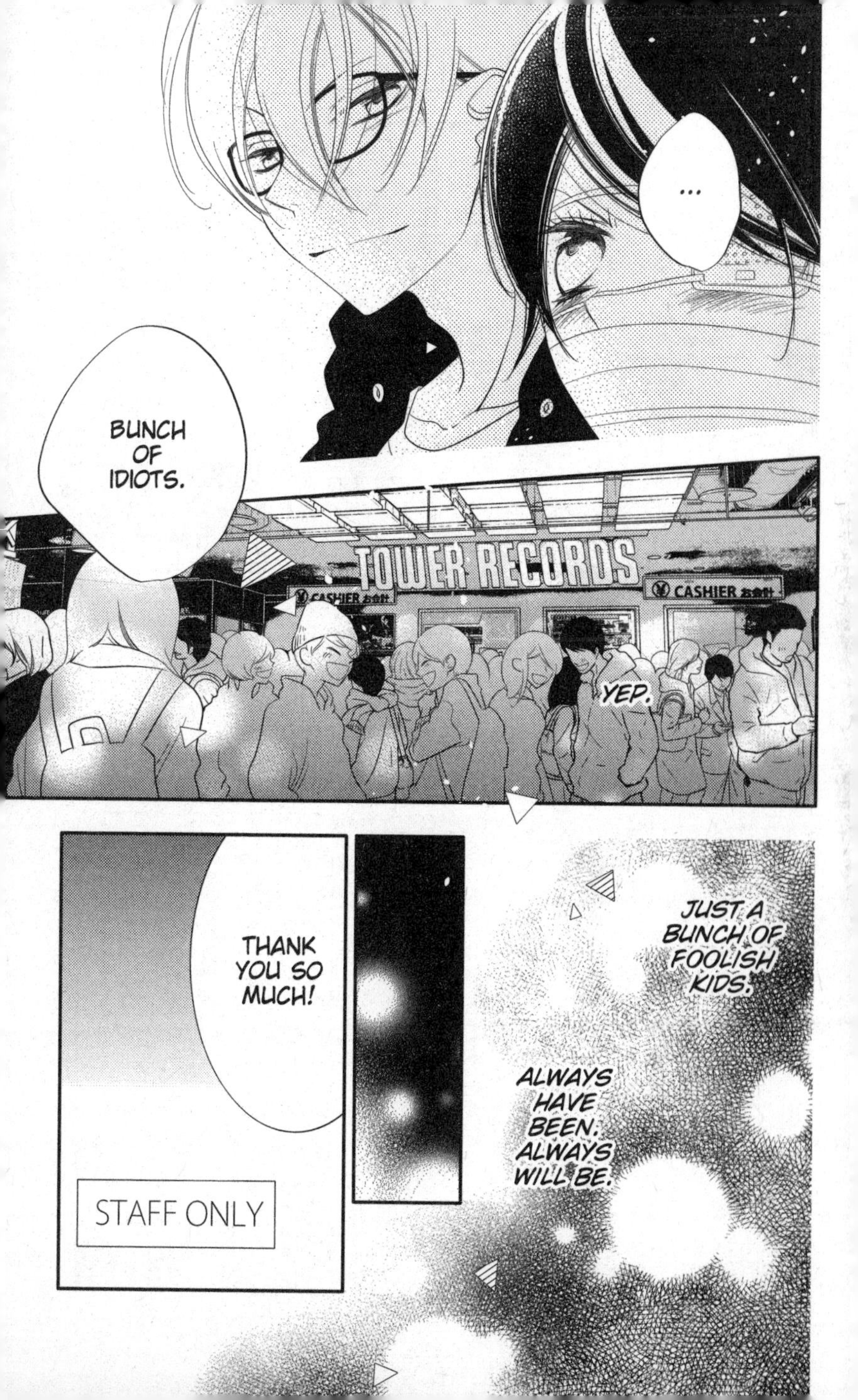
...
BUNCH OF IDIOTS.
TOWER RECORDS
CASHIER
CASHIER
YEP.
JUST A BUNCH OF FOOLISH KIDS.
ALWAYS HAVE BEEN. ALWAYS WILL BE.
THANK YOU SO MUCH!
STAFF ONLY

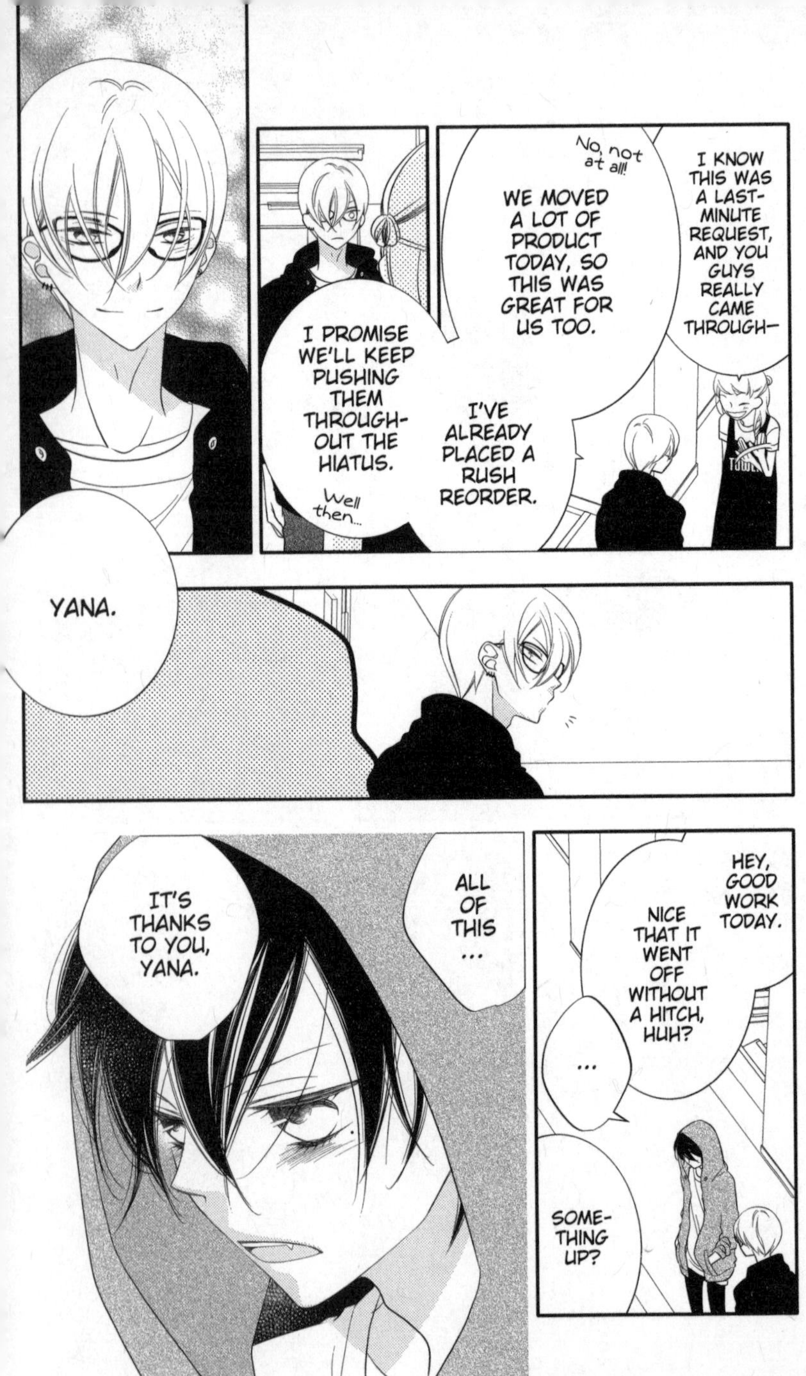
I KNOW THIS WAS A LAST-MINUTE REQUEST, AND YOU GUYS REALLY CAME THROUGH—
No, not at all!
WE MOVED A LOT OF PRODUCT TODAY, SO THIS WAS GREAT FOR US TOO.
I'VE ALREADY PLACED A RUSH REORDER.
I PROMISE WE'LL KEEP PUSHING THEM THROUGH-OUT THE HIATUS.
Well then...
YANA.
HEY, GOOD WORK TODAY.
NICE THAT IT WENT OFF WITHOUT A HITCH, HUH?
...
SOME-THING UP?
ALL OF THIS ...
IT'S THANKS TO YOU, YANA.

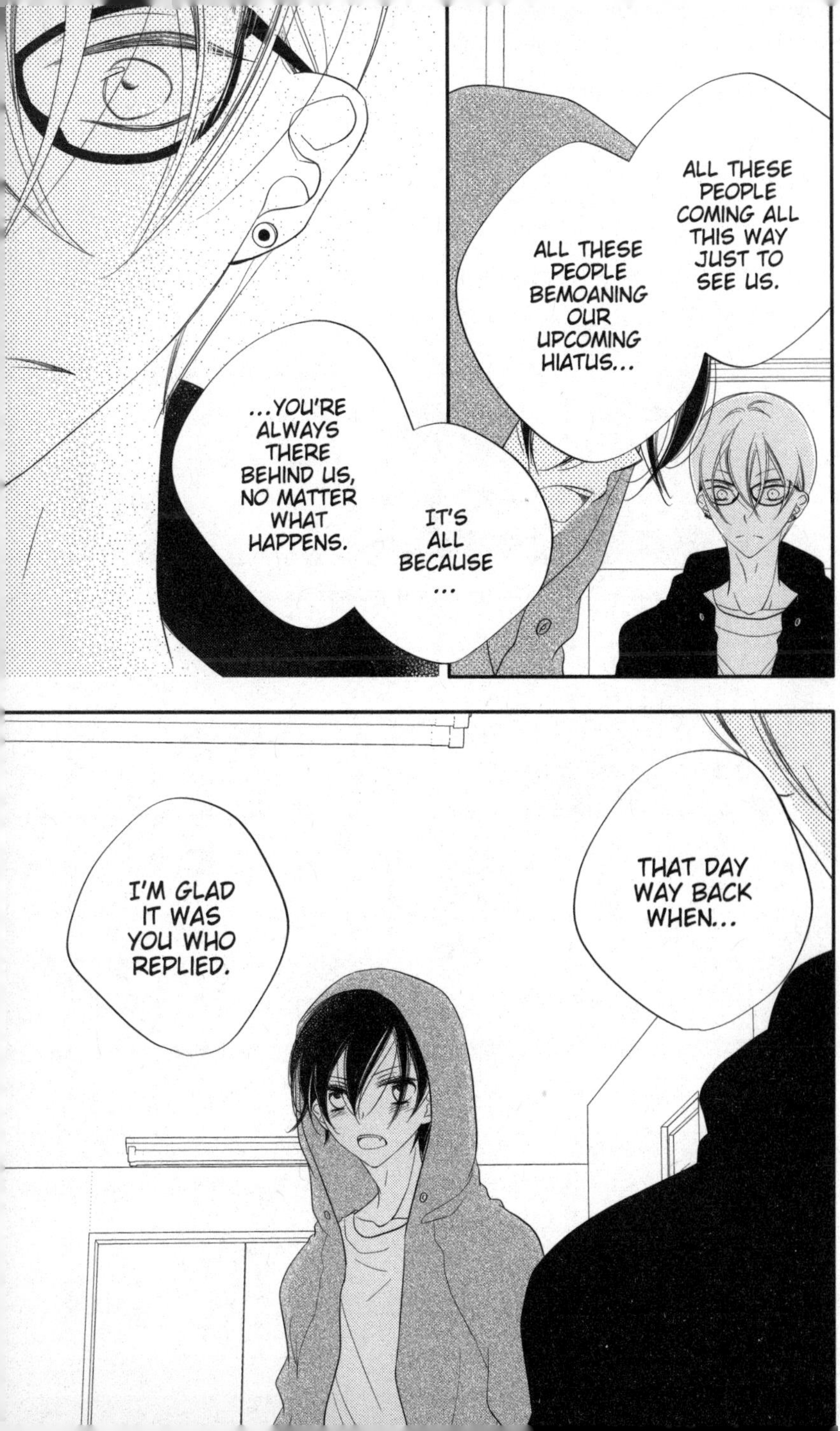
ALL THESE PEOPLE COMING ALL THIS WAY JUST TO SEE US.
ALL THESE PEOPLE BEMOANING OUR UPCOMING HIATUS...
IT'S ALL BECAUSE...
...YOU'RE ALWAYS THERE BEHIND US, NO MATTER WHAT HAPPENS.
THAT DAY WAY BACK WHEN...
I'M GLAD IT WAS YOU WHO REPLIED.

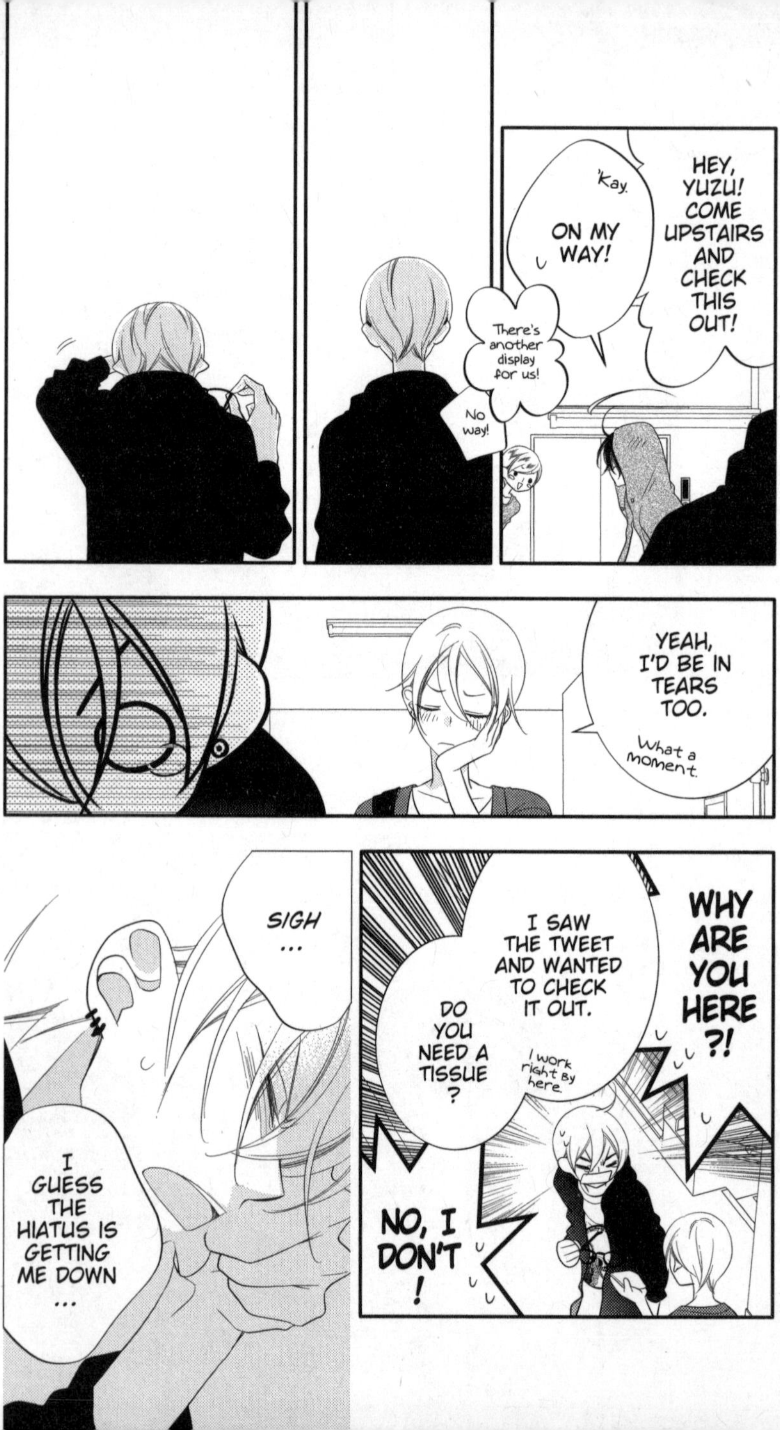
HEY, YUZU! COME UPSTAIRS AND CHECK THIS OUT!
'Kay.
ON MY WAY!
There's another display for us!
No way!
YEAH, I'D BE IN TEARS TOO.
What a moment.
WHY ARE YOU HERE?!
I SAW THE TWEET AND WANTED TO CHECK IT OUT.
I work right by here.
DO YOU NEED A TISSUE?
NO, I DON'T!
SIGH...
I GUESS THE HIATUS IS GETTING ME DOWN...

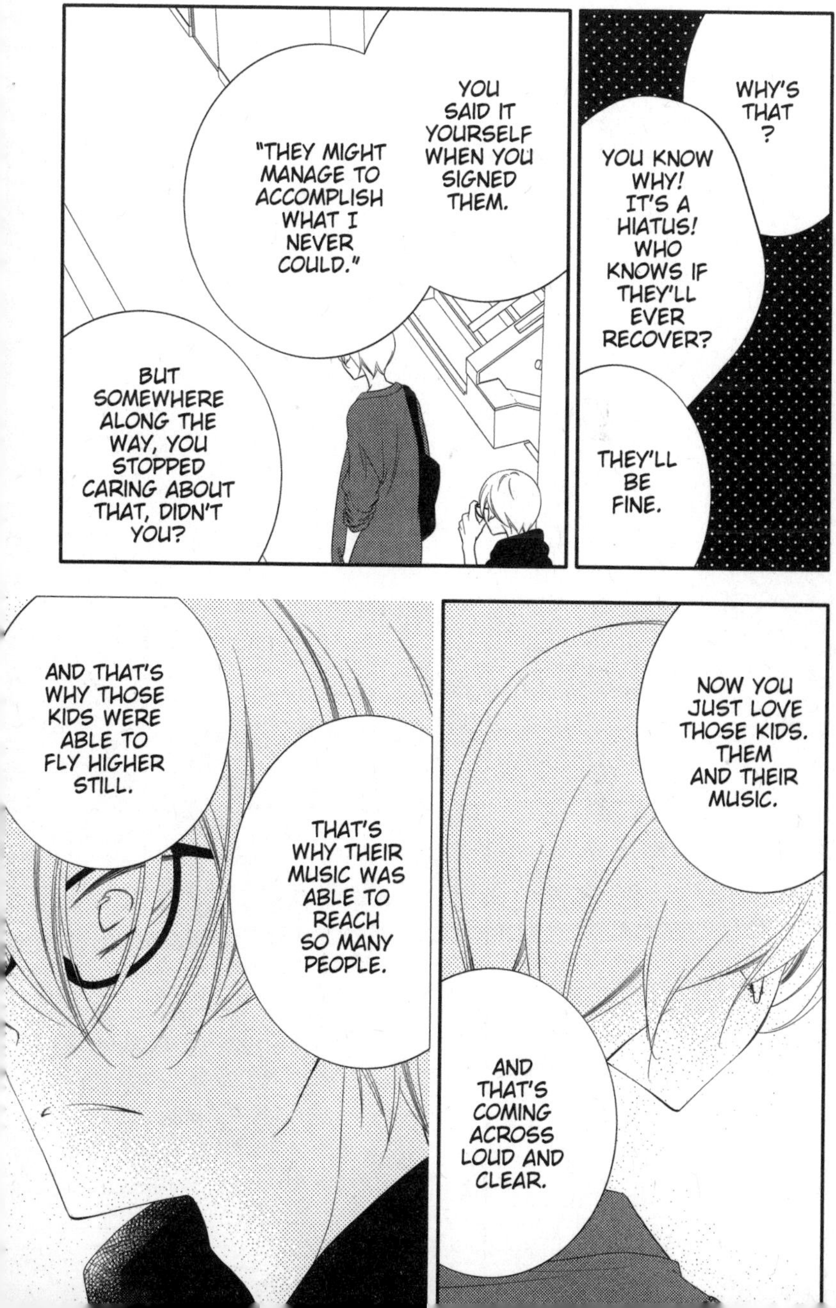
WHY'S THAT?
YOU KNOW WHY! IT'S A HIATUS! WHO KNOWS IF THEY'LL EVER RECOVER?
THEY'LL BE FINE.
YOU SAID IT YOURSELF WHEN YOU SIGNED THEM.
"THEY MIGHT MANAGE TO ACCOMPLISH WHAT I NEVER COULD."
BUT SOMEWHERE ALONG THE WAY, YOU STOPPED CARING ABOUT THAT, DIDN'T YOU?
NOW YOU JUST LOVE THOSE KIDS. THEM AND THEIR MUSIC.
AND THAT'S COMING ACROSS LOUD AND CLEAR.
THAT'S WHY THEIR MUSIC WAS ABLE TO REACH SO MANY PEOPLE.
AND THAT'S WHY THOSE KIDS WERE ABLE TO FLY HIGHER STILL.

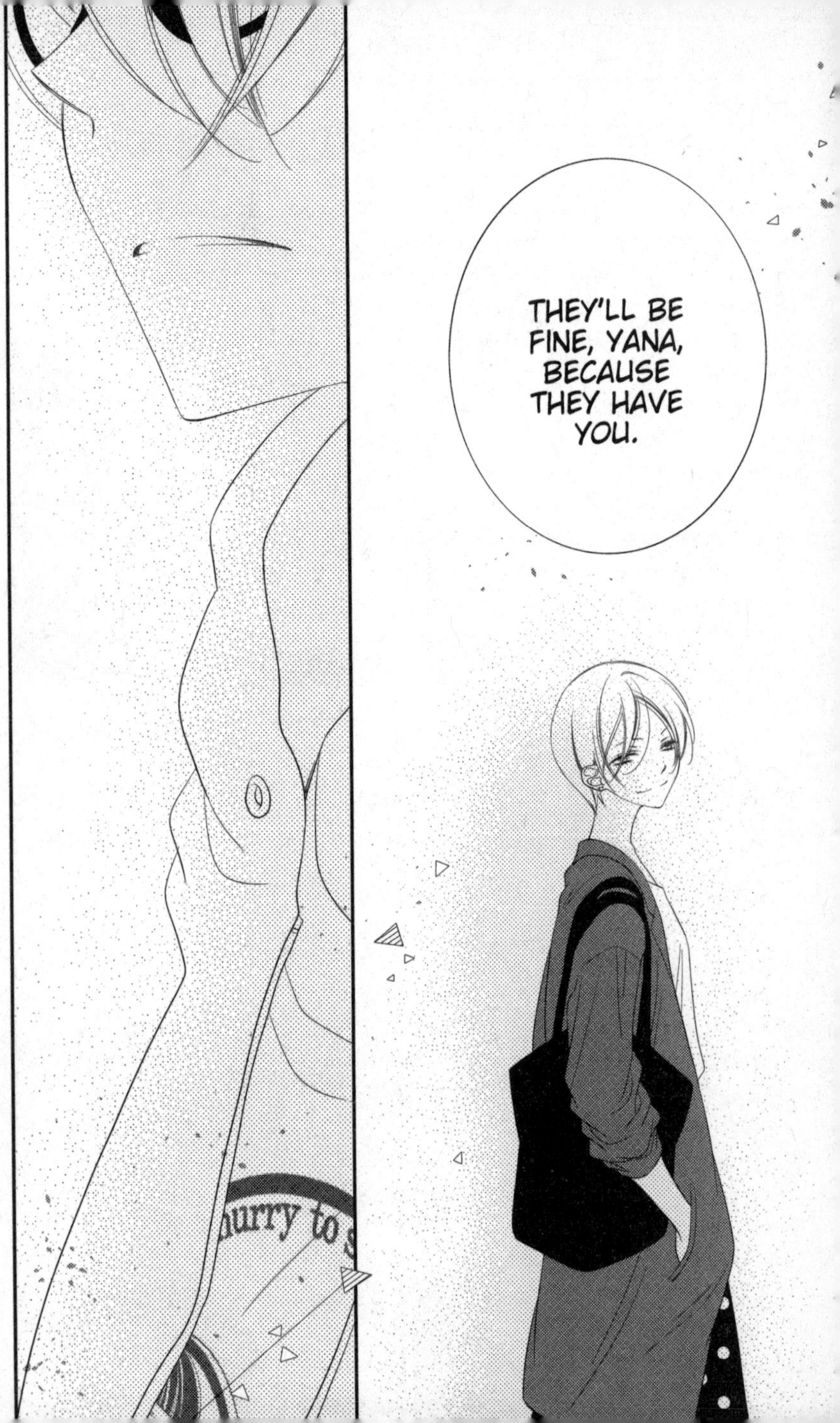
THEY'LL BE FINE, YANA, BECAUSE THEY HAVE YOU.
hurry to s

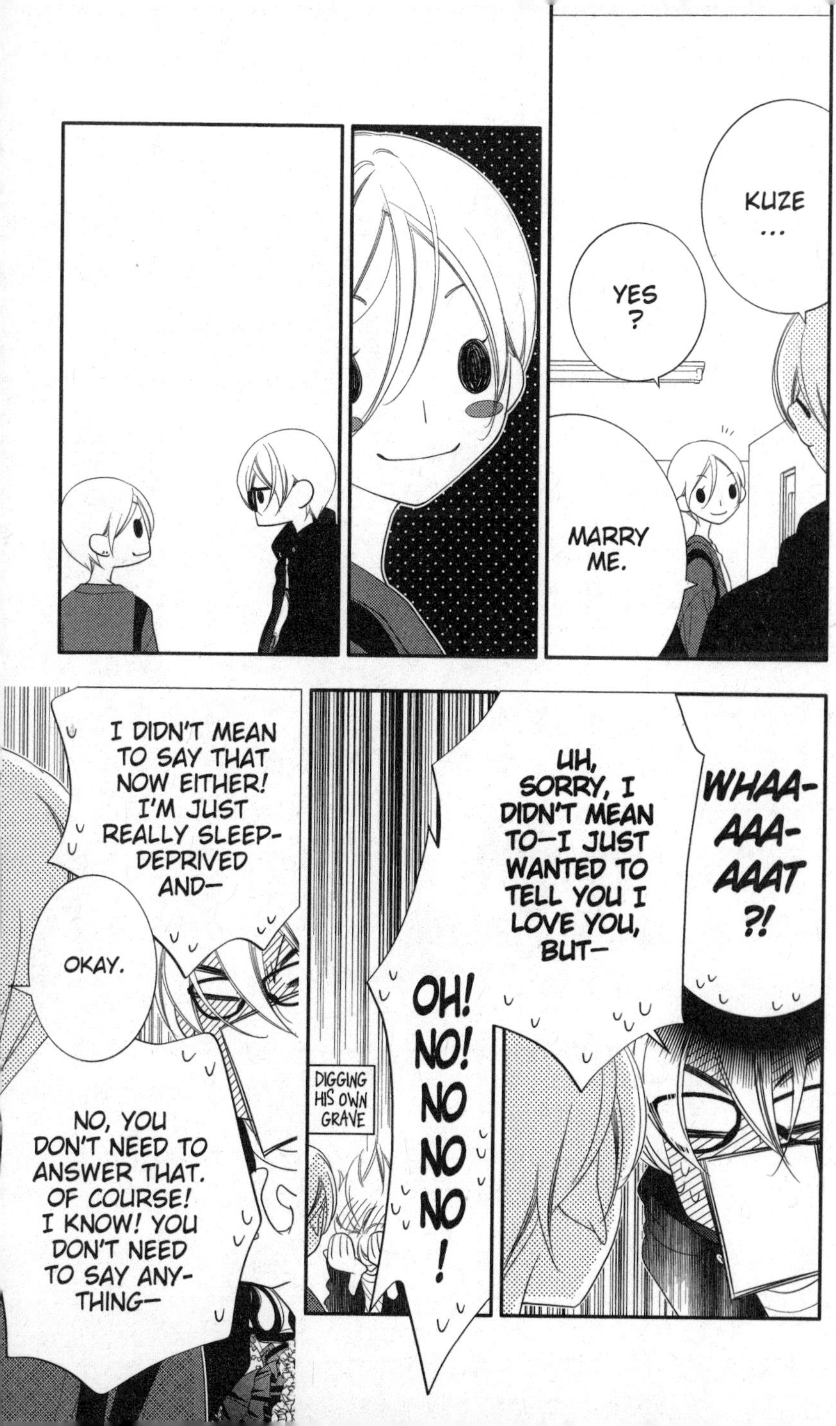
KUZE ...
YES ?
MARRY ME.
WHAA-AAA-AAAT ?!
UH, SORRY, I DIDN'T MEAN TO—I JUST WANTED TO TELL YOU I LOVE YOU, BUT—
OH! NO! NO NO NO !
DIGGING HIS OWN GRAVE
I DIDN'T MEAN TO SAY THAT NOW EITHER! I'M JUST REALLY SLEEP-DEPRIVED AND—
OKAY.
NO, YOU DON'T NEED TO ANSWER THAT. OF COURSE! I KNOW! YOU DON'T NEED TO SAY ANY-THING—

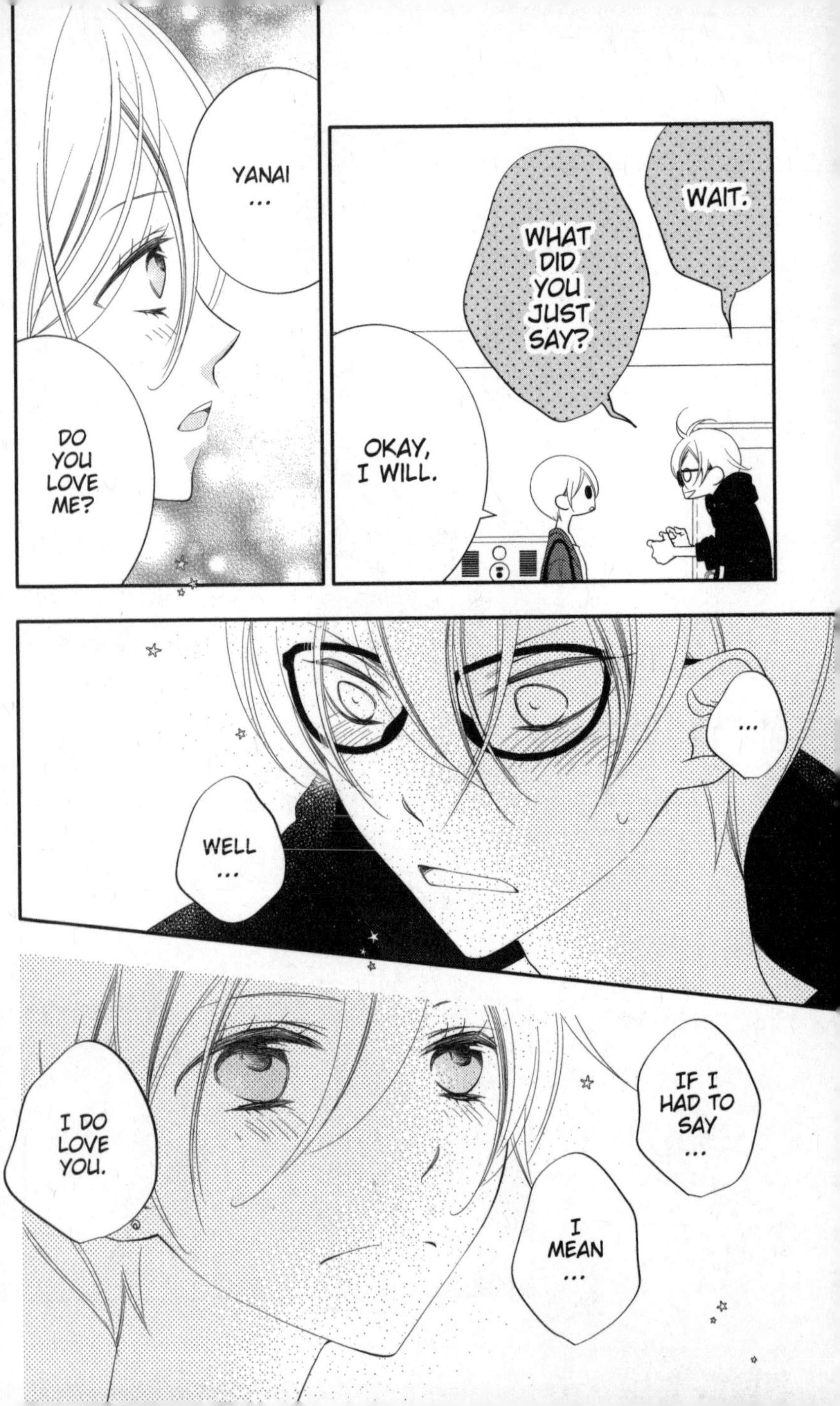
WAIT.
WHAT DID YOU JUST SAY?
OKAY, I WILL.
YANAI ...
DO YOU LOVE ME?
...
WELL ...
IF I HAD TO SAY ...
I MEAN ...
I DO LOVE YOU.

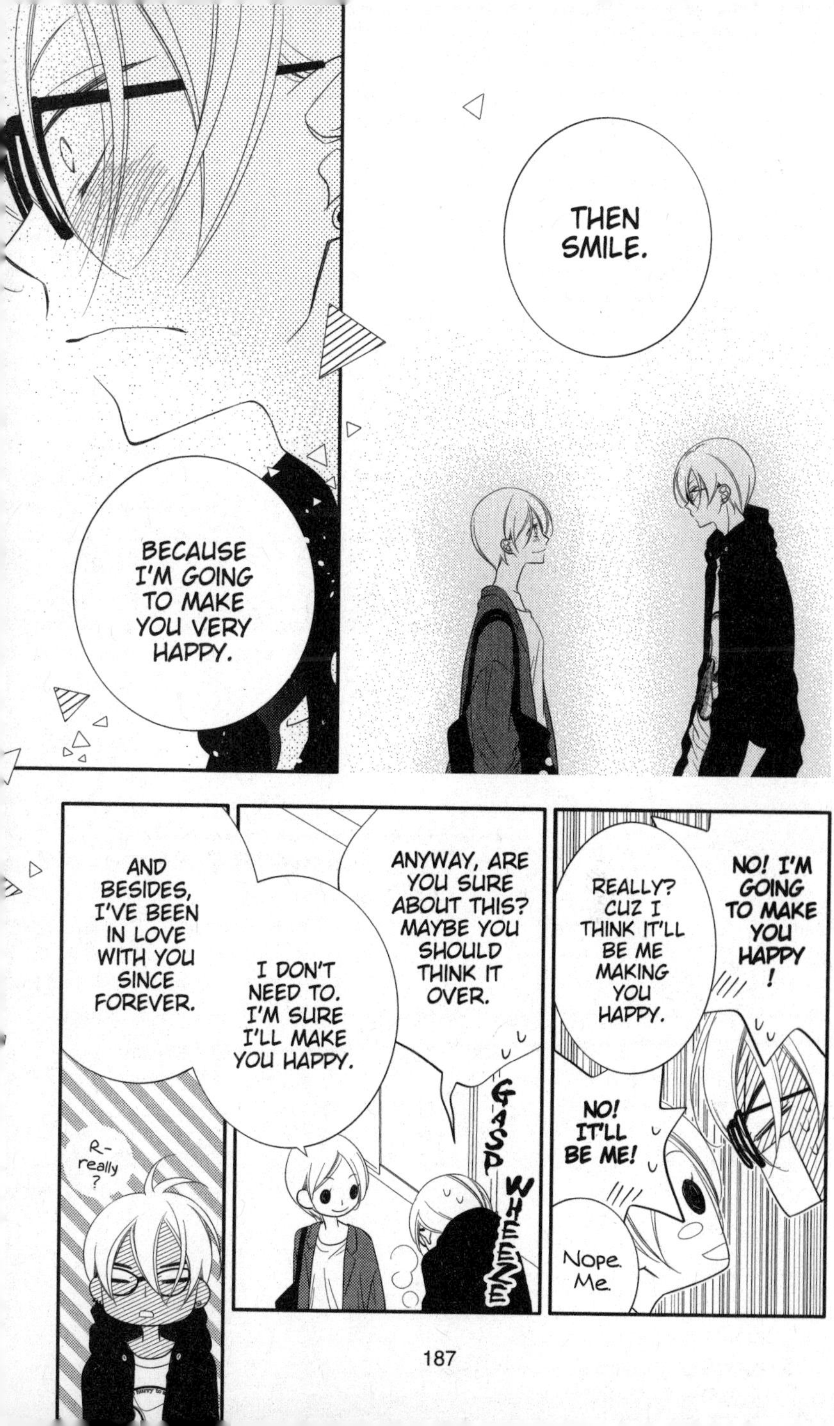
THEN SMILE.
BECAUSE I'M GOING TO MAKE YOU VERY HAPPY.
NO! I'M GOING TO MAKE YOU HAPPY!
REALLY? CUZ I THINK IT'LL BE ME MAKING YOU HAPPY.
NO! IT'LL BE ME!
Nope. Me.
ANYWAY, ARE YOU SURE ABOUT THIS? MAYBE YOU SHOULD THINK IT OVER.
GASP
WHEEEZE
I DON'T NEED TO. I'M SURE I'LL MAKE YOU HAPPY.
AND BESIDES, I'VE BEEN IN LOVE WITH YOU SINCE FOREVER.
R-really?

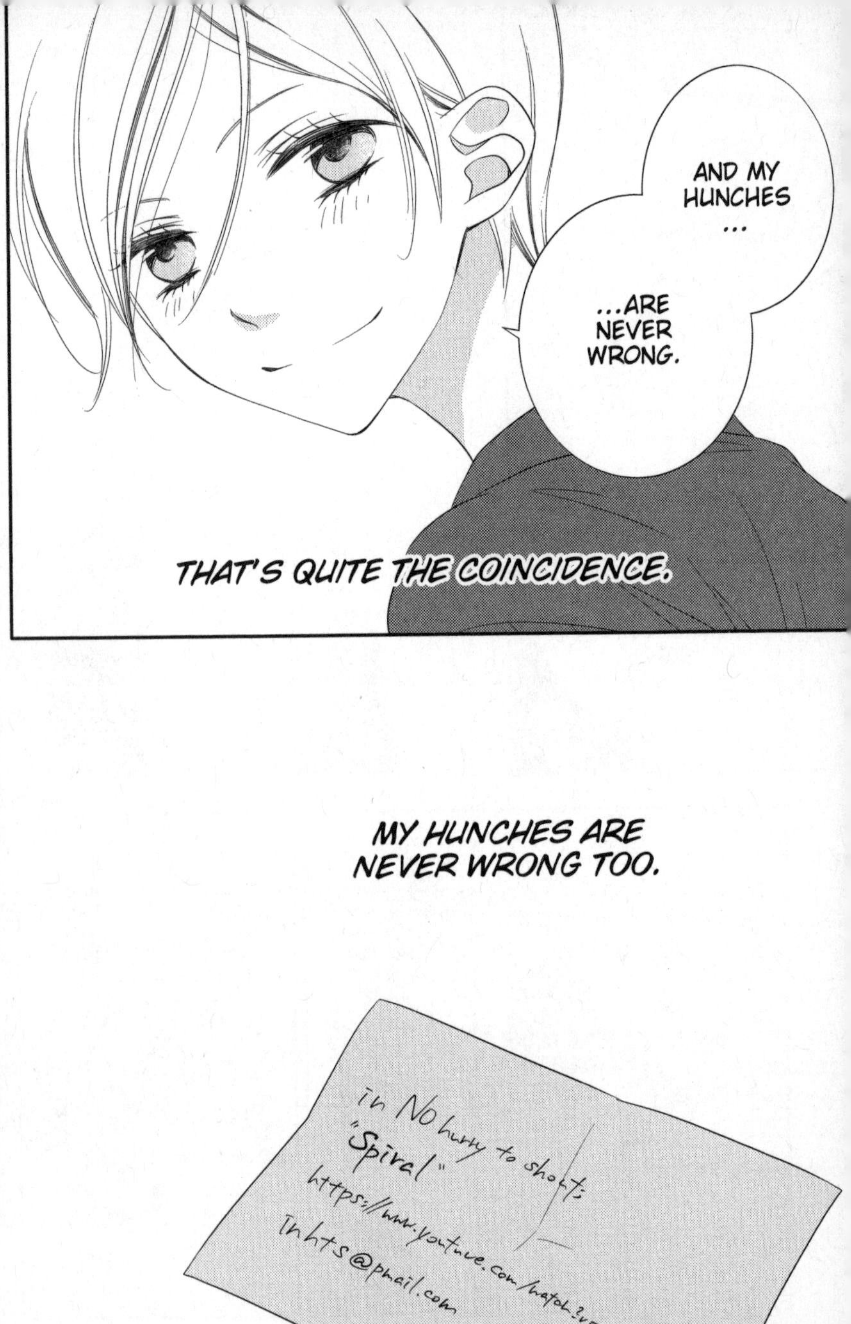
AND MY HUNCHES ...
...ARE NEVER WRONG.
THAT'S QUITE THE COINCIDENCE.
MY HUNCHES ARE NEVER WRONG TOO.
"Spiral"

ANONYMOUS NOISE ⑯ / THE END

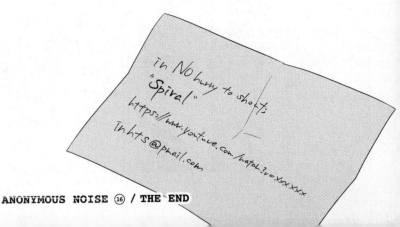

TO BE CONTINUED IN ANONYMOUS NOISE 17

I've just begun work on the final
serialized chapters of *Anonymous Noise*
(at the time of this writing). Whether
it's me pulling the characters to the
finish line or them pulling me, I intend
to enjoy it to the fullest!

- Ryoko Fukuyama

Born on January 5 in Wakayama Prefecture in
Japan, Ryoko Fukuyama debuted as a manga
artist after winning the Hakusensha Athena
Shinjin Taisho Prize from Hakusensha's *Hana to
Yume* magazine. She is also the author
of *Nosatsu Junkie*. *Anonymous Noise* was
adapted into an anime in 2017.

ANONYMOUS NOISE
Vol. 16
Shojo Beat Edition

STORY AND ART BY
RYOKO FUKUYAMA

English Translation & Adaptation/Casey Loe
Touch-Up Art & Lettering/Joanna Estep
Design/Yukiko Whitley
Editor/Amy Yu

Fukumenkei Noise by Ryoko Fukuyama

First published in Japan in 2018 by HAKUSENSHA, Inc., Tokyo.
English language translation rights arranged with HAKUSENSHA, Inc., Tokyo.

Printed in the U.S.A.

Published by VIZ Media, LLC
P.O. Box 77010
San Francisco, CA 94107

10 9 8 7 6 5 4 3 2 1
First printing, September 2019

ratings.viz.com RATED T TEEN

PARENTAL ADVISORY
ANONYMOUS NOISE is rated T for Teen and is recommended for ages 13 and up. This volume contains suggestive themes.

VIZ MEDIA
viz.com

Shojo Beat
shojobeat.com

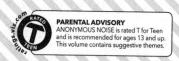

Surprise!

You may be reading the wrong way!

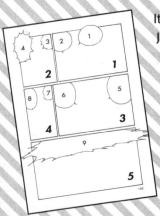

It's true: In keeping with the original Japanese comic format, this book reads from right to left—so action, sound effects and word balloons are completely reversed. This preserves the orientation of the original artwork—plus, it's fun! Check out the diagram shown here to get the hang of things, and then turn to the other side of the book to get started!